Governance Reforms

About the Author

Karunakar Patnaik is a retired officer of Indian Administrative Service. With thirty five years of experience in public service as a civil servant in different capacities, he witnessed and watched with keen interest the operationalisation of mechanisms and machinations of administrative knitty-grities from the grassroots level to higher echelons of power that be in the important spheres of administration. As a student of political science and a practitioner of public administration, he was immensely encouraged by the recent trends and developments in public governance to write this book on "Governance Reforms", a topic which is currently and widely interntionalized, nationalized and to speak the least, localized. His passionate areas of keen interest are, of course, local administration, institutions and their operationalisation in the midst of developing and emerging issues that challenge governance problems. After year of retirement he has been closely associated with non-governmental and community stakeholders at the grassroots. Besides a number of publications on local government, tribal issues, he has authored several articles and books on governance. The writer is a Senior Fellow in the Institute of Social Sciences and a visiting fellow to institutions of social and economic research and analysis.

Governance Reforms
Critical Issues and Challenges

Karunakar Patnaik

CONCEPT PUBLISHING COMPANY PVT. LTD.
NEW DELHI-110059

ISBN-13: 978-93-5125-277-1 (HB)

First Published 2017

Published and Printed by

Concept
Since 1974

Concept Publishing Company Pvt. Ltd.
Regd. Office:
A/15-16, Commercial Block, Mohan Garden,
New Delhi-110059 (INDIA)
Phones : 25351460, 25351794, *Fax* : 091-11-25357109
Email : publishing@conceptpub.com
Website: www.conceptpub.com

Editorial Office: H-13, Bali Nagar, New Delhi-110 015, India.

Cataloging in Publication Data—DK Courtesy: D.K. Agencies (P) Ltd. <docinfo@dkagencies.com>

Patnaik, Karunakar, author.
Governance reforms : critical issues and challenges / Karunakar Patnaik.
pages cm
Includes bibliographical references and index.
ISBN 9789351252771 (HB)
ISBN 9789351252788 (PB)

1. Administrative agencies—India—Reorganization. 2. Public administration—India. I. Title.

JQ229.O73P38 2017 DDC 352.20954 23

Preface

Governance as such, embraces the unfathomable and impenetrable areas in management techniques of public administration in the present day context. In the years gone by, it was government and not governance that mattered to the public at large in any form of government whether democratic, despotic, monarchy, military or any other. With unfolding democratic process in many of the countries around the world, governance in common parallence related to governments and their administration machinery that existed to ensure good governance for the governed. In the concept of "the king can do no wrong" and democracy as a form of government "of the people, by the people and for the people", democratic, accountable and responsible governments brought into their fold the ultimate wisdom that governments should be responsible, responsive, accountable, people-centric and participatory with the stake of equality, equity, fraternity, freedom of expression etc. These budgewords found expression in the written and unwritten constitutional patterns which gradually led to establishment of democratic values in the national and international fora of organisations trying to find out as to what a best form of government could be? India's story of governance is well visualized in Kautilya's Arthastastra. What is good for the people is said to be the best form governance "Sarbajana Hitaya", "Sarbajana Sukhaya" were not merely rhetorics but the essence of governance.

With India adopting a written Constitution since 1950, governance structure centred round the three pillars of democracy, namely the Executive, Legislative and Judicial organs which, as instruments of governance, were expected to provide the much-hyped good governance to the country and the people ultimately. Sixty five years of operationalisation of these structures have landed up with an unique experiment of democracy where exceptions are high, deliveries controverted every now and then and structural changes ordained. Successes are many but much less than expectations in high galore treading in limitless sea of experimentation without either trying to understand what a good transparent, accountable, responsible and responsive governance system could be. I have tried to find out some of the issues that have confronted our democratic structures. Most of the contents of this book are not deliberately text-book-centric nor arranged from academic literature exclusively but based mostly on the important events that have traversed through the working of our democratic institutions over the years and the views and expressions reflected in several newspapers, journals, reports of commissions and committees.

The book contains six chapters. Administrative and civil service reforms are often clubbed together because of multiple issues that warrant a vibrant and workable civil service which practically is the olden framework of governance, India has inherited from the colonial past. As civil servants continue to work under the clock of ministerial responsibility, you can neither make any one of them responsible to each other although both are accountable to the people. Committees and commissions have gone through the problems of public administration in India but administration in the executive is more reflected as fallen short of accountability, responsiveness and transparency. India is credited with one of the best examples of conducting elections to its Parliament and the State Assemblies. In spite of several lapses, the electoral process has undergone wide and far-reaching changes. The chapter on "Electoral Reforms" indicates the basic issues that confront our entire electoral process. Attempt has been made to analyse the multiple issues of Indian elections. Indian Judiciary is credited with the distinction of being one of the best democratic institutions but issues and problems are not of common nature. The people of this country have great respect and adoration to our judicial process and expect administration of justice to maintain its impeccable dignity and wisdom. Judiciary must rise to the occasion. The public institutions which are as old as our social structure have gone through several odds and obstacles. We inherited the police as we did the civil service. It has been difficult for the police to maintain its clear and undisputable image as it is often criticized and looked upon as a foe rather than a friend of our society. Administration in India is, therefore, placed at a critical juncture whether it relates to the executive, the legislature, the judiciary or the police for achieving a transparent and accountable governance.

In this book I have tried to analyse various aspects of the above institutions and place before the readers a bibliographical developments in the recent history of our democracy and pointed out a few of the remedies required towards ensuring a better, vibrant, responsible and responsive governance system.

Karunakar Patnaik

Contents

Abbreviations

ACR	-	Annual Confidential Report
ADR	-	Association for Democratic Reform
AIADMK	-	All India Anna Dravid Munetra Khazagam
ARC	-	Administrative Reforms Commission
BDO	-	Block Development Officer
BJD	-	Biju Janata Dal
BJP	-	Bharatiya Janata Party
BPRD	-	Bureau of Police Research and Development
BSF	-	Border Security Force
BSP	-	Bahujan Samaj Party
CAG	-	Comptroller and Auditor General
CAPAM	-	Commonwealth Association of Public Administration
CCR	-	Confidental Character Roll
CEC	-	Chief Election Commissioner
CGAR	-	Core Group on Administrative Reforms
CHRI	-	Commonwealth Human Right Initiative
CIC	-	Chief Information Commissioner
CISF	-	Central Industrial Security Force
CJ	-	Chief Justice
CJI	-	Chief Justice of India
CM	-	Chief Minister
CMO	-	Chief Minister's Office
CMP	-	Common Minimum Programme
CPI	-	Communist Party of India
CPI	-	Corruption Perception Index
CPIM	-	Communist Party of India Marxists
CrPC	-	Criminal Procedure Code
CSDS	-	Centre for Study of Developing Societies
CVC	-	Chief Vigilance Commissioner
CWG	-	Common Wealth Games

DARPGP	-	Department of Administrative Reforms, Public Grievances and Pension
DCBI	-	Director of Central Bureau of Investigation
DFID	-	Department of Foreign Direct Investment
DG	-	Director General
DGP	-	Director General of Police
DM	-	District Magistrate
DMK	-	Dravid Munetra Khazagam
DOPT	-	Department of Personnel and Training
DSPE	-	Delhi Special Police Establishment
EBC	-	Economically Backward Class
EC	-	Election Commission
ECI	-	Election Commission of India
EVM	-	Electronic Voting Machine
FCI	-	Food Corporation of India
FR	-	Fundamental Rules
GDP	-	Gross Domestic Product
GoI	-	Government of India
GoM	-	Group of Ministers
IAS	-	Indian Administrative Service
IB	-	Intelligence Bureau
ICAC	-	Independent Commission Against Corruption
ICS	-	Indian Civil Service
ICT	-	Information Communication Technology
IFC	-	Information and Facilitation Centre
IFS	-	Indian Forest Service
IGP	-	Inspector General of Police
IIAS	-	International Institute of Administrative Service
IIM	-	Indian Institute of Management
IIT	-	Indian Institute of Technology
INC	-	Indian National Congress
INLD	-	Indian National Lok Dal
IT	-	Information Technology
ITACT	-	Income Tax Act
ITBP	-	Indo Tibetan Boarder Police
JAC	-	Judicial Appointments Commission
JD (U)	-	Janata Dal (United)
JWGCS	-	Joint Working Group on Civil Service
LJP	-	Loktantrik Janata Party
MCD	-	Municipal Corporation of Delhi
MIS	-	Management Information System
MLAS	-	Members of Legislative Assembly

MOPPGP	-	Ministry of Personnel, Public Grievances and Pensions
MP	-	Members of Parliament
NCMP	-	National Common Minimum Programme
NCP	-	Nationalist Congress Party
NCRB	-	National Crime Records Bureau
NCT	-	National Capital Territory
NDA	-	National Democratic Alliance
NGO	-	Non-governmental Organisation
NIC	-	National Informatic Centre
NISG	-	National Institute of Smart Government
NJC	-	National Judicial Council
NOTA	-	None of the Above
NPC	-	National Police Commission
NPM	-	New Public Management
OBC	-	Other Backward Castes
OM	-	Organisation and Management
PAC	-	Pradeshika Armed Constabulary
PAR	-	Performance Appraisal Record
PAS	-	Performance Appraisal System
PCA	-	Prevention of Corruption Act
PCI	-	Press Council of India
PERC	-	Political and Economic Risk Consultancy
PESA	-	Panchayats Extension to Scheduled Areas
PGRAMS	-	Public Grievances Redressal and Monitoring System
PIL	-	Public Interest Litigation
PMO	-	Prime Minister's Office
PSU	-	Public Sector Undertaking
RI	-	Rigorous Imprisonment
RJD	-	Rashtriya Janata Dal
RPACT	-	Representation of Peoples Act
RTI	-	Right to Information
SAD	-	Shiromani Akali Dal
SC	-	Scheduled Caste
SIT	-	Special Investigation Team
SP	-	Samajvadi Party
SP	-	Superintendent of Police
SPE	-	Special Police Establishment
ST	-	Scheduled Tribe
TMC	-	Trinamul Congress
ToI	-	Times of India
TV	-	Television

UK	-	United Kingdom
UN	-	United Nations
UNDP	-	United Nations Development Programme
UP	-	Uttar Pradesh
UPA	-	United Progressive Alliance
USA	-	United States of America
UTP	-	Under Trial Prisoner
VIP	-	Very Important Person
VVIP	-	Very Very Important Person
WB	-	West Bengal

Glossary

Abatement: The action of abating or being abated; ending or subsiding.

Activism: The policy or action of using vigorous campaigning to bring about political or social change.

Ambivalent: Having mixed feelings or contradictory ideas about something or someone.

Archaic: Old, Out Dated.

Bountiful: Large in quantity; abundant.

Bureaucracy: A system of Government in which most of the important decisions are taken by State officials rather than by elected representatives.

Bureaucrat: An official in a Government department, in particular one perceived as being concerned with procedural correctness at the expense of people's needs.

Burgeon: Begin to grow or increase rapidly; flourish.

Capitalism: An economic and political system in which a country's trade and industry are controlled by private owners for profit, rather than by the state.

Capitalist: A person who uses their wealth to invest in trade and industry for profit in accordance with the principles of capitalism.

Civil society: Society considered as a community of citizens linked by common interests and collective activity.

Coalition: A temporary alliance for combined action, especially of political parties forming a Government.

Corporatization: It is the process of transforming State assets, Government agencies, or municipal organizations into corporations.

Collegium system: Collegium system is a process through which decisions related to appointments and transfer of judges in Supreme Court and High Court is taken by a collegium which consists of CJI, four senior most judges of Supreme Court and three members of concerned High Court (in the matter related to High Court) including chief justice of High Court.

Communal Disharmony: It refers to the principle that different peoples within a community or society must live together peacefully and in pursuit of mutual goals.

Conservatism: Conservatism is any political philosophy that favours tradition (in the sense of various religious, cultural, or nationally—defined beliefs and customs) in the face of external forces for change, and is critical of proposals for radical social change.

Conscientious: Wishing to do one's work or duty well and thoroughly.

Court of record: A court whose proceedings are recorded and available as evidence of fact.

Criminalization: The process by which behaviours and individuals are transformed into crime and criminals. Previously legal acts may be transformed into crimes by legislation or judicial decision.

Cynicism: An inclination to believe that people are motivated purely by self-interest; scepticism.

Democratization: It is the transition to a more democratic political regime. It may be the transition from an authoritarian regime to a full democracy, a transition from an authoritarian political system to a semi-democracy or transition from a semi-authoritarian political system to a democratic political system.

Denunciation: Public condemnation of someone or something.

Disenchantment: A feeling of disappointment about someone or something you previously respected or admired; disillusionment.

Diktat: An order or decree imposed by someone in power without popular consent.

Disparate: Essentially different in kind; not able to be compared.

Dither: Hesitate.

Doctrine: A stated principle of Government policy, mainly in foreign or military affairs.

Draconian Provisions: Provisions or their application which are excessively harsh and severe.

Dynamism: The quality of being characterized by vigorous activity and progress.

Emphatic: Expressing something forcibly and clearly.

Enticement: Something used to attract or to tempt someone; a lure.

Equivocal: Open to more than one interpretation; ambiguous, uncertain or questionable in nature.

Equality: Equality is ensuring individuals or groups of individuals are treated fairly and equally and no less favourably, specific to their needs, including areas of race, gender, disability, religion or belief, sexual orientation and age. Promoting equality should remove discrimination in all of the aforementioned areas.

Expeditious: Done with speed and efficiency.

Extremist: A person who holds extreme political or religious views, especially one who advocates illegal, violent, or other extreme action.

Fissiparous: Inclined to cause or undergo division into separate parts or groups.

Formidable: Inspiring fear or respect through being impressively large, powerful, intense, or capable.

Fraternity: A group of people sharing a common profession or interests.

Globalization: The process by which businesses or other organizations develop international influence or start operating on an international scale.

GNP: Gross National Product (GNP) is a broad measure of a nation's total economic activity. GNP is the value of all finished goods and services produced in a country in one year by its nationals.

Governance: The action or manner of governing a State, organization, etc.

Heirarchy: A system in which members of an organization or society are ranked according to relative status or authority.

Humanistic: Humanistic philosophy and values reflect a belief in human dignity and science — but not religion. A humanistic philosophy refers to a few specific ideas. For one thing, humanistic thinkers are not religious; they donot believe in a god or gods. ... This philosophy is called humanism.

Hype: Promote or publicize (a product or idea) intensively, often exaggerating its benefits.

Impeccable: In accordance with the highest standards; faultless.

Imperialism: A policy of extending a country's power and influence through colonization, use of military force, or other means.

Impersonation: An act of pretending to be another person for the purpose of entertainment or fraud.

Indelible: Something which cannot be forgotten or removed.

Indignation: Anger or annoyance provoked by what is perceived as unfair treatment.

Individualism: A social theory favouring freedom of action for individuals over collective or state control.

Individualistic: More interested in individual people than in society as a whole.

Inexorable: Impossible to stop or prevent.

Infringement: The action of breaking the terms of a law, agreement, etc.; violation.

Insurgency: An insurgency is a movement within a country dedicated to overthrowing the Government. An insurgency is a rebellion.

Insurgencies are movements to overthrow Governments.

Internalization: Internalization is the process of consolidating and embedding one's own beliefs, attitudes, and values when it comes to moral behaviour. The accomplishment of this may involve the deliberate use of psychoanalytical or behavioural methods.

Institutionalization: Institutionalization refers to the process of embedding some conception (for example a belief, norm, social role, particular value or mode of behaviour) within an organization, social system, or society as a whole.

Intimidation: The action of intimidating someone, or the state of being intimidated.

Judiciary: The judiciary (also known as the judicial system or court system) is the system of courts that interprets and applies the law in the name of the state. The judiciary also provides a mechanism for the resolution of disputes.

Justiciable: Subject to trial in a court of law.

Legislature: A legislature is a deliberative assembly with the authority to make laws for a political entity such as a country or city. Legislatures form important parts of most Governments; in the separation of powers model, they are often contrasted with the executive and judicial branches of Government.

Liberalization (or liberalisation): It is a relaxation of Government restrictions, usually in such areas of social, political and economic policy. This may be similar to deregulation.

Liberty: The State of being free within society from oppressive restrictions imposed by authority on one's behaviour or political views.

Linguistic: Linguistics is the scientific study of language, specifically language form, language meaning, and language in context.

Mandamus: A judicial writ issued as a command to an inferior court or ordering a person to perform a public or statutory duty.

Marxist: It is a method of socioeconomic analysis that analyzes class relations and societal conflict using a materialist interpretation of historical development and a dialectical view of social transformation. It originates from the mid-to-late nineteenth century works of German philosophers Karl Marx and Friedrich Engels.

Materialize: To come into perceptible existence; appear; become actual or real; be realized or carried out: Our plans never materialized. 2. to assume material or bodily form; become corporeal.

Morphological: It is a branch of biology dealing with the study of the form and structure of organisms and their specific structural features.

Nationalization: is the process of transforming private assets into public assets by bringing them under the public ownership of a national government or state.

Nepotism: The practice among those with power or influence of favouring relatives or friends, especially by giving them jobs.

Obiter dicta: A judge's expression of opinion uttered in court or in a written judgement, but not essential to the decision and therefore not legally binding as a precedent.

Objectivism: The belief that certain things, especially moral truths, exist independently of human knowledge or perception of them.

Oligarchic: A small group of people having control of a country or organization.

Ombudsman: An official appointed to investigate individuals' complaints against a company or organization, especially a public authority.

Ordeal: A very unpleasant and prolonged experience.

Ostensibly: As appears or is stated to be true, though not necessarily so; apparently.

Parallel economy: Parallel economy, based on the black money or unaccounted money, is a big menace to the Indian economy. It is also a cause of big loss in the tax-revenues for the Government.

Pauperization: A state of extreme poverty or destitution.

Pernicious: Having a harmful effect, especially in a gradual or subtle way.

Pervasive: (especially of an unwelcome influence or physical effect) spreading widely throughout an area or a group of people.

Platitude: A remark or statement, especially one with a moral content, that has been used too often to be interesting or thoughtful.

Plea: A request made in an urgent and emotional manner.

Pliable: Who can be easily influenced.

Polarized: To divide into sharply opposing fractions, political group etc.

Populist: A member or adherent of a political party seeking to represent the interests of ordinary people.

Precept: A general rule intended to regulate behaviour or thought.

Predicament: A difficult, unpleasant, or embarrassing situation.

Predictive policing: Predictive policing refers to the usage of mathematical, predictive and analytical techniques in law enforcement to identify potential criminal activity.

Predilections: A preference or special liking for something; a bias in favour of something.

Probity: The quality of having strong moral principles; honesty and decency.

Privatization: The transfer of ownership, property or business from the government to the private sector is termed privatization. The Government ceases to be the owner of the entity or business. The

Government ceases to be the owner of the entity or business. The process in which a publicly-traded company is taken over by a few people is also called privatization.

Probity: The quality of having strong moral principles; honesty and decency.

Promptitude: The quality or habit of being prompt, promptness.

Professionalism: The practising of an activity, especially a sport, by professional rather than amateur players.

Prophency: A prediction of what will happen in the future.

Prosecutor: A person, especially a public official, who institutes legal proceedings against someone.

Protagonist: An advocate or champion of a particular cause or idea.

Protracted: Lasting for a long time or longer than expected or usual.

Puisne: denoting a judge of a superior court inferior in rank to chief justices.

Queer: Spoil or ruin (an agreement, event, or situation).

Quixotic: Extremely unrealistic and impractical.

Recalcitrant: Having an obstinately uncooperative attitude towards authority or discipline.

Red-tapism: Refers to excessive regulation or rigid conformity to formal rules that is considered redundant or bureaucratic and hinders or prevents action or decision-making.

Refurbishing: Renovate and redecorate (something, especially a building).

Revere: Feel deep respect or admiration for (something).

Romanticism: A movement in the arts and literature which originated in the late eighteenth century, emphasizing inspiration, subjectivity, and the primacy of the individual.

Rule of law: The restriction of the arbitrary exercise of power by subordinating it to well-defined and established laws.

Sabotage: Deliberately destroy, damage, or obstruct (something), especially for political or military advantage.

Scrupulous: Very concerned to avoid doing wrong.

Self-Aggrandizing: Exaggerating one's own importance or power.

Separatists: a person who supports the separation of a particular group of people from a larger body on the basis of ethnicity, religion, or gender.

Simulacrum: An image or representation of someone or something.

Sinequanon: It is an indispensable and essential action, condition, or ingredient

Socio-political: Combining social and political factors.

Sovereignty: The authority of a state to govern itself or another state.

Sporadic: Occurring at irregular intervals or only in a few places; scattered or isolated.

Subjectivism: The doctrine that knowledge is merely subjective and that there is no external or objective truth.

Succumbed: Fail to resist pressure, temptation, or some other negative force.

Summon: Order (someone) to be present.

Suo motu: *Suo motu*, meaning "on its own motion," is a Latin legal term, approximately equivalent to the term *sua sponte*. For example, it is used where a Government agency acts on its own cognizance, as in "the Commission took *suo motu* control over the matter."

SWOT Analysis: Strengths weaknesses opportunity threat analysis, A study undertaken by an organization to identify its internal strengths and weaknesses, as well as its external opportunities and threats.

Totalitarian: Relating to a system of government that is centralized and dictatorial and requires complete subservience to the state.

Tribalism: The behaviour and attitudes that stem from strong loyalty to one's own tribe or social group.

Tribunal: A body established to settle certain types of dispute.

Tyranny: Cruel, unreasonable, or arbitrary use of power or control.

Unimpeachable: Not able to be doubted, questioned, or criticized; entirely trustworthy.

Urbanization is a population shift from rural to urban areas, "the gradual increase in the proportion of people living in urban areas", and the ways in which each society adapts to the change.

Wilful disobedience: Willful disobedience is the intentional disobedience by a free agent who knows what he is doing, although not necessarily acting with malice or evil intent.

Writ: A form of written command in the name of a court or other legal authority to act, or abstain from acting, in a particular way.

Zamindars: A landowner, especially one who leases his land to tenant farmers.

1
Administrative Reforms

Introduction

Administrative system is an ongoing process and therefore, reforms in administrative system is never a one-time job. No administrative structure can be reflective of a continuing governance pattern at a given time and with change of times, is bound to experience gradual transformation either in the positive or in the negative. The inexorable Parkinson's Law of Bureaucracy indicates that bureaucracy has the inherent tendency to expand even though work remains constant. A hierarchical existence makes it inwards-looking, secretive and self-defending. Moreover, the monopoly of power enjoyed by it makes it self-aggrandizing and therefore, makes it alienated from society. This most embedded challenge in the drive for administrative reform can be better explained in the words of Woodrow Wilson as "it is harder to run a constitution than to frame one". In view of the multi-dimensional areas of state action, reforms have to be multi-dimensional including political and economic reforms. The context of reforms correspond to the socio-political and economic changes introduced to the governance pattern of any country from time-to-time. There could be vested interests both in introducing reforms and in preventing reforms. Therefore, instead of going for radical changes, reforms should come in small packages or quantums unless the total state structure is changed, say from democratic to despotic, from socialist to capitalist, from religious to secular and so on. Mere creativity and innovative ideas are not simply enough to set in agenda for better reforms. Reforms have, therefore, to come in the midst of common responsibilities of all agents of society.

British Legacy

The history of Administrative Reforms in India has been a quixotic search for balancing politics with the ideals of welfare state. The unparalleled treatise of Kautilya's "*Arthashastra*" dealing with administration as a state-craft is one of the best examples suggesting for an ideal balancing between the demands of the Mauryan state and Brahmin-dominated society. It suggested continuous action for maintaining State superiority rather than King's superiority over other institutions. During the British administration, the context and content of administration changed. The legal and regulatory frame of reference was, therefore, of British rather than the one already embedded into local understanding and institutions. Although intentions were benign, they had not reached to local problems and therefore, remained only on files. The increasing gulf between the government and the people and the inability of the people to influence and change of guard polarized the state and its people. All these made rebellious, destructive and pauperization of state property a matter of pride and chivalry. Thus, the main concern of reforms undertaken during the British period were the prevention and control of corruption and indiscipline through imposition of severe penalties. The Regulating Act of 1773 is the best example in this regard. Reforms were more or less an "administrative engineering" to cleanse departmental functioning through the penalizing effects of a coercive and centralized state authority (Keith, 1992). The purpose of administrative reforms was to increase the power of the departmental head to control subordinate offices. It was this principle which led Warren Hastings for reorganization of both revenue administration and criminal justice, besides expanding control over the district police by the District Collector. The distancing from local institutions antagonized two powerful groups in native society: the administrators of the East India Company and the Zamindars or powerful land-owning class who felt that their control over land was weakening. Therefore, the next spate of reforms by Lord Cornwallis were undertaken to rectify this neglect and to re-establish the control of Zamindars over land which was the prime resource for colonial power. In the absence of local linkages in terms of language, culture and institutions, these reforms always tended to be carried away by dominant voices, thus, creating greater imbalances instead of the balance sought to be attained by reforms.

In the context of British reforms, revenue and judicial reforms received priority. The Permanent Settlement of 1793 separated the revenue and judicial functions which had come to be united under the District Collector since the time of Warren Hastings in 1772. A separate post of Civil Judge was created as the District Magistrate became the head of the district administration. It was around this time 1792 that the Daroga system was introduced in which an Indian officer of the rank of Daroga was to replace the Thanedar as the head of the Thana (police station). The old rural police called the ancient militia (Mishra, 1984) or Chowkidars who functioned during the reign of Marathas and the Mughals were replaced by regular policemen. These reforms even distanced the Zamindars from the management of local affairs and from undertaking responsibilities of local administration for which the Thanedars and Chowkidars provided strong support. This set of reforms strengthened the state as a powerful instrument of coercive power to restructure power distribution at the grassroots. Thus, land became the focal point for intense administrative restructuring and a cue for further reforms which came as packages for generating powerlessness among the indigenous communities.

At this point of time in 1789, the world witnessed the first revolutionary upsurge in the form of the French Revolution which led to a disarticulation of the British monarchy and a transformation of purely commercial image of British administration overseas. Reform emphasized as never before the need for maintaining the *status quo* of British control in India. Lord Wellesley realized that in the civil service the instruments merely would not be sought by which kingdoms could be overthrown and revolutions accomplished or wars conducted but an inexhaustible supply of useful knowledge, cultivated talents and well-ordered and disciplined morals were needed the most. Thus, under Regulation IX of 1800, the college for Fort William was established in Calcutta by the Governor General-in-Council to provide a system of higher education towards the end of a highly disciplined and morally and intellectually committed life-long career of civil service in India. Later, however, the East India Company denounced Wellesley's plan of raising such an All India Service. But this was later-on revived when the Directors of the

Company re-established such a training college, first at Hertford and then later at Haileybury. The intention was to create a steel-framed bureaucracy which could ensure uninterrupted business in India. The long probationary training period of three years, the subsequent determination and placement in rank on the basis of a final examination, and the importance to conduct rules and character certificates from the principal of the college only ensured that the objective was attained. The unimpeachable steel-frame system was sustained on an extremely superior level of privileges and salary, not only to attract the best brains and youth of the upper strata of Indian society but also to alienate them from the masses as a class of superiors.

It is noticed that from this period onwards, the state continued to expand into the domain of Panchayats (village councils), civil administration and district administration probably, for considerations of economy and efficiency. A large number of regulations were enacted to streamline and restructure civil and criminal justice and to get rid of some prevailing unhealthy practices and social customs. Two new positions, namely the Chief Commissioner appointed in 1853 and the Lieutenant General appointed in 1854 helped in the further centralization of administration after the Charter Act of 1833. Provincial governments were brought under the control of the Governor-General-in-Council. A system of annual reports integrated the departments vertically and made centralization much more effective. Macaulay was appointed as additional member to the Executive Council for making laws and regulations. The Law Commission was appointed to design civil, penal and procedural codes so that the administration of justice could be based upon the principles of equity and equalitarianism. This extensive jurisdiction only strengthened executive authority in the implementation of policies and ensuring regulatory interventions. In 1870, James Stephen justified the centralization of Indian administration as absolutely essential to the maintenance of British Rule in India.

The passage of the Government of India Act of 1858 was followed by the deputation of H. Rickett to examine the frame of the prevailing company administration in India. The Act replaced the Court of Directors and Board of Control by a cabinet minister called the Secretary of State for India. By the time the Rickett report on 'Civil Establishments and Salaries' came up in 1866, several centralizing tendencies continued in various appointments. The introduction of the portfolio system entrenched departmental administration which further consolidated the position of the Governor General who was designated as the Viceroy of India. The Secretary of State controlled the Governor General, who also further extended his control over the Lieutenant General. Paradoxically, however, the legislative councils continued to grow and with the Indian High Court Act of 1861 and the creation of courts at Calcutta, Madras, Bombay and Allahabad, it was evident that administrative reforms were open to the concerns of legitimacy of the regime. Simultaneously, judicial administration was growing and emerging as a check to executive powers at every level.

While all that was taking place in executive and judiciary, police reforms ironically lagged behind except in Sindh where Charles Napier's personal initiative and efforts led to the Viceroy to appoint a Police Commission in 1860. This Commission recommended certain changes which were put together under the Police Act (V) of 1861. By this arrangement Provinces could then onwards take charge of their own establishments headed by an Inspector General of Police. The district police were also restructured to be headed by a District Superintendent of Police who was immediately responsible to the District Magistrate. In 1905 another position of a Deputy Superintendent of Police under the District Superintendent was created for the Indian officer to look after the intricacies of Indian life. In 1902, Lord Curzon appointed another Police Commission to focus further on structural and organizational problems. This led to the creation of a separate bench of 'Criminal Intelligence' under the Home Department of the Government of India to co-ordinate inter-provincial crimes.

The next attempt came as a realization that power had to be decentralized with the local governments which had been totally subsumed in neglect and disarray. In 1687, the first Municipal Corporation was set-up in Madras. James II sought an arrangement to broaden the People's Participation Act XIV of 1856 to establish Conservancy Boards with administrative powers for Calcutta, Madras and Bombay. The respective District Commissioners were made the head of these Boards. In 1870, Lard Mayo's resolution set this trend moving towards decentralization and which finally evolved into Lord Ripon's resolution for local governance. The importance of this resolution lay in the belief that local decentralization and self-government was a means for imparting political education both in cities and villages. He observed:

> "As we have entered upon a period of change in India—such measures (elected local bodies) will not only have an immediate effect in promoting gradually and safely the political education of the people which I hold to be a great object of public policy, but will also pave the way for further advances in the same direction—this subject of local government is a broad question of political principle."

In 1882, his government issued the epoch-making resolution on local governance which led to the enactment of the Local Boards Act of 1885. The recommendation of the Act included that the smallest administrative unit, the Sub-division or Taluk or Tehsil, shall ordinarily be placed under a Local Board which would further be controlled by the District Boards. Lord Ripon recommended elections to local bodies, decentralization of financial structures and reduction of the number of official members to just a third of the total members. The efforts made by him towards administrative decentralization influenced the post-independence reforms in Panchayat administration. However, this was found to be too radical by his successor Lord Curzon. Instead of broadening this process of decentralization, his government confined itself to achieving 'efficiency and economy' through a centralized bureaucracy and draconian disciplinary laws. But the Corporation of Madras being already in existence since 1688 and the municipal bodies for Calcutta and Bombay since 1726, despite Curzon's indignation, decentralization had already taken root in Indian administration. In the meantime, besides Curzon's apprehensions, these developments had challenged the focus of reforms towards local decentralization. Firstly, the rise of middle-class Indian nationalism among the English-speaking educated Indians questioning police autonomy and bureaucratic control. Secondly, the emergence of a new class of industrial workers who consolidated themselves after learning about the Russian revolution. Thirdly, disenchantment of middle-class as it was losing control over land. Certain legislative attempts such as the Punjab Land Alienation Act and Tenancy legislations decreased the flow of rent to them from the land.

Ripon's drive for administrative decentralization at the level of local administration could not go very far. The size and complexity of British bureaucracy continued to grow. It was not only the police but failure of the bureaucracy in providing relief services during famine, floods and water which enlarged the number of administrative departments in the Viceroy's Executive Council. This laid the foundations of the Planning and Development Department which converged into a Planning Commission after Independence. In 1907 the Royal Commission on decentralization emphasized once again the indispensability of decentralization at the local level. Only Punjab adopted its recommendations in its Municipal Act of 1911. Panchayats became legal bodies under the Government of Indian Act of 1919 but the Act of 1935 ironically made them a provincial subject and subservient to Provincial Governments. This legacy passed through independence to the new constitution of the republic prevented Panchayats from evolving into self-governing institutions.

Many dilemmas of the British government about administrative reforms in India took back seat when His Majesty's government in 1917 decided to clarify the goals of British governance in India in the Secretary of State Edwin Montesque's declaration, which mentioned about the "increasing association of Indians in every branch of administration and the gradual development of self-governing institutions with a view to the progressive realisations of responsible government in India." The system of 'Diarchy' as a measure of reform made restructuring and Indianisation of the administrative machinery indispensible to its functioning. The Lee Commission of 1922 provides proof that the British government realized the indispensability of Indianisation of civil services in India.

Chaturvedi and Maheswari (1984) have mentioned about three landmarks of administrative reforms in the period preceding independence. The first landmark was the 1919 Montesque-Chelmsford reforms which made a beginning towards democratization by restructuring bureaucracy according to the new demands set by 'dyarchy'. The second was the introduction of Provincial Autonomy in 1935 and the third landmark was the

1945-46 'Report of Richard Tottenham' on the Indian Civil Service which laid the foundations for a development-oriented public administration in India. Despite this, the steel frame bureaucracy was always in demand to establish law and order in an otherwise fearfully centralized state, and as expressed by Morley the Secretary of State to Minto, the Viceroy, "Bureaucrats in their hearts believe in nothing but the virtue of will and arbitrary powers". This also led to the decadence of bureaucratic organizational practices. Strict adherence to the two important principles of hierarchy and neutrality supported by laws such as the Official Secrecy Act of 1923 overlooked and consistently marginalized the need for transparency and accountability in administration. The mass exodus of British and Muslim administrations due to partition of India came as a terrible tragedy, and laid the foundations of a highly non-secular and passionately communal, casteist and despotic system of administration in India.

Reforms on the Eve and After Independence

The political context of administration changed after Independence and so did the nature of the state. The inadequacy of decision-making processes was evident as these took place in the institutions raised during colonial times and these remained victims of what Ferrel Heady termed as 'operational autonomy'. Functions of bureaucracy increased after independence due to adoption of a welfare state model which extended jurisdiction of the government from 'cradle to grave' concerns. While efforts were being made for redefining the functional goals of Government, the bureaucracy continued to perform the conventional role of maintaining law and order. There were two models for the Indian bureaucracy to adopt for welfare state functions. One was the 'Soviet Model' and the other was the 'Beveridge Model'. The Soviet Model was characterized by a bureaucratic rather than a professional principle of organization. This entailed a higher role to the generalist and a subservient status to research-oriented organizations which provided analytical information. Hierarchy, unity of command and neutrality as bureaucratic features makes public organizations more inward-looking and closed. The Beveridge model emerged from the report prepared by Sir William Beveridge (1942), a highly esteemed economist and expert on unemployment problems in

Britain. The report entitled "Social Insurance and Allied Services" aimed to provide a comprehensive "cradle to grave" social insurance to all citizens. The huge success of this report indicated the shift of a sizable British population to the left which resulted in the victory of the Labour Party in the 1945 elections. The significance of this report for administrative reforms is that the principle of state intervention for collective welfare found place in governance in contrast to the selective, charitable and philanthropic activity undertaken by Victorian non-state actors. While the Soviet Model focused upon fair distribution and investment in industrial development, the Beveridge model focused upon the 'cradle to grave' responsibility of the state towards its citizens. These developments have, however, greatly influenced the ideological stands of Indian reforms.

In post-Independent India, the civil services were confronted with the arduous task of implementing socio-economic programmes within the democratic constitutional framework. The whole mechanism of service delivery for the people threw an open challenge to the assertion that the British system of civil service had the skills to govern India (Mathur, 2004). This was based on three essential myths. The first was about the popularity of civil service as a profession that attracted the best minds, the second was its efficiency in administering India and the third was the sacrificial spirit-de-corps of the ICS which ostensibly infused the government with the primary concern of working for the welfare of the people. These myths helped to perpetuate colonial legacies of administration in Independent India and weaken policy implementation in the developmental state. These were major shortfalls in the basic requirements of good governance besides acute shortage of skilled as well as non-skilled personnel. These initial difficulties led to the appointment of a six-member committee under Girija Shankar Bajpai in August 1947 for 'secretariat reorganization'. In 1948, a committee was set-up 'to review increase in civil expenditure of the Central Government since 1938-39 and to make recommendations for the promotion of true economy in administration by the elimination of un-necessary, wasteful or extravagant expenditure'. Incidentally, this committee was headed by the Industrialist Kasturbhai Lalbhai but had members from bureaucracy as well as elected political representatives. This led to a more comprehensive review undertaken by the Gopalaswami Ayyangar Committee in 1949. In 1951, a retired civil servant A.D. Gorwala was asked by the Planning Commission of India to assess the capability of existing public administration for undertaking the demands of developmental planning. He submitted two reports-one on public administration, and the other on the efficient conduct of state enterprises, which reflected upon the increasing role of public enterprises in Indian economy. Nehru's enthusiasm for reforms brought Paul H. Appleby from Syracuse University in the USA for a survey of public administration in India. His studies appeared in the form of two reports: 'Public Administration in India: Report of a Survey' in 1953 and "Recognisation of India's Administrative system with Special Reference to Administration of Government's Industrial and Commercial Enterprises" in 1956. These two reports suggested stream-lining organization, procedures, work methods and relations with the Parliament. As a result, an "Organization and Methods" (O & M) division was setup in the cabinet secretariat. Appleby's reports have been one of the most influential documents since independence to direct the future course of reforms in India. At least two out of the 12 recommendations that Appleby made in his first report were immediately accepted. One was about the need for setting up of an 'Institute for Public Administration Research' and the other for setting up an O & M organization in the Central Government. The rest of the reports including Gorwala's report would not inspire the government to undertake administrative reforms despite its growing need to do so.

With the launching of the First Five Year Plan (1951-1956), new administrative agencies were identified for development purposes with new responsibilities for administration. The O & M division was setup as the standing machinery for administrative improvement which later in 1964 was merged with the Department of Administrative Reforms. By virtue of its location in the cabinet secretariat, this division was able to co-ordinate activities of various Ministries. Two documents which initiated the future course of reforms were published in 1961-62. The first was the 'Statement of Administrative Procedure' and the second was the 'Report on Indian and State Administrative Services and Problems of District Administration' by V.T. Krishnamachari. Both documents recommended series of improvement in simplifying procedural aspects of administration, better training for public conduct, effective performance and measures for reduced corruption. These reports also suggested an improvement in the pre-entry training at the National Academy of Administration. A central council for local-self- government was constituted by an order of the President in 1954. Initially it dealt with problems of both rural and urban governments, but later urban government was placed in Entry 5 list II of the VII Schedule and Entry 20 of List III while rural government was placed in List II of Schedule VII and Article 40 of the Directive Principles of State Policies.

The decade of the 1960s was a most challenging period for India. A severe economic crisis, speedily lengthening unemployment list, scarcity of civil supplies, technological and scientific backwardness and rampant corruption called for some severe reform measures. Several efforts were made by the Planning Commission, Estimates Committee of Parliament, two Pay Commissions (1946 and 1958), reports on public administration and lastly, K. Santhanam's Committee on the Prevention of Corruption in 1964, which engaged themselves in the ordeal of reforms. During Indira Gandhi's reign and due to her call for greater commitment for the bureaucracy, administrators started hovering around politically powerful offices, especially the Prime Minister's Office. These institutions mauled hierarchy principles so much that the Prime Minister's personal secretary became more powerful than the cabinet secretary. P.C. Alexander and later P.N. Haksar became the chief advisers on bureaucratic restructuring. Few secretaries such as Nirmal Mukherjee and later T.N. Chaturvedi had the courage to question the Prime Minister about several unilateral decisions taken during period of intense politicization of bureaucracy. The distinguished scholar on administration C.P. Bhambri (1972) commented that the British genius was given all credit for creating a neutral civil services but it was forgotten that a neutral and value-free bureaucracy was only possible in a society where consensus existed on values. Considering from this angle, the aforesaid reforms were mere readjustments and improvements over the pre-existing designs of administration. It may be appropriate here to recall what the Secretary of State Morley lamented to Viceroy Minto in 1907 about Indian bureaucracy: "The government of India will be pure bureaucracy and neither you nor I can help it".

Administrative Reforms Commission, 1966

The constitution of the Administrative Reforms Commission (ARC) in 1966 has been a major landmark in the history of administrative reforms in India. It provided inumerable literature for researchers who intend to understand the complexity of reform processes. The Fourth Five Year Plan stated that, "administrative development" set for itself a direction for 'administration for change' which attempted to replace 'development administration'. Thus, the setting-up of the Department of Administrative Reforms in 1964 under the Ministry of Home Affairs was intended to speed up efforts for reforms. In January 1966, the ARC was setup by the Government of India (GoI) under the Chairmanship of Shri Moraji Desai. The Commission had wide terms of reference ranging from the structural study of the machinery of government at both the central and state level to the administration of the agricultural and economic programmes adopted by the government. The Commission had adopted 10 broad rules undertaking the survey. These relate to:

(i) The machinery of the GoI and its work procedures,
(ii) The machinery of planning at all levels,
(iii) Centre-State relationships,
(iv) Financial administration,
(v) Personnel administration,
(vi) Economic administration,
(vii) Administration at the state level,
(viii) District administration,
(ix) Agricultural administration, and
(x) Problem of redressal of citizen's grievances.

The Commission submitted as many as twenty reports between 1968 and 1970 with about 537 major recommendations.

Some of the major recommendations relate to:

(i) need for specialization,
(ii) unified grading structure,
(iii) requirement,
(iv) requirement agencies,
(v) training,

(vi) promotions,
(vii) conduct and discipline,
(viii) service conditions etc.

The Commission followed the model of the Hoover Commission on organization of the executive branch of the Government (1953-55). While the Hoover Commission restricted itself to the specific area of the reorganization of the executive branch of Government despite its lengthy terms of references, the ARC, in contrast, dealt with a large number of issues which made its study too comprehensive and at many points bloated and unnecessary. Analysists state that the Commission would have contributed more meaningfully if it had restricted its terms of reference like the Fulton Committee on Civil Service Reforms which proved to be an effective agent of reform in Britain. C. Subramaniam speaking at the Business Relations Conference at Bangalore in 1968, remarked that the 'Commission had got itself bogged-down with unessential'. The Fulton report on the committee on civil services (1968) pointed-out that many of the findings of the departmental restructuring had a strong bearing upon the work and organization of civil service in the country and by restricting its terms of reference the inherent inter-dependencies of government departments were missed-out. Chairman K. Hanumanthiya also defended ARC against this charge when at a press conference in Bangalore he explained how steadily the task of the Commission was being done because the terms of reference were not as detailed as was assumed to be by the critics. He claimed that the Commission's investigations were already completed and all its recommendations were being accepted except the one which said that the Prime Minister could not be Chairman of the Planning Commission. However, the principal criticism was about its too wide-ranging terms of reference. The ARC also was encountered with the criticism about its timing and its composition. Many felt that it was too early to study changes in Indian administration and the 1960s were turbulent for the nation both externally and internally due to the Sino-Indian war in 1962 and later, the loss of two Prime Ministers, Jawaharlal Nehru and Lal Bahadur Shastri. This Commission, however, coincided with the Minnowbrook Conference (1968) in USA both in its turbulent political and social climate and in its efforts to explore standards of sustainable administrative practices capable of universal application around the globe even though the term 'sustainable' was nowhere mentioned in the conference papers.

Another criticism against the ARC was about its composition because its Chairman Moraji Desai preferred to include only members of Parliament and not experts from the bureaucracy and other public sector organizations. Incidentally, at least its Member Secretary came from the civil services. This Commission functioned till June 1970 when it was suddenly dissolved by its Chairman Hanumanthaiya but throughout its short tenure, it was ridden with internal wrangles and authoritative dispositions of its Chairman. The Commission had also to face a lot of uncertainty when its first Chairman Moraji Desai became the Deputy Prime Minster in 1967 and later when its revered member H.C. Mathur passed away suddenly in 1968.

On examination of some of the features of the Commission's findings, it is clear that it attached a sense of urgency to do the need for 'economy and efficiency' and therefore, suggested a combined approach to improving structures, methods and personnel. It recommended weeding-out of all obsolete administrative practices, but had clearly put up a warning against those rushing to 'transplant foreign practices' (ARC, 1968). As a consequence of this report, the Ministry of Home Affairs had to shed a lot of extra flab which it had accumulated since colonial times. It was also able to retain the Department of Administrative Reforms. Its Department of Personnel was shifted to the cabinet secretariat. Some powerful functions such as the appointment and transfer of judges of High Courts and Supreme Court were given to the department of justice within the Ministry of Law and Justice. The Prime Minister's position was strengthened by receiving the CBI from the Ministry of Finance and also the Department of Personnel. In 1985, a full-fledged Ministry of "Personnel, Public Grievances and Pensions" was established directly under the Prime Minister. As a measure of economic efficiency, and out of the need for better coordination, a separate "Ministry of Programme Implementation" was established. On the recommendations of the L.K. Jha Commission, the concept of performance appraisal and management by objectives was introduced in the form of annual action plans for ministries and departments as well as MoUs with public sector undertakings. Most of these changes were done to improve coordination between ministries, departments and cabinet committees. The ARC also came up with the pruning of public sector undertakings. Field agencies were given more freedom and responsibilities in an effort to make them more receptive to local needs. But, one of the suggestions regarding entrepreneurial development which was not accepted by the government related to the setting up of sectoral corporations in eight industries or manufacturing areas and for air transport, shipping and tourism. However, these reforms indicated the need for greater accountability of public officials, need for transparency of procedures and the right to information, but above all, it was efficiency and economy which were the driving force behind reforms.

The increasing criminalization of electoral politics and rampant corruption in high offices hindered some of the most important requirements of the ARC. Ironically indeed, since the ARC of 1969 no other comprehensive commission till the 2nd ARC headed by Virappa Moilly, was formed in 2005. *Ad-hocism* has marred many good practices. It is only in the recent past that few State Governments have come up with few initiatives for reform to improve their governance. The Government of the National Capital Territory (NCT) of Delhi was the only state government to have constituted a permanent ARC consisting of a Chief Secretary, two Principal Secretaries, three Secretaries, one Additional Secretary and two Commissioners (NCT order dated 7th September, 2001). The functions of this commission also suggest the official seriousness towards the need for reforms since it had to furnish its first report within a period of 60 days and annually, by the first day of May each year. But less fortunate states like Karnataka dissolved its ARC within days of its presentation of the final report by its former Law Minister Haranallah Ramaswamy. In Rajasthan also, the ARC which was constituted under the former Chief Minister Shri Shiv Charan Mathur in May 1999 and had submitted its recommendations soon thereafter, did not see them implemented. Except having a department or a skeleton of that on administrative reforms in some of the states, no state government have actually gone for a full-fledged Administrative Reforms Commission in the state. For a long period, the setting up of a Second Administration Reforms Commission was being contemplated. Reminded of the pulse of recommendations of First Administrative Reforms Commission, the gossip of non-action as a tradition was conspicuous in the backdrop of setting a Second Administrative Commission. With the experience of the First Commission's recommendations, there was enough justification to believe that Parkinson's Law may apply where bureaucracy may only grow in size without commitment and normal danger could also be expected from a Second Administrative Reforms Commission as well.

Globalization and Administrative Reforms

Development of technology and modern inventions have led to increased global interaction and communication. The invention of cycle, steam-engine, telephone, electric bulb and various technological equipments and machineries have decreased gaps between people and influenced inter-personal relationships. But technological advancements also affect the wider processes of democratization of political systems which bypass the logical institutional change. Globalization, while opens up new opportunities for any nation, it also threatens small and weak societies and their self-governed institutions. In 1991 when the new economic policy was launched in India, a lot of publicity was given by the international financial donors. Many usages like de-regulation, out-sourcing, dismantling, restructuring and downsizing came into vogue in the reform literature. The post-Second World War period saw the rise of command economics. Writers like A. Lerners (1944), Gunnar Myrdal (1957) and Paul Samuelson (1973) made a strong case in favour of command economies. Samuelson even predicted that these economies would grow faster than the market economy of the USA and the Soviet economy would catch-up with that of USA by the 1990s and most surely by 2010. Many developing countries also adopted this model as the surest way to grow fast and grow meaningfully. However, the intellectual convergence after the collapse of communism and the reunion of the two Germanys gave cue to neo-liberal economy of the World Bank looking for a more cost-effective service delivery system.

The first fallout of globalization on administrative reforms came in the form of bureaucratic-bashing which spread through literature coming from all disciplines of social theory. Some well-established constitutional practices regarding the relationship of bureaucracy to parliamentary democracy such as that of ministerial responsibility and civil service neutrality were opened to public scrutiny. As public choice theorists questioned the altruism of welfare state model, bureaucratic-bashing became a fashionable intellectual exercise towards the end of 1980s. Many questions about the economics of bureaucracy such as (i) Why bureaucracies fail to provide goods and services in an efficient manner? (ii) Why do governments continue to adopt policies from which there are no discernible benefit for its citizens and on many of the precepts of the theory of bureaucracy like hierarchy, neutrality, utility of command, impersonality and superior-subordinate relationship in an organisation were raised. Many writers like Gordon Tullock (1965), Luduig Von Mises (1944), Anthony Downs (1967) and William A. Niskanen (1971) provided an inside vision into the operations and economics of bureaucracy. Niskanen treated the bilateral relationship between bureaucracy and representative government as one of bilateral bargaining between an 'information supplier' and the sponsor. The bureaucrat has a monopoly over information which is in demand by the sponsor who is the monopoly-demander for this information. This is called the "Monopoly and Bilateral Bargaining Model". Another model, i.e. the principal-agent model propounded by Weingast (1984) and Moe (1984) found that the model Niskanen may not be actually a trouble free and smooth model for transfer of information since all individuals are 'rational utility maximizers'. From the above analysis it transpires that the whole politics can be seen as a chain of principal-agent relationship, from citizen to down the hierarchy of government to the lowest level bureaucrats who actually deliver services directly to citizens (Moe, 1984). Even it remains a fact that politics and administrative reforms also become ingredients of the market. The economics of the bureaucratic system which guided the NPM (New Public Management) reforms refers to certain ingredients such as to maximize profits by firms, utility by consumers and political support by policy-makers (Shughart, 1999). However, the public choice model stands in direct contrast to the public interest model previously developed by A.C. Pigou (1932) which asserts that markets cannot be trusted to supply public goods as they are more prone to enter into undesirable activities than their counter-parts in government. But, this theory gradually weakened by attacks from other theory groups. But, it was Williamson's (1990) 10 propositions of policy reforms universally referred to as the "Washington Consensus" were even considered as a more notorious prescription for reforms. The main tenors of this proposition are: (i) Fiscal discipline, (ii) Redirection of public expenditure priorities towards fields offering both high economic returns and the potential to improve income distribution such as primary health care, primary education and infrastructure, (iii) Tax reforms (to lower marginal rates and broaden the tax base), (iv) Interest-rate liberalization, (v) A competitive exchange rate, (vi) Trade liberalization, (vii) Liberalization of FDI inflows, (viii) Privatization, (ix) Deregulation (to abolish barriers to entry and exit), and (x) Secure property rights.

The above mentioned propositions reflect the re-liberal agenda of the World Bank. The WB, UNDP and DFID have published extensively on the need for NPM reforms for overcoming financial stagnation and social backwardness which the bureaucratic model failed to achieve (DFID, 1997; UNDP, 1995; World Bank, 1995, 1996, 1997). Success stories of small states such as Mauritius "Managing Success 1985" or "The East Asian Miracle 1993" and "Debacles in Sub-Saharan States" or in "Latin Interpretations of Good Governance" are constructed as the freedom to invest and de-invest to achieve the agendas of donor programmes. Even though the policy thrust of the Washington Consensus has also been criticized as a sort of new imperialism, its author Williamson has tried to justify this version of reform as potentially poor-poor. But this theory has failed in practice at least in the first generation NPM reforms as revealed from the reforms in Brazil and other Latin American countries as not contributing to reducing poverty and inequality. Therefore, the post-Washington Consensus Reforms "need to focus on improving the quality of investment, promoting the development of sound and efficient financial markets enhancing the legal and regulatory environments and improving the quality of the public sector including the judiciary" (Burkey and Perry, 1998). Even Stiglitz (1998) goes a step further to suggest the need for three ideals which have gone unrecognized, i.e. sustainable development, equalitarian development and democratic institutions besides electing the need for financial regulation, competition and transparency. The term NPM has recently become a brand name for administrative reforms all over the world. It is both a new institutional philosophy for the transformation of the public sector and a plea for economy and efficiency through managerialism and technological sophistication. The term was first used by Hood (1991). Many writers have viewed and branded this model of reform from different perspectives. Christensen and Laegreid term it as a loose and hybrid concept because it tries to balance the demands of participatory management, scientific management and business management. However, NPM suggests the principles of old scientific management but diminishes the accountable and controlling layer of Weberian bureaucracy as a result of which it becomes centralization through managers.

It is imperative that the running of government should be professionalized. All senior level posts need to be thrown open for competition for candidates not only within the civil services but also competent professionals. In countries like UK, Australia, New Zealand, all top posts in civil services have been thrown open to competition and selection is done by getting the best men for each job as recruitment will be job specific. This will take away the power of appointment of top posts from the hands of politicians and depoliticize the services. Presently, the provisions of discipline rules are so cumbersome and tortuous that it becomes very difficult to take action against a delinquent employee for in-subordination and misbehaviour. Once appointed, it is also impossible to remove or demote an employee. The provisions of Civil Service Conduct and Discipline Rules are porous and complicated with numerous loopholes and invariably weighted in favour of the delinquent. The Commission to Review the Working of the Constitution (2002) headed by Justice Venkatachaliah observed that "the constitutional safeguards have, in practice, acted to shield the guilty against swift and certain punishment for abuse of public office for private gain" and suggested for re-visiting the issue of constitutional safeguards under Art 311 of the Constitution. The second ARC has also said that it created a climate of excessive security without fear of penalty for incompetence and wrong doing. There is, therefore, a need to recast the disciplinary procedure so that quick and summary punishment could be given to delinquent employees while keeping in view the principle of natural justice.

Impact on Local Government

NPM reforms have made serious impact upon local government. The grassroots levels have become more consolidated, turbulent and resource sensitive. Activity charged civil society groups at the local level are close to resource use groups. A substantial part of administrative problems at the lower level of administration such as Panchayats and Municipalities are the consequences of inadequate assessments, half-hearted surveys, uncommitted investigations and bad evaluation of resources. Local communities both rural and urban throughout the world have struggled to design new and innovative practices to deal with the problems as the state apparatus has failed to answer their common daily problems. A network of civil society groups which surround the Panchayats in the phase of global reforms indicate the failure of bureaucracy and the emergence of "Governance" as a new multi-disciplinary synthesis to deal with this problem of fragmentation and consolidation at the grassroots level. Considering the various problems at local level in the mid-1990s came about a realization of the need to adopt global practices to local norms and community institutions. The CAPAM conferences in 1994 on 'Government in Transition' and in 1996 on 'The New Public Administration Global Challenges—Local Solutions' were attempts to focus upon the new role of public managers in providing high quality services that citizens valued and bridging the gap that occurs between comprehensive country strategy for global reforms agenda and local experiments. These conferences advocated a new paradigm which is explainable under five components, namely (i) delivery of high quality services, (ii) increasing managerial autonomy, (iii) rigorous performance measurements of individuals and organizations, (iv) managerial support services to facilitate achievement of policy targets, and (v) receptiveness to competition. This change was visible even in the Terms of Reference (TOR) of the Fifth Pay Commission (1998) which indicates a conscious departure from the TOR of ARC of 1966. The Fifth Pay Commission suggested the following steps:

- The core functions of the government should first be defined.

- The distribution of work between the three-tiers of governance will have to be restated.
- The number of Central Ministries and departments should be reduced drastically.
- The size and construction of Central Ministries and departments should be redefined. All functions that should be performed by the State Government and Panchayati Raj Institutions may be transferred to them.
- All functions that do not involve formulation of policy should be delegated to agencies.
- Recruitment to the different services may be reduced.
- There should be a sound legal architecture.
- The Government office itself will need a heavy dose of restructuring.
- The financial management and budgetary system will have to be totally re-written.
- There will have to be a simplification of procedures and formulation of accountability norms in government (Report of the Fifth Pay Commission, 1997: 113-14).

The purpose of these recommendations was to make administration more citizen-friendly and cost-effective. In fact, the number of departments in the Government of India had increased from 35 in 1962 to 50 in 1972. The Tata Consultancy Group invited by GoI for classifying various services suggested a three-fold classification basing upon the roles performed by them. These were core services, participatory services and auxiliary services. The core functions are those given in the Constitution for which the Government is the sole trustee for delivering social goods and services. Participatory functions are those policy-making functions which require a partnership of public and private sectors but the Government has the responsibility for production and trading of goods and services. Auxiliary functions are only regulatory functions of the Government where it is not responsible for the delivery of goods and services. Besides the Pay Commission's recommendations, many new practices have been incorporated such as corporatisation, privatization exploring the possibilities of linking the private sector as suppliers to the core functions of Government such as defence, atomic energy, space research, railway infrastructure and other sensitive installations and areas of mixed economy in order to have greater competition and contracting out of services. This is the first time that a Pay Commission has undertaken to serve as a commission for administrative reforms also. But, due to lack of political will and stability and rising electoralism in public life many of its recommendations failed to make any changes and the privatization factor had some elements of rationalization of services. These reforms also remained handicapped because of the need for reforms in the electoral system, the judiciary and the right to information.

Reform Initiatives after 2000

A few important initiatives were taken after 2000 to overcome some of the implementation handicaps of reforms undertaken in the early era of global integration of India. 'Law and Governance' was recognized as one of the most perplexing areas and lack of research as a major hindrance to sustainability of reforms. The existence of obsolete laws of colonial era prevented any progress towards a transparent, accountable and speedy service delivery to citizens and in implementation of pro-poor programmes. Thus, a commission on 'Review of Administrative Laws' was setup on 8th May 1998 under the Chairmanship of Shri P.C. Jain which submitted its report on 30th September, 1998. To monitor the follow up action on the implementation of the Commission's recommendation, a Standing Committee was also constituted under the Chairmanship of Secretary, Personnel Department. Some of the major recommendations which were highlighted as areas in need of urgent attention were, repeal of more than 50 per cent of Central Laws (1132 out of 2500 laws), expeditious amendments to a critical list of about 109 Acts, documentation of administrative laws, rules, regulations and executive instructions etc., harmonization of statutes and laws from the perspective of domestic and foreign investors, trade and industry, consumers, exporters and importers and development of a viable alternative dispute resolution machinery (Annual Report MOP PG&P, 2003-04). By 2003, four hundred and five (405) Acts including 5-war-time permanent ordinances were repealed. Forty Six (46) Acts have already been amended and 18 Amendment Bills introduced in Parliament. However, Ministries and some departments decided to retain 819 Acts which are mostly the Appropriation Acts and Recognisation Acts. Many Acts were at various stages of processing.

Thereafter, a 'Core Group' on Administrate Reforms (CGAR) was constituted under the cabinet secretary and its composition revealed the need for a composite and more coordinated efforts in the future. The group included the Secretaries from Planning Commission, Expenditure, Legal Affairs, Information Technology, Statistics, Scientific and Industrial Research, Personnel and Public Grievance and Administrative Reforms. In 2004 a Committee (better known as the Hota Committee) was constituted under the Chairmanship of Shri P.C. Hota, IAS (Retd.) former Chairman of Union Public Service Commission (UPSC). Out of its many recommendations, the need for a responsive and citizen-friendly, transparent, accountable, ethical and e-governance friendly civil service tops the list. Some conventional areas of reform such as de-politicization of civil services and methods to decentralize process have featured again but the most important one is about putting a premium on intellectual growth of civil servants and on upgrading their domain of knowledge.

The government also tried to initiate a "Minimum Agenda for E-Governance" for the use of information technology along with reengineering processes in government towards greater transparency, accountability and speed. A high power committee with cabinet secretary as its chairperson was constituted for this purpose. This minimum agenda *inter alia* ensures provision of a basic minimum infrastructure as well as certain government to government and government to citizen transactions (Annual Report Ministry of Personnel, Public Grievance and Pensions, 2002). The Department of Administrative Reforms, Public Grievances and Pensions (DARPGP) has taken initiatives to document and disseminate best practices in the area of e-governance. As a result of these initiatives, at least four good practices received International Innovative Awards 2000 from Commonwealth Association of Public Administration and Management (CAPAM). These practices are the following:

- Bhoomi—online delivery of land records—Government of Karnataka.
- Trichy community policing. A novel experience, Government of Tamil Nadu.

- Kudumbshree—An innovation in tackling urban poverty, Government of Kerala.
- National Child Labour Project, Government of Tamil Nadu.

A 'Digital Repository' information centre has been set-up by DARPGP to disseminate all good practices and experiments in e-governance which is connected to select 'knowledge centres' in the country. A National Institute of Smart Government (NIGS) has been setup at Hyderabad on Information Technology and Software Development to bring about a change of the face of Indian bureaucracy. In 2002-03, a composite plan scheme under the nomenclature of 'Plan Scheme on Administrative Reforms' has been formulated by merging two earlier reform efforts of government, i.e. modernization of government offices of 1986 and the scheme on Administrative Reforms of 2000. This has encouraged and inspired greater interaction with professionals and research agencies in the areas of evaluation and bench-making, application of information technology, research projects in administrative reforms, development of knowledge management system and assessment of quality in government.

E-governance implies a smoother interface between government and citizens. Although, it cannot entirely replace manual governance, even its limited application could be good enough to effect day-to-day living. It can reduce distances to nothing, linking remote villages to government offices in the cities and can reduce staff, costs and check leakages in government system and can make citizen-government interaction smooth, without queers and tyranny and harassment of clerical staff in offices where citizens generally interact in respect of payment of taxes, bills, user fees, conduct registration formalities and try to secure driving licences etc. On the whole, e-governance is only a tool for good governance: E-governance initiatives have, during the last decade or so, transformed the administrative landscape in the country. While in the past the administration grappled with the issue of making the bureaucracy responsive to the needs of the people on one hand and reducing the interface between the administration and the public on the other to reduce rent-seeking behaviour, ICT provided the ideal solution by speeding up government processes and increased accountability and transparency in the government. There has been considerable effort in organizing internal Management Information System (MIS) to support decision-making. But despite promises and hypes, these have performed well below requirements. One major problem in this area is the lack of systematic evaluation of the value addition provided by IT system. For ensuring a successful information-based decision support system, some minimum design requirements are needed. These relate to (a) maximum capacity for analysis and use of information at the intermediate level of management, (b) system development for data uploading and integration, (c) no peripheral service provider to have entry more than once, (d) formulation of a data policy, (e) engagement of independent agency to certify capacities of each software, and (f) development of capacity-building of Block, District and State levels to analyse and interpret data.

The citizen's charter initiative in the government started in 1996-97 and was endorsed by State and Union Territory Administration in the conference of Chief Ministers held in May 1997. In 2002, a core group under the Chairmanship of Secretary (Consumer Affairs), Director General National Informatics Centre (NIC) and Additional Secretary (Administrative Reforms and Personnel Grievances) was formed to improve upon the functioning of these charters. This initiative of citizen's charter and sway of ICT in governance has led to the setting-up of computerized Information and Facilitation Counters (IFC). The NIC has also developed an uniform software called Public Grievance Redressal and Monitoring System (PGRAMS) as an effort towards capacity building for good governance.

The discourse on government in public administration across the world has swung between two extremes, i.e. "the government that governs least governs the best" and the government that governs and looks after its citizens "from cradle to the grave" is the best. In India, the concept of welfare state is enshrined in the "Directive Principles of State Policy" of the Constitution. Over the years, the focus on administrative reforms in India has changed. The earlier policies were mostly related to "efficiency, economy and effectiveness". The subsequent thrust has changed over to "responsive administration and participatory governance" with focus on "transparency and accountability". Good governance has been emphasised by successive Five Year Plans. The Twelfth Five

Year Plan envisages that "good governance" is increasingly viewed as an essential element of any well functioning society. It ensures the effective use of resources and deliverance of services to the citizens and also provides social legitimacy to the system. The problem of governance needs to be tackled in systematic improvements, improvement in consumer satisfaction and of course, corruption. Therefore, the government needs to provide people-centric administration for which "citizen's charter" has been drawn up. The citizen's charter is based on the premise that the citizen is the king and government organizations exist not to rule but to serve the citizens.

The Twelfth report of the second ARC on "citizen centric reforms" has listed a large number of reform measures which include (i) providing certain rights to people through legislation, setting up of new institutional mechanism to redress citizens grievances, improving accessibility to citizens, simplifying procedures to reduce bureaucratic delays, using technology to improve internal efficiency, rewarding government employees who perform well, improve discipline within the organization, reduce regulatory control and holding public contract programmes etc. Many piece-meal and sporadic experiments have been done in the past to address these issues. But now there is a growing realization that stakeholder participation is essential for the efficient delivery of services to the people and for improving transparency, accountability and responsiveness in public services. It is now widely observed that India's dismal record in economic and social development is largely due to poor performance in public services. The administrative machinery is not designed to provide people-friendly services as inefficiency and multi-functioning is marbled into the bureaucracy. The second ARC (Tenth report) had observed about "often systematic *regidities*, needless complexities and over-centralisation that make public servants ineffective".

Spearheading reform process for the twenty first century, the DARPGP has started collaborating with DFID, WB, CAPAM, International Institute of Administrate Sciences (IIAS) and has signed an MOU with Malaysia forming a Joint Working Group on Civil Services (JWGCS) to speed up reforms in the area of service delivery and productivity enhancement. But the process and methodology of administrative reform is faced with certain paradoxes due to the demands of improving pro-poor service delivery and at the same time increasing direct and foreign institutional investments. While certain requirement such as transparent, accountable and speedy administrative system is common to both areas of poverty eradication and increasing foreign investments, for the former there is need for a revolutionary restructuring towards empowerment of local administration and community institutions which would protect their rights over land, water and forest and this is true not just for the tribals status as given in the PESA (Panchayats Extension to Scheduled Areas) Act of 1996 and the Forest Rights Act, 2006 but to all Panchayats in the country. Sustainability demands action at the level of grassroots governance which includes amendment of procedure laws, electoral laws, Panchayat administration and laws for the protection of agricultural and Panchayat land. Three structural areas where reforms are most needed are the Tehsildar's office, Thana and the office of District Collector. Three legal areas where reforms are urgently required are the laws governing police investigations and collecting evidences, laws for land acquisition and laws for the implementation of citizens charter.

References

A.D. Gorwala—*Report on Administrative Reform.*

Administrative Reforms Commission Reports—1966.

Administrative Reforms Commission Reports—2005.

B.K. Chaturvedi—*Core Group Report on Administrative Reforms.*

Brazier Rodney—*Constitutional Reforms* (1998).

Chaturvedi and Maheswari—*Administrative Reforms*—1984.

Core Group on Administrative Reforms under Chairmanship of Cabinet Secretary.

Dixon, J. and Kouzmin, A.—Management Innovations for Improving Governance.

Fifth Pay Commission Report.

H.C. Mathur—2004—*British Civil Service.*

K. Santhanam—*Report on Prevention of Corruption*—1964.

Kaul, M.N. and Shakdar, S.L.—*Practice and Procedure of Parliament* with particular reference to Lok Sabha.

L.K. Jha Commission—*Report on Performance Appraisal and Management.*

Official Secrecy Act—1923.

P.C. Hota—*Committee Report on Civil Service Reforms,* 2004.

P.C. Jain Committee Report on "*Review of Administrative Laws*" — 1998.

Paul Appleby—*Public Administration in India*, Report of a Survey, 1953.

Paul Appleby—*Recognition of India's Administrative system* with special reference to administration of government's industrial and commercial enterprises – 1956.

Pay Commission Reports—1946 and 1958.

Pradeep Saxena—*Administrative Reforms*—A study of major countries.

R. Coupland—*Britain and India*, 1941.

R.B. Denhart and Denhart—*Public Administration and the Critique of Domination*.

Review of Working of the Constitution, 2002—*Vankatachaliah Commission Report*.

Second Administrative Reforms Commission, 2005—*Moily Commission Report*.

Sir Ivor Jennings—Cabinet Government, 1961.

Sir Ivor Jennings—*Parliament*, 1961.

2
Civil Service Reform

Introduction

If we turn to history, there was a time when there were no services. But for ordinary citizen, the country was better governed than it is at present. Akbar introduced an imperial service which was viewed as "the steel frame of the Moghul edifice". A pool or group of young nobles appointed and promoted (even dismissed) by imperial favour administered the *subhas, sarkars* and *praganas* as bearers of states, districts and sub-divisions. These officials were salaried and transferable. The system continued until the empire itself dissolved under the later Moghuls. In 1765, the East India Company acquired the Dewani of Bengal, Bihar and Odisha and entered the area of governance. Step-by-step, therefore, a civil service evolved until it blossomed into the Indian Civil Services (ICS). The ICS set a pattern of how a cadre should be organised to attend to the tasks of governance. All other "All India Services" set up later after Independence, used the ICS as the model. The service cadre system it pioneered was adopted by every central and state service after 1947. Its members were assured complete security of service. Once someone managed to get in, he remained virtually untouched. The Constitution of Independent India guarantees similar security for all existing services, All India, Central and State.

The Indian Administrative Service (IAS) which is the inheritor of the ICS has been subjected to serious criticism in the recent periods. Sometime back, Mr. Narayan Murthy, Chief of Infosys went to the extent of suggesting that the IAS should be replaced by Indian Management Service (IMS) which had triggered then a lot of debate. It was generally accepted that such change by itself may not be very meaningful as the environment in which the civil services function is very different from the management services working in business and industry. The business management theories and techniques cannot, therefore, automatically be transplanted to public administration without taking into account the different political environment. It is often alleged that even though enough power and resources are available, government organizations do not function effectively and efficiently. The system lacks work-ethic and realization of goal among the majority of public servants. It is equally difficult to trace-out a handful of so called efficient and competent civil servants in any office or department now. A microscopic minority of them who are conscientious with a high sense of responsibility, sincerity and commitment could be traced with difficulty. Curiously and unfortunately government job has been taken as one where there is less of work or no compulsion to work and less or no responsibility direct or indirect but more facilities for comfort are available. In the present era of information technology and globalisation, young ones are now able to start on a very handsome salary. This makes government job irresistible and therefore, Paul H. Appleby rightly described government culture of non-performance as "action-shy".

Modernised British Civil Service

The fact that modern day public administration is bound to undergo reforms and transformation due to several factors is well demonstrated from the recent past British Civil Service Reforms and multi-dimensional changes which have taken place in recent years in British Civil Service which is the product of Northcote-Travelyan report of 1854. This report envisaged that civil service would be non-political, anonymous and life-time with adequate security. There would be no arbitrary dismissal. Security of service has to be modest with decent remuneration. There would be no written contract between the government and the civil servant although the Civil Service Handbook embodied the norms, standards, traditions and code of conduct of the civil service. In the process, the value of civil service was slowly inculcated in the new recruits through an internal process of socialization. In the situations, the civil service was essentially generalist in nature though it could function in various specialized areas. The shake-up in recent past years has gone to such an extent that some writers have started saying that the traditional civil service no longer exists. This had terrific consequences on the working of public administration not all of which could be considered desirable. The Fulton Committee report of 1968 made a strong case for managerial orientation of British Civil Service. The Committee indicated that the present civil service with its leisurely ways would not be able to provide the necessary dynamism. Fulton Committee's report made Margaret Thatcher more determined to introduce radical conservative philosophy into governance. She appointed Sir Derrick Rayner to scrutinise whole range of public expenditure with a view to curb it. This was the beginning of the process of down-sizing the government. As a result, the number of civil servants came down from 7,50,000 in 1970 to 5,00,000 in 1990. The change was not just quantitative but was structural and qualitative as well. The traditional department structures were replaced with executive agencies of an adhoc nature numbering 102. Sixty per cent of civil servants started working under these agencies. The Chief Executives of these agencies were made directly and personally accountable to the Minister for achieving results. They had direct access to the Minister by-passing the permanent Secretary. The Civil Service Commission and its central recruitment system was abolished and was replaced by its own recruitment by the agencies who also had fixed pay and other allowances. The agencies could enter into individual contracts with their civil servants and could even offer preferential pay. In the new system, the emphasis was on measuring performance in relation to pre-determined targets of business. The system of bureaucratic rules and procedures was replaced by a mission-driven mechanism with an entrepreneurial, flexible and innovative approach to achieve better results. The managerial orientation and the structural changes in the character and behaviour of civil servants and their relation with ministers which were not all very desirable, public spirited civil servants considering themselves as philosopher-guardians of public interest above everything else including their own self-interest gave way to 'cando' 'yes men' committing themselves to minister's ideology or even his whims and fancies and in return, seeking maximum personal benefits. The anonymity of civil servants and the long standing position in the parliamentary government that the minister is constitutionally responsible and accountable for the actions of civil servants, gave away to a position where the ministers were quick to pass on the blame to their civil servants or use them as buffers and shock-absorbers by exposing them to public scrutiny. The ministers themselves did not hesitate to accept lucrative positions in companies whose interest they promoted while in the office of the new era of liberalization. Similar benefits accrued to the civil servants on their retirement even before the traditional stipulation of two years after retirement had expired. All this meant a noticeable decline in the ethical and moral standards of the British public life.

The aforesaid issues attracted intensive and extensive public debate. In the famous Belgrano Sinking case when Dr. Punting who was serving as Deputy Secretary in the Defence Ministry conveyed the facts to the Members of Parliament which were kept back by the Prime Minister. He was promptly dismissed from service. In the memorandum that followed thereafter, the Cabinet Secretary Armstrong categorically laid down that the loyalty of the civil servants was not to public good as he sees it but to the Minister under whom he was serving. The same Cabinet Secretary was forced by the Prime Minister Mrs. Thatcher to defend in an Australian court the British government's decision to prevent the publication of the book "Spy Catcher" by a former secret service officer. One case of the exposure of the anonymity of the civil servants relates to Dr. David Kelly who was the senior scientist in the Defence Ministry. The Defence Minister Hoon leaked his name as the mole in the Ministry who passed on the information of "sexing up" the intelligence report to the press. He was forced to appear before a parliamentary committee whose members subjected him to critical scrutiny. Unable to bear the strain, Dr. Kelly committed suicide. Thereafter, some steps have been taken to bring back the focus on public interest and to ethical norms. The concept of "citizen's charter" was evolved to emphasize the public orientation of the services delivered by the government and to redress public grievances and complaints.

In the post-Independent India, reforms in the Central and the State Administrations were attempted many times, but unfortunately all added with some cosmetic changes. This has demonstrated clearly that government lacked political will for a thorough restructuring and re-orientation of the administrative principles and ethics. Starting with the report of the Secretarial Reorganization Committee (SRC) headed by G.S. Vajpayee (1947) to the Surindernath Committee (2002), B.N. Yugandhar Committee (2003) and P.C. Hota Committee (2004), reports on various aspects on administration are stored in Home Ministry's archieves. Besides many seasoned administrators, judges and academics have contributed to the sizable volumes of literature on civil service reforms. The last committee was headed by P.C. Hota, a distinguished civil servant in February, 2004 to examine the whole gamut of civil service reforms in India with elaborate terms of reference. They enjoin upon the committee, among other things, to recommend ways and means to make the civil service responsive, citizen-friendly, accountable and ethical and to protect the members of the services from wrongful pleasure exerted by political executive, business and other vested interests. The government wanted the Committee to suggest steps for a corruption free civil service and for intellectual growth and up-gradation of the "domain knowledge" of members. The majority of the eleven members of the Committee including the Chairman were drawn from all India and Central services. The time limit of six months was scrupulously adhered to and the report of nearly 150 pages was submitted in July 2004. The Committee had cut-out all grills of legal and academic jargon and had come straight to the core issues. It has recommended changes which are clear, unambiguous and, on the whole, implementable. A few of the recommendations, however, may appear to be rather one-sided and narrow but evidently the recommendations are the products of sound practical knowledge, a deep appreciation of public needs and a very lively concern for deteriorating values and vanishing principles of honesty and integrity in civil service.

The Committee focused on three all-India services and all central services. Both these categories jointly make a formidable total of more than 80 thousand officers which is nearly three per cent of the total strength of the Central Government employees in India. The members of these services hold the highest position in various branches of administration at the Centre and the States. The Committee appeared to be deeply concerned with the growing influence on the services of political and other vested interests. The political executive ruthlessly uses the stick of posting and frequent transfer, ignoring the merit and capability of an officer to break the backbone of civil services. To remedy the situation the Committee has, *inter-alia*, suggested the introduction of the system of "tenure posting" in all posts from Cabinet Secretary to District Magistrate. The Committee observed that the recommendation of the Chief Ministers' Conference in 1997 for the creation of State Civil Services Board with the Chief Secretary as Chairman to put a stop to frequent and arbitrary transfer of public servants has not been followed by most of the states. Only a few states have created such Boards which generally remain non-functional or heavily influenced by political executive. Therefore, the Committee recommended for "a statutory barrier" to frequent transfers by the enactment of a Civil Services Act which will create not only the Civil Services Board but also a three-member ombudsman, the Chairperson of which will be "a retired official of proven honesty and integrity" and before which the agrieved officers will be at liberty to agitate their grievances. The proposed Civil Services Act will incorporate the code of ethics of the civil services giving the code a statutory sanction and making the ethics of civil service not merely platitudes by an enforceable rule. While the Civil Services Board is expected to insulate the civil services from political influence, the committee recommended that for the police force, independent commissions with suitable composition may also be set up in each state to protect police officers from *mala fide* transfers, suspension orders and to ensure a statutory tenure. It is expected that this will enable the police to stand up effectively against unhealthy pressure. The State Commission will also continuously monitor the performance of the police forces. In this connection, the committee endorsed the recommendations of the National Police Commission (NPC) on this issue and observed that "even if there is delay in the government's taking a final view on the NPC's recommendations, the above recommendations should be accepted and acted upon as they are essential for upholding the rule of law and good governance."

To stem the burgeoning corruption in the civil services, the committee recommended amendment to Article 311 to provide for summary removal of corrupt officers by an order of the President or the Governor. To identify corrupt civil servants, the committee cites the example of the UP IAS Officers' Association, which some time ago selected three most corrupt officers by secret ballot. The committee holds that peer perception of a civil servant is usually accurate and as such, the service associations may be encouraged to identify the corrupt and the inefficient by secret ballot. This will certainly be a novel method; but it is doubtful how far such a course of action will be procedurally appropriate and legally tenable, even if the inescapable aberrations in such a course of action are ignored. The committee has not only dithered but also bent backward while recommending measures against corruption in commercial decisions. The dimension of such corruption, it is well known, is enormous. On the ground of probable harassment of an honest officer acting in good faith, the committee recommends the revision of section 13(1)(d)(iii) of the Prevention of Corruption Act, 1988, which provides for prosecution of an officer whose decision benefits a person without public interest. The committee pleads for going back to the 1947 position when this section was not there. On similar plea of promptitude in implementation of government decision and *bona fide* intention, the committee recommends the enforcement of the single directive, which necessitates prior permission of the government before launching an inquiry into the allegation of corruption against an officer of the rank of Joint Secretary and above. It is now common knowledge that in all commercial deals, officers of and in the rank of Joint Secretary are involved and since generally all high-ups get big slices of the cake, no Minister/ Secretary will ever give the clearance for an inquiry. The Supreme Court struck down the single directive in 1998; but under pressure of the rich and the corrupt, it was restored soon after. In view of these two recommendations, the committee's forceful denunciation of corruption in civil service sounds somewhat hollow. The committee has, however, very rightly suggested that no officer after retirement should be appointed to constitutional posts like member of Public Service Commissions or Governor of a State. This suggestion was likely to be resented and it has been done so. But the fact remains that there are a few officers who had an impeccable reputation of honesty, but succumbed to temptation and shamelessly scrambled for post-retirement gubernatorial or other appointments. The committee suggests a two year cooling off period after retirement for those who want to join politics. To make the civil service citizen-friendly, the report suggests empowerment of citizens as represented by non-governmental organizations, consumer groups, media with a view to building up partnership for formulating the programmes and for their proper implementation. Although such partnership falls far short of empowerment in a democratic set up, it is worth trying and if it succeeds, its ambit and power may be amplified. This is definitely welcome as a starting point. To ensure transparency, the committee recommended the implementation of the "Freedom of Information Act, 2002" at a very early date, although the committee noted with dismay that the rules under the Act had not been finalized and the date of implementation not notified. The committee also recommended re-examination of the Official Secrets Act so that it is reduced to "essential minimum" for the purpose of national security, public order and privacy. It is good that the Government of India have already enacted the Right to Information Act, 2005 and rules there under, the details of which are incorporated therein. The committee has made many other worthwhile recommendations, but it all depends upon the dispensation in New Delhi to consider them seriously. Let us hope that these recommendations are not sent to the archives because the committee was set up under a different political dispensation.

Over the years, the bureaucracy, has also developed the knack of even thwarting the court judgements taking full advantage of the imperfect and over-stressed judicial system. It is, therefore, imperative that the victim's grievances are heard at a level where quick redressal is possible. Severe punishment may be meted-out to those who fiddle with cases and deliberately delay the processing of files concerning promotion, confirmation and appraisal or who indulge in harassing officers who want to do correct things and are honest. But what happens at the political level? No reform of administration is possible unless the administration is insulated from political pulls and pressures and there is a commitment at that level also to improve the system. It was hoped that the Prime Minister would include this issue in his agenda for administrative reform. The second Administrative Reforms Commission was expected to suggest ways and measures to insulate the bureaucracy from politician's self-promotion agenda without minimizing the sanctity of authority at political level. The other areas of reform which needs to have been addressed by such a commission would be transparency, integrity, attitude of civil servants towards public, sensitivity of the needs of the people, efficiency for which recruitment and training procedures may also require to be overhauled. But no exercise of administrative reforms would be complete without pruning the size of the bureaucracy. The right way to do this would be not to cut down on the number of vacancies at the higher level but to review and abolish all departments and offices which have ceased to be relevant and there is hardly any work. A good number of such non-entities could be identified. Such an exercise could have been undertaken to identify such departments towards "operation governance" without waiting for another Administrative Reforms Commission to come-up. But however, the second Administrative Reforms Commission set up in 2005 has already made several recommendations on which the Central Government and State Governments need to take reformatory measures.

The IAS Impact

The IAS impact on the overall civil services is the principal bone of contention but the service seems to be sinking under the weight of its own number. Earlier, the cadre-size and annual intake were kept under leash. But gradually, cadre and intake began leaping up through unchecked recruitment producing an eventful glut, so much so that the states are not inundated with IAS officers. In many states there are multiple secretaries for the same job and officers of Chief Secretary's rank are two a penny. In the early years corrupt officers were rare and communal ones rarer. But today, the reverse is true. The politician-bureaucrat nexus has thrived in state after state to undermine probity in services. Even though politicians are subject to social audit by people through electoral choice every five years, bureaucrats cannot be thrown out since they wear the chastity belt of security of tenure, though the only security for a civil servant should be integrity and performance. The sad fact is that rarely an IAS official in this country was found to have been dismissed from service for inefficiency or lack of performance until recently when such actions were taken in a very few cases across states. Being conversant with the statute and rule-book, and having clout in the corridors of power, such officials have no peer in the art of wriggling out of any corruption charge which is why they have a high demand among corrupt and shady Ministers and politicians. A lot of research is required to find out as to how many IAS officers have been charge-sheeted, tried, convicted and served a jail sentence for corruption and financial impropriety under the various provisions of the Prevention of Corruption Act and related statutes. Apologists may argue "why pick on the IAS". Are other services and indeed society itself not equally infected? But if the IAS has sunk so low, it has lost its *raison d'etre*. The traditional argument that All India Services promote the unity and integrity of the country by combating *parochial* attitudes, since the officers of these services are generally posted in the states other than their own and therefore are less susceptible to local and regional influences than the officers from within the state would be, has lost much of its value. In fact, in almost all states, most of the officers are posted to their own state because they opt for it. The other requirement that the inter-change of officers (sharing of All India Services between the States and the Centre) provides the Central Administration with officers having field experience in the states and the state also having the advantage of such officers who have held Central Government posts, is also not very tenable if one takes into consideration the large numbers of IAS officers who have never been to the Centre and for all practical purposes, have spent their entire service career in the states even though nominally belonging to the All India Services. Majority of IAS officers of state cadres attempt to avoid Central deputation on some pretext or the other. Some of them even have managed to stay during the whole service tenure in the concerned State. Conversation continues in several fora as to the willingness to go on Central deputation or to avoid but when preferred, many have also manoeuvred to continue in Delhi beyond the normal period. Many hang on to Delhi and the role models are some of those seniors who reached the highest level of secretary to GoI without having served in the State except for the "cooling off" period. A State cadre officer of IAS is required to spend his parent state after completion of a central-stint which is usually five years. The period is even stretchable to seven years if one is willing to serve in vigilance organization of a Central undertaking. The facility of retaining of Central Government flat at the last place of posting for three years particularly in Delhi creates a strong incentive to bounce back to Delhi after the expiry of the cooling off period. There has been some attitudinal and perceptional change in these officers now preferring to stay for longer period under Central deputation because of prevailing chaotic political climate in state governance pattern and behaviour of political masters.

Dr. Manmohan Singh's UPA Government constituted the second Administrative Reforms Commission with Mr. Virappa Moily as its Chairman to bring in further reforms in administration. The first Administrative Reforms Commission was constituted in the sixties headed by Morarji Desai. We are probably not conscious of what happened to the recommendations of Desai Commission. Did any tangible reform take place in administration on the recommendation of that Commission? Appointment of commission and commissions are often resorted to as time-consuming efforts and hardly any attempt is made for effective and real action. In the backdrop of this non-action tradition, hardly there was any guarantee or possibility that the second Administrative Reforms Commission's recommendations will bring in any dramatic change in the existing administrative structure which lacks accountability and performance. Dr. Manmohan Singh had taken some other initiatives for bureaucratic reforms besides setting up of the second Administrative Reforms Commission. He met the Secretaries to Government of India of various departments in meetings where he advised them to be proactive, responsive and work without fear or favour. He emphasised on a "fair, just and equitable system of governance". This was definitely a timely initiative. Regrettably today politicians seem to have become suspicious of bureaucrats. This has resulted in the formentation of a "spoil system" under which, when a different political party comes to power, its first task is to shift government servants posted by previous political executive and place its favourites in crucial posts. This has enabled the politicisation of bureaucracy. It is hard to think as to why politicians expect government employees to be committed or partial? Does it not amount to abuse of discretionary powers of political masters to transfer bureaucrats at will without any justification even though the Constitution of India has special provisions to the effect that a 'permanent executive' can function at the optimum level as against the political executive which changes from time to time in our democratic parliamentary system?

In the recent years, there has been lot of discussion on civil services reforms. It was being contemplated to stop making civil services a lifelong career for some as there was proposal to weed-out unsuitable officers along the way. There is also a recommendation to reduce the age limit for those entering the service to 25 from the current 30. While various panels in the past have looked into such issues, the latest proposals are significant as they have been made by a powerful committee specially set up by the government to look into administrative reforms. This core group was headed by former Cabinet Secretary B.K. Chaturvedi himself. Adding more weight to the recommendations are the six secretary level officers among its members including the Secretary of the Department of Personnel and Training (DOPT) to oversee the civil service reform initiatives. The core group reportedly decided to reduce the age limit for those taking the civil services examination to between 21 and 25 against the currently upper age limit of 30 years. In the new initiative proposal, the OBCs and SC/ST candidates were to be given the usual concessions. For OBCs the current relaxation is three years while for SC/ST it is five years. The core group decided to put in place a mechanism to weed-out corrupt civil servants. Performance of civil servants would be reviewed at different points of their careers. This proposal is given effect to 15, 25 and 30 years of service. To protect honest civil servants, however, a review of section 13 of the Prevention of Corruption Act and protection against unjustified prosecution after retirement, had been suggested. The general idea behind these reform initiatives seem to make the civil service more accountable and better geared towards dealing with people's problems. The core group reportedly recommended the immediate need to introduce a psychological test, aptitude assessment and group discussions. The idea behind this recommendation was to see public dealing and general presentation skills of candidates. The group also suggested that accountability be woven into the performance of civil servants and government departments. To solemnise this, each department would be required to lay-down performance targets to be outlined in its annual report. Departments would also have to spell-out final deliverables to consumers, citizens and the common man and devise mechanisms to evaluate successes. Outstanding public servants should be publicly recognized. A transparent and objective mechanism for evaluating performance and selecting civil servants for public recognition through civil services awards may be evolved by the Department of Personnel and Training (DOPT). In addition, validation checks by a high level committee would be necessary to eliminate single-point assessments.

India has the largest bureaucracy with an estimated Rs. 7000 crore of the tax payer's money spent on footing the 'babudom's pay bill.' To make it trim and efficient and improve the standards of governance, there have been various suggestions for reforms in the civil service, including induction of age at the entry level for the civil services examination as in the Armed Forces. The sincerity of the UPA government in setting up of the second Administrative Reforms Commission for refurbishing the image and efficiency of civil services was beyond suspicion particularly of Prime Minister's initiative and genuine desire to make the bureaucracy more responsive. Yet the fact remains that in the last 67 years after Independence, all initiatives for transforming the present bureaucracy into a genuine public service have remained on paper only. Any attempt to implement them has been systematically sabotaged. The morale of the bureaucracy is so low in public's eye that the man in the street has a very poor opinion of the bureaucracy as a whole. To him, after all, the fine distinctions between All India Services and State Services or Clerical Cadre matter little. In his vision, with few exceptions, bureaucrats are as responsible for the sorry plight and that of the country as the political class. It would be simplistic to argue that the entire blame lies with the politicians as many stout defenders of the services tend to do. They take comfort in the fact that federal democracy has not been able till now to evolve a system of governance that would take care of the people and their concerns, speaks volumes of the bureaucracy itself which has become a burden for the country. It is an unpleasant truth which has to be faced squarely. Some years back reports from two state capitals, i.e. Bangalore and Hyderabad spoke of a certain dissatisfaction at the lower level of top political leadership over the performance of the bureaucracy. In Karnataka, both the then Chief Minister and the Dy. Chief Minister expressed a clear warning to the district level officers to deliver or "to be at home". In Andhra Pradesh, a SWOT analysis of the performance of officials was initiated. It was suggested that Chief Ministers should go for review of the performance of, not only of officials, but also of Ministers. Such an assessment of performance should be entirely professional and objective-based without any politicization. If this is done government in states will be approaching the corporate culture of a continuing performance evaluation and consequential insensitive for performers and disincentives for those who fail the test. In our present system of governance, the district level administration is at the cutting edge of the delivery of government services and programmes. However good the policies and programmes may be, everything depends on delivery by officials at the district and grassroots levels. It is the responsibility of the state administration to monitor the performance of the entire bureaucracy as well as the local bodies administration and report to the government. Because of the development activities, emergence of a power-centre in the Chief Minister's Office (CMO) in some states are reportedly not easily digested by several officials and politicians with the functioning of CM's office. Because of the functionaries in CMO's office becoming too close to the centres of power and arrogating to themselves some of the powers of government, senior government officials heading key departments were distanced from the decision-making process. This extra-bureaucratic channel has not been seen well with the administrative system in some of the States also. At the National level, the Office of the Prime Minister (PMO) is also similarly graded. The present PMO under the Narendra Modi government is reportedly branded as the most powerful agency of governance in the country.

When we turn to past history we find that no major structural changes have taken place in the Indian Civil Service after Independence. There has been a much steeper decline in the standards of public life. Scandals after scandals have defaced the face of public administration. Corruption at the top has become pervasive and India has been adjudged as one of the most corrupt countries in the world. The Santhanam Committee had recommended appointment of Vigilance Commissioners. Some time back the Supreme Court itself looked into the need for strengthening the machinery dealing with corruption and ordered that the CBI should work under the supervision of the CVC and laid down the procedure for appointment of the CVC. In recent years, civil servants have been seen as puppets in the hands of the ruling politicians. Politicians have effectively used the power of postings and transfers to bend the civil servants to their will. Honest civil servants are side-tracked, marginalized, given unimportant or difficult postings or even penalized. On the other hand, civil servants who are prepared to dance to the tunes of the Ministers are favoured and are rewarded by giving them prize postings. No wonder, this has led to a steep decline in the standards of public administration. One of the ways to halt the decline is to eliminate the nexus between politics and administration. The politicians should work in the representative assembly, pass laws and lay down policies. The civil servant should be required to administer policies and programmes strictly according to law and rules without any political interference. This change is difficult to come about but has now become urgent and imperative.

Dr. Manmohan Singh's initiative towards administrative reforms was accepted as timely and genuine as evinced from his address to the Nation on 24th June, 2004 when he bemoaned the fact that "the government at every level is today not adequately equipped and attuned to deal with the economic and social challenges facing the nation." He promised that the reforms of administration and of public institutions to improve efficiency and the quality of delivery services will be the priority of his government. With the setting up of the Administrative Reform Commission (Second Administrative Commission) in 2005 to prepare a detailed blue print for revamping the public administration system and the Common Minimum Programme (CMP) drawn up by the UPA government at least gave an impression that his declaration was not an empty rhetoric only. It is a fact that the existing machinery of governance has almost failed. All efforts at economic growth, development with social justice, have not met with the desired success because the instruments of administration are ineffective, inefficient and corrupt. The need to improve the system to make it more responsive had been felt all through since independence. The British had developed a perfect system to achieve the goals relevant to the British Empire. Even R. Coupland in his book "*Britain and India*" (Longmans Green & Co., 1941) has said that "no bureaucracy has ever been better officered". When India became free, the same bureaucracy was found by our first Prime Minister Jawaharlal Nehru to be "fossilized to by-gones and absolute methods" and refused to move with the times. This civil service we inherited from the British was the subject matter of Constituent Assembly debate too. We were not sure if this civil service could be relied upon to be loyal to the new order. Mr. B. Das, a member of the Constituent Assembly had this to say "I hope and pray God that from 26th January, 1950, the indigenous spirit of administration will come into existence." The indigenous spirit did come into existence with time but the administrative machinery time and again failed to deliver the goods in our democratic welfare state. Bureaucratisation with its hallmark of red-tapism, rigidity and adherence to rules rather than results, lack of integrity and commitment became a hurdle rather than help in the way of rapid growth and development. Therefore, the concern for administrative reforms was there all along. Many initiatives were undertaken to improve the system. Several committees and experts looked into it and some alternations were made and institutions created to streamline government machinery and prevent corruption. The only major exercise in administrative reforms was undertaken in 1966 with the setting up of the Administrative Reforms Commission to conduct a comprehensive review of administration, followed by second administrative Reforms Commission (Moily Commission) in 2005. Some of the recommendations of the commissions were/are being given effect to. However, with passing years and growing challenges on the social, economic and political fronts, the inadequacy and ineffectiveness of the system grew. The gap between what was expected of civil servants and their actual performance became wider and wider resulting in all schemes and plans for improving the lot of masses of this country going away with inefficient and corrupt delivery mechanism. It was late Rajiv Gandhi as Prime Minister himself who told the people that out of Re 1 only 15 paise reached the beneficiaries for whom it is meant. The rest 85 paise were either pocketed or wasted on the way. His was, therefore, another sincere attempt at improving the system. In his 5th January, 1985 address to the nation after being elected with a massive majority, he gave a call for responsive administration. His mandate to the bureaucracy was to simplify rules and procedures, reduce the level of decision-making, delegate powers, reduce paperwork; cut down on in-essential staff; make use of improved technology for communication. It was during his time that computerization was introduced in Government office. In spite of all these attempts during the last half-century and more since Independence, the administrative machinery remains what the first Prime Minister of the country called "fossilized". It only grew in size. While the staff strength of Union Government in 1948 was

14.4 lakhs, it is nearly 40 lakhs today. The all-pervasive menace of corruption has made life for every citizen difficult as it subordinates completely the public good to individual greed. India has attained the dubious distinction of being among the 30 most corrupt countries, according to the Corruption Perception Index (CPI) of Transparency International. Nor has its rank risen very much in the Human Development Report of UNDP in spite of substantial resources assigned to literacy, health and growth of per capita income. It is still among the medium human development indexed countries. Bad governance is indeed wasteful, anti-development and anti-people and in the face of current challenges to the security of the nation, anti-national too. Therefore, there is urgent need for radical reforms in the administration. Now the question arises as to where from should it start? Obviously, there should be clear goals which should be defined. Productivity, accountability, transparency, integrity and sensitivity are the most important characteristics that a citizen expects from the public service. Therefore, he wants the police to protect his life and property and to maintain law and order. He wants the municipal bodies to provide him with basic services, clear drinking water, sanitation and good roads. This warrants the administrative system to gear itself in such a way that the people do not face situations to die of starvation while foodgrain rots in the godowns of FCI, the people do have school with thatched roofs and missing teachers, where primary health centres go without doctors or equipments and no employment available in spite of employment schemes being implemented. The situation is such that law and order machinery is mal-functioning and has failed to protect the people. The police is accused of killing rather than protecting, robbing rather than catching the thief, helping rather than prosecuting the scamsters, extorting rather than punishing the extortionist. Cases in different courts do not get settled for years. Delays take heavy toll of physical and financial health of the litigants. Denial of justice is common and the judiciary particularly at the lower level is equally suspect so far as corruption is concerned. The task is, therefore, stupendous. The entire machinery of the Government at the political decision-making and implementation levels needs overhauling. But for administrative reforms to succeed, sustained political commitment is required. Therefore, the initiatives of the former Prime Minister with two very important planks of administration, i.e. stability of tenure and raising the motivation and morale of officers who get punished by doing the right things or by being honest seems to be a right step in the right direction and at right time. The present Prime Minister Narendra Modi has also stressed on administrative and civil service reform to provide a "minimum government and maximum governance".

Recruitment

Civil servants are expected to have skills, knowledge and values with integrity, commitment to public service and above all, commitment to the ideals and philosophy embodied in the Constitution. These call for a transparent, objective, fair and equitable recruitment process to ensure recruitment of the right type of people for selection to the civil service. This process of recruitment to civil services in India could be traced back to several years of the past both during the British Raj and after Independence. A. D. Garwal's Report 1951, report of the committee 1956 on the public services (qualification for recruitment) known as the Ramaswami Muralidhar Committee, Report of V.T. Krishnamachari 1962 on Indian and State administrative services and problems of District administration, Report of the 1st ARC 1969, D.S. Kothari Committee Report on recruitment and selection methods 1976, Satis Chandra Committee report on review of scheme of civil service examination, Prof. Yoginder K. Alagh Committee report on civil services examination, review 2001 and P.C. Hota Committee report 2004 have contributed to the bulk of recommendations on recruitment to civil services. These Committees broadly recommended issues relating recruitment, among them being (i) Recruitment to all grades conducted to eliminate patronage (A.D. Agrawal Committee) and (ii) university degree should be the minimum qualification for recruitment to higher services and age limit between 21-23 years but need not be insisted upon for secretarial and ministerial services. The V.T. Krishnamachari Committee recommended recruitments to be made annually. The 1st ARC recommended for a single examination to IAS/IFS and other non-technical class-I services through a single competitive examination. It recommended to enhance the upper age limit to 26 years. The Yugandhar Committee

(2003) recommended on in-service training mechanism including three mid-career training programmes in the Twelfth, twentieth and 28th years of service prescribing the tenure of each programme.

For the first time in the realm of civil service, the first ARC outlined some of its philosophical thoughts to reform civil service in suggesting recruitment of qualified and competent persons to build up specialization particularly in the secretariat level. It suggested to select senior management personnel across relevant sources for induction to higher management positions and provide adequate opportunities to talented personnel on basis of competence and performance. Eight broad areas of specialization, namely: (i) economic administration, (ii) industrial admministraction, (iii) agriculture and rural development, (iv) social and educational, (v) personnel, (vi) defence and internal security, and (vii) planning, were identified. But all these were not actually implemented over the years although sporadic instances of pick and choose of personnel were restored to. The Surindernath Committee identified almost eleven domains for officers some of which were already suggested by the first SRC. The Hota Committee also recommended introduction of domain assignment to encourage skill acquisition, professional excellence and career planning. It suggested empanelment and posting of joint secretaries, additional secretaries and secretaries to be done through domain assignment competitive selection and matching of skills with job requirements. The second ARC (Moily Commission) has recommended permissible age for appearing in civil service to be 21 to 25 years for general candidates, 21 to 28 years for OBC and 21 to 29 years for SC/ST and physically challenged categories. The permissible attempts in civil service examination should be 3, 5, and 6 for the above-mentioned categories respectively. The existing age limit with cut-off date, i.e. 1st August may continue.

Training

Training is critical to human resource development. A distinguishing civil servant L.K. Jha (ICS) once observed that "administrators are not born but made". This happens through adequate training which a civil servant goes through in service career. In the pre-Independance period higher civil services had an organized training system particularly for ICS officers in England followed by field posting training in the districts.

In the aftermath of Independence, training programmes underwent changes with emphasis on socio-economic development rather than regulatory functions. While little spectacular was noticed during 1950-1980, the training structure was revamped with emphasis on mid-career training during Rajiv Gandhi premiership. One week vertical training, periodic (4 week) programme was made mandatory for middle level IAS officers and number of national academic institutions got involved in the training of senior civil servants. But importance of training as a continuing regular programme got diluted. With economic liberation in the 1990s, training programmes were bound to be reoriented keeping good governance, transparency and objectivity in view. The National Training Policy containing training needs of civil servants, i.e. (i) updating and enhancing professional knowledge and skills, promotion and sensitization to professional, socio-economic and political environment in work and right attitudinal orientation was an appreciable attempt. This policy laid emphasis on responsiveness, commitment, awareness and accountability. But this policy lagged behind in implementation due to absence of a proper monitoring mechanism. While the present training system in civil services is wide open in content varying from service to service, a "foundation course" is common to all of them. This course is intended to develop spirit de'corps among officers of different sources, fostering the attitudes and values of civil servants and basic understanding of government functioning. Besides the foundation course for IAS and other civil services in the Lal Bahadur Shastri National Academy of Administration, professional training for all-India and other organized group—"A" services are also provided by their respective training institutions. The National Police Academy at Hyderabad, Foreign Service Institute, New Delhi, Railway Staff College at Vadodara, National Forest Academy, Dehradun, National Academy for Direct Taxes, Nagpur, Audit and Accounts Staff College, Simla etc. Besides professional training, mid-career training is also arranged and such a structured system of compulsory mid-career training for IAS particularly started from 1986. From 2007, a new and comprehensive system of mid-career training was introduced for the IAS.

While over the years, based on the recommendations of various committees and commissions, training programmes have been designed to five (V) phases for senior civil servants particularly the IAS, these trainings are imparted in important training institutes in the country and abroad. Phase I and II trainings are conducted after "Foundation Course" and "District Training" are over. Phase III and IV are imparted after specific years of service and the Vth phase training of 4 weeks is supposed to be between 26 and 28 years of service. For group A and other services, different training modules are designed. The main purpose of all the training programmes is to enhance academic qualification and professionalism in public policy. But these training programmes suffer from several basic shortcomings cutting cross all services. These could be attributed to attaching less importance to "Foundation Course", seeking leave to write civil service examination by officers of other group 'A' services, deficient and inadequate display of importance in the training curriculum. To re-evaluate the design and contents of training programmes, the committee headed by Dr. R.V. Aiyyar was constituted in respect of IAS officers but other services were not covered.

The first ARC recommended for formulation of a national policy on civil service, creation of 'Training Division" and cell for promotion, coordination and facilitation of training programmes, and extension of 'foundation course' to all technical class I services. The second ARC has recommended for mandatory training for all groups of officers at induction stage and periodical training as a condition to confirmation in service, promotion and determination of inter-se-seniority. A monitoring mechanism should be set up for overseeing implementation of the National Training Policy, 1996. The practice of "Common Foundation Course" for all group 'A' services should continue. For group 'B' and 'C' services, thc Institute of Secretarial Training and Management (ISTM) may be the nodal agency to design and deliver common foundation courses. A few select institutions may be identified for capacity building and upgradation of skill and knowledge of civil servants. The composition of governing bodies of national training institutes be broadened by inducting eminent experts and one of the national institutes be upgraded to a national institute of good governance.

Transfers

Another important facet of bureaucratic illness is the problem of transfers. It has been alleged against the bureaucratic system that transfers have become instruments of award and punishment and even for making money by politicians and bureaucrats. Transfers of civil servants in some of the states have become so frequent and irrational that their tenures are not only made unstable and unpredictable but susceptible to mental and psychological impact on the officials. In Uttar Pradesh, at one point of time, about 500 officers were transferred in five months by the Chief Minister at the behest of MPs and MLAs. One police officer was transferred thrice in two days. Some officers were even transferred five to eight times in two months. Transfer has been converted to an industry in several states where money gets exchanged for lucrative posts. An officer who offers money to get a good post is bound to make money by illegal and fraudulent means several times the amount he has paid. This leads to more corruption. Therefore, the officers with short tenure can hardly ensure governance and proper delivery of service. If the District Magistrate stays in the district for less than a year, how can he perform and show results? It is, however, heartening that the former Prime Minister Manmohan Singh initiated the reforms process in civil service by emphasizing the need for stability of tenure of officials in key positions. He aptly reminded that frequent transfers of public servants has a debilitating impact not only on their performance or morale but also on the whole process of governance. To raise the morale and motivation of officers, institution of a grievance mechanism to deal with grievances of officers regarding delay in posting, promotion, victimization, lack of support etc. is a welcome and much needed step. It is a fact that civil servants themselves become victims of bureaucracy, especially those who are honest and transparent. The functionaries at the lower level handling personnel matters relating to seniority, confirmation, promotion, transfer and other career-related files are alleged to be playing nasty games with the officers concerned. Consequently, these officers become victims of their bosses, peers and even sometimes their subordinates. That is one reason why a large number of court cases from employees are filed against their departments. Officers get demoralised when superiors show no inclination to right the wrong done intentionally or even unintentionally at the lowest level. This also helps in swelling of cases in tribunals where affected officers seek justice for redressal of grievances.

Some years back, after the BJP Government came to power in Rajasthan, (not after the elections in 2013) a press report highlighted the mass transfer of officers in the State. The State government which had halted the transfer spree during the budget session that year, suddenly transferred about 50,000 of its own employees including several hundred of teachers. It simply created chaos since in a large number of cases, teachers of a particular subject were being transferred to schools where such subjects were even not being taught. Government employees were being transferred to places where there was no slot for them. These mass transfers resulted in protests that became violent in places. The result was that practically the entire machinery of the State Government was paralysed for weeks during which allegations of favouritism, vindictiveness and corruption were hurled. In Madhya Pradesh, a new government after being installed, began to shuffle as many as 90 IAS officers at one point of time. In a few cases, officers were shifted again even before they were in the process of joining after the transfer orders. Officers were at a loss to understand the criteria adopted by the government in carrying out such transfers. The Chief Minister, during the short period in office, was so pre-occupied with transfers at the behest of official and non-official advisers that it had no time for governance. The worst situation took place in the number of transfers they ordered within a very short span of time in which officers were transferred five to eight times in a two-month period. There have been instances of IAS and IPS officers being transferred twice in a single day. Transfers have been traditionally considered inevitable in the career of a civil servant probably for the reason that it is considered necessary either to give wider exposure to the employee which would broaden his/her horizons or to prevent any vested interest in getting developed in a particular post or place if an employee is posted there for too long. But, today transfer is used as a weapon for reward or alternatively for punishment. Politicians use this for their personal ego and to demonstrate their hold on the bureaucracy. Caste considerations also weigh with them. But the worst motive for transfers has come to be for monetary considerations. The transfer industry has come to be a lucrative business for politicians in some cases. Prize posts are open to the highest bidders. Money is allegedly made by people's representatives, MLAs and MPs in recommending such transfers. The result is that transfer has become one of the major causes of corruption in almost all states. If money is exchanged for giving a post, the employee thus posted is bound to be corrupt. Frequent transfers do not inspire or motivate. Transfer is also often meted-out as punishment not for being inefficient or corrupt but for not toeing the line. An officer is given a 'good' posting if he/she is co-operative and helps in the pursuit of personal agenda of such politicians so as to build their office for personal gains. Under these situations, how will the bureaucratic system work? The stability of an officer has to be ensured if he/she is expected to deliver. If the average tenure of a District Magistrate is just a few months, how is he/she expected to perform? He/she does not get sufficient time even to get acquainted with his district. It is, therefore, necessary to bring order to the chaotic business of 'transfers' as a step towards administrative reforms. Keeping these in view, the Prime Minister of UPA Government had written sometime back in the past to the Chief Ministers on the need for stability of tenure. But given the nature of present politics, such voice of decency was almost ignored. Some time back, in the conference of Collectors of districts of the country, the Prime Minister had reiterated his concern for tenure of District Collectors, in particular. Mr. H.D. Shourie of "common cause" had once approached the Supreme Court asking for a direction for framing of rules governing the process of transfers of government servants. The Supreme Court refused to interfere since it thought the guidelines for taking such administrative decisions should satisfy the rule of non-arbitrariness. Unfortunately, the malaise has worsened since then. It is time that the Apex Court takes note of the present situation and helps in laying down certain guidelines in the public interest. Transfers and postings of government servants are the prerogatives of the Central/State governments. With the passage of time, in recent period, the political elected representatives continue to play dirty game pressuring the political masters to transfer officers of their choice at various levels. Regrettably some of the pliable officers continue to dance to the tunes of political masters for temporary gains.

The authority of State and Central Governments in matters of transfer of officials/employees is very often challenged in appropriate courts and courts of administrative tribunals. In most of the cases, illegal and unreasonable transfer orders are challenged and employees/officials seek justice through courts placing both the government servants and governments in embarssing situations causing financial and administrative losses. Existing circulars and instructions regulating transfers are flouted and disobeyed. Circulars/guidelines issued from time-to-time regulating transfer and postings are violated more often on various considerations particularly at state government levels. Elected representatives particularly MPs and MLAs, in the transfer seasons, initiate recommendations for transfer of government employees within and outside their political constituencies on various considerations. Ministers including Chief Ministers face this challenging threat from political colleagues and mostly succumb to the pressures and counter-pressures. This has adversely impacted proper functioning of bureaucracy. Policy of transfer, therefore, is recommended by many, should be based on non-political and ethical norms, whatever be its tenor of influence on political governance spectrum even though bureaucracy thrives under the "cloak of ministerial responsibility". The recent trend of governance in some states due to formation of new governments by state level political parties has caste an indelible mark in the bureaucracy a situation of vendeta against bureaucrats on the ground of allegiance or closeness to the political parties/masters of the governments of yester-year/s.

It is alleged that the present system of transfers, postings, promotions, disciplinary and other personal matters pertaining to the higher civil service are *adhoc* and non-transparent. Transfers are often used as instruments of reward and punishment with officials being frequently transferred on the whims and caprices as well as the personal needs of the local politicians and other vested interests. Officers, especially those in the All India Services serving in the state governments have no stability or security of tenure. The "transfer industry" is backed by entrenched and powerful vested interests, as frequent transfers generate huge amounts of black money for corrupt officials and politicians, both directly and indirectly. Almost all commissions and committees in the past dealing with administrative reforms have stressed the need for transfers at all levels to be handled in a non-partisan, open and transparent manner. The conference of Chief Ministers (1997) had observed that frequent and arbitrary transfer of public servants affects the ability of the system to deliver services effectively to the people. It recommended the constitution of Civil Services Boards in different states. Direct political control or direction in the management of transfers, postings, promotions, inquiries, disciplinary proceedings, rewards and punishments has adversely affected the morale, capability, efficacy and morality of civil services. These matters need to be depoliticized and entrusted to independent Civil Service Boards which will closely monitor and ensure accountability at all stages, regulate transfers in a transparent and national manner, protect the honest civil servant and identify and recommend punishments for those who betray the public trust. Therefore, implementation of civil service reforms and institution of a rational and transparent policy on transfers would go a long way in insulating civil servants from wrongful and extra-legal pressure from the political establishment.

The recent order of the Supreme Court seeking to insulate bureaucracy from political executive has been flogged for all the unjust and unfair reasons. The recent incident of suspension of a young woman IAS officer in Uttar Pradesh without proper inquiry who was reinstated a few days thereafter when baseless charges could come to the public domain is a vivid example. Another case of atrocious charges against the then Coal Secretary P.C. Parikh was an instance of painful and alarming agony of an upright senior bureaucrat. Civil servants these days are being subjected to draconian provisions of section 13 (i), (d) (iii) of the PC Act 1988 for criminal conduct. There exists a "Spoil System" where transfers and postings have been described as an industry. Political interference and pressure on civil servants has become cancerous. The second Administrative Reforms Commission has observed that over 600 committees and commissions have looked into various aspects of civil service reforms. It is important to eliminate the *adhoc* and non-transparent transfers and postings which often reflect the whims and caprices of political functionaries. There are states where the district magistrates and SPs have an average tenure of about six months. Although the conference of Chief Minister's resolutions were passed to constitute "Civil Service Boards" to depoliticize the so called transfer of posting industry, nothing concrete has come out across many states. The Civil Service Board, properly constituted, may be entrusted with the task of managing personnel. It has been suggested that all premature transfers need to accompany a detailed reasoned order so as to become subject matter of scrutiny of legislature, media and civil society. Normally, a civil servant should be given a fixed tenure of minimum three-four years to foster fair and objective decision along with accountability and performance.

The Central Government's decision some time back to provide minimum two-year term in any posting to officers of IAS, IPS and IFS Cadres is a welcome step towards insulating them against political pressure to facilitate good governance. This important decision of government would not have come but for the directives of the Supreme Court. Frequent transfer of usually upright officers or those who are on the wrong side of government have adversely affected such officers. Provision of fixed tenure at least would come as a boon for officers like Ashok Khemka in Harayana and Durga Shakti Nagpal of Uttar Pradesh. Following the directives of the Apex Court, every State Government will have to make appointment of cadre officers on the recommendation of a Civil Service Board under the minimum specified tenure which can be done only on the recommendation of the board. Now, according to the amendments effected to IAS, IPS and IFS officers cadre rules, an officer appointed to any cadre post shall hold office for at least two years unless, in the meantime, he/she is promoted, retired or sent on deputation outside the state or training exceeding two months. Now, it is to be seen as to what extent the State Governments are sincere in setting up of Civil Service Boards and how effectively they function with total transparency.

Performance Appraisal

In spite of several recommendations made in the past by commissions and committees on administrative reforms, the existing culture of non-accountability and non-performance in the government structure still persists. There is still enough ground to believe that Parkinson's law applies to bureaucracy which has grown in size without commitment. To ensure real change in performance and improvement in delivery system, the problems of non-accountability and non-performance need to be addressed first. This may be difficult to achieve unless Art 311 of the

Constitution which provides enough protection as a cover for ineffective, inefficient and corrupt public servants is amended. Therefore, this provision in the Constitution requires to be thrown-out or modified drastically. Article 311 of the Constitution provides that no public servant could be removed, dismissed or reduced in rank without an enquiry in which he should be informed about the charges made against him/her and given a reasonable opportunity of being heard in respect of the charges. Therefore, this provision stands as a stumbling block for taking any effective and immediate action for lack of accountability and non-delivery of services by the erring civil servants. The disciplinary rules for civil servants provide for time-taking processes and procedures. Therefore, the effect of deterrent punishment is hardly visible and existent in the aforesaid rules. It has been often alleged that enquiry officers appointed in the disciplinary proceedings cases are mostly non-motivated and therefore, conviction or punishment rates are very low in such proceedings. Therefore, many have pleaded that even though natural justice is thrown out, Article 311 must be replaced by a system of running contracts under which the public servants will be engaged and based on their performance, contracts would be renewed. Suggestions have also been mounted that there is need for reviewing the prevailing system of assessment of performance. It is debated and held that the existing system of grading performance of public servants into different categories like poor, fair, good, very good and outstanding is rather debased. Due to this grading classification, there is almost a running competition among public servants to secure the best category of performance, i.e. outstanding and this seriously does oblige on many counts, not on actual assessment of target-oriented appraisal. As a result of this system of appraisal, sometimes it is noticed that almost ninety per cent of government servants are rated as "very good" or "outstanding" by the reporting officers due to influence, temporary impression of general nature and the disinclination to defend an average, bad or adverse grading. Sometimes, reporting and countersigning officers are also influenced by other fraudulent means. Even some civil servants manage to manipulate to continue in particular department and particular desks/seats for several years to establish an impression that they have developed expertise in specific subjects and are, therefore, indispensable. In this process, under the artificial cover of efficiency, they continue to secure outstanding remarks in the confidential character rolls.

The first ARC recommended use of the term "Performance Record" instead of confidential report. At the end of every assessment year, the civil servant was required to furnish an account of the work done by him/her during the year to the reporting officer who should take note of this report while grading the civil servant. Grading of performance was to be categorized to three categories, namely: (i) out of turn promotion, (ii) fit for promotion, and (iii) not fit for promotion. It had emphasized the need for specialization by civil servants as per pre-qualification for holding senior level posts and had suggested that all the services should have an opportunity to enter middle and senior level management levels in central secretariat and selection should be made by holding mid-career competitive examination which should include interview to be conducted by the UPSC.

The second Administrative Reform Commission noted that the existing system of performance appraisal is unsatisfactory and suggested that it should be transparent with 360 degree feedback and there should be numerical rating on the pattern of armed forces and an independent third party be associated with the assessment. Today, there is hardly any emphasis on job performance and incentive for hard and meritorious work. The rules relating to promotion with excessive reliance on Annual Confidential Report (ACR) are also framed that everyone gets his/her promotion when his/her turn comes and encourages mediocrity. ARC's most important suggestion is comprehensive in-depth assessment at important milestones in an officer's career, the first review being done on completion of 14 years of service and another on completion of 20 years. If he/she is found unfit after second review, the service may be terminated. A government servant's promotion, career advancement and continuance in service should be linked to his actual performance on the job and the dead wood should be weeded out.

The Surinder Nath Committee, as a measure of administrative reforms, had suggested the system of Annual Confidential Report (ACR) to be replaced by Performance Appraisal Record (PAR) maintained in the computerised system for effective monitoring and timely assessment of performance. Under this system, the officer could be allowed to see the PAR after the reviewing officer has completed the report with the provision that he can comment on factual observations made on his performance. There could be a Referral Board which shall adjudicate in case of difference of opinion between the officer reported upon and the reporting/ reviewing officer. Many of the earlier recommendations which find place in the statute book (Fundamental Rule-56J) even today have hardly been implemented because for every such action taken on the recommendations, the documents must stand the scrutiny of judicial interpretation. Above all, the present system of ACR writing does not inspire much confidence for the system to get reformed. In the circumstances, replacement of the system of ACR rating by Performance Appraisal Record (PAR) seems to be a reasonable and welcome recommendation. All said and done, the fact remains that the system of ACR writing has been reduced to a mockery and breeds sycophancy. The assessment made in the present format has practically no relevance in actual performance of the officer reported upon. The report can contain an assessment which has no relevance to the reality of an officer's efforts. The report can be very laudatory when it is least warranted or downright condemnation when nothing of the kind was ever palpable. This has put a serious impact on the system. Given the ground rules, it would take only the naïve and the bold to workout schemes and take initiatives without defining the mind of the superiors. The present system is such that it encourages employees to maintain the equilibrium and coupled with this, is the corruption network. It is so active and pervasive that either one has to be inside it or outside it. If inside, you can do no wrong as the British Crown and the gifts are bountiful for such people. On the contrary, nothing good or excellent that the outsider does, would merit mention in the report confidentially written and maintained.

The Performance Appraisal System (PAS) has the advantage of ending the traditional review system which merely intended for granting promotions. This system of subjectivism would rather invite objectivism instead. Under the new system (PAS) bureaucrats would be required to stand on performance with the necessary and adequate dose of transparency injected into it. The focus would automatically shift from loyalty, sycophancy and blind-following to performance only. Of course, there are and could be many cases where bureaucrats who never worked all their lives and knew nothing of their jobs except how to extract maximum benefit for themselves went up the slithery pole with impunity and without a hiccup. This is because they never had the acid test to be assessed against any objective standards. The recommendations of Surinder Nath Committee for transparency in appointments to posts under the central staffing scheme that includes selection through interview for posts of Joint Secretary and above, would mean loosing of hold over men and matters. Selection of persons on merit would breed a team of workers always on trial to prove their worth for the future advancement. In the circumstances, they may have no time to worry about anything save their work and targets assigned to them. But given the existing network of nexus in the system, it is least to believe that such changes are a distinct possibility. But it positively strikes to mind that this may result in the death-knell of the existing system and pave the way for a cleaner public life.

In spite of several shortcomings in the appraisal system of performance evaluation of bureaucrats, annual evaluation is definitely a good practice. But the service record (confidential annual report) more often than not stands in the way of empanelment of Joint Secretary level posts in the Government of India which reflects only on the efficiency and suitability of the officers. Non-performance is the basic problem of governance. When public servants, whether appointed or elected, know that their performance is being appraised, they tend to perform better. When non-performing elected public servants get re-elected and when pen-pushing, bureaucrats get their time-bound assured promotions—the message to them is obvious. The appraisers are the voters in the case of elected public servants and the government in case of the bureaucracy. While the bureaucracy has the appraisal system known as confidential reports written annually on their performance, conduct, character and qualities, their merit, competence, initiative, leadership qualities, planning and policy-making which are judged from these confidential reports for the purpose of their career advancement, the very use of annual confidential reports, instead of annual performance reports, has created an environment of non-transparency in performance appraisal. The fact remains that the present system of performance appraisal has several weakness. In the existing system, performance reports are not shown to officers. Only adverse reports are communicated to officers. If the reports are shown to officers, they would come to know of their strengths and weaknesses and the reports will help them utilize their strengths better and overcome their weaknesses. In any case, the performance reports are the assets of officers who have to work hard in-order to earn the report. They are entitled to see their reports so that representations can be made against adverse remarks and not against under-reporting, mis-reporting or non-reporting of performance. Experience reveals that if an officer does not like his junior, he gets away merely by non-reporting which is not communicated and when exposed, the senior acquits himself by saying that he is the best judge of the individual performance of an officer even in the face of *prima facie* record of qualitative and quantitative performance of the junior. There is no independent or neutral forum like a committee of officers who may, in disputed cases, be asked to appraise the performance on the basis of the record of qualitative and quantitative performance.

The committee appointed under the Chairmanship of Lt. Gen. Surinder Nath, former Chairman, Union Public Service Commission (UPSC) had recommended that performance reports should be shown to officers and that the representations received should be examined by a "Referral Board". In addition, the committee had recommended a 10-point grading system in place of the existing five-point grading system. This recommended procedure was intended to facilitate for better differentiation and help in identifying the really outstanding from the rest of the lot. The committee also referred to the problem of inflated assessments for keeping officers in good humour and hoped that the nine-point grading system will take care of this problem. To all these problems the obvious remedy was to release all CRs on a website accessible to all officers. As a result, when the assessing officers know that the CRs written by them should be seen by others, they would tend to report more truthfully based on qualitative and quantitative record of performance. The committee had also recommended interviews to be conducted by a panel including UPSC Chairman.

At present, one of the biggest problems of governance is the declining ethical and moral standards of public servants. In the existing confidential reports format, there is a column on "integrity". But unfortunately, the usual report on integrity is rather dumb. The usual report which is recorded against this column is "beyond doubt", or "nothing adverse came to notice" etc. The fact remains that the integrity of officers is not really hidden from their superiors and colleagues but its reporting is vague. It is possible to grade officers on the basis of their integrity much like the grading based on other qualities. If the integrity column of the annual performance report provides for detailed reporting and grading of integrity, an integrity record of public servants, maintained in the ordinary course of business, would be available to the government. This record would be of great value in identifying public servants for sensitive jobs. While the writing of confidential reports of All India Services is regulated by the All India Service (Confidential Rolls) Rules, 1971 framed under the All India Service Act, 1951, the process of promotions or empanelment for senior positions in Government of India is left to executive instructions. That there is enough anomaly on this score is evident from the objects and reasons of the All India Services Act, 1951. A reading of provisions would sufficiently justify this. Article 312 of the Constitution provides that Parliament may, by law, regulate the recruitment and conditions of service of persons appointed to the All India Services, common to the Union and the States. At present, these All India Services are mainly the Indian Administrative Service, the Indian Police Service and the Indian Forest Service. In the absence of any provision in the Article 312 similar to that included in Article 309, the Government of India is now compelled to deal with many of these matters by means of non-statutory executive orders. This arrangement is neither satisfactory nor quite justifiable. Statutory executive orders in matters concerning service conditions of all India services were probably intended to protect the independence of the members of the higher civil services in dealing with public work, including the political agenda for changing governments. But, if only writing of CRs is regulated by statute and the process of promotion itself including the rules of promotion is left to the executive discretion without any transparency, the ultimate objective is diluted. In fact, according to Article 320 (b) of the Constitution, the Public Service Commission is consulted in the matter of promotions to civil services. Article 323 (c) mandates consultation with the Public Service Commission on all disciplinary matters. Consultation with an independent Constitutional Authority reduces the scope for arbitrariness in promotions and disciplinary action. But a provision in the same Article has been used to dispense with consultation with the UPSC in the case of All India Services where the need for protection from arbitrary treatment is the greatest. This sometimes results in long spate of suspension of All India Service officers as it happened in States like Uttar Pradesh and some other states. Such situation could be avoided if the UPSC is consulted under Article 320 (3) (c) in all such matters.

Under the existing system, the most senior level appointments in the Central Secretariat as well as top field level posts are made from amongst the Indian Administrative Service (IAS) officers who are normally generalists although in the recent years, many candidates with technical and professional background are getting into IAS examination through open competitive examination. The second ARC has observed that the present process of empanelment of officers for the post of Joint Secretary and above is not fair, objective and transparent and overlooks the real merit of the officer and his suitability for a particular job. It has identified 12 domains in which officers should specialize. It has recommended that domain should be assigned to all the officers of All India Services and Central Civil Services on completion of 13 years of service. Vacancies at the level of Deputy Secretary/Director should be filled only after matching the domain competence of the officer for the job. The Commission also recommended introduction of competition for senior positions in the Senior Administrative grade and above (Joint Secretary level) by opening these positions to all the services. For higher administrative grade posts (Additional Secretary and above) recruitment for some of the posts could be done from open market. The other recommendation of the Commission relates to constitution of a statutory Central Civil Service Authority which should deal with matters of assignment of domain, preparing panel for posting of officers at different levels, fixing tenures and determining which posts should be advertised for lateral entry.

Former Prime Minister Manmohan Singh's proposal to reform the appraisal process for senior bureaucrats addressed a grey area in administrative appointments. The Annual Confidential Report (ACR) is meant to serve as a stringent check on a civil servant's ability and responsibilities. Over the years, however, the exercise has become increasingly *adhoc*. At its worst, palpable politicisation has rendered the procedure as an easy tool for the administration of the day to promote favoured bureaucrats and suppress others for reasons other than the strictly professional. At a relatively inadvertent yet equally destructive level, apathy has leached out diligence and rigour from the entire procedure. In other words, lobbying and drift tend to guide the empanelment of high officials. This should, hopefully, change. A panel of experts may assist the appointment committee of the Cabinet in assessing the performance of those in running for posts of Secretaries, Additional Secretaries and Joint Secretaries. This seems to be done now. That the service record (confidential annual report) more often than not stands in the way of empanelment of Joint Secretary level posts in the Government of India reflects only the efficient and suitability of the officers. Sadly, the events of the last 60 years have not fulfilled the hope and expectation of Sardar Patel that the IAS would provide the cementing factor and hold together the various parts of India. In spite of the growth in the size and influence of the service, one witnesses increasingly fissiparous tendencies in many parts of India which are posing a threat to the political and administrative unity of the country. One may, therefore, have to look for an alternative model which will not supplant but at least supplement the civil services, keeping in view the legitimate aspirations of the people in a federal polity. The cutting edge of the administration in most assignments of the higher civil services starts from jobs which carry the rank of a Joint Secretary to the Government. Under the present dispensation, no lateral entry is permissible to such a post. Only officers who have worked in the junior posts over the years are appointed. Places above the rank of Joint Secretary, Additional Secretary, Secretary and Private Secretary are almost the monopoly of the IAS. Promotion and appointment to the posts are automatic, efficiency and integrity do not count for much. Consulting the service record is only a technical formality.

The second ARC has suggested to strengthen the existing performance appraisal taking in to consideration the following factors, namely: (i) performance appraisal should be more consultative and transparent; (ii) it should be modified on the lines of latest PAR system for all India Services; (iii) Performance appraisal format to contain generic details of the particular service to which the office belongs, the goals of the department he is working with and the requirements and targets of the department; (iv) Performance appraisal should be year round for drawing up a detailed work plan and mid-year review of performance; (v) assignment of numerical ratings; (vi) expanding the scope of performance appraisal to a comprehensive performance management system (PMS) appropriate to particular Ministry/ department/organization; (vii) annual performance report to be signed by the Minister and Secretary/head of department containing physical and verifiable details of work to be done in a particular financial year; and (viii) Verification of actual performance by a third party.

A very strong case exists for throwing all these jobs open to the market. It may be worthwhile to consider that a broad-based independent committee with representatives from Government, industry and civil society under the aegis of the UPSC, are associated with the recruitment process. All members of various cadres/services fulfilling the eligibility criteria may compete with the candidates from the market. Appointments may be contractual initially for three-five years renewal being strictly contingent on performance. For proven incompetence and even a share of doubt of integrity, services should be terminated with only one right of all to an independent tribunal. The requirement of government permission before proceeding against civil servants in a Court of Law should be waived. Critics may argue that the market driven approach is flawed since district experience will be given the go-by. But this suffers from superficiality if experience is any guide, where everyone rises in a "hierarchy of incompetence" on the basis of the rule of automaticity. But the tremendous merit of the market-friendly mechanism of recruitment to higher civil service lies in the fact that it will generate a spirit of competition among the bureaucrats who will not remain smug in their approach to work after entry into the constituted services. Consequently, governance at all levels of administration will improve. The man on the street will be the ultimate beneficiary from the proposed reorganisation of the civil services.

The second ARC has made several other recommendations on issues relating to motivation, accountability, disciplinary proceedings, civil service code, civil service law etc. But an exclusive chapter is devoted to the relationship between the political executive and civil servants.

The basic norm of civil service in a Parliamentary Democracy is to ensure political neutrality. But such a proposition may not be emphatically said to be possible in state civil services as they have no "fall back" position unlike the All-India services. In the present day set-up, the District Magistrate and the Superintendent of Police are in a hopeless minority who have no axes to grind and are not free from local political influence even though they are under the ultimate protection of the centre. The position of DM and SP has been weakened overtime by not allowing them a fixed tenure. In many states, they are under the mercy of local governments. In absence of a fixed tenure, democratic governance suffers. It compromises the political neutrality of the civil service. Without a fixed tenure for government servants who are subordinate to the ruling political executive, all talks of political neutrality becomes meaningless. The case of lady IAS Officer Durga Shakti Nagpal of UP Cadre is only one such reflection at the micro-level of what has been happening over the years at the macro-level.

The latest civil list of All-India Services indicates that the intake in IAS has been reduced to a fraction of what was earlier whereas induction of State services has multiplied several fold. In larger States like Karnataka and Punjab, the intake of federal services in the last few years has been reduced to a trickle in face of flood of state 'promotees'. When the idea of All-India services materialized, the state civil services were conceived as "Feeder Services". Another damage has been inflicted on the constituted civil services. A number of posts under the Union Government have been thrown open to the "experts" from the free market. It has been alleged that many of the "experts" end up damaging the system. Rightly or wrongly, in their greater wisdom, the Central Government appointed a committee headed by a brilliant academic D.C. Kothari to suggest reforms in recruitment to civil services. The Committee suggested abolition of the earlier system of constituted civil service consisting of the IAS and the IFS and provided the option to successful candidates to choose any of the services of IAS, IFS and other allied services.

Most of the government departments both at Central and State levels suffer from poor work culture and low out-turn of performance or productivity in terms of positive end-products. It has been often suggested to down-size the government, improve work environment and privatise some of the services. The vast sprawling bureaucracy needs to be down-sized. The Fifth Pay Commission (1997) as well as the Expenditure Reforms

Commission headed by K.P. Geetha Krishnan (2000-01) had given vast array of measures for restricting, re-organizing and down-sizing various Ministries and departments which would bring greater efficiency and cut cost. Some of the key recommendations cover (a) the multi-level hierarchical structure should be reduced and an officer-oriented system with level jumping be introduced to speed up decision- making; (b) in the policy-making Ministries, the system of section be abolished and the desk officer system introduced; (c) the existing system of Ministerial staff be abolished and replaced by a multi-skilled position to be called as "Executive Assistant" who should be computer savy; and (d) government offices must be remodernised with provision of computer and other gadgets. It has been felt that a large number of rules and procedures relating to citizens day-to-day inter-face with government in matters relating to issue of passport, registration of property, sanction for construction of dwelling unit, licence etc. are outdated and dysfunctional which should now be updated, simplified and discretionary powers of public servants in these matters be eliminated. The rules relating to personal management are outdated and rigid providing no flexibility. The existing rules relating to budgetary allocation and utilization leads to huge wastage of money. Although most countries like UK have shifted to multi-year budgeting, India is still far behind those countries. There is, therefore, a need for privatization and out-sourcing of large number of services which the government is directly doing in order to improve efficiency and reduce cost. The working of the government is highly centralized with all powers concentrated in Ministers and departmental heads. There is, therefore, a need for paradigm shift in the approach. Advanced countries like Britain, New Zealand, Australia, Canada, Singapore, Japan and USA have revamped their bureaucratic system and shifted to professional management of the bulk of the government activity through creation of "Agency" or "Performance Based Organisations" (PBOs). Britain, one of the leading countries for reforming public services, now selects "Chief Executives" of agencies through open competition open to public and private sectors including hiring on the basis of a contract. The creation of "Executive Agencies" has resulted in substantial gains in efficiency of public services so much so that a "Treasury and Civil Service Committee" of the House of Commons in Britain has observed that Executive

Agencies have brought about "over all transmission in government" and termed it as "the single most successful reform programme in recent decades". It is time that India draws lessions from the experience of other countries and moves towards creation of "Performance Based Organizations" to make the government efficient, economical, sensitive to citizen's needs and transform into a professional and performance oriented management system of governance.

References

B.N. Yugandhar Committee - 2003 on *Administrative Reforms.*
Fulton Report – 1968.
G.S. Vajpayee (1947) *Committee on Secretarial Reorganization.*
K.P. Geetha Krishnan - 2000-01 *Expenditure Reforms Commission.*
P.C. Hota Committee (2004) on *Civil Service Reform.*
Robert Armstrong—*Management in Civil Service.*
Second Administrative Reforms Commission – 2005.
Surindernath Committee (2002) *Report on Administrative Reforms.*

3
Electoral Reforms

Introduction

In a democracy, free and fair election is an essential ingredient of democratic governance. Transparency and purity in election is the key to a successful and sustainable democracy. Conduct of free, fair and peaceful elections contribute to the making of a deep-rooted democracy. Since, rule of law and democracy are intimately interlinked, rule of law pre-supposes a democratic government to be representative, responsible and responsive. To ensure these traits, political institutions like the Parliament and State legislatures have very important role to play. Unlike totalitarian and despotic governments, democratic governments need to be based on the trust of the governed. Free and fair elections can be ensured if the machinery which conducts elections is independent and the law under which elections are conducted, is faultless.

In India, under Article 324 of the Constitution, the superintendence, direction and control of all elections to Parliament and State legislatures are vested in the Election Commission. Under this article, elections connote a wider sense to include the entire process of election. The Election Commission is endowed with all powers necessary for smooth conduct of elections. Under sections 14 and 15 of the Representation of People Act, (RP Act) 1951, the Election Commission is mandated to hold genuine elections to Lok Sabha and State Legislative Assemblies anytime within a period of six months before expiration of the term of the house concerned. During the early years of our democracy, political idealism and morality were appreciably noticed. Therefore, elections during these periods were by and large, free and fair. Subsequently, say towards the 70s, a remarkable and steady decline in the moral standards of political parties, politicians and the voters was noticed. Over the years by the end of 80s, money and muscle power along with gross misuse of government power and machinery became integral parts of political culture. These intended to erode the credibility of the electoral system. One of the main reasons for all pervasive corruption in the country is attributed to unbelievably enormous expenditure collected through dubious means by political parties and their candidates. Apart from the adverse consequence, the growing influence of money-power has also the effect of promoting criminalization of politics.

At one point of time, muscle power almost acquired a kind of legitimacy in the electoral system starting with booth capturing by organized and armed goons and hoodlums in some places. These were subsequently followed by impersonation, intimidation or violence to win elections. In some states ruled by cadre-based parties, electoral malpractices led to scientific rigging of elections. This practice led to the exclusion of genuine voters sympathetic to the revival of political parties and inclusion of bogus voters in the electoral rolls and manipulation of election results at the time of counting. From the 1980s, persons with criminal records were fielded in the Lok Sabha elections in the States like Bihar and Uttar Pradesh on account of the so called '*Babu-Neta*' syndrome'. This process has been euphemistically called the "criminalization of politics" over these years. The system degenerated to such an extent by 1990 that the Election Commission had to be proactive for upholding the constitutional mandate of conducting free and fair elections. A paradigm shift was noticed in the role of Election Commission from a passive to a proactive body, from a low profile organization to a catalytic agency committed to the cleansing of electoral system. A lot of debate regarding a transparent and accountable electoral system in the elections to State Legislative Assemblies and Parliament has taken place in the past. It is often alleged that our democratic institutions are sandwiched between push and pull of money and use of muscle power in elections. The democratic institutions have been unable to attract genuine, fair, honest and the incorruptible, intellectuals from different walks of lives in society to participate as genuine representatives of the people. The electoral system has become so ugly that honest and genuine persons are loosing interest in joining politics. It is like bad elements driving away good elements. Reforms in electoral system have, therefore, been suggested from different quarters. Of several reform measures suggested, a few important issues call for intense debate.

The present system of governance is almost going downhill in terms of values. Now, there is a wide variation between the rich and the poor because of divisiveness, acquisitiveness and the intent for possessiveness. While some remain happy, a large chunk of populace remain poor. "No one can be perfectly moral till all are moral, no one can be properly happy till all are happy" (Herbert Spencer). The only practical means of political equality for all is democracy through periodic free and fair elections where everyone exercises his/her votes through franchise and ballot it where ultimately the majority governs. The party system is, therefore, inevitable in a democracy when plural views threaten to create chaos. Therefore, discipline and well organized expression in governance through well-settled ideology is the means for better and stable administration in society. To ensure this, elections must be fair and clean and candidates of parties should be persons of integrity and not crooks.

About two decades ago, Gorbachev, the Russian leader, had set-up an institution in Moscow called the "Independent Initiative" where intellectuals from world-over were invited to express their opinions freely and fearlessly on system of government whether centralized democracy, oligarchic or people-oriented. The idea was to promote through the ballot, a set of people on policies of government, selection of candidates who are clean and independent, non-communal and non-corruptible and who could maintain high standards of morality. Regrettably, we do not have an established institution like that till now. When elections approach, large scale processions, propagandas, marches and slogans become abundant. Vote banks become the strategy and money power is adopted as the key to buying votes. Candidates with influence and wealth but without social commitment and integrity manage to manipulate constituencies and betray the masses through the bedlam process and end up with a system of governance where the voice of the common people is relegated to the last. It is a travesty of democracy that a creamy-layer holds the public money to its own advantage. In spite, this, a simulacrum of people's sovereignty survives. Therefore, the country needs an independent initiative to scrutinize the candidates and the electoral process. This is possible if positive response from individual institutions and political parties would be forthcoming. Such an attempt also made in the past through an independent initiative institute of which Late Justice V.R. Krishna Iyer was the president. There seems to be hardly any trace of it now.

Money and Muscle Power

Elections at every tier of governance, be it at Panchayat level, Assembly or Parliament, has become phenomenally costlier. Expenses in an election in Assembly and Parliament constituencies despite restrictions/limits prescribed by the Election Commission reaches abnormally, a very high level. This leads to artificial generation of black money which influences the political system very badly. This has been accentuated more particularly after the ban on company donations. After 1968, the priority or importance of political leaders was judged by the Congress party within its party-fold who could raise maximum money (black money) for the party. Those who raised black money were able to raise funds to strengthen their own political base. While the party men got scope to raise money, the inner-party democracy started dwindling and party's total power continued to get centralized with "High Command" or the "Party Supremo". As a consequence of this open licence granted to party men, raising and distributing money started before and after elections which ultimately made elections more expensive for the party. This corrupted the political system enabling MPs, MLAs, Ministers and other party functionaries to collect money openly. Gradually, this system reflected in the elections to local bodies. Functionaries of local bodies like Sarpanchs, Chairpersons of Panchayat Samitis and Zilla Parishads continued to collect money to meet election expenses and amassed huge sums to themselves at the expense of development works. The high cost of elections resulted in high corruption, disorderliness and distortion of democratic values.

A.J. Liebling long years ago in 1947 had observed that anybody with 10 million dollars would be free to try get himself nominated and the rest of the people would be free to vote for their favourite millionaire or even to abstain from voting. He also warned in 1960s that the business models of newspapers would one day prove their undoing. This prophecy has come true in Indian context. By and large, political parties collect funds to build and sustain the organization, to train party cadres and fight elections. Many countries including India have helped cushioning their expenses at public cost. But the major share of funding still comes from corporate industrial houses and voluntary organisations as contributions. Unreliably, the major source of such funding influences voting behaviour and that is why the subject impacts directly on democratic rights. While all important institutions of governance including Parliament, the Judiciary and the executive have attracted intense public litigation, the financing of political parties has been left untouched.

A rough eye estimation indicates that in every general election to all State Assemblies and Parliament, about one lakh crore black money goes into circulation in the country. The recent trend of elections has established that more of rich people of trading and business community, industrialists, corporate houses vie for becoming candidates and win elections. This trend has spread across the country. Use of money in elections has become so widespread and communicating that even a small and poor state like Odisha witnesses instances of moneyed people vying for electoral benefits in contesting elections with the assumption that higher the assets, more are chances of winning elections. The 2009 elections to the 15th Lok Sabha divulged that 543 MPs elected were worth close to Rs. 28 billion of which 64 members of Union Cabinet accounted for Rs. 5 billion. Therefore, the links between wealth and winning elections are strongly grounded than before. It has been approximately calculated that if a person is worth Rs. 50 million, he has 75 chances more likely to win an election to the Lok Sabha than any other person under Rs. 1 million worth. About 23 of 64 members of the UPA cabinet whose assets were already in public domain fell in to the Rs. 50 million plus category. It was reliably learnt that in the entire UPA Cabinet, only one came into the Rs. 50 million plus category which could provide greater chances of winning but those with less than a million, have 43 times chances more likely to win. This analysis of the report of the National Election Watch (NEW) of the 15th Lok Sabha is the result of a fine research. This report further reveals that 3437 candidates with less than Rs. 1 million were in the fray. Of this, only 15 (0.44%)

could be successful on the highest income category. Out of 1785 candidates in Rs. 1-5 million group, only 116 (6%) won election. But the win ratio went up to 19 per cent of candidates within the Rs. 5-50 million segment. Of 322 candidates in the 50 million plus or so called platinum tier, about 106 (33%) romped home. For non-billionaires, the chances of getting elected are bleak. India had an estimated 53 dollar billionaires before economic meltdown but regrettably about 836 million human beings are those who 'get by' on less than Rs. 20-30 a day. Incidentally, India ranks 66th amongst 88 nations on the Global Hunger Index (GHI), just one position above Zimbabwe.

Figures furnished by the elected representatives indicate that the number of crore-patis in the 15th Lok Sabha was 306 which was up by 98 per cent compared to 2004 Lok Sabha with 154 crore-patis only. The net-worth of the candidates in Vidarbha area only rose over by 160 per cent between 2004 and 2009. Out of 306 crore-patis, 141 come from Congress, 58 from BJP and SP, BSP and the DMK and respectively contributed 14, 13, and 12 multi-millionaires. Shiv Sena and NCP had nine and seven respectively. This means that the Shiv Sena and NCP had 80 per cent of their elected MPs as crorepatis. In the United States, collective net-worth of elected representatives in Washington was 172 billion in respect of both the Senate and the House of Representatives against 28 billion of India in respect of the Lok Sabha only. In fact, the growth rate in terms of money for second and third term MPs seems better than others. The fact remains that both in USA and in India, money plays a very important role in election and money from big corporates clinches victory. That money plays a very important role in elections was clearly visible in the run-up to 2008 "trust vote" in Indian Parliament. This trend has spread across the country.

Table 3.1: Status of Assests of Canditates

Value of Assets	*No. of Candidates*	*No. of MLAs*	*% of MLAs*
Very high (5 crore above)	15	6	40
High (50 lakh to 5 crore)	174	50	29
Medium (10 lakh to 50 lakh)	344	54	16
Low (less than 10 lakh)	755	37	5

In the 2009 General Elections to Odisha State assembly, about 40 per cent of the candidates that had declared assets of Rs. 5 crore and above, had won elections. Table 3.1 indicates the status of candidates in terms of assets declared by then.

In 2014 elections to Odisha Legislature Assembly, there has been a marginal increase in the number of members (MLAs) having criminal background. In the 147, member Assembly, 52 candidates have criminal cases pending as against 48 in 2009 elections. Of fifty-two winners who have declared criminal cases, 41 have serious criminal cases involving attempt to murder, rape, kidnapping and crimes against women. If an offence for which maximum punishment is of 5 years or more, non-bailable electoral offence and offence related to loss to exchequer are considered as serious offences like assault, murder, kidnap and rape. The party-wise criminal cases indicate that 32 out of 117 winners of BJD have declared criminal cases pending against them while 9 out of 16 Congress winners and 8 out of 10 BJP winners have criminal cases pending against them. Eight winners have declared attempt to murder-related cases in their affidavits, three robbery and dacoity, four kidnapping, six crimes against women. All together 218 candidates with serious criminal cases lost the election in 2014. (*Source*: Odisha Election Watch). There is 8 per cent fall in young legislators in the 14th Assembly. The age-groups of MLAs indicate that in the age group of 25-30, there are only 3 members, 20 in the bracket of 31-40, and 73 in the age group of 25-50 years. There are 63 members in the age group of 51-70 and only 11 in the age bracket of 70 and above.

In the 2014 Assembly Elections, thirty eight per cent of candidates who have properties worth more than 5 crore have managed to win elections while 28.1 per cent of rich candidates in the bracket of Rs. 2–5 crore have emerged victorious. Around 24.5 per cent of candidates have assets worth between Rs. 50 lakh and Rs. 2 crore who have made it to the Odisha Legislative Assembly (OLA). On the contrary, only 1.5 per cent of candidates with property value below Rs. 10 lakh could win elections. Around 62 MLAs in Odisha have the highest declared assets in their constituency while 34 have second highest asset position among the candidates in their respective seats. The preference for wealthy candidates seems to have gone up in this election as 76 of the 147 MLAs are crore-patis. In the 2009 elections, only 33 MLAs had declared assets over a crore. The average assets of winners in 2014 Assembly elections is around Rs. 3.22 crore against Rs. 1.71 crore among 134 winners in 2009 Assembly. Sixty-two of the 117 MLA's of BJD who got elected in 2014 elections are crorepatis along with 9 of the Congress and 4 of the BJP. Election analysis indicates that 52 per cent of elected members are corepatis.

With regard to age and education factors it is seen that about sixteen per cent are below the age of 40. Thirty four per cent of lawmakers are not graduates. Eight members are not even matriculates while 17 members have cleared class X. As regards educational qualification of BJD, out of 117 elected members, two members have passed 5th class, 5 eighth pass and 12 are tenth pass. Twenty five have passed Twelfth standard, 33 are graduates and 29 graduate professionals. The new Assembly has 32 post-graduates with 28 from BJD, 3 from Congress and one from BJP. BJD has two doctorates. Congress has three post-graduates, five graduate professionals and three graduates, two each with Tenth and Twelfth pass. Only one BJP MLA is a post-graduate, two graduate professionals and one graduate. One has passed class 5th. Total number of women candidates is 11 against one (1) in 2009, four (4) are post-graduates, three (3) graduates, two Twelfth class pass and one Matriculate and one class 5th.

It has been pleaded that money power attracts muscle power and both create havoc in the electoral process. Due to large number of constituencies, multiplicity of political parties and numbers of candidates, absence of clear ideology, politicisation of caste and communal identities on the basis of which vote banks are created, elections in India have become not only expensive but boiling points of corruption and grounds for generation of black money leading to criminalisation of politics. Because of lacuna in the RP Act in putting a ceiling on election expenditure incurred by a candidate or his agent only and not on the party or anyone else, huge amounts are being spent freely for the candidate or the party beyond the ceiling fixed by the EC for candidates. This has affected the level-playing ground between parties and candidates which directly or indirectly adversely affect the economic system of the country. The statutory ceilings on election expenditure by candidates are patently unrealistic and inadequate compared to the actual expenditure incurred by a candidate and therefore, have no bearing on the maximum limits laid down. Considering the lifestyle of the political leaders, the cost of their travel, the huge amount that is spent during elections, it is obvious that parties and party leaders accept money from business houses whereas their followers are extorting money from business houses. After all, why should a business house give any money to any politician unless he is convinced that this is a form of investment which can be encashed at huge profit to the advantage of politicians and also for overlooking malpractices of the business houses? It was reported that the house of Tata and the family of Jamnalal Bajaj, particularly Rahul Bajaj claim to be not falling to this trap and are principled. But this is not true of many other business houses. Therefore, party funds are largely dependent on contributions from blackmarketeers, people engaging in illegal business and business houses. Considering the index of individual rising of politicians acquiring huge sums from different sources and their lifestyle ridden with luxury, high comfort and richness through acquisition of property disproportionate to their known or declared sources of income, one wonders where dose all these money come from?

One of the emerging trends of 2014 elections for the 16th Lok Sabha is that this Lok Sabha had the highest share of crorepati candidates. Four out of five winners in this election were crorepatis. Of the 2209 crorepati candidates who contested this election, only about 20 per cent won which is sharply lower than the earlier elections. In 2004 elections, only 12.7 per cent were crorepati candidates, 15.9 per cent in 2009 elections and now 26.8 per cent in the 2014 elections. Out of these, the percentage of crorepatis who own the elections was respectively 30 per cent, 58 per cent and 82 per cent. In 2004 elections, the wealthiest 5 per cent of candidates stood almost on 50 per cent chance of winning. By 2009 and 2014, their chances had dropped to less than a third. In the 2004 elections about 45 per cent candidates in the wealth bracket were winners whereas in 2009 elections 35 per cent won and in 2014 elections it has marginally comedown below 35 per cent of 2009 level.

An investigation by "*Times of India Group*" analysed the status of states in the 2014 elections in regard to percentage of rich and poor with average assets in crores, the most and least of women MPs and tainted and cleanest MPs with criminal cases as percentage to total MPs in the States, the oldest and the youngest. The position is reflected in Table 3.2.

Table 3.2: Percentage of oldest and youngest criminals

Rich and Poor average assets in Crores		*Most and least women MPs elected*		*Tainted and cleanest MPs with Criminal cases as % to total MPs from the State*		*Oldest and Youngest average age*	
Name of the State	*Amount in crores*	*Name of the State*	*No. of MPs*	*Name of the State*	*% of MPs*	*Name of the State*	*Average age*
AP	58.3	WB	29	Delhi	71.4	Uttrakhand	62
Meghalaya	35.6	MP	17	Bihar	67.5	Punjab	59.9
Himachal	2.00	UP	16	Maharashtra	63.8	J&K and Himachal	59
Tripura	0.6	Karnataka	4	Punjab	7.7	Tamil Nadu	50.9
		Rajasthan	4	Rajasthan	4	Delhi	47.3

The state-wise position of average assests of candidates in crores is indicated in Table 3.3 below.

Table 3.3: Position of average assests of canditates in crores

Sl. No.	*Name of the State*	*Average assets of candidates in crores*	*Sl. No.*	*Name of the State*	*Average assets of candidates in crores*
1.	Andhra Pradesh	58.3	15.	Gujarat	9.3
2.	Meghalaya	35.6	16.	Jharkhand	8.5
3.	Uttarakhand	34.7	17.	Bihar	7.7
4.	Nagaland	31.6	18.	Tamil Nadu	7.1
5.	Punjab	25.5	19.	Arunachal Pradesh	5
6.	Haryana	23.4	20.	Manipur	4.9
7.	Maharashtra	15.9	21.	Sikkim	3.2
8.	Odisha	15.8	22.	Chhattisgarh	2.9
9.	Karnataka	14.5	23.	West Bengal	2.7
10.	Delhi	12.6	24.	Kerala	2.6
11.	Madhya Pradesh	11.7	25.	Goa	2.2
12.	Uttar Pradesh	11.2	26.	Himachal Pradesh	2
13.	Rajasthan	10.1	27.	Tripura	0.6
14.	Assam	9.4			

Another analysis of affidavits filed by winners suggests that voters do not mind electing candidates with criminal cases and money power. A third of candidates have criminal cases and more than two-third of the candidates are millionaires. In the 2009 elections, out of 158 with criminal cases, 30 won and in 2014 elections out of 186 with criminal cases, BJP with 98 have won 35 seats, Congress 8 out of 18, AIADMK 6 out of 16 and Shiv Sena 15

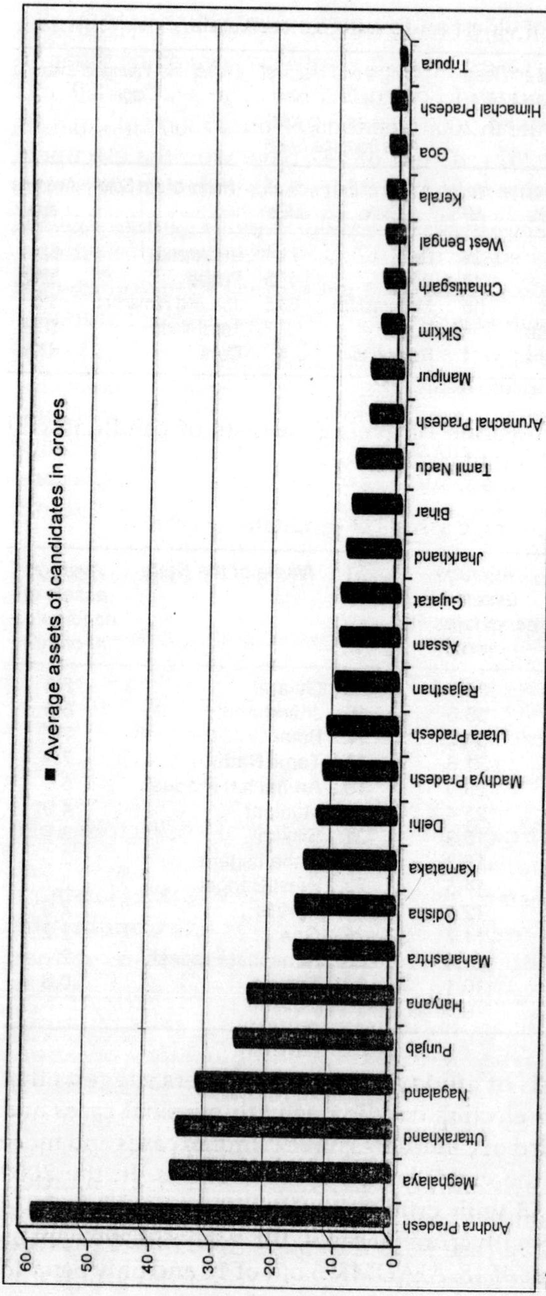

Fig. 3.1: Average assets of candidates in crores.

out of 83. In Maharashtra, 31 have won with criminal cases and 18 with serious criminal cases. In Uttar Pradesh 22 out of 28, Bihar 18 out of 28, Andhra Pradesh 13 out of 20, Karnataka 4 out of 9 and Gujarat 7 out of 9. While in 2009 elections, 58 out of 300 millionaires won the election, in 2014, 82 out of 442 have won the elections. Before the 2014 elections to Lok Sabha it was calculated that Indian politicians were expected to spend about five billion dollars against seven billion dollars spent in 2012 U.S. Presidential elections. Although, people's representatives get elected to operationalise democracy, peoples choices are restricted by the candidates put up by various political parties and those independents who contest mostly as dummy candidates.

Nine out of ten Ministers in the present team of Modi are crore-patis [Association for Democratic Reform (ADR)]. The average assets of the 46 Members Council of Ministers is Rs. 13.47 crore. Of them, 13 Ministers have declared criminal cases against themselves. The National Election Watch (NEW) and the ADR analysed the self-sworn affidavits of the 44 of 46 new-elected Ministers including the Prime Minister. Details of Prakash Javadekar and Nirmala Sitharaman were not analysed as they were not MPs by that time. Of the 44 Ministers, 40 (90%) are crorepatis. As per ADR report, five Ministers have declared assets over Rs. 30 crore each. Arun Jaitley had declared assets worth over Rs. 113 crore, Harsimrat Kaur Badal had declared assets worth Rs. 108 crore, Gopinath Munde (now dead) Rs. 38 crore, Maneka Gandhi Rs. 37 crore and first time Minister Piyush Goyal Rs. 30 crore. Total assets include assets of self, spouse and dependants.

Five Union Ministers, namely Arun Jaitley (BJP), Harsimrat Kaur Badal (SAD), Gopinath Munde (BJP), Maneka Gandhi (BJP) and Piyush Goyal (BJP) declared their assets worth more than Rs. 30 crore (Jaitley with 113 crore, Badal Rs. 108 crore, Munde Rs. 38 crore, Meneka Gandhi Rs. 37 crore and Goyal Rs. 30 crore). Only four Ministers who are in the bracket of less than one crore are (i) Mansukhbhai Dhanjibhai Vasava (BJP) 65 lakh, Thawar Chand Gehlot (BJP) 86 lakh, Sudarsan Bhagat (BJP) 90 lakh and Ram Vilash Paswan (LJP) 96 lakh. Eight Ministers had declared serious criminal cases including cases related to attempt to murder, communal disharmony, kidnapping and electoral violations. Uma Bharati had declared a case related to attempt to murder, a case promoting enmity between different groups on the ground of religion, race, place of birth, residence, language and doing acts prejudicial to maintenance of harmony and a case related to illegal payments in connection with election. Upendra Kushwaha and Paswan have each declared a case related to bribery. Munde had declared a case related to kidnapping.

As elections cost huge sums of money, it is obvious that political parties cannot afford to give every candidate crores of rupees for an assembly or Parliamentary election. A candidate who spends Rs. 5 crore and wins a seat has to collect money by illegal means to recoup what he has spent. Thereby, he becomes corrupt and corrupts the system by focusing the civil servant to assist in collecting money. The civil servants, in their turn, find that it is lucrative to be corrupt. Unscrupulous contractors and businessmen take advantage and corrupt the bureaucrats and the politicians. Consequently, persons like Dawood Ibrahim flourish and scams occur on a national scale. Political corruption has become so deep-rooted particularly in the coalition structure both at the states and national level that politicians like Mayawati and Mulayam Singh Yadav and many others who are accused of having disproportionate assets to their known source of income prefer their cases to linger on whether it is the DMK, AIADMK, the Congress, the BJP, the Janata Dal, the Reddy brothers in Bellary or Y.S. Reddy of Andhra Pradesh.

At the core of business model politics involving cash economy, the problems of election accentuate to the spiralling trend of corruption. The E.C. requires candidates to declare expenditure but no questions are asked on the source of election spending. The limit of Rs. 16 lakh per assembly and Rs. 40 lakh per Lok Sabha (revised to 40 lakh and 70 lakh before 2014 elections) seat makes no sense. Why sky limit expenditure is incurred by candidates? What is the use of knowing candidates assets when there is no compulsion to reveal the source of funds. According to statements of poll expenditure submitted by the parties to the Election Commission, the BJP spent Rs. 448.66 crore in the general elections, 2009. The ruling Congress spent Rs. 380.04 crore which is Rs. 68.62 crore less than the poll expenditure of the opposition parties. Of the total Rs. 443.66 crore spent by BJP, the Party Central Office spent Rs. 162.68 crore while Rs. 285.98 crore was spent at the level of the states. An analysis of expenditure of statements submitted by various political parties reveals that majority of donations came in shape of cash rather than through transparent means of funding. Data analysis results indicate that only 24 per cent of the total election funding received by Congress party was received through cheques and demand drafts and the rest received in cash. The BJP received about 49 per cent of their funds through cheques and demand drafts. The Congress received a total of Rs. 313.74 crore as election funding out of which a whopping Rs. 237.36 crore was received in cash and Rs. 76.38 crore in cheques and drafts. The BJP received Rs. 478.61 crore through cheques and demand drafts out of which Rs. 239.73 crore was received both at central and state levels. Among the other national parties, the BSP spent Rs. 21.13 crore. This party got a total of Rs. 33.16 crore from the date of announcement till the date of completion of the poll process in 2009 elections. The party received Rs. 20,000-00 through cheques and drafts and the rest in cash. The NCP incurred Rs. 26.17 crore of which Rs. 18.26 crore was received at state level and Rs. 7.91 crore at national level. But the major chunk of funds was received in shape of cash. The CPM incurred Rs. 10.26 crore which included Rs. 6.53 crore spent on individual candidates, Rs. 2.6 crore at district level and Rs. 1.47 crore at state level. If that was the self-declared source of funding, why no attempt was made to ascertain the sources more particularly the cash deposits/receipts.

In spite of declarations false or otherwise, none of the parties addressed the fundamental need to regulate political finance which political parties in many countries like U.S., U.K., Japan, Canada, France, Germany and Thailand have enforced long since as reported by the International Institute of Democracy and Electoral Assistance (DEA). In about 45 countries around the world including the above mentioned countries have banned anonymous donations to political parties. India now happily has a provision for public disclosure of expenditure of political candidates but there is no ceiling on expenditure of political parties. That indirect spending on election is so huge and gigantic that Gopinath Munde, a former MP publicly said that he spent nearly Rs. 8 crore in his own election against the stipulated limit of Rs. 25 lakh which invited the wrath of the Election Commission. Political parties very well realize that civil society in general and RTI activists can do little except to pursue PIL route. Disclosure of political finance should be warranted under the important consideration to promote a healthy political competition which requires sharing in sources and quantum of funding of each party with the voter.

India, therefore, now needs a law to bring it on a par with progressive countries worldwide. That would mean mandatory disclosure and reporting to provide clarity about political funding, their sources and utilization. To ensure this, creation of an enforcement agency modelled after the Federal Election Commission created under the Federal Election Campaign Act, 1974 of the United States may be thought of. This body would supervise all financial transactions of political bodies that have solicited or spent money to support candidates. This body shall verify all reports presented and disclose the same to the public and the media. In India, ideally the ECI should be empowered to do this job after which there may be no need for individual parties to give responses under RTI. Worthwhile to mention that in 2011, two RTI querists namely the Association for Democratic Rights, an NGO and an individual named Subash Agarwal appealed to the CIC against refusal of political parties to share information although, by all accounts, they were public bodies. The appeals were upheld by the full bench of CIC in an order dated 3rd June, 2013 ruling that six national parties needed to provide information as sought for on the ground that they were recipients of valuable state resources in the form of land, accommodation and tax exemptions which amounted to 'substantial funding' from the public exchequer. Accordingly, they were to be treated as public bodies and made answerable as such. It was expected that most of the political parties would come together to annul the damage done by the CIC in seeking judicial intervention or introducing fresh legislation to overturn the CIC's order. Knowing this, the applicants further filed a caveat to forestall the grant of a likely stay against the order of CIC. But subsequently, it was floated in the newspapers that a bill had been kept in readiness to be introduced in the forthcoming session of parliament seeking to exclude political parties from the ambit of RTI. The Government headed by the Congress party with tacit consent of other leading political parties except probably the CPI wanted to change the definition of 'public authority' mentioned under Section 2 of RTI Act in order to keep all recognized political parties out of the jurisdiction of RTI. The Government was also reportedly trying to seek approval of cabinet to bring in amendment to Whistle Blowers

Protection Bill to keep information that could compromise the strategic and economic interests and impact on foreign relations out of the ambit of the bill. The Law Minister, however, peddled the theory that "political parties are not public authorities. A political party is a voluntary association of persons. People can join or leave a party. Political parties are registered and recognized under the RP Act. They also come under IT Act which throws sufficient transparency in financing and funding". The whole issue of election funding veers round some of the major points, namely (i) unfurling the RTI umbrella over political parties that would have implications for political strategy and functioning. Once conceded, information even as distribution or denial of tickets can be sought for which may be untenable given the competitiveness, secrecy and intricacy of political decision making. (ii) Political parties do not maintain the documentation needed to respond to wide ranging RTI queries and they cannot be expected to establish a new organization only to fulfill the sweeping questions that will come in under the RTI. (iii) If political parties received substantial funding, the same logic should be applied to all similarly placed NGOs. (iv) It is well known and publicly admitted that most political funding comes from black money sources and in cash. It is, therefore, impossible to declare whose contribution it was without first cleaning up the unaccounted (number two) accounts. The above mentioned argument cannot be ruled out altogether as without validity.

The CIC verdict should have been looked upon as an opportunity and not a threat. It was a priceless moment for political parties to collectively break themselves loose from criminal elements unaccounted and excess money power to resolve remove illegitimacy from the power game. Political parties should pledge to support a law to ban anonymous donations and cash contributions beyond a threshold and put a ceiling on election related expenditure of individual political parties. The ECI or any other agency created and empowered should have full authority to oversee the inflow and outflow of political finance and institute legal action, if scrutiny is stone-walled. If a model code of conduct for election could be evolved simply through consensus, why not a model code for political funding? The explanatory role to section 77 (i) of the PR Act had put a ceiling on election expenditure incurred by the candidate or his/her agent. But in real practice, ceilings are patently unrealistic and inadequate to meet even a small fraction of expenditure being incurred. The Supreme Court had also clearly expressed its anxiety in 1974 against unchecked use of 'party funds' for candidates in the elections. In the case *C. Narayanswami vs. Jaffer Sharif* the Apex Court observed "If the call of purity of elections is not to be reduced to a lip service then the persons investing funds in furtherance of the prospect of election of a candidate must be identified and listed."

Criminalisation of Politics

Criminalization of politics is a recent and serious trend in the present day politics of the country. That a number of criminals are entering into politics is a bare truth. Political parties are unable to deny tickets to such people whose number is gradually increasing. Apart from arranging and spending huge amounts in the elections and in spite of regulation under section 8 of RP Act, 1951, entry of persons with criminal background is increasingly distinct. In the Eleventh Lok Sabha, a large number of MPs had criminal charges against them. In the Thirteenth Lok Sabha, one-fifth of the members irrespective of the political party, had criminal records. The RJD has 43.5 per cent, BSP 27.8 per cent, Samajvadi Party 19.4 per cent, the Congress 7.6 per cent and the BJP 10.9 per cent of MPs with criminal background. Although the BJD of Odisha has least number of MPs with criminal cases, the 2009 election to State Assembly in Odisha indicates that out of 1388 candidates who contested, 295 candidates had pending criminal cases. This covered almost all parties irrespective of their number. The ECI had once recommended that a person against whom a charge has been framed under relevant sections of the IPC, Unlawful Activities (Prevention) Act, 1967, the Narcotic Drug and Psychotropic Substances Act, 1985 or any other offence punishable with imprisonment for life or death under any law, shall be disqualified for a period of five years, from the date of framing charges provided he or she is not acquitted of the said charge before the date of scrutiny notified under section 36 of the RP Act. Almost all committees on politics and electoral reforms have acknowledged unanimously about criminalization of our political system. The core committee on electoral reforms in its "Background Paper on Electoral Reforms" recommended two measures, namely enforcement of disclosure of criminal antecedents of candidates and eligibility restrictions for candidates with criminal cases pending against them. The Vohra Committee on criminalization of politics was to identify the extent of politician-criminal nexus and recommend ways and means to combat this menace. The "National Commission to Review the Working of the Constitution" citing the Vohra Committee recommendations observed that nexus between the criminal gangs, the police, bureaucracy and politicians has surfaced openly so much so that some political leaders have become leaders of these gangs/armed Senas and over the years, have themselves got elected to local bodies, state assemblies and National Parliament. Madhav Godbole reports that over 20.25 per cent MLAs and MPs have had criminal record in successive elections.

Of several remedies proposed by various committees on criminalization of politics in the country, two important remedies deserve attention, namely, (i) under rule 4A of the "Conduct of Election Rules", 1961, each candidate is required to file an affidavit (form 26 appended to Conduct of Election Rules, 1961) regarding cases in which the candidate has been accused of any offence punishable with imprisonment for two years or more in a pending case in which charges have been framed by the court and cases of conviction for an offence other than any of the offences mentioned in section 8 of RP Act, 1951, and sentenced to one year or more, and (ii) Secondly, in pursuance of the order of Supreme Court, the ECI in March 2003 issued an order that candidates must file an additional affidavit stating information relating to all pending cases in which cognizance has been taken by a Court, assets and liabilities of the candidate and his educational qualification. Section 125A of the RP Act, 1951, also prescribes penalties for withholding or providing incorrect information which amounts to imprisonment up to six months, or fine or both. Section 8 of RP Act provides for disqualification of the candidates from contesting an election on conviction by a court of law. Sub-section (i) of section 8 of RP Act lists certain crimes and stipulates a disqualification period of six years from the date of conviction. In sub-section (2) it lists out a different set of crimes for the candidates to be disqualified from the date of conviction and six years since release. Sub-section (3) provides that any candidate convicted for a crime for which the minimum imprisonment is two years shall also be disqualified from the date of conviction and will continue to be disqualified for six additional years after his release.

The Law Commission of India, way back in 1999, suggested that an amendment be made to the RP Act to insert a new section as 4A to make declaration of assets and criminal cases pending against the candidate as part of the qualifications necessary for membership to the House of the People. The "National Commission to Review the Working of the Constitution" proposed several measures. It proposed amendment to section 8 of the RP Act to provide that a candidate accused of an offence punishable with imprisonment of 5 years or more, be disqualified. On the expiry of one year from the date of charges framed against him and unless cleared during that one year period, shall remain disqualified until the conclusion of the trial. The Commission also proposed that in case a candidate is convicted by a Court of Law and sentenced to imprisonment of six months or more, he shall be disqualified during the period of the sentence and for six additional years after his release. Candidates violating this provision should be disqualified and political parties nominating such candidates with knowledge of his antecedents should be de-recognized and de-registered. The other recommendation of the Commission related to the person convicted of any heinous crime such as murder, rape, smuggling, dacoity etc. should be permanently debarred from contesting political office. It also proposed establishment of special courts to decide cases against candidates within a period of six months or less. The Law Commission in 1999 had also taken a different stand in suggesting section 8 to remain unchanged. It suggested addition of a new section as 8B to the RP Act to provide for a set of penalties for electoral offences particularly having bearing upon conduct of elections under section 153A and 505 of the IPC and serious offence punishable with death or life imprisonment. The new section would provide for framing of charges to be the ground of disqualification which shall last only for a period of five years or till the acquittal whichever is earlier. If a candidate is found guilty, he would automatically be disqualified under section 8 of RP Act.

The ECI had proposed in 2004 that section 8 of RP Act 1951 should be amended to disqualify candidates accused of an offence punishable with imprisonment of 5 years or more even when trial is pending provided the Court has framed charges against the person. Anticipating the possibility of misuse of such provision by the ruling party, the ECI suggested a compromise where only cases filed prior to six months before an election would lead to disqualification of a candidate. The ECI also suggested that candidates found guilty by a 'Commission of Enquiry' should stand disqualified. The historic verdict of the Supreme Court in 2013 bars a person in jail/police custody from contesting an election has been widely welcomed by the public though many raised certain misgivings on the ground that the court did not appear to have taken into consideration the views of the ECI. The ECI had held that those, against whom criminal charges have been admitted in the Court, should not be allowed to contest. The EC had not been able to implement this. On a representation submitted by "Nandini Voice for Deprived", a Chennai based NGO with appeal that the ECI should use its residual and inherent powers to bar such persons from contesting the polls, the ECI rejecting the appeal observed that "the Supreme Court has held that Article 324 operates in areas left unoccupied by legislation". In other words, in matters that are covered by law, the Commission cannot issue directions contrary to the provisions of law. On this issue, the ECI was subjected to criticism that it looks up to the Court to issue directives on its powers and functions and not playing the role of a constitutional entity but functions as an administrative body.

The Apex Court in its July 2013 judgement held that convicted MPs and MLAs will be disqualified with effect from the date of conviction, i.e. the date from which they will lose their posts even if they appeal to a higher court. They will be disqualified even during the pendency of the appeal. This strikes down a provision in the electoral law that protects a convicted law-maker from disqualification on the ground of pendency of appeal in higher courts. Instead of welcoming the decision of the Court, some politicians and political parties had openly opposed judicial intervention on the ground that the Supreme Court does not have the power to frame laws and regulate elections. This argument falls flat when questioned as to how convicted legislators are entitled to participate in the exercise of formulating law. When persons with criminal background are not eligible for government job, how a corrupt and convicted legislator can take part in election and become a policy maker? The order of Supreme Court intends to rectify such a system in order to bring in reforms in electoral reforms. The Supreme Court has directed the ECI to frame guidelines for regulating the contents of election manifestoes of political parties and bring them within the ambit of code of conduct even if the manifestoes were announced before the notification of election. This order of the Court was issued to ECI entrusting the responsibility of conducting elections in a free and fair manner. This landmark decision of Court will ensure transparency and accountability and level playing field to all political parties. Against the above order of the Apex Court, even petition was filed challenging the impugned judgement on the ground that section 8 of the RP Act has been declared unconstitutional without tracing its history. The Court passed an erroneous judgement which shall have serious repercussion in the functioning of Parliament, state legislature and democracy. The issue of constitutionality of sub-section (4) of section 8 of the RP Act had already been settled by a five-judge bench in 2005. The recent verdict in two cases i.e., (i) Parliament exceeding its power by enacting the provision in section 8 (4) of RP Act that gives a convicted law-maker the power to remain in office on the ground that appeals have been filed and pending, and (ii) a person who is in jail or in police custody cannot contest elections to legislative bodies since only an elector can contest polls and he/she ceases the right to cast vote due to confinement in prison or being in custody of police, should have been decided by a constitutional bench. However, the leaders of parties cutting across political lines urged the government to bring amendment to the RP Act to overturn the Apexs Court's ruling. They held that the verdict will lead to atrocious consequences as any government can detain its political opponent even one day before the poll nomination. This is of course an individual view.

Legislatures do not seem to be representing the people. Instead, they represent the political class. When legislatures pass irresponsible laws to protect criminals in the house, the political class as a whole, stands condemned. It has so happened that murderers and rapists function as law makers included therein Ministers also. This is a disgraceful trend of Indian democracy. In recent years, Indian Parliament tends to give protection and immunity to criminals who are blocking Parliament's proceedings altogether. This is abuse of democracy. No sincere efforts seem to have been taken to stop criminalization of legislators. Therefore, the oblivious expectation with a lot of doubt is weather the judiciary can do what politicians refuse to do? It is not surprising but ironic that because elected representatives fail to address their legitimate duties and functions, judiciary penetrates to the area of failure of legislators. The frequent acid attack on women is one example where no action was taken until the Apex Court intervened to direct the government to regulate the retail sale of acid failing which the Court would impose ban on all sales.

The decision of Supreme Court in July 2013 in *CEC vs. Jan Chowkidar* has attracted significant attention to address the issue of criminalization of politics. Justices A.K. Patnaik and S.J. Mukhopadhaya ruled that it is established by law in India that individuals in lawful custody of the police, under-trials and those serving a sentence of imprisonment after conviction, cannot vote. This reasoning of Supreme Court has entertained several views from different quarters. Besides, significant debates in our constitutional jurisprudence on the nature of right to vote it has been established through judgement of Supreme Court in the past that the right to vote is not a fundamental right or a constitutional right but only a statutory right. Being a statutory right, the legislature can determine the term on which the right to vote is to be enjoyed by the people of the country subject to Articles 325 and 326 of the Constitution. One such condition is to be found in section 62 (5) of the RP Act which explicitly provides that "no person shall vote at any election if he is confined in a prison whether under a sentence of imprisonment or transportation or otherwise or in lawful custody of police". The Court probably relied upon this provision of law. The constitutionality of section 62 (5) of the RP Act was challenged earlier before the Supreme Court in Anukul Chandra Pradhan *vs.* Union of India (July, 1997) as being violative of the right to life under Articles 14 to 21 of the Constitution. Through an unanimous opinion authored by the late Chief Justice J.S. Verma, the Supreme Court rejected this challenge. Even though this judgement appeared to be unconvincing, the Supreme Court took the view that it was reasonable to deny voting rights to convicted prisoners under trial and those in police custody with a view to curb criminalization of politics. The Court took into account of practical considerations and ruled that the additional resources that would be required in terms of infrastructure, security and deployment of extra police forces were legitimate justifications in denying the right to vote to prisoners and those in custody. The court held that a prisoner was "in prison as a result of his own conduct and therefore, deprived of his liberty during the period of his imprisonment (and) cannot claim equal freedom of movement, speech and expression with others who are not in prison."

The above mentioned judgement of Supreme Court was slated to be unconvincing on the ground that the court did not consider it necessary to distinguish between convicted prisoners and under trials and those in custody on the other. While judicial sanctity and honesty of the principle of "innocent until proven guilty" is embraced in our criminal justice system, the presumption that under-trials and those in custody are yet to be guilty as far as voting rights are concerned, negates the very fairness of justice. The fact remains that those in custody are yet to be found guilty and therefore, to be exempted while determining the contours of the right to vote. It has been urged that the right to vote lies at the very heart of the idea of full and effective citizenship and by denying voting right to prisoners, the state effectively negates their citizenship status. By virtue of being incarcerated with very little access to outside world, this opportunity to participate in the political process is integral to further alienation from society. While the stated goal of our criminal jurisprudence is to reform prisoners and reintegrate them into society, the denial of voting rights to prisoners treats them as outcasts. In many other countries like South Africa, Canada and European countries the constitutional courts have ruled that a blanket ban on voting right for all convicted prisoners is discriminatory and violates their dignity. One is reminded of what Winston Churchill as Home Secretary said in the House of Commons in July 1910 "The mood on temper of the public in regard to the treatment of crime and criminals is one of the most unfailing test of civilization of any country." True, prevention of criminalization of politics is essential but not at the expense of denial of voting rights to those in custody and in prison.

There has been a growing tendency for all the established political parties to choose crorepatis as their candidates. Pursuant to the Supreme Court Order (2002) all candidates are required to furnish sworn-in affidavits to the ECI declaring their education, wealth and criminal cases. Non-Governmental Organization (NGOs) seem to have collated those figures and put in on their websites forgetting that at-times, those may lead to draw wrong conclusions. With rising cost of property in recent years, lakhpatis of yester-years could be easily crorepatis in recent years, and the established parties seem to be deliberately preferring to handout tickets to such wealthy candidates. This trend has been elaborately analyzed by the Association for Democratic Reform (ADR) over the last several elections to both the Parliament and State Assemblies. In the elections (2013) held to the State Assemblies of Delhi, Rajasthan, Madhya Pradesh, Chhattisgarh and Mizoram, the figures reflected in the ADR website indicate that in Delhi, the cumulative percentage of crorepatis was 33 per cent. The SAD party had all candidates, as 'crorepatis' followed by INC with 87 per cent, the BJP 85 per cent, the AAP 47 per cent. Incidentally, the average asset of INC candidates was 14+ crore of rupees, the BJP 8+ crore, and the AAP 2+ crore. In Madhya Pradesh, the BJP had 70 per cent crorepatis, the INC with 66 per cent and the BSP 18 per cent. In Rajasthan, the BJP had 75 per cent and the INC 70 per cent. In Mizoram, the MPC fielded eight candidates, all crorepatis, while INC had 73 per cent and the MNF 65 per cent. In Chhattisgarh, the average figure of all crore parties was 22 per cent with INC at 68 per cent and the BJP 66 per cent.

Electoral money power has been a most difficult problem to solve. It is frustrating to observe that despite presence of election observers during elections, candidates continue to use all manners of deception to distribute money and freebies to lure voters. There being no end to human ingenuity, large sums of cash are ferried in the most unlikely of private and public vehicles. In Karnataka elections of 2008, even milk vans and ambulances were not spared from the most blatant misuse. While over Rs. 40 crore of cash and freebies were seized by vigilance officials, unknown amounts of clandestine sums would doubtless have reached their destinations. The bye-election to Thirumangalam (Tamil Nadu) in (December 2008-January 2009) marked a low point in this regard. Elections in Bellary in Karnataka too provided another amusing case study. During the elections, a number of criminal cases were registered but the first task of the newly elected State Government was to withdraw all these cases in connivance with the bureaucracy and the public prosecutors. But the EC passed orders that all election related cases be contested in court on their merits and could not be withdrawn by executive orders. The High Court upheld the EC's stand.

In spite of these, India has been a stable democracy. Elections have been held on mandated time every time. There has been invariably a willing acceptance of the people's mandate. The Election Commission has been viewed as fair and impartial. Court orders in election related petitions have been accepted without demur. The recently held elections (November-December 2013) in Delhi has demonstrated that elections can be won without resorting to calls of caste, religion, subterfuge, muscle power and money. The importance of AAM ADMI PARTY's stunning triumph lies in its being able to win a clean election without having to resort to money and muscle power or without having to exhort caste, creed, class or religious loyalties. It kept its expenditure within the statutory limit of Rs. 16 lakh for an election to the State Assembly of Delhi. That any candidate can win an election within the limits set by law even without support of party cadres is a fact to be applauded. It is all the more remarkable when a party wins an election without breaking the election code in any significant respect and that too under harsh media glare in the national capital. In recent years all parties having declared 'winnability' to be their 'mantra' have really ended up in giving tickets to those wealthy enough to fund their own elections. Muscle power, even criminality, has often been viewed as bonus points. In the midst of this situation, the success of AAP becomes both a fascinating case study and important bench-mark towards cleaner elections.

Given the low level of convictions of MPs and MLAs, political parties are not deterred from continuing to hand out party tickets to persons with criminal backgrounds, says the Law Commission report on electoral reforms, which was presented to the Supreme Court. The report, penned by Commission Chairman Justice A.P. Shah, pointed out that a person with criminal background seems to be at an advantage as far as his political career is concerned. "Candidates charged with a crime have a 2:1 chance of winning the election over candidates with no criminal backgrounds. This means that political parties liberally and repeatedly hand out tickets to criminally charged candidates and seventy four per cent of candidates with criminal backgrounds have re-contested elections in the last 10 years," the report states. The report also analysed "as to how people with criminal backgrounds are among winners as well criminal backgrounds are not limited to contesting candidates, but are found among winners as well. Of the 5253 candidates with serious criminal charges against them, 1187 went on to win the elections. About 13.5 per cent of the 8882 winners were analysed from 2004 to 2013. Over all, including both serious and non-serious charges, 2497 (28.4% of the winners) had 9993 pending criminal cases against them," the report stated. The report also found a disturbing trend that the percentage of winners with criminal cases pending is higher than the percentage of candidates without such backgrounds. "While only 12 per cent of candidates with a clean record win on average, and 23 per cent of candidates with some kind of criminal record win. This means that candidates charged with a crime actually fare better at elections than clean candidates. Probably as a result, candidates with criminal cases against them tend to be given tickets a second time. Not only do political parties select candidates with criminal backgrounds, there is evidence to suggest that untainted representatives later become involved in criminal activities. The incidence of criminalization of politics is thus pervasive making its remedy an urgent, the report stated. In the 10 years, 18 per cent of candidates contesting either National or State elections have criminal cases pending against them. In 5253 cases, the charges are of serious criminal offences that include murder, attempt to murder, rape, crimes against women, cases under the Prevention of Corruption Act, 1988, or under the Maharashtra Control of Organised Crime Act, 1999 which, on conviction, would result in five years or more in jail. In the current Lok Sabha, 162 sitting members have criminal cases pending against them, of which 76 members have serious criminal cases. Further, the prevalence of MPs with criminal cases pending has increased over time.

Booth Capturing, Poll Rigging and Malpractices

Booth-capturing and tearing of ballot papers, snatching away ballot boxes, pre and post-election killings and commission of crimes resulting in kidnapping and murders has been a trend during electoral processes in the country for quite some. In fact, influence of money and muscle power was reportedly in existence since the first general elections of 1952 but with a limited rather negative scale. In the sixties, the criminals and anti-socials used to play as second fiddle to politicians with a view to secure gains and get protection from them. The influence of muscle power in Indian politics has been increasing since then. Between 1990-1998, as many as 371 political workers in 302 incidents and 5 MLAs in Bihar were reportedly murdered. The State Governments in some cases, tried to protect these gangsters. Even the police of concerned States provided security to these elements and many of them became either MLAs, Ministers, MPs, etc. Of them, Kalpanath Rai, Anand Mohan Singh, Pappu Yadav, and Phoolan Devi could be cited as instances. Such was the presence of these people in politics that even a Governor like Satyanarayan Reddy, Governor UP had had to candidly say that government was protecting as many as 938 politicians out of which about 222 were history-sheeters or under-trials involved in cases relating to extorsion, kidnapping, rape and murder. The Vohra Committee (1993) highlighted about the nexus between politicians, administrators and criminals. The Committee, in its report, mentioned as to how criminals enjoyed the patronage of local politicians and protection of government functionaries in States like Bihar, Haryana and Uttar Pradesh. In course of time, this epidemic spread to other states. But with introduction of electronic voting machines and photo-identity cards in elections, the culture of booth capturing seems to have been reduced a lot.

Poll-rigging encompasses areas of exclusion of names from voter's list, intimidation and impersonation. Impersonation and bogus voting becomes a reality in absence of strong opponent. Cadre-based parties were alleged to have enrolled their supporters at times, excluding their opponents. Instances of high percentage of polling in some polling stations by intimidation of bogus voting in connivance with polling officers were reportedly common in some elections. In some cases, actual voters were prevented and others in their place exercised franchise. Coercion to vote for a particular party or to stay away from the polling booth is inflicted by political parties through anti-social elements. In some states ruled by organized or cadre-based parties, electoral malpractices led to "scientific rigging of elections". This is a very sophisticated subtle technique applied at every stage of electoral process from exclusion of genuine voters sympathetic to the rival of political parties and inclusion of bogus voters in the electoral rolls to manipulation of election results at the time of counting. During the 1980 elections, notorious history-sheeters or people with criminal records or background were fielded for the first time for

Lok Sabha seats especially in Bihar and UP. Involvement of these unscrupulous elements strengthened what is called the '*babu-neta*' syndrome in politics. Over the years, this process has been euphemistically called the "Criminalization of Politics". By 1990, politics had degenerated to a very low level warranting the Election Commission to become proactive for upholding the constitutional mandate of conducting free and fair elections. With growing trend of criminalization of politics, there had been a paradigm shift in the role of Election Commission from passive to a proactive body, from a low-profile organization to a catalytic agency committed to the cleansing of the electoral system.

The Goswami Committee, in its report of 1990, recommended to empower Election Commission to take strong action on the report of returning officers, election observers or of civil society in regard to booth capture or intimidation of voters. The "National Commission to Review the Working of the Constitution" also recommended that the EC should have power under section 58A of RP Act, 1951 to order for a fresh election, declare election results void or even to order for a re-poll in such cases. It recommended to make use of electronic surveillance equipment as a deterrent to booth capture or intimidation of voters.

Pre-election Larges

As a sequel to attracting voters, Chief Ministers of many states in recent years have opened up state coffers to make the voters happy on the eve of elections. In Rajasthan, the then Chief Minister gifted to the electorate cash doles, pensions, laptops and sponsored pilgrimage. His populist schemes cost the exchequer an additional amount of about Rs. 3000 crore at a time when the state was reeling a debt of Rs. 1.71 lakh crore. In the budget he had allotted Rs. 300 crore for free *sarees* and blankets for families below poverty line. Subsequently, the budget had been doubled and later on, instead of sarees, the beneficiaries got cash. The Delhi Chief Minister left no stone unturned to please the voters. She announced a slew of schemes for slums and unauthorized colonies to please the huge voter base. Freebies and welfare schemes were seen as an easy way to neutralize anti-incumbency. The Delhi Government cleared around 200 cases for regularisation of irregular colonies with ownership rights given to residents in about 45 resettlement colonies. In BJP ruled Chhattisgarh and Madhya Pradesh, identical populist schemes, be they financial assistance to women for marriage, pilgrimage for the elderly, free powers for farmers, laptops for college students or almost free ration etc. were introduced to woe voters. Both the states were brimming over with schemes where tax payers' money was being doled out. In Chhattisgarh, rice was given at 1 rupee a Kg to the poor. The Chief Minister's re-election in the last assembly polls is largely attributed to the popularity of the schemes. The same type of schemes were introduced in Odisha by providing rice at Rs. 2.00 per Kg to the poor and the Chief Minister's re-election in 2009 and 2014 is attributed to as one of the reasons for his getting re-elected and forming government.

The freebie culture originated in south India. Political parties in Tamil Nadu have been bedazzling voters with promises in the last few elections. If it was grinders and mixtures that churned on positive vote for the AIADMK in 2011 as against Karunanidhi's riding to power offering television sets to voters five years before. The Schemes that are being currently offered by the present Chief Minister J. Jayalalitha range from gold for women who need marriage assistance to subsidised bottled water. This continued even when the State's economy was in a mess with outstanding debt of Rs. 1.31 lakh crore in 2012-13 and in 2013-14 at Rs. 1.55 lakh crore. The idea of giving laptop which is now a staple scheme in election bound states was pioneered by the Samajvadi Party in Uttar Pradesh. It earmarked Rs. 2721.24 crore for 15 lakh free laptops for students who passed class XII. The Nitish Kumar government in Bihar introduced distribution of bi-cycles to students which was followed by some other states like the Naveen Pattnaik Government in Odisha.

The worrying aspect of all these welfare schemes is the alleged corruption and partnership. In Rajasthan, numerous reports have come to say about diversion of medicines meant for free distribution to patients diverted to open market and for that middle-men charging from poor patients. In Delhi, a scam of about Rs. 28,000 crore in the regularization of unauthorized colonies was reported in which PWD officials, government functionaries and contractors were reportedly involved. In Madhya Pradesh, it was alleged that those close to BJP leadership got advantage of such schemes. This type of allegation has also come from other states.

Despite allout efforts of politicians, voters remain an elusive target. But most voters can distinguish between a genuine welfare scheme and a poll gimmick. Unbridled welfare schemes, have more bearing on the system than the financial burden. None of the states has any mechanism to check if the welfare schemes serve the purpose of greater interest of mass of people in general.

The issue of election freebie has become a very important issue. Freebie connotes anything given without charge. If something is given free of charge promised by political parties to the electorate, the logical deduction would be that it amounts to inducement of voters. In the meeting of Election Commission with political parties, some time back to frame guidelines on election manifesto, nothing concrete emerged and it is the EC which is now to decide and draw a distinction between a legitimate welfare scheme and a measure that is undertaken with the sole intention of attracting voters. In July 2013 the Supreme Court, while dismissing a special leave petition filed by Chennai-based lawyer S. Subramaniam Balaji held that although the promises in an election manifesto cannot be construed as "corrupt practice" under section 123 of the RP Act, it cannot be ruled out that distribution of freebies of any kind influenced the people as it shakes the root of free and fair election to a large degree, the Court said. It asked the EC to consult all political parties to formulate guidelines for election manifesto and noted the need for a separate legislation in this regard. The EC's stand has been that freebies disturb the level playing field in elections. Surprisingly, except for the Bahujan Samaj Party and three other parties from the North East, all major political parties like the BJP, Congress and the Left have defended their right to announce freebies on the plea that these were welfare measures meant for the betterment of the lives of the poor and in their meeting with the EC have made it clear that neither the poll panel nor the courts had any right to intervene in their manifesto. Sensing the belligerent mood of political parties on the issue, the EC asked them to send their written submission to proceed further in the matter. To sort-out this critical but important issue, two options emerge in the forefront. One option could be to put in place a system of self-regulation by the parties which seems very difficult to achieve. The second option could be to formulate a set of guidelines that allows freebies only if they are intended for the poor, the disadvantaged and the marginalized. But all depends upon the timing of launching or declaring the freebies. Declaration or launching of the pre-election largesse should not be implemented at least within the last six months to one year before the elections are due. Distribution of freebies like laptops, rice, *sarees*, T.V. sets, cycles, scooters, gas cylinders etc. should have the prior approval of legislature based on a clear budgetary allocation duly passed by the legislature and no *post-facto* approval process be adopted.

The Supreme Court disposed of a petition which argued that the announcement of pre-poll freebies like free laptops, mixers, grinders, television sets etc. specially by DMK first and then by AIADMK in Tamil Nadu which tantamounts to bribery, is violative of Article 14 and defies the definition of "public purpose" and is a corrupt electoral practice. The petitioner S. Subramaniam Balaji sought for an end to this practice and requested the Court to formulate necessary guidelines. As it exists now, if an individual candidate makes promises to influence voters, he/she can be hauled up for 'corrupt practices' under section 123 of the RP Act, but the same does not apply to a party if it presents a parade of pre-poll sops and freebies to the voters. The RP Act is silent about promises made by parties. Parties argue that promises are implemented only when schemes are passed by an elected legislature and hence are valid. The first amendment to the Constitution circumscribed freedom of expression and right to own property to the diktat of 'public interest' and 'public purpose'. But in the instant case, the CJ of Supreme Court observed that "distribution of freebies of any kind undoubtedly influences all people. It shakes the root of free and fair elections to a larger degree." The Court directed the ECI to frame guidelines on the contents of election manifesto released by parties which should be included in the 'model code of conduct'. But the public in general, are not that optimistic because of several instances of inaction in the past. The class of 'corrupt practices' came into the RP Act in 1956 but had to wait till the 1990s for Seshan, the then ECI to implement it. Generally, political parties release their election manifesto before the announcement of the election date and the EC cannot regulate any act done before announcement of the election date. But the CJ in this case held that "an exemption can be made as the manifestos purpose is directly associated with elections".

Open solicitation of voters with virtually rice, bicycles, computers, *mangalsutras* and the like is making a mockery of elections. All political parties jump into the freebie racket with competitive fervour. The Supreme Court had to cry a halt to this evident malpractice. The Election Commission has reportedly made several recommendations with a view to putting an end to the practice of legalized fraud. The government could have kept the criminal elements out if the recommendations of ECI were adopted and acted upon. Instead, it became a party to the outrageous malpractices in which jailed candidates holding dance-and-dinner parties inside high security prisons as elected criminals to Parliament going under police escort to take oath and then returning to their prison cells. Even though the political class has welcomed the recent judicial rulings for public consumption, it has not really digested internally because every party without exception has goons and mafia dons in its leadership list. Facts indicate that as many as 1406 MPs and MLAs in office today have criminal cases against them. Even though the Supreme Court is candid in its judgement that criminals be kept out of Parliament and Assemblies, the legislators have not paid or are inclined to pay attention to this issue of electoral reform. In fact, the strength of criminal class has become indistinguishable from the political class. The muscle and money power of dons are the lifeblood for parties and therefore, they try to frustrate the law and cheat the voters.

Corruption Influencing Voter's Choice in Election

There was overwhelming consensus that the Congress-led UPA II performed very poorly in the 2014 elections owing to charges of massive corruption at the highest level, besides lack of leadership and the government's ability to control price rise. Political commentators and the BJP-led NDA made repeated references during election campaigns to the Coal Scam, the CommonWealth Games (CWG) and the Adarsh Housing scam among others. The BJP also shared its own trouble in matters relating to favouring Adani Business Group and Nitin Gadkari's alleged involvement with Purti Group. Notwithstanding the campaign rhetoric, corruption seems to be mattering little in spite the way commentators and political parties think it does. Recent studies have shown that voters in India do not care about corruption. There is a crucial difference in how voters think about corruption and how political parties and leaders represent this issue in their campaigns. In fact, voters care more about the corruption they encounter on an everyday basis whereas parties make issue a spectacle. A large section of the electorate has never heard of the corruption scams that occupy newspaper headlines and prime time television space. In July 2013, "Lokniti-CSDS" contacted more than 18000 citizens and found that awareness among the general public on scams such as 2G and Coalgate was quite low. Only half of the sampled respondents said that they had heard of coal scam, 40 per cent knew of the 2G scam. Less than a third of the citizens responded that, they heard of them. It revealed from the study that awareness on all the issues relating to scams was much lower among women, the poor and respondents residing in rural areas. The 2013 tracker poll had asked respondents whom they would vote for in this election. They found that there was no statistical significant influence of the knowledge of scams on the respondent's presence for the two parties—the Congress and the BJP. Table 3.4 below will show that the likelihood of a voter preferring the Congress remained almost the same whether or not she/he had heard of the party's involvement in scams. Those who heard of scams were a little more likely to vote for the BJP but the difference in the probability of a voter voting for the BJP was no more than 10 per cent. In these situations, the question arises as to why scams have no bearing on vote choice? One section of scholars think that it is the corruption at local level institutions which matters more to voters. The National Survey 2011 shows that people are much more concerned with the everyday corruption they face while interacting with local-level state institutions like Police, BDO etc.

The below graph indicates the link between scams and vote choice :

Table 3.4: Impact of Scams on Voter's Choice

Name of the Party	*1*	*2*	*3*	*4*	*5*	*6*
BJP	0.32	0.23	0.32	0.74	0.34	0.24
Congress	0.26	0.29	0.26	0.29	0.26	0.28

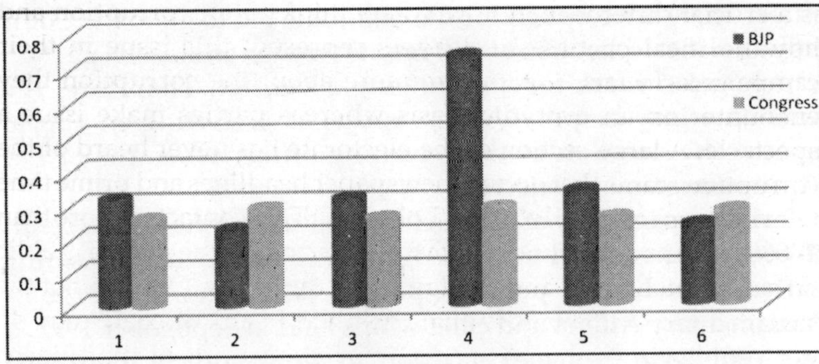

Application of Model Code of Conduct

The Parliamentary Standing Committee on Personnel, PG, Law and Justice, in its 6th report on Electoral Reforms, recommended that the powers to de-recognise political parties on account of violation of model code of conduct may be incorporated in the RP Act, 1951 itself. The Committee recommended that the provision of the model code be made part of RP Act, 1951, or the rules framed there under for ensuring free and fair election in the country. The Committee headed by Shantaram Naik also sought revision in the election expenditure limit of a candidate to make it more realistic and setting up of first-tract courts to dispose of election disputes within a period of 12 months. The Committee sought to remove the powers of Election Commission to de-recognize a political party on account of violation of model code of conduct and suggested to incorporate it in the RP Act, 1951. It also suggested that persons other than members of houses of Parliament and Assemblies should not be given powers to make application to disqualify an MLA or an MP and recommended to reconsider different criteria provided to nominated and independent members under the Tenth Schedule to join any political party in the same manner as in the case of nominated members. It has been observed that instructions or orders issued by Election Commission under Article 324 of Constitution sometimes appears to be encroaching upon legislative power of Parliament. Therefore, such instructions or orders issued by EC may be suitably incorporated in the RP Act, 1951 or rules made thereunder. When the nomination paper of a candidate is rejected by a presiding officer, there is no option for the candidate but to go to the Court only after the declaration of poll results through an election petition which takes years for announcing a verdict. Therefore, the candidate may be provided an option of preferring an appeal against the decision of the returning officer when his or her nomination paper is rejected.

The present code of conduct for political parties is the result of consensus evolved in the "All India Conference of Presiding Officers, leaders of political parties, Ministers in-charge of Parliamentary Affairs and chief whips held in September 1992. It was resolved in the same conference to evolve and observe a code of conduct for legislators. The resolution could not be implemented because the government in power could not muster enough strength and courage. The proposal to prescribe certain minimum qualification for contesting the election and holding the posts of legislators could not materialise besides the qualification required for a legislator on the basis that no court cases or convictions would be pending against the candidate seeking to contest elections. The responsibility of enforcing the model code of conduct, however, lies with the ECI.

The "Model Code of Conduct" was formulated on the basis of a consensus among political parties. This was made effective since the seventh general elections to the Lok Sabha in 1979. This innovative document has been hailed by many democratic countries across the world as a significant contribution by the Election Commission of India (ECI) to the cause of free and fair elections. It contains guidelines for the ruling parties both at the Centre and in the State to ensure that a level playing field between the candidates of ruling and the opposition is maintained and that the party in power does not enjoy any disproportionate advantage over its rivals during election. It also lays down as to how political parties and candidates should conduct themselves, during the election campaign. Though the model code of conduct, in some form or the other, had been in existence from the 60s, its observance was mainly left to the good sense of the political parties and the candidates. It was only during the Tenth general election to the Lok Sabha in 1991 that the EC became very proactive in the implementation of the model code of conduct. Since then, the ruling parties at the Centre and the States are trying to ensure its enforcement and observance.

Use of Electronic Voting Machine (EVM)

The introduction of Electronic Voting Machine (EVM) by the ECI is a new innovation in the electoral process. Besides EVM, issue of voter identity card and review of electoral roll with photo of the voter are the commendable reform measures adopted by the ECI. These measures aim at generating voter's right from threat of a validation and impersonation. EVM was first applied in 1982 in one of the constituencies in Kerala on experimental basis. In 2004 Lok Sabha elections, EVM was used almost all over the country. This initiative of ECI was intended to make the electoral process, simple, quick, trouble-free and reduce malpractices and improve efficiency in the conduct of elections. The use of EVM although has been very useful in matters relating to counting of votes within shortest possible time and in reducing chances of booth capturing, several doubts and allegations of manipulation through the use and management of used chips had been raised against use of EVM. In spite of these, the election process itself is not free from errors. It is alleged that it weakens the democratic process, and is also influencing and encroaching upon the right of voters. But experience obtained in the last two-three general elections with the application of EVM has demonstrated that it is almost a fool proof system and a better and improved process of voting. The system of EVM facilitates for "no-invalid-votes" as every vote recorded in the machine is accounted in favour of the candidate for whom it is voted when the button is clicked. During the non-EVM period in the past, the number of invalid votes (both protested invalid and ignorant invalid votes) used to be increased in successive elections despite improvement in literacy rate. In 1989 Lok Sabha elections, about 76 lakh votes were declared invalid. In 1992 Presidential Election, 67 votes were invalid with a value of 17199 votes. Therefore, introduction of EVM in Indian elections guarantees the voter's right against the threat of invalidation of their votes and against hijacking of poor voter's votes through money and muscle power.

The use of electronic voting machines (EVMs) instead of traditional system of ballot boxes and ballot papers, is a revolutionary step taken by the EC to make the electoral process simpler, smoother and speedier. This machine has been manufactured by two public sector undertakings, namely : (1) Bharat

Electronics Limited, Bangalore and (2) Electronic Corporation of India Ltd., Hyderabad. In spite of initial technical flaws, these machines were used for the first time in the general elections to the legislative assemblies of Madhya Pradesh, Rajasthan and Delhi in 16 constituencies in 1998 on experimental basis. Subsequently, more and more constituencies were covered. The advantage in use of EVCs is that it quickens the process of counting of votes and makes the electoral process far cheaper by dispensing with printing of hundreds of millions of ballot papers. Another advantage of EVMs is that there are no invalid and wasted votes at all as every single vote recorded in the machine is accounted for. Added to these, is the possibility of eliminating looting or snatching ballot papers or ballot boxes which account for more transparency in actual polling and counting of votes.

In many elections at State and Central levels it was pointed out that failure to use Electronic Voting Machine (EVM) contributed largely to booth capture. Booth capturing can be defined as seizing of polling station, intimidating polling officers, and casting their votes. The marking system of voting was introduced in 1962 to make it possible for a substantial number of illiterate voters to indicate easily their preference in choosing representatives. Over the years, with tremendous increase in the volume of work, crores of ballot papers had to be printed and lakhs of ballot boxes had to be prepared, transformed and kept in storage resulting in huge expenditure in terms of money and time. To overcome these difficulties, the Election Commission of India (ECI) thought of introducing electronic gadget. The Electronic Corporation of India Ltd (ECIL), Hyderabad and Bharat Electronics Ltd. (BEL), Bangalore developed the electronic voting machine in 1981.

When the ECI used EVM in 1982 on experimental basis, in Assembly poll in Kerala, an election petition was filed questioning the statutory authority of the Commission to introduce use of EVM in election. The Supreme Court decided that voting machines could be used even without a necessary provision under the law. With amendment to the election law adopted in December 1998, the ECI had prepared to use voting machines in 1999 Lok Sabha poll. However, it had to be postponed as political parties aired apprehension about a possible manipulation or distortion of the electronic instrument to favour some candidates or party symbols.

The question of reliability was taken up in March 1990 for consideration by the "committee on electoral reforms" appointed by the V.P. Singh Government. The committee headed by the Law Minister Dinesh Goswami with other members like L.K. Advani (BJP), H.K.L. Bhagat (Congress), Somanath Chatterjee (CPIM), Homi Daji (CPI) and Era Sezhiyan (Janata Dal). The Committee collected copious evidence from experts of ECIL and department of electronics and got clearance from the experts committee for technical education of the EVM in respect of doubts and apprehensions about the credibility of voting machines. The Committee recommended use of voting machines in all future bye-elections and general elections to Lok Sabha, State Assembly and also Panchayat and local bodies with suggestion to educate the electorate and familiarize them with the working of the machine.

While rigging is not possible with EVMs as against such possibilities in the ballot paper making system, a vote once recorded in an EVM cannot be tampered with. The EVMs are capable of retaining the memory of the votes recorded for a period of three years. If the machine is tampered with in any respect either during the poll time or at any other time before the counting of votes, that will be easily detectable so that a fresh poll can be ordered. The 2004 Lok Sabha elections were held with more than a million EVMs. Thereafter, EVMs have been used in bye and general elections. The Election Commission of India has earned the reputation and honour of sincerely discharging its constitutional obligations in conducting free and fair elections in the world's largest functioning democracy. In order to ensure that elections are conducted in a free, fair and peaceful manner, the EC seems to have taken several innovative and protective steps in the recent past. Computerization of electoral rolls is one such innovative effort as a result of which computerized electoral roll is now available in almost all constituencies. The other innovative scheme is "Elector's Photo Identity Card" (EPIC) introduced and completed for about 370 million electors in the country in order to improve the accuracy of voter's list, prevent electoral fraud and protect citizen's right to vote. Introduction and implementation of Model Code of Conduct (MCC) warranting political parties and contesting candidates to abide by the Model Code of Conduct, has been formulated on the basis of consensus among political parties.

NOTA Option

That people should have the option to reject any or all the candidates in an election if they are unfit to hold office has been the centre of discussion and debate for quite some time. The "Peoples Union for Civil Liberties" (PUCL) pleaded before the Supreme Court in a case it filed that the Court should direct the Central Government to provide a choice in the Electronic Voting Machines (EVMS). The purpose of the argument was to provide an opportunity to dissatisfied elector to express his/her dissent against the contesting candidates. This would also provide the benefit of reducing bogus voting.

The Constitution provides for universal adult franchise in all elections of public nature *vide* Articles 324 to 329. But in no election, there is any option allowing "None Of The Above" (NOTA). Articles 327 and 328 enable Parliament and State Legislatures to make provisions for the conduct of elections. Article 325 converts the right to vote as a fundamental right of an individual who is eligible. Even though some activists and political thinkers across the world have been advocating for the option of rejection and/or recall of a particular candidate, regrettably different strategies in India concerning election did not have any specific provision for this. Possibly, law makers could not foresee such situations while formulating laws. In fact, "NOTA" thinking is neither revolutionary nor novel. In some countries of the world, a limited number of political parties follow this practice. The main countries that have such a provision in their ballot practices are France, Spain, Ukraine and Nevada state in the U.S. Although Russia had such a provision, it was abolished in 2000. A system called "RON" (Reopening Of Nominations) is followed by some student unions in Great Britain. The first voter consent law containing a binding "NOTA" ballot option was introduced in the Massachusetts Legislature in 2007. In the US, a non-political organization called "Voters for None Of The Above" has also been running campaign for "No Vote" option as one of the options in the ballot. It has been argued that "None Of The Above" (NOTA) allows voters to send a message that they want change in the quality of candidates which ultimately would send signals for more fundamental reforms in finance and direct democracy.

In India, electoral reforms have been taken up in right earnest and Election Commission and the Central Government have taken several steps to clean up electoral process. But the fact, however, remains that Indian elite continue to remain apathetic and unconcerned with the process of selection of candidates. The crisis of choice manifested in absence of inspiring names on the ballot has indeed fuelled voter apathy towards the secret duty of voting. It is a fact that NOTA option will not address all the issues relevant to electoral reforms. But, it will ensure that people can voice their disapproval of the candidates by the positive action of casting their vote instead of absenting. This will have a positive impact on the voter mindset by showing that their choice at a polling station has a direct effect. One of the most important questions raised is as to what happens after NOTA gets the highest number of votes? Two options seems to be very often debated. First, the real candidate who gets the highest number of votes after NOTA can be declared as elected. He or she will assume office in the knowledge that he or she was not the first choice and therefore, would be expected to act more responsibly. The second option will be a re-election with new candidates. But this could mean repeating the entire process twice or even thrice causing huge expenditure to the public exchequer and other attendant complications. Moreover, it is possible in the theory that a particular constituency may return a NOTA verdict continuously on more than three or four occasions thus creating farcical situation. However, attractive and romantic NOTA may appear, this idea has inherent problems emerging from issues related to expenditure, time factor, morale of voter and stability of the governments. Therefore, a larger debate is required.

The recent judgement of the Supreme Court (2013) on NOTA is among the series of judgements towards electoral reforms. One of these judgements relate to the attempt made to save MPs found guilty of offences that would instantly un-seat them. The attempt to thwart this decision through the RP (Amendment and Validation) Ordinance had to be given up because of public pressure and the President of India's reported reluctance to sign the Ordinance. The courts have had to intervene because of government's reluctance to move ahead in bringing meaningful electoral reforms. This has led to restoration of public's faith in the system. The NOTA case is the classic example of government's failure to do the right thing at the right time. In fact, the ECI had moved the Law Ministry as early as 2001 for an amendment to the rules to provide for a button in the EVM in order to protect the identity and secrecy of a voter who does not want to vote for any candidate. This was the equivalent of the unmarked ballot paper of earlier era. The ECI did receive no response. In 2004, the EC reiterated the earlier proposal after christening the button as 'None of The Above' with clear articulation to enable a voter to reject all candidates. The PUCL filed in the meantime came for hearing in 2009 although the protagonists of "No Vote" accepted it as an attribute of "Rejection" of candidates. This was obviously a misconception as votes recorded against this button would have the same fate as the "Invalid Votes" of the ballot paper era without any role in determining the winner. With EVMs the "Invalid Vote" category got eliminated as mistakes like wrong marking and multiple marking. When the matter came up in the Supreme Court in 2009, the government realized the importance of this button to create a negative impact leading to the demand for a right to reject candidates and seek fresh elections.

The government reacted very strongly to the aforesaid situation and pleaded that since the right to vote was not a constitutional right but only a statutory right, the petition filed under Article 32 was not maintainable. The matter ultimately went to a larger bench and now has come with the historic verdict. The recent verdict on NOTA has witnessed several reactions. Some describe the issue of "NOTA" as a minor issue. Others hold that it may increase voters turnout which the court also held. Some others feel that it will make parties more responsible to nominate better candidates. The Judges pronouncing the judgement have held that it can widen participation and curb impersonation. A reading of the judgement indicates that the judges strove to make it a reality by an innovative interpretation of past judgements of the Supreme Court and provisions of the constitution and the nature of right to vote with the sole objective of giving the voter a wider choice. To quote a portion from the verdict. "Democracy is about choice. This choice can be better expressed by giving the voters an opportunity to verbalise themselves unreservedly and by imposing least restrictions on their ability to make such a choice." The Court declared that the provision of negative voting would be in the interests of promoting democracy. The Court further clarified between the right to vote which it confirmed as a statutory right and the act of exercising the right by the casting of a vote which it confirmed as a constitutional right as enshrined in Article 19(i)(a), the right to freedom of speech and expression. It added a Constitutional lustre to 'negative voting' by declaring "not allowing a person to cast vote negatively defeats the very freedom of expression and the right enshrined in Article 21, i.e. the right to liberty." The right of negative voting with consequence of vote for rejection of all candidates instead of the current status of merely being 'no vote' or 'negative vote' would be a logical step forward. This step would inevitably have to follow if political parties do not accept the inevitable in selecting candidates. NOTA will indeed compel political parties to nominate a sound candidate. A time may come with demand for fresh election with a fresh set of candidates, if in the first election, NOTA scores the highest vote. With 12 crore first-time voters in the 2014 election to parliament, the stage was set for the electorate to challenge political parties' commitment to decriminalizing the legislative bodies.

The "National Commission to Review the Working of the Constitution" headed by Justice M.N. Venkatachaliah considered and rejected both the concept of 'negative voting' and 'recall' of elected representatives on grounds of being either impracticable or unnecessary. However, it gave serious thought to making 50 per cent of the total votes plus one vote as the minimum for a candidate to get elected and a run-off if no candidate met that requirement. But the Commission stopped short of including it as a recommendation, and instead, suggested that the government and the Election Commission will study the issue more carefully. In the circumstances, the Commission while recognizing the beneficial potential of the system for a more representative democracy, recommended that the government and the Election Commission of India should examine the issue of prescribing a minimum of 50 per cent plus one vote for election in all its aspects, consult various political parties and other interests that might consider themselves affected by this change and evaluate the acceptability and benefits of this system. Instead of waiting for NOTA to emerge as a spring board for change, this could be made the starting point for reform.

Taking a liberal view both from the judgement of the Supreme Court in the Peoples Union on Civil Liberties (PUCL) case and the recommendation of the M. N. Venkatachaliah Commission, the common assumption is that implementation of both view points is not an easy door to open up. Application of NOTA and its implementation while not an easy experiment at least in the preliminary years till its systematic application is stabilized after some years of franchise exercise in elections, implementation of Venkatachaliah Commission recommendations seem to be not feasible in the present context of voters turnout in elections if results of total voting pattern for several elections to Parliament and State Assemblies are of any indication. In both the circumstances, the issue of mandatory voting assumes importance as a measure of electoral reform.

NOTA option in 2014 Lok Sabha elections hardly generated 1.1 per cent of total vote share as nearly six million voters opted for this option. The number of votes registered under NOTA is above the votes garnered by many regional parties such as Janata Dal (United), Lok Dal, Lok Janashakti Party, Shiromani Akali Dal and even the left parties. Following is the party-wise NOTA share reflected in Table 3.5.

Table 3.5: NOTA Share

Sl. No.	*1*	*2*	*3*	*4*	*5*	*6*	*7*
Name of the Party	*JD (U)*	*CPI*	*JD (S)*	*SAD*	*Lok Dal*	*UIP*	*JMM*
Vote Share (in percentage)	1.1%	0.8%	0.7%	0.7%	0.5%	0.4%	0.3%
Total votes secured	5992196	4327298	3731481	3636148	2799899	2295929	1637990

Prominent among states where percentage of NOTA option exercised include Andhra Pradesh 0.7 per cent (340615), Bihar 1.6 per cent (581011), Maharashtra 0.9 per cent (433180), Tamil Nadu 1.4 per cent (582062) and Uttar Pradesh 0.7 per cent (592211). The disproportionately high use of NOTA particularly in reserved constituencies was seen to be continuing. This could be on account of upper caste candidates preferring to vote for no other than vote for a *dalit* or a tribal candidate. On an average, 10000 votes were cast in every constituency. In 46 constituencies, over 20000 NOTA votes were cast. All but one of the ten constituencies in which the most NOTA votes cast were reserved constituencies. Eight of them were for scheduled tribes and one for Scheduled Castes. Over twice as many NOTA votes were cast in Scheduled Tribe constituencies than in general constituencies. Similarly, more votes were also cast in Scheduled Caste constituencies as compared to general caste constituencies. The proportion of negative vote was higher than the national average in Chhattisgarh (1.9%) followed by Gujarat (1.8%), Jharkhand (1.5%) with the highest of all in the two Scheduled Tribe constituencies in Meghalaya. The number of NOTA votes was the highest of all the Scheduled Caste constituencies of Nilgiris in Tamil Nadu (over 46000) where the margin of victory between the AIADMK candidate and the DMK's A. Raja was one lakh votes. In Nilgiris, NOTA got more votes than the votes secured by the Congress candidate. Similar position was obtained in South Bangalore where NOTA votes were more than the votes received by the independent candidate Pramod Muthalik.

The status of application of NOTA in the major states and Union Territories in the 2014 elections is indicated in Table 3.6 below.

Table 3.6: Status of application of NOTA in the Major States and Union Territories

Sl. No.	*1*	*2*	*3*	*4*	*5*	*6*	*7*	*8*	*9*	*10*	*11*
Name of the State	UP	WB	TN	Bihar	Gujarat	Maharashtra	MP	Rajasthan	Karnataka	Odisha	Puducherry
Votes	591603	567868	556668	555418	454888	391814	391814	327902	257822	292349	22268

Comparing the number of NOTA votes with total number of votes cast, Puduchhery leads the least at 3 per cent followed by Meghalaya 2.8 per cent, Chhattisgarh, Gujarat and Union Territory of Dadra & Nagar Haveli at 1.8 per cent, Odisha at 1.6 per cent, Jharkhand, Mizoram and Daman-Diu at 1.5 per cent, Madhya Pradesh 1.3 per cent and Kerala 1.2 per cent. Out of nearly 60 lakh voters who opted for NOTA, Nilgiris in Tamil Nadu and Nabarangpur in Odisha were the two Lok Sabha constituencies that saw the maximum NOTA votes while Nilgiris saw 46559 NOTA votes (5% of total votes) Nabarangpur had 44408 (4%) followed by Baster in Chhattisgarh with 38772 votes (5%). Like many other States, in Odisha, NOTA was chosen by more voters than the number of votes polled by the AAM Admi Party (AAP) in the State. In parliamentary constituencies, 332780 electorate hit the NOTA option where as AAP candidates got about half (147898 votes). In the Assembly elections of Odisha, AAP shared 0.6 per cent votes against NOTA's share of 1.3 per cent. The overall national position indicates that despite being widely seen as an option that empowers the educated voter, the proportion of NOTA was lower than the national average in states and Union Territories and only slightly above the national average was in Kerala (1.2%). It may be recalled that the Supreme Court in September 2013 upheld the right of a voter to reject all candidates contesting the elections in a constituency which would go a long way in cleansing the political system. The observation of the Supreme Court seemed to be tending towards protection of rights enshrined in the Constitution but exercise of right to vote using NOTA option has really transformed nothing spectacular in the 2014 elections. It is, however, important to note that NOTA is not an endorsement of the right to reject. Even if 99 voters opt for NOTA, the only one voter for a candidate becomes the winner in the existing electoral system of our country. The 99 voters are simply to be considered as blank or "invalid" votes. The Election Commission of India had proposed for provision of NOTA option with a view to ensure secrecy of neutral or non-voting. The Supreme Court granted this provision in 2013 but not to create the right to reject.

Mandatory Voting

People's participation in the democratic process of voting in elections is an important feature of democracy. While voting is a right it should also be a duty as well. The Gujarat Assembly passed a mandatory voting bill making voting as much a right as a duty. In 2009, the Gujarat government's attempt to pass the mandatory voting bill, i.e. the Gujarat Local Authorities Law Amendment Bill, 2009 was made applicable to all qualified voters of Municipal and Panchayat bodies. The bill provided for penal action for defaulters. The argument of the government in favour of the bill was that the legislation would eliminate passive voters, bring voters to the polling booths to ensure maximum participation and eliminate money and muscle power which is being increasingly used by political parties and politicians in elections. If mandatory voting is introduced, it is likely to eliminate communal elements from politics because of large turnout of voters. Considering the present low turnout in many elections in the country, when a person with mere 21 per cent votes out of 40 per cent total votes polled even though 79 per cent may be against this individual, is elected and that sounds highly unreasonable.

Compulsory voting is not altogether a new concept. Out of about 32 countries having provision for compulsory voting, only 19 countries have enforced such laws relating compulsory voting. Belgium provides punitive action whereas Australia, Brazil, Egypt, Greece have compulsory voting. Even some countries like Netherlands and Venezuela which practiced compulsory voting at one point of time, have since abolished the system. Since, compulsory voting does not always mean that one has to vote under any circumstances, therefore, it does not violate individual freedom. Compulsory voting could be in the shape of right to vote or right not to vote. One can now choose the "none of the above" option. The Gujarat Governor returned the Gujarat Local Authorities Laws (Amendment Bill, 2009) which contained provisions for compulsory voting in election to local bodies on the ground that (i) compulsory voting violates the citizens right to freedom of speech and expression guaranteed under Article 19 of the Constitution; (ii) to punish voters who fail to vote violates their fundamental freedom in the matter of voting; and (iii) experience of other countries shows that it is difficult to implement compulsory voting. The Supreme Court in the Peoples' Union of Civil Liberties (PUCL) held that 'vote' is a form of speech as the voter indicates his preference for one of the contesting candidates silently (secretly). Under Article 19 (i), all citizens have the right to freedom of speech and expression. The freedom to vote also includes the right not to vote. This right is subject to any law made by the state which imposes reasonable restrictions in the interest of the sovereignty and integrity of India, the security of the State and many other conditional restrictions. But compulsory voting does not fall under the above categories. Several arguments have been advanced against voting being made compulsory. Some argue that it is undemocratic to force people to vote which would mean infringement of liberty. With many ignorant and having little interest in politics, any sort of compulsion may lead to increased number of invalid votes and encourage reckless voting behaviour.

The Election Commission of India had held the view that it is impossible to have compulsory voting in India in view of the large-scale work force in unorganized sector. If candidates set-up by political parties at elections are not acceptable to the voters because of their criminal background or antecedents, corrupt practices or incompetence, it would be oppressive and unethical to compel voters to vote. Besides the Gujarat government's bill on compulsory voting, a private member's bill on compulsory voting was also defeated in the Lok Sabha. The Supreme Court also rejected a petition seeking to make voting compulsory in 2005. In 2009, the Supreme Court also dismissed a plea made by one Atul Sarode from Maharashtra to make voting compulsory and for not allowing anyone to represent a constituency unless he/she secures a minimum of 51 per cent of votes. The bench of Supreme Court consisting of former Chief Justice K.G. Balakrishnan and Justice P. Sathasivam dismissed the plea and observed that greater turnout of voters could be ensured only by increasing people's awareness and even 60 per cent turnout could be fairly a satisfactory position.

Introduction of NOTA option seems to have prompted a clamour for mandatory voting especially from the Bharatiya Janata Party (BJP). The two concepts are related but not in-separately intertwined. The former BJP President Lal Krishna Advani reasoned that NOTA option serves the purpose of those who want to stay away from voting for political reasons but voters have no longer any justification for not going to the polling station. He wrote on his blog as "As things stand to-day, voters who without any legitimate justification have not been exercising the valuable right of franchise the Constitution of India has conferred on them have, unwittingly thus, been casting a negative vote against all the contesting candidates, without intending to do so. I hold, therefore, that a negative vote would become really meaningful if it is accompanied also by the introduction of mandatory voting." But the fact remains that there could be many who may not have faith with electoral or even democratic system. In that case, should there be objection to voting not politically valid? If voting were to be made compulsory, a negative vote is, of course, integral to the process but the reverse is not true. If a negative vote were to be made mandatory, compulsory voting need not follow. Mandatory voting will be meaningful when accompanied by negative vote but negative does not need any infusion of meaning from mandatory voting. The principle behind the negative vote is that no voter should be forced to choose a representative he does not approve of. But merely because a voter is free to reject all candidates, he/she cannot be forced to go to a polling station. Making voting compulsory will more than negate the gain made with the introduction of the negative vote. The negative vote emanates from a negative right to stay away from a political process free from any government control. To make participation in the political process mandatory will be in violation of the very same negative right. After all, in a democracy, the voters have the right not to participate in voting. The right to vote whether it is a fundamental right or a mere statutory right, if it is a right at all, implies the right to not vote. The NOTA option is a step forward. It should be used to further widen democratic choices, and not allowed to bring in coercive means to increase voter participation.

Of several electoral reforms suggested from time-to-time, making voting compulsory for every voter has been agitating the minds of those concerned with it since recent trends in elections particularly in urban areas reflects that percentage of voting has been very low at many places. Therefore, many protagonists of democracy have suggested for incorporation of punishable provisions in the election laws against those absenting from voting without sufficient and valid reasons. In addition to this, the most important argument placed in public domain for quite some time is the right of voter to rejection of any candidate/s along with the right to election. The general suggestion has, of course, been that election procedure must be made easy and transparent. Among the important suggestions made towards further electoral reforms through different state and national level discussions and debates are : (i) one voter list for all elections including Panchayat, Assembly and Parliament. This proposal was even endorsed by the Chief Election Commission; (ii) that voters card must be made compulsory for all and shall be provided to the voter in the election booth itself if the voter has defaulted in securing the Identity Card; (iii) election should be held in one day throughout the State for Assembly/Parliament elections and in three-four phases in different states; and (iv) total election process should be over within 21 days at the latest.

It was incidentally discussed in the Constituent Assembly that every candidate should get at least 1/3rd of the total votes of the constituency. An honourable member Lokanath Mishra moved an amendment to {8(A) (i)} and said that "every candidate will be elected by the people and even if there is no rival, no candidate shall be elected unless be gets at least 1/3rd of the total votes ......". There was a lot of deliberation in the Constituent Assembly on the issue of reservation of seats in constituencies. It was advocated that it should be mandatory for all political parties to reserve seats for women, SC, ST and minority communities of their own choice. While allotting seats, parties have to follow the guidelines of election not to go below the bottom line fixed by the Election Commission. The present day cry for recall was also discussed in the Constituent Assembly when Mr. Mishra delivered a very meaningful speech with the following words: "the primary members shall have the right to recall the member they elected to the Assemblies or the Assembly of the State. It is a fundamental right. We know that when we are returned to the Assembly we come there as representing the masses for five years. But what we care for is the party caucus, the "High Command" and if it is pleased, we are alright. We don't care for the people. I, therefore, submit that if we are the real members representing the people, our first concern should be the people. They must be our masters. If we serve them well, we are there; if we do not, we must go out. But this does not *happen now.* It is, therefore, essential that if the people have a right to elect members, they must have the right to recall them if things go wrong. The right to recall is a fundamental right in democracy...." When all eligible voters voluntarily come forward or otherwise compelled to enter into the polling stations, the entry of unwarranted persons in the law making bodies can be reduced to a large extent. It has been noticed that the rate of no-voting is gradually decreasing election after election say 61.70 per cent in 1951-52 elections, 61.33 per cent in 1969, 60.48 per cent in 1977, 60 per cent in 1999, 58.40 in 2009. In the last elections held to State Assemblies of four states namely Rajasthan, Chhattisgarh, Madhya Pradesh and Delhi in 2013 that the rate of no-voting has also decreased. With a view to expanding voter participation, the RP Act was amended in 2010 effective Tenth February, 2011 to allow Indian citizens residing abroad to enroll in voters list and exercise franchise. In the assembly elections held in April 2011 in Kerala,

Tamil Nadu, Pondicherry, West Bengal and Assam, the impact was not that encouraging. Only 52.60 per cent NRI voters exercised their votes.

Compulsory voting is another mode of electoral reform mooted against chronic voter apathy especially in urban areas. But compulsion and democracy hardly go together. The ECI has been consistently laying emphasis on voter's education which has started paying dividends from the elections held in 22 states since 2010 and the general elections of 2014 to the 16th Lok Sabha where even the percentage of voting crossed 80 per cent in some states. The 2014 elections, as pointed out already, crossed sixty per cent in the electoral history. Therefore, motivation and facilitation rather than compulsion should be the correct method for ensuring maximum voting in elections.

Election Expenditure

During 1995-96, India received about Rs. 10000 crore Foreign Direct Investments (FDI). It was anticipated that in the 2009 elections to Lok Sabha polls, equal amount of FDI would be spent in the said elections. The official spending was likely to be about 20 per cent of total expenses including Rs. 1300 crore by the EC and the rest by political parties in campaigning as estimated by Centre for Media Studies (CMS). An amount of Rs. 2000-2500 crore was estimated to be spent in form of un-official money or cash paid to the voters. The CMS survey indicated that in States like Andhra Pradesh and Karnataka half of voters were likely to be paid cash for vote about 24 hours before the polling day. The ECI was likely to spend about Rs. 1300 crore and other State government agencies were to spend about Rs. 700 crore towards photo identity cards, EVMs and polling booths. Various political parties were expected to spend about Rs. 1650 crore from their party funds in addition to the direct and indirect spending by the individual candidates. Candidates of national parties were estimated to incur about Rs. 4350 crore while those from regional parties expected to spend another Rs. 1000 crore. Money was to be spent generally on canvassing (Rs. 3500 crore), printed materials (Rs. 2000 crore), other media channels such as video, audio, cable, cinema, SMS, TV advertisement (Rs. 1500 crore). Another Rs. 1500 crore was to go for public meetings, wages and rallies. The 2004 Lok Sabha elections had cost the country about Rs. 4500 crore against Rs. 3200 crore in 1998 and Rs. 2100-2200 crores in 1996 Lok Sabha elections. It is an open secret that political parties continue to receive funding from the corporate world. In fact, corporate funding for election cannot be prevented but there could be some mechanism to make the funding public. Media had been greatly influenced by different power centres and the fairness expected from the fourth estate had been lost somewhere. From the ground level itself, leaders are straying un to unscrupulous sources of funding election expenses which could be arrested if good people do not shy away from politics. The ECI has fixed limits on the expenditure of candidates in election from time to time. During 2004 elections, the ceiling on expenditure varied between Rs. 10 lakh to Rs. 25 lakh, for assembly seats from Rs. 5 lakh to Rs. 10 lakh. Apart from fixing limits on election expenses, the EC has fixed time limit of 30 days on candidates to file details of election expenditure. To further reduce quantum of election expenditure, it has reduced the campaign period from 21 days to 14 days. This move is in the right direction. It has been suggested that a comprehensive legislation be brought out to regulate both income and expenditure of political parties. Although the ECI, following the judgement of Supreme Court in the *"Peoples Union For Civil Liberties" and another vs. Union of India* (2003) made it mandatory for candidates to submit affidavit disclosing assets and liabilities, unfortunately, the order did not apply to political parties.

The present election law fixes a ceiling on the election expenses of individual candidates but not of political parties. There is no regulation of the manner of raising and spending funds nor are their accounts in public domain for scrutiny by the people at large. The Election Commission, with a view to bring transparency, has proposed the accounts of political parties to be audited by the chartered accountants from a list specified by the EC. There seems to be no reasonable and appreciable steps taken to address this issue as yet.

Fast-Past-The System (FPTP)

The essential features of Indian electoral system broadly consist of the First-Past-The Post (FPTP) system as against proportional representation. This system enables a candidate to win an election when he gets more votes than his strongest single competitor, not necessarily polled a higher total than the combined opposition. In India, the ballot structure is categorical than ordinal. When voting is an act of choice, the function of ballot is to structure that choice. The ballot structure is of two types, namely (i) categorical and (ii) ordinal. The categorical ballot asks the voter to decide which one of the candidates, he prefers. The ordinal ballots allow the voter to express a more complex, equivocal preference, a more by rank-ordering the candidates. The significant difference between these two types of ballots lies in the nature of the role imposed by each upon the voter. Experience of last elections has shown that several flaws exist in the Indian electoral system which lives with the feeling that majority of Indian voters are not really represented in the Parliament. The system does not take care to see that minority groups, women and other marginalized sections are all adequately represented in the legislature. In the general elections of 1952, 1957, 1962 the Congress Party bagged 75 per cent seats each in Lok Sabaha with 45 per cent, 48 per cent, and 45 per cent of votes, respectively. In 1967 and 1971 it had own 54 per cent, 68 per cent of total seats with a vote share of 40 per cent and 44 per cent respectively. The experience was repeated even in 1977 when the Janata Party got 55 per cent seats with 43 per cent votes. Even when Rajiv Gandhi led the Congress in 1984 it got only 48 per cent of votes but mustered a huge share of 77 per cent of seats. In the 2004 elections, MPs who got the support of less than 30 per cent of total votes polled, got elected. Three hundred and twenty two (322) of 539 newly elected MPs were returned with less than 50 per cent of voter support. The number of winning candidates who secured 50 per cent of more of the valid votes polled has varied between 121 and 221 during the last five general elections. The Venkatachalliah Commission which surveyed the record of three general elections concluded that over 2/3rd of the members of the Lok Sabha and almost 90 per cent of the members of some State Legislative Assemblies were elected on a minority vote. The fact remains that a large chunk of population (voters) abstains from voting bespeaks of the malady of our democratic system. From the total voting percentage in all the general elections to the lower house of parliament, it transpires that the voting percentage has been within the range of 55 per cent to 63 per cent maximum. The first general elections to the Lok Sabha recorded 61.2 per cent, the second 62.2 per cent, third 55.42 per cent, fourth 61.33 per cent, fifth 55.29 per cent, sixth 60.49 per cent, seventh 56.92 per cent, eighth 63.56 per cent, nineth 61.95 per cent, tenth 56.93 per cent, eleventh 57.94 per cent, twelfth 61.97 per cent, thirteenth 59.99 per cent, fourteenth 57.65 per cent and 15th 56.97 per cent, a decline from 57.65 per cent in the preceding house (*Source*: ECI). The results of the recently held elections to legislative assemblies, in five states in 2013 could also lead to the presumption that besides wave for a change due to high inflation, unemployment and corruption, a new wave of voters largely first-timers, women voters and those from blue collar sections particularly from reserved constituencies, probably thronged the polling booths as against a mere 47 per cent of voters in 2003 elections in these states. But the fact remains that prevailing electoral politics dose not ensure a majority democracy by and large. A majority of all MLAs and Lok Sabha members are elected by minority of votes, even with less than 15 per cent of votes polled.

In the elections held in 2013 to five legislative assemblies of Rajasthan, Delhi, Madhya Pradesh, Chhattisgarh and Mizoram, except Mizoram, the average voting percentage in all the four States has swollen significantly from their previous record. With 72 per cent in Rajasthan, 67 per cent in Delhi, 75 per cent in Madhya Pradesh and 81 per cent in Mizoram which is marginally one per cent lower compared to 2008 elections, such high turnout has puzzled many. While equally this is an encouraging trend, it is an enigmatic call for increasing mobilization of voters especially in the erstwhile BIMARU States, i.e. Rajasthan, Madhya Pradesh and Chhattisgarh. Although many explanations including new initiatives taken by ECI to raise voters consciousness and revision of voter lists are attributed as factors but these seem to be not necessarily sufficient causes for enlarged voter's participation. Irrespective of the factors attributed, the fact remains that a silent wave was sweeping across the country demanding a change against high inflation and unemployment particularly, besides all-pervasive corruption.

Under the present law, there is no right of negative voting that enables a voter to refuse to vote for a particular candidate or to cast his vote against all candidates. This is different from a voter refusing to exercise his franchise at all. In a writ petition filed in the Supreme Court by Peoples Union for Civil Liberties (PUCL) it is submitted that a citizen's right to vote at an election in secrecy includes the right of negative voting *qua* all candidates. Another plea is that the EC is bound to provide appropriate mechanisms in the EVMs for effective exercise of such a right. Incidentally it is noteworthy that the EC in its letter dated 10.12.2001 supported the elector's right to negative voting. The council for the Commission submitted before the Supreme Court that PUCL could seek directions for appropriate modification in the EVMs to enable the electors to exercise their right of negative voting. The Union of India contended before the Court that the right to vote was a mere statutory right, neither a fundamental right nor a constitutional right. A division bench of the Supreme Court comprising Justices B.N. Agarwal and G.S. Singhvi dealt with the issue. Justice Singhvi elaborately referred to previous Supreme Court judgements and succinctly enunciated the principles laid down in them. But the division bench found it difficult to reconcile the divergent observations made on this issue in the different three-judge bench decisions. Therefore, it directed the matter to be placed before the CJI for appropriate orders.

The results of Bharatiya Janata Party (BJP) with vote share of 31 per cent in the 2014 Lok Sabha elections has been dubbed as too low a legitimacy to rule India. Critics say that since 69 per cent of votes did not favour the Bharatiya Janata Party (BJP), it had no moral ground to rule the country. But those favouring the BJP have contended that in our system of first past-the-post, it is ultimately seats and not votes that count. On this score, BJP's performance has been striking. It may be seen from the Table 3.7 that no party has ever won majority of votes cast. Even in 1984, the mother of all landslide victories, the Congress secured only 49.1 per cent of votes. Until 1989, national elections were dominated by a single party, i.e. the Congress party. Vote share were routinely above 40 per cent and the victory margins over the runner up were huge. In the changed era of coalition politics, the winning party's vote share plunged and victory margins narrowed dramatically. For example in the 2009 election, Congress's vote-share was 28.5 per cent and the UPA at 37.2 per cent as against 18.8 per cent for runner up, i.e. BJP, but it was sufficient for the Congress-led UPA to capture majority seats. In the 2014 elections, the Congress's vote share has plunged to 19.3 per cent, its lowest ever against BJP's 31 per cent, which is its largest ever with a larger victory margin than the

Congress enjoyed in the last two elections. The NDA accepted Narendra Modi as Prime Ministerial candidate and therefore, the BJP and its allies together have secured 38 per cent plus votes.

The outcome of an election needs to be reviewed in the context of the electoral system in which it occurred. In our system, the party which wins the most seats, even if a majority, does not win the majority of votes. If, hypothetically India were to move to some version of proportional representation system, it will be naïve to assume that voting behaviour and election strategies will remain unchanged. With our current system, parties' rational strategy is to target resources to seats in which they are competitive, try to swing seats that are tightly contested and more broadly, maximize the vote to seat multiplier, that is, squeeze as many seats as possible out of votes cast. The Congress seemed to have managed that in the past as may be seen from Table 3.7.

Table 3.7: Status of Vote castes in Lok Sabha Election

Sl. No.	*Year of Election*	*1st Place Party*	*Percentage (%)*	*2nd Place Party*	*Percentage (%)*
1.	1951-52	Congress	44.9	CPI	3.2
2.	1957	Congress	47.7	CPI	8.9
3.	1962	Congress	44.7	CPI	9.9
4.	1967	Congress	40.7	Swatantara Party	8.6
5.	1971	Congress	43.6	CPI-M	5.1
6.	1977	Janata Party	41.3	Congress	34.5
7.	1980	Congress	42.6	JNP	9.3
8.	1984-85	Congress	49.1	CPI-M	5.8
9.	1989	Congress	39.5	Janata Dal	17.7
10.	1991-92	Congress	36.2	BJP	20.1
11.	1996	BJP	20.2	Congress	28.8
12.	1998	BJP	25.5	Congress	25.8
13.	1999	BJP	23.7	Congress	28.3
14.	2004	Congress	26.5	BJP	22.1
15.	2009	Congress	28.5	BJP	18.8
16.	2014	BJP	31	Congress	19.4

The fact remains that elections to Lok Sabha and Legislative Assemblies are held from single member territorial constituencies through direct elections under the FPTP system but elections to Rajya Sabha and Legislative Councils are held under the system of proportional representation through single transferrable vote. In spite of alleged deficiencies in the FPTP system, the system has several advantages like easy access to voters, simple method of vote counting, immediate result on declaration of winning candidate's name. Under this system, voters elect representative of their choice identified as representative of the constituency. The system, however, by and large provides a stable government. But the 2014 Lok Sabha elections has demonstrated that a party like the BSP has ended up without a single representative despite capturing over 20 per cent of vote share.

State Funding of Elections

The major electoral reform veers around the issue of state funding of election expenses. This important issue was discussed elaborately in the Constituent Assembly. A portion of the discussions was recorded as "It is necessary that the state must see that election expenses are borne by the State. Otherwise, some landlords, capitalists will built up a party to set up candidates and those candidates will be returned. Lets us say there is poor but good and honest man, but he has neither the money nor to contest from a party without money. What would be the fate of such people? The result is, he cannot stand for election. If he stands, he comes to ridicule. The state means both the provinces and the Union Government. Therefore, only cost towards party manifesto, one party poster, party appeal and two or three public meetings could be allowed. Candidates may be allowed to have limited scope of expenditure with at best one or two vehicles, postal expenses and one CD containing activities of the party for each which could be adequate. As the voter has the right to election, the cost of elections should be met by the state because getting elected to the legislature is not to be presumed as a profession or profiteering business. The elected person comes to the legislature to serve the people and not otherwise". This was, in fact, the spirit of discussion held in the Constituent Assembly.

Any electoral reform becomes meaningless if the Election Commission is not empowered to regulate, evaluate and monitor the democratic norms of political parties. The CEC had proposed in 1998 to the Law Ministry to confer on the CEC, instead of the Central Government, the rule-making power under the RP Act, 1951. Some have even suggested to insert another clause in section 29 of RP Act authorising the EC to issue necessary orders to regulate registration and de-registration of political parties. In fact, the constitution was silent on functioning of political parties until the inclusion of Tenth schedule and the 42nd Amendment in 1976. It has also been argued that party whip in any form for electing member/s or open voting system curtails the democratic rights of voters. This also negates the democratic value of any person entitled to exercise voting right. It is also argued that instead of the Speaker of both houses of Parliament and Legislative Assembly, the EC should be empowered to decide on issue of defection and his decision can only be challenged before the Supreme Court. Political parties are being subjected to the dictum of "High Command", "Supremo", "Couteri", "Caucus". Therefore, they do not have transparency in fund channalisation, submission of returns on activities, funds, audit and expenditure. There is no prescribed or mandatory mechanism to control party affairs. Even though the idea of proportional representation in the Parliament and Legislative assemblies on the lines of Justice V.M. Tarkunde Committee's, recommendations (1974) and the recommendations of the Law Commotion in 1999 have been suggested by a school of thought on electoral reforms but not much in terms of massive electoral reforms and democratisation of political parties has been effected. It has been suggested by some that proportional representation should be adopted in the election on the basis of population to cleanse politics of crime. They hold that the recent judgement of Supreme Court barring jailed leaders from contesting elections was no solution to break 'politicians-crime' nexus. It has been apprehended by some political leaders that they will be forced to quit public life if the norm indicated in the Supreme Court judgement was implemented. In fact, crime is only one aspect. People entering politics bring with them caste, money and political infrastructure that shielded their criminal background. In fact the Court did not touch upon the constitutional validity of election process. The unfortunate tendency developing in our political structure that those responsible for law-making are mostly the law-breakers is a great threat to our democracy.

It has been suggested that EVM should have the option of "none of the above". If the election in a constituency results in "None of The Above" (NOTA) getting the maximum number of votes, there should be a re-poll and the candidates who contested should not be allowed to re-contest in the election. General voters are more often left with no option but to vote for candidates whom they did not like. An election watch-dog had suggested that any person who had been charged by a court of law of serious offences like murder, attempt to murder, rape, kidnapping and extortion should not be allowed to contest elections. A comprehensive electoral reforms bill to regulate political parties covering the issues of internal democracy, financial and procedural transparency may be kept in place. The Law Commission had already drafted such a bill which need to be translated in to action by the government.

Paid News

Of late, since the 2009 elections, a pernicious practice of publishing "paid news" by some newspapers and television channels has been the bone of contention in the effort for safeguarding and ensuring free and fair elections. This has almost threatened to undermine the very foundation of our democracy. In this process, media houses aggressively sell their space for sponsored news items that favour candidates. Prospective candidates, not only buy space but buy these newspapers in bulk for circulation in their constituencies to influence voters. Morever, this blurres the distinction between news and advertisement. This not only deceives the voters but impairs the prospects of candidates, with limited resources. The ECI can hardly do anything substantially legal against the media house and the citizens/consumers, instead of becoming consumers of such information, should desist the trend. The courts can hardly do anything since right to unbiased information is not explicitly guaranteed under the Constitution.

As regards, publication of pre-poll and exit-poll survey during elections which political parties have been clamouring for ban, the ECI decided to ban publication or telecast of opinion exit-polls 48 hours before the last hour of polling in single phase balloting. The Press Council of India (PCI) had been considering in consultation with the ECI, a mechanism to look into complaints of 'paid news'. Stringent regulatory steps or even an amendment to the RP Act may be required to tackle this issue. Besides, the ECI and the PCI, the civil society should take strong action against politicians and media personnel for 'paid news'.

In the elections held in the last two-three decades both in the Central and State levels, movie celebrities, stars, singers, cricket and hockey players etc. seemed to be endorsing candidates.

Bollywood celebrities and state level cine stars are being used in the election campaigns to influence voters. Of course, in States like Tamil Nadu this practice is as old as 60-70 years. There is no mechanism to stop it except to leave it to film industry for self-regulation. Committees in the past have debated regarding opinion polls and their impact in influencing the voters. The ECI also recommended to put in place restrictions on publishing results of opinion polls for specific period during election process. In the recent amendment of the RP Act, 1951, a new section 126A was inserted prohibiting conduct of exit polls and publishing results during the period starting from 48 hours before the close of poll in an election. But the amendment did not cover opinion poll. There is no restriction for determination through print media as section 126(1) does not apply to print media. The ECI has recommended that section 126 should also be applied to print media as well. Print media and electronic media are becoming part of the business activity today as against TV channels and newspapers in the past. Several news channels are seen to be under the control of the same company. For purchasing news, parties/candidates pay more than crores of rupees. This is a dangerous trend. If media is controlled by rich people, there would be effort for "manufacturing the consent" in favour of certain political parties and candidates. Secondly, the democratic responsibility of giving the news of different candidates who are contesting elections and their views on various issues will be denied thereby.

Sometime back, the Chairman of Press Council of India Justice Markandey Katju while suggesting for a statutory regulator with punitive power for media, expressed his anxiety over media indulgence in the practice of "paid news" in some of the elections held in recent years. The ECI was reported to have received 766 complaints of "paid news" during January-March Assembly elections of which 253 were found to be true. Notice had been issued in 581 cases. The amount paid towards "paid news" were to be added to the poll expenditure of the 253 candidates. In the 2011 Assembly polls, the ECI had taken action in 250 cases. It caught about 121cases in 2010 Bihar polls alone. In Tamil Nadu and West Bengal political parties even had their own media which were not reported. Under the RP Act, "paid news" had been made a cognizable offence as it can be prejudical and affect the prospects of candidates. In spite of this, media agencies continue to approach political leaders demanding money in exchange for publishing news in their favour. The EC has proposal amendment to the RP Act, 1951, to provide that publishing and abetting the publishing of "Paid News" for furthering the prospect of election of any candidate or for prejudicially affecting his prospect be made an electoral offence under Chapter III of Part IV of Representation of People Act, 1951 with punishment of a minimum of two years imprisonment.

Election Petitions

It is a recurring phenomenon in every election, be it to the Lok Sabha, State Assemblies or local bodies that petitions are filed in many courts challenging the elections on diverse grounds. The long inevitable procedural delays in courts ensure that a substantial number of these petitions remain pending in courts even after the term of the office to which the election relates comes to an end. In such cases, the election petitions are dismissed by most courts as having become in-fructuous. This kind of disposal seems to be not the correct recourse in law. Section 86 (6) of the Representation of People Act, 1951 mandates that trials in election cases shall, as far as is practicable, proceed on a day-to-day basis and section 86 (7) directs the Court to endeavour to conclude the trial within six months from the date on which the petition is presented to the High Court. Following the 2009 Lok Sabha elections, nearly 110 election petitions were filed in various High Courts across the country challenging the election of various candidates. Not one of the 110 petitions was concluded within the period of six months. Twenty-five of them remained pending even at the end of the five years term of the 15th Lok Sabha. Election is not merely a matter involving two individuals only. It is more than that. The Supreme Court in *Sheodhan Singh's vs. Mohan Goutam* had clearly observed that "no one can be allowed to corrupt the course of an election and get away with it either by resigning his membership or because of the fortuitous circumstance of the Legislative Assembly being dissolved. The public are interested in seeing that those who had corrupted the course of an election are dealt with in accordance with law." The law relating to withdrawal and abatement of election petitions is exhaustively dealt with in Chapter IV of Part VI of the RP Act. Those provisions do not provide for abatement of an election petition either when the returned candidate whose election is challenged, resigns or when the Assembly is dissolved. As emphasised by the Supreme Court, an election petition is not a *lis* between two individuals but an attempt at preserving the purity of the electoral process. Therefore, the judiciary, instead of closing such cases as infructuous, would be doing salutary service to the spirit of election laws by not closing such pending cases but proceed with these cases to their logical end.

Saving of Security Deposit

Besides the candidates who are elected, those defeated try to console themselves if they have finished reasonably well and particularly if they have saved their deposits. They see this as a matter of pride as their deposit is saved but do not mind for humiliating defeats but feel humiliated if the deposits are lost. As per ECI rules, if the candidate fails to get a minimum of 1/6th of the total votes polled, the deposit is forfeited and goes to the government treasury. In the first Lok Sabha elections in 1951-52 about 745 candidates out of 1874 (40%) forfeited their deposits. In the Eleventh Lok Sabha election in 1996, 91 per cent or 12688 out of 13952 candidates lost their deposits. This was the elections which saw highest number of candidates contesting for the Lok Sabha. In 2009 elections as many as 85 per cent of them lost their deposits, percentage-wise the third highest after 91 per cent in 1996 elections and 86 per cent in 1991. Generally, it has been observed that the

Table 3.8: Year-wise contestants who lost their deposits

Sl. No.	*Year*	*No. of Contests*	*No of Contestants for feting deposits*	*%*
1.	1952	1874	745	40
2.	1957	1519	494	33
3.	1962	1985	856	43
4.	1967	2369	1203	51
5.	1971	2784	1707	61
6.	1977	2439	1356	56
7.	1980	4629	3417	74
8.	1984-85	5492	4382	80
9.	1989	6160	5003	81
10.	1991-92	8749	7539	86
11.	1996	13952	12688	91
12.	1998	4750	3486	73
13.	1999	4648	3400	73
14.	2004	5435	4218	78
15.	2009	8070	6829	85
16.	2014	N.A	N.A	N.A

candidates from national parties have fared well in saving their deposits. The 1977 general elections witnessed best performance ever by national parties as only 100 out of 1060 candidates of national parties did not fare well and also every second candidate, lost their deposits. Out of 779 of 1623 candidates from national parties lost their deposits. In fact, about 49 per cent of national party candidates in the Eleventh Lok Sabha (897 out of 1817) lost their deposits. The above Table 3.8 indicates the election year-wise position of contestants who lost their deposits.

Dimensions of Indian Elections – Analysis of 2004, 2009 and 2014 Elections

Fourteenth Lok Sabha and Assembly Polls 2004

The Fourteenth Lok Sabha election along with some Assembly polls which staggered over five phases between April 20 and May10, 2004 was a historic election as claimed by the then CEC T.S. Krishna-murthy. The unique features of this election were, (i) Inclusion of candidates' declaration on criminal, educational and financial antecedents through affidavit to accompany nomination papers; (ii) Introduction of Electronic Voting Machines (EVMs) in 750000 polling booths; (iii) Winding up of counting in one day instead of three days; (iv) Overseeing of entire process by remote control through electronic devices by EC through only 400 staff; (v) Engagement of five million polling personnel and security forces in the conduct of elections; (vi) Deployment of 2000 observers to monitor polling across the country; (vii) Estimation of 10 billion rupees on poll expenses; and (viii) Phase-wise spreading of elections—J&K—4 phases, Bihar and UP—3 phases, AP, Assam, Jharkhand, Karnataka, MP, Maharashtra, Manipur and Odisha—2 phases and 24 States and Union Territories wrapped up in a single phase.

This election also had far-reaching implications due to the following important events, namely : (i) the India shining advertisement campaign of the BJP led by National Democratic Alliance (NDA) government just after the dissolution of Lok Sabha in January 2004 and before the announcement of elections. The attempt of BJP was severely criticized by all sections. The EC legally could not do anything even though the CEC T.S. Krishnamurthy expressed concern; (ii) The other important event related to the distribution of sarees in Lucknow on the birth day celebrations of BJP leader Lalji Tandon where 22 poor women died in the stampede; and (iii) The fourteenth Lok Sabha and some Assembly polls witnessed unprecedented media craze for opinion and exit polls. There was demand by many political parties to ban opinion polls and not to announce results of polls before the end of last phase of polls.

Fifteenth Lok Sabha Elections, 2009

With the world's biggest and most complex democratic exercise India had gone to the 2009 elections with 714 million eligible voters in five phases between April, 16 and May, 13 to elect 543 members to the 15th Lok Sabha. Despite an increase of 43 million voters and 141402 polling stations, the ECI decided against stretching the election schedule beyond a month. The trick was to strike a delicate balance between taking care of security and logistics which dictate a spread out schedule and avoiding an unduly long process which would make electioneering even more punishing than it is during an Indian summer. The entire process arrangement appeared to be mind-boggling in which about 4 million civil staff members; 2.1 million securities personal were to be deployed. The enhanced complexity was the phasing and sequencing of the election against what the ECI described as "cross-border influences" in the peaceful conduct of polls. The 2009 election was the election in which photo electoral rolls in the whole country with the exception of Assam, Nagaland and Jammu & Kashmir were adopted. In an effort to prevent impersonation and bogus voting, a stimulus package for photography of about 585 million photographs in the electoral rolls was a gigantic step. Considering this to be not enough, a special drive was launched to maximize coverage.

At present, about 82 per cent of voters are covered. For the 2009 Lok Sabha elections, preparations started right from 2008. One of the important features of this election was introduction of Photo Identity Cards. Of several measures undertaken to ensure more transparency in the elections and to cleansing of rolls of the names of dead voters, duplicate names, shifting to new locations, new eligible voters and inserting photographs against voter details were some of the markable initiatives taken for this election. About

7.6 million new voters were registered, 1.2 million names were deleted and number of registered voters rose to 716 million from the figure of 671 million in 2004 elections. About 82 per cent of the electorate had their image on the photo rolls and the turnout was 58.2 per cent. About 834944 polling stations, 1.18 million EVMs were in place and mobilized. Over 11 million personal including about 8 million civilian staff and 3 million central and state police forces were deployed.

The Election Commission of India introduced some major changes in this election. Booth-level officers were appointed to handle between 1000-1500 voters at a particular booth. They were responsible for the veracity of the electoral rolls pertaining to a geographical area. For the first time, the Commission initiated "vulnerability mapping" to identify villages and hamlets that could be vulnerable to intimidation. As many as 86782 villages were identified as "vulnerable" and 373886 persons identified as potential troublemakers and action was initiated against them. One of the distinguishing features of this election was that polling stations were equipped with mobile connectivity, landline phones, satellite phones, high frequency communication equipment. The normal practices that had shown favourable results in the previous Lok Sabha and Assembly elections were also followed in this election. Besides, observers and micro-observers were deployed to ensure transparency in the election process. On the schedule of elections which was conducted in five phases, sections of media and stakeholders, however, felt that the duration of election schedule could have been shorter. Computerisation of electoral rolls is one of the major efforts made by the ECI to bring transparency in electoral process. The computerization of electoral rolls is available in almost all constituencies besides photo cards. The other initiative in the scheme of "Electors' Photo Identity Card" (EPIC) was introduced and completed for about 370 million electors in the country in order to improve the accuracy of voters list and prevent electoral fraud and protect citizen's right to vote.

The 2009 election was a closely fought election since after Independence. The number of major contestants in a constituency was at the highest 2.91 per cent beating records of 1952 and 1996 at 2.88 and 2.88 respectively. The victory margins in this election was the lowest at seven per cent against 14.4 per cent of 1952 elections. There has been a continuous fall in victory margin per cent to to single digits after the 1996 elections. Similarly, after 1952 elections, the voter's share of votes has been reducing. Table 3.9 illustrates the victory margins and winner's share of voters since 1952.

Table 3.9: Victory Margins and Winners Share of Voters

Sl. No.	*Year*	*Victory margin %*	*Winners share of votes*	*Sl. No.*	*Year*	*Victory margin %*	*Winners share of votes*
1.	1952	14.4	47.0	9.	1989	12.7	51.0
2.	1957	11.1	50.4	10.	1991	10.8	47.9
3.	1962	12.2	48.4	11.	1996	N.A	45.3
4.	1967	11.7	47.6	12.	1998	N.A	47.0
5.	1971	21.5	55.3	13.	1999	N.A	48.5
6.	1977	24.8	59.3	14.	2004	N.A	48.5
7.	1980	16.7	51.1	15.	2009	N.A	44.6
8.	1984	17.9	53.1	16.	2014	N.A	N.A

Source: Election Commission.

Elections 2014

The 2014 general election was predicted to be a close electoral race. The 2011 census data indicated a dramatic demographic shift in the electoral framework in which about 149.36 million out of the total electorate of 725 million estimated by the ECI would be the number of first-time voters. These young adults were estimated to be anywhere between 18 and 23 years of age. These young voters belong to a generation particularly those living in urban areas, have seen the good times when India's growth rate was almost 9 per cent and consumer economy was acquiring a very overt form, the proliferation of malls, multiplexes and so on. Now they have come up to a stage at present to see a closed aspiration of an economic crisis and incestuous and closed system that has corroded beyond repair. Now the question arise did they vote along castes and communal lines? Do they feel let down? This group, even though seemed to be a handful as an aggregate but was very unpredictable as individuals. The census also indicated that this demography was likely to be concentrated in the battle ground states and had a greater proportion residing in rural areas. Incidentally, the male to female ratio of the young first time voters was a little less than equal.

Of the new total voters of the country, males constitute 10.88 per cent and the females 9.73 per cent and taken together, they constitute 20.6 per cent. In the rural areas both males and females consist of 14.32 per cent and in the urban areas 6.28 per cent. The top 10 states in which first time voters were to be coming in largest numbers are respectively Uttar Pradesh (3.9%), Maharashtra (1.82%), Bihar (1.63%), West Bengal (1.55%), Andhra Pradesh (1.42%), Madhya Pradesh (1.27%), Rajasthan (1.26%), Tamil Nadu (1.06%), Karnataka (1.01%) and Gujarat (1%). Given the so called demographic dividend, the question was often put as to whether these voters could form a constituency which may be called political constituency by themselves. Basing on the census data if it is presumed that those who were 15 and above in 2011 and will be able to vote in 2014, their total number would be 830 million. Of this, 290 million will be aged 30 or below, i.e. 35 per cent of the eligible voters. If the definition of youth is liberally interpreted and kept at the cut off point at 35 years, the number of youth voters might peg at a whopping 47 per cent of eligible voters. All that depended on the enrolment of young voters and willingness of such voters to cast their ballots which may be crucial for political party/parties. In a tight fight, the first time voter has the potential to swing the outcome. Pratap Bhanu Mehta, President of the Centre for Policy Research (Delhi-based think-tank) points out that this generation which comes without any baggage was better placed to stoke a new debate that would move the country away from the business as usual approach. In fact, out of the total voters of the country pegged at 833124487, the young voters in the age bracket of 18-35 age-group were expected to be 395088197.

In fact, the voter count for 2014 elections has gone up by more than 97 million of which nearly 46 million are women according to final revision of data released by EC ahead of elections. As of 14th February, 2014, there were 814.5 million registered voters, i.e. up by 13.6 per cent from 717 million voters during 2009 elections. The States account for 98.27 per cent of voters. The male and female ratio of voters during 2009 elections was respectively 37.47 crore with a total of 71.69 crore including others whereas for the 2014 elections, the projected ratio between male and female was estimated at 42.66 crore and 38.79 crore excluding 28341 belonging to others. The total voter base was, therefore, estimated at 81.45 crore.

Size of Electorate - 2014

Initially the size of India's electorate was estimated at 81.5 crores for the elections after the summary revision of data. The electorate is now nearly five times than it was when India first voted about 60 years ago. The electorate has grown at double the space between the 2009 general election and the 2014 elections than the elections between 2004 and 2009. About 10 crore new votes are added to the electoral role between 2009 and 2004. About 52 per cent of the electorate is male. The census data shows roughly 83.3 per cent people are 18 years and above in the 2014 elections. The ECI seems to have achieved a commendable and incredible registration rate enrolling almost 98 per cent eligible voters. Uttar Pradesh, Maharashtra, West Bengal, Andhra Pradesh and Bihar account for half of country's electorate. Over the last twenty years, the electorate of the country has become well over 1.5 times its size. The electorate grew by 64 per cent over the last twenty years even while the overall population grew by just 43 per cent. The electorate of some states have grown much faster than other states. Delhi has doubled its electorate size in 20 years. Uttar Pradesh grew by

Table 3.10: Size of Indian electorate since First general election

Sl. No.	Year	Electorate size	Male	Female
1.	1951-52	173212343	NA	NA
2.	1957	193652179	NA	NA
3.	1962	216361569	NA	NA
4.	1967	248904300	NA	NA
5.	1971	274189132	43564829	130624303
6.	1977	321174327	16701951	154155176
7.	1980	356205329	185539439	170665890
8.	1984-85	400375333	208040256	192335077
9.	1989	498906129	262045142	236860987
10.	1991-92	511533598	268962610	242570988
11.	1996	592572288	309815776	287756512
12.	1998	605880192	316692789	289187403
13.	1999	619536847	323813667	295723180
14.	2004	671487930	349490864	321997066
15.	2009	716985101	374758801	342226300
16.	2014	814591184	426651513	387911330

Source: Election Commission.

70 per cent while Madhya Pradesh and Bihar grew at around 25 per cent. Looking at the last 10 years only, West Bengal seems to be having the fastest growing electorate with increased percentage of 30 per cent between 2004 and 2014. Table 3.10 indicates the size of the Indian electorate over the last general elections.

Political Parties: Status and Vote Share

The number of political parties registered with the Election Commission and those contested the elections has increased over the years. In the initial elections starting from 1952, the Congress party used to roast. By the late 1980, the picture began to change. With a fragmented polity, coalition governments became the norm. After a spell of 25 years, the BJP has changed the spirit in the 2014 elections winning a decisive majority. The year-wise and election-wise results of largest, second largest and other parties since 1952 is shown in Table 3.11.

Table 3.11: Largest, second largest and other parties

Sl. No.	*Year of Election*	*Name of the Largest winning party*	*No. of seats won*	*Name of the second largest party*	*No. of seats won*	*No. of total seats*
1.	1952	Congress	364	CPI	16	489
2.	1957	Congress	371	CPI	27	494
3.	1962	Congress	361	CPI	29	494
4.	1967	Congress	283	Swantanta	44	520
5.	1971	Congress	352	CPI	25	518
6.	1977	BLD	295	Congress	154	542
7.	1980	Congress	353	JNP (s)	41	542
8.	1984	Congress	414	TDP	30	514
9.	1989	Congress	197	JD	143	529
10.	1991	Congress	244	BJP	120	521
11.	1996	BJP	161	Congress	140	543
12.	1998	BJP	182	Congress	141	543
13.	2004	Congress	145	BJP	138	543
14.	2009	Congress	206	BJP	116	543
15.	2014	BJP	282	Congress	44	543

During the last three general elections to the Lok Sabha, the number of political parties that registered with the EC and those participated in the elections has an increased trend. During 2004 elections, 764 political parties were registered and 215 participated. In 2009 elections 1060 political parties and, 1657 parties in 2014 were registered with the EC. In these three elections, the number of contestants were respectively 5435 (2004), 8070 (2009) and 8251 (2014) with 2385, 3831 and 3234 independents respectively. Of these, 5 (2004), 9 (2009) and 3 (2014) were independent women MPs.

In 2014 elections, for the first time in the electoral history of independent India, a non-Congress party secured a majority on its own. The BJP with its unprecedented tally of 282 on its own and with its allies which got +338, obtaining a huge mandate since 1984. The Congress bagged only 44 seats (19.4%) against BJP's share of 31 per cent followed by other regional parties with slander number and percentage. AIADMK and TMC got 3.2 per cent and 4 per cent vote share respectively. The BJP became the first party to win a majority on its own in 30 years but the record it set was to win the highest margins in the past three decades. In the past several elections effective from 1952, the victory margin taken for each year as the median of all margins across constituencies, indicate that except 1952 (14.5%), 1971 (21.5%), 1977 (25%), 1980 (16.6%), 1984 (17.9%) elections, the 2014 elections registered 13.6 per cent vote share. The lowest ever vote share was registered in 2009 (7%) elections. The 2014 elections indicate that victory margins were also strong not only in the areas which have been BJP's strong holds, i.e. Gujarat and MP but also key states where the party made in-roads such as UP and Bihar. Victory margins across Telengana and Seemandhra were lower than elsewhere in the Country. The BJP has become a dominant party in states like Gujarat, UP, Bihar, Rajasthan, MP and Chhattisgarh. But, despite the dominance of BJP, the number of parties with significant vote-share at the constituency level continue to remain at an all time high except 2009 indicating the fragmented vote in different parts of the country. All said and done, the 2014 elections was a record setting/breaking election that set many records as mentioned in the fore-going analysis.

The fact that the BJP has won a majority on its own in the 16th Lok Sabha has inevitably drawn comparisons with previous polls in which parties won a majority on their own. What has not quite figured in most of the constituencies is the fact that no party has ever before won more than half the seats with a vote share of just 31 per cent. The previous lowest vote share for a single party majority was in 1967 when Congress won 283 out of 520 seats with 40.8 per cent of total valid votes polled. Far from spelling a fractured polity, the 2014 results show just how fragmented the vote has been. It is because the vote is so fragmented that the BJP was able to win 282 seats with just 31 per cent votes. Thus, in the ultimate analysis, it shows that less than 4 out of every 10 voters that opted for NDA candidates and not even one in three chose somebody from the BJP to represent them.

It may be seen that in the elections of 1957, 1962, 1967, 1971, 1980 and 1984-85, the vote share of winning political parties, i.e. the Congress and the Janata Party (1977), was always above 40 per cent. The Congress party had the vote share of 47.8 per cent in 1957, 44.7 per cent in 1962, 40.8 per cent in 1971, 43.7 per cent in 1980, 48 per cent in 1984-85. In the 1977 elections, the Janata Party won 295 seats out of 542 seats with a vote share of 41.3 per cent. Thus, the BJP's performance in 2014 elections securing 282 seats out of 543 with vote share of 31 per cent is really not astounding. This could happen because of fragmentation of vote share.

Voting on Caste-Lines

Politics in several parts of India is still mired in caste and religions. Identity politics lurks below the surface when it is not front and centre. Perhaps nowhere no more so than in UP and Bihar which with 120 seats between them account for close to a quarter of total Lok Sabha seats. Candidates are often chosen on the basis of whether they are *Dalit* or OBC or Thakur or Bhumihar or Brahmin or Muslim and the like. The TOI group combed through the entire list of candidates of the major leaders in the two important leading States, i.e. UP and Bihar where caste politics plays a big role. In other States like Andhra Pradesh, Tamil Nadu, Karnataka, Punjab, Haryana, Rajasthan, and Maharashtra, the caste factor is evident more or less. If it is not caste, it is religion. But nowhere does it cast such as long and imposing shadow and over such a huge block of seats as the two "heartland" states, namely UP and Bihar. Bihar has altogether 6 reserved constituencies and UP with seventeen. The TOI report found mind-boggling array of castes from Dusadh, Jatar, Dom, Pasi, and Musahar (all SC/Dalit) to Koeri, Yadav, Dhanuk, Kurmi and Barhai (all OBC) to Kahar, Mallah, Gangota and Tanti (all EBC) somewhere between SC and OBC to upper Caste Rajputs, Bhumihars, Kayasthas and Brahmins. The 2014 election results have shown that in UP, out of 80 candidates contested in the reserved seats under the banner of BJP symbol, 73 got elected accounting for

91 per cent. For the Congress against 76 contested, only two were elected with only 3 per cent win. The SP had fielded 78 candidates against which only 5 got elected with 6 per cent win. The BSP fielded 80 candidates against which none was elected. In UP, a total of 314 candidates were fielded against reserve seats of 17. The un-reserved categories belong to Brahmins, Thakurs, Bhumihars and other OBC, Yadav, Jat, Vaishya, Dalit, Muslim and others. Similarly, in Bihar, altogether 160 candidates contested under the banner of BJP, Congress + NCP, RJD, JD (U) LJP and others against 6 reserved constituencies. Tables 3.12 and 3.13 below indicates the party-wise

Table 3.12: Uttar Pradesh

Sl. No	*Name of the caste*	*BJP*			*Congress*			*SP*			*BSP*			*Total*
		C	*E*	*W*	*C*	*E*	*W*	*C*	*E*	*W*	*C*	*E*	*W*	
1.	Brahmin	14	13	93	11	0	0	5	0	0	21	0	0	53
2.	Thakur	15	14	93	8	0	0	11	0	0	8	0	0	42
3.	Bhumihar	1	1	100	3	0	0	1	0	0	0	0	0	5
4.	Other OBC	21	19	90	8	0	0	22	0	0	14	0	0	65
5.	Yadav	1	0	0	0	0	0	11	5	45	1	0	0	13
6.	Jat	4	4	100	4	0	0	0	0	0	0	0	0	8
7.	Vaishya	3	2	66	7	0	0	1	0	0	0	0	0	11
8.	Dalit	17	17	100	19	0	0	14	0	0	17	0	0	67
9.	Muslim	0	0	0	11	0	0	13	0	0	19	0	0	43
10.	Others	4	3	75	5	2	4	0	0	0	0	0	0	7
	Total	80	73	91	76	2	3	78	5	6	80	0	0	314

Note: C: Contested, E: Elected, W: Winning%

Table 3.13: Bihar

Name of the caste	*BJP*			*Congress + NCP*			*RJD*			*JD (U)*			*LJP*			*Others*	*Total*
	C	*E*	*W*	*C*	*E*	*W*	*C*	*E*	*W*	*C*	*E*	*W*	*C*	*E*	*W*		
Brahmin	3	3	100	1	0	0	1	0	0	2	0	0	0	0	0	2	9
Rajput	7	5	71	1	0	0	3	0	0	2	0	0	1	1	100	2	16
Bhumihar	3	3	100	1	0	0	—	—	—	3	0	0	1	1	100	6	14
Kayastha	1	1	100	0	0	0	1	0	0	1	0	0	0	0	0	4	7
Yadav	4	4	100	1	1	100	9	2	22	6	0	0	0	0	0	6	26
OBC	7	4	57	1	0	0	3	0	0	11	2	18	1	0	0	8	31
MBC/EBC	4	2	50	0	0	0	2	1	50	2	0	0	1	0	0	4	13
Dalit	3	3	100	5	0	0	2	0	0	6	0	0	3	3	100	8	27
Muslim	1	0	0	2	2	100	6	1	17	5	0	0	1	1	100	4	19
Sikh	0	0	0	1	0	0	0	0	0	0	0	0	0	0	0	0	1
ST	0	0	0	0	0	0	0	0	0	0	0	0	0	0	0	1	1
Total	33	25	83	13	3	23	27	4	15	38	2	5	8	6	85	45	164

Note: C: Contested, E: Elected, W: Winning %

and cast-wise position of candidates belonging to different castes who contested, won and the percentage of win.

While the Congress had the worst disaster in the 16th Lok Sabha elections and the party performed poorly among its traditional voters, namely—Dalits and Tribals, the grand old party still continues to have the overall support of Muslims, India's largest religious minority. The National Election Study (NES) shows that nation-wide Muslim vote for the Congress was 38 per cent (excluding allies), almost the same as in 2009 elections. The question, in fact, arises as to why the party did not get more votes among Muslims given the community's aversion to the BJP. NES data clearly shows that in states where the Congress is in direct competition with the BJP, it got nearly three-fourths of the Muslim votes. States in which there is presence of strong regional parties (Uttar Pradesh, Bihar, Andhra Pradesh, Tamil Nadu, West Bengal, Delhi, Assam etc.), the overall Muslim support for Congress dropped to about one-third as the community voted for the non-Congress options. Interestingly, the BJP also saw its vote share among Muslims rise to about 8 per cent at the national level compared to the four per cent it had five years ago. While this undoubtedly indicates greater support for the BJP among Muslims, the increase in Hindu support from 22 per cent in 2009 to 36 per cent is proportionately greater. While two out of every Muslims voted for the Congress in the 2014 elections, upper caste support for the BJP was one out of two. Even as the Muslims rallied behind the non-BJP options, a counter Hindu upper caste and OBC consolidation much greater in magnitude seems to have rendered the Muslim votes ineffective even in states where Muslims have always been in a position to make a difference to the final outcome. In fact, of the 87 seats where Muslims are over twenty per cent of the population, the BJP won 42 as opposed to just 15 seats in 2009. That the voice of 15 per cent of the country's population could be rendered ineffective expresses a paradox present in our democracy.

However, the voting pattern of Muslims for the Congress, BJP and others in the past six elections from 1996 to 2014 and the comparison of Muslim votes for BJP and Congress is reflected in the Tables 3.14, 3.15 below.

The 2014 election was expected to witness an unusually high religious polarization following Modi's elevation and charged campaign that followed with BJP sweeping across the country and

Table 3.14: Voting Pattern of Muslims

Year of election	*Congress*	*BJP*	*Others*
1996	36%	2%	62%
1998	32%	6%	62%
1999	40%	7%	53%
2004	36%	7%	57%
2009	38%	4%	58%
2014	38%	8%	54%

Source: National Election Study conducted by CSDS in 2014, 2009, 2004, 1999, 1998 and 1996.

Table 3.15: Comparative Voting Pattern of Muslims for BJP and Congress

Year of election	*Upper Caste vote for BJP*	*Muslim vote for Congress*
2014	47	38
2009	29	38
2004	35	36
1999	40	40
1998	47	32
1996	35	36

Source: NES conducted by CSDS in 2014, 2009, 2004, 1999, 1998 and 1996.

expectation of experts that Muslims voted in large number for the BJP, the CSDS post-poll survey found the truth to be just the opposite. In the last six elections since 1996, the vote share of the Congress among Muslims had been 33 per cent. But for the first time in the 2014 elections, the proportion has risen to 44 per cent. This is undoubtedly a big increase in Muslim polarization towards Congress. Moreover, in bipolar states like Chhattisgarh and Madhya Pradesh, the Muslim vote share for the Congress goes even higher in to the 70 per cent and it rose above 90 per cent in the election. This indicates that not only a significant proportion of Muslims appeared not to have voted for the BJP but the representation of Muslims in Parliament has dropped to a historic low. The preference for Congress among Muslims in this election is 44 per cent against the historic preference for the party among Muslims at 33 per cent.

Voting Pattern of OBC

The Other Backward Classes (OBCs) comprise a multitude of disparate castes, sub-castes and traditional occupational groups.

Accounting for about 41 per cent of population of the country (NSSO 2004-05), they form the largest socio-political bloc. The National Election Study data show, most of the OBC votes during the past two decades have gone to regional and/or "social justice" parties. Evidence shows that while the Congress and the regional parties put together lost among the OBCs, the BJP increased its vote share by impressive 12 percentage points (from 22% in 2009 to 34% in 2014). At one level, the BJP gained at the expense of the Congress. However, the BJP's spectacular success among the OBCs is largely driven by a huge surge for it among the lower OBCs, who are said to have gained the least from the reservation regime. The BJP polled a whopping 42 per cent of the lower OBC votes as against 30 per cent of the upper OBCs. But the aggregate picture often conceals more than it reveals. In fact, the OBC votes in the past, have taken different routes in different political contexts. This holds true even in 2014 elections. In many States such as Kerala, Odisha, Tamil Nadu and West Bengal, the BJP failed to make much impact among the OBCs. However, it almost swept the OBC votes in States such as Gujarat, Madhya Pradesh, Maharashtra and Rajasthan. It also did quite well in those states that have long been the laboratory of OBC politics. In Uttar Pradesh and Bihar, not only did the BJP amass an overwhelming majority of the lower OBC vote but also got significant support from the upper OBC voters who have been religiously supporting prominent OBC leaders like Mulayam Singh, Lalu Prasad Yadav and Nitish Kumar.

Vote Share of Political Parties in 2014

Table 3.16 below reflects the vote share of political parties in the 2014 elections in respect of the OBCs.

Table 3.16: Share of Political Parties in 2014 Elections

Categories	*BJP*	*Congress*	*Left*	*Others*	*Shift from BJP*	*2009 elections% Congress*	*Left*	*Others*
All OBCs	34	15	3	49	+12	–2	–2	–1
Upper OBC	30	15	3	52	+8	–7	+1	–2
Lower OBC	42	16	3	39	+20	–11	–6	–3

Note : Figures are in per cent rounded off and weighed by actual vote share of parties.
Source: NES 2009, 2004 CSDS, Delhi.

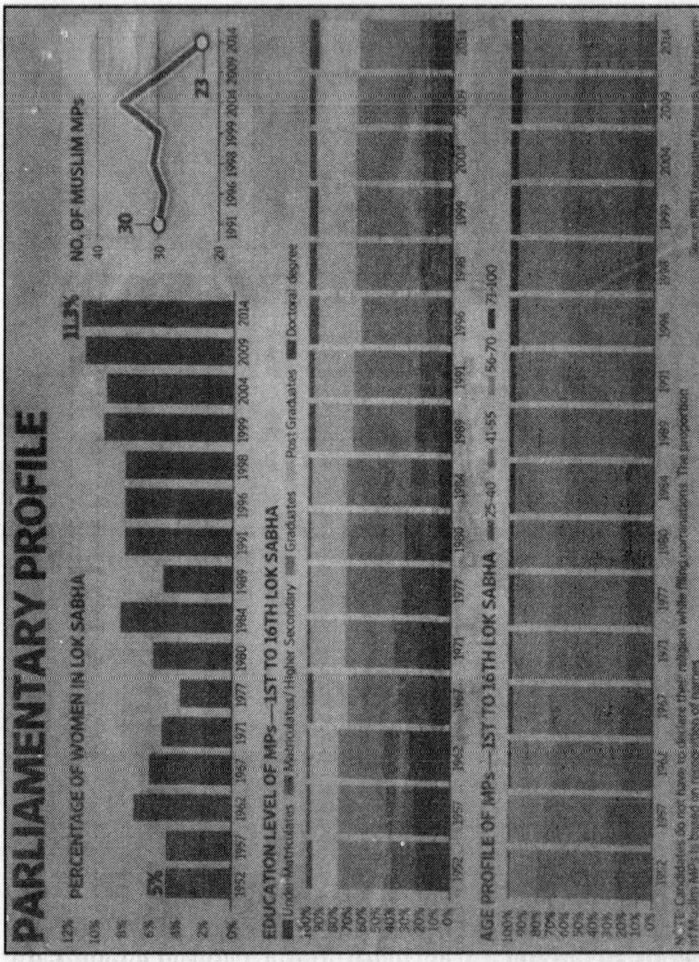

Fig. 3.2: Parliamentary Profile

In view of the above analysis, can it be concluded that the rising popularity of the BJP among the OBCs signifies the end of "Caste politics" more strictly of OBC politics? It yet remains to be seen whether this shift of the OBC voters towards BJP is because they believe this party to be a better vehicle of their interests or whether this shift is part of the larger process of consolidation of the Hindu vote.

Profile of MPs including Women MPs

The following graph reflects the parliamentary profile in respect of percentage of women in Lok Sabha, education level of MPs and their age profile from the first general elections 1952 to 2014 and the representation of Muslim MPs from 1991 to 2014.

Photo Copy: Parliamentary Profile

Of all the elected MPs including women MPs, in the 2014 Lok Sabha elections 71 (13%) are in the age bracket of 25-40 years, 216 (40%) in the age group of 41-55 years, 212 (39%) in the 56-70 years group and 41 (8%) in the age-bracket of 70-100 years. Age details of three MPs were not available. Information collected with regard to educational qualification of MPs elected to the 16th Lok Sabha can be seen from Table 3.17 below:

Table 3.17: Educational qualification of MPs elected in 16th Lok Sabha

Qualification	*Under Matriculates*	*Matriculates*	*Graduates*	*Post-graduates*	*Doctorates*	*Not available*
No. of MPs	69 (13%)	56 (10%)	225 (42%)	150 (27%)	33 (6%)	10 (2%)

Analysis of the data indicates that majority of MPs elected (42%) are graduates followed by Post-graduates (27%). This is an encouraging trend beyond the demand for legal reservation of seats for women.

As regards educational qualification of Ministers of Modi government 8 Ministers (around 18%) have declared that they have educational qualification of Twelfth standard or below while 35 (80%) are graduates or above. Table 3.18 below indicates education group and the number of Ministers in the Modi Cabinet (position of Ministers included in the expansion phases excluded).

Table 3.18: Education group and No. of Ministers in Modi Cabinet

Qualification	5th pass	10th pass	12th pass	Graduate	Graduate professional	Post-Graduate	Doctorate	Others	Total
No. of Ministers in Cabinet	1	5	2	6	17	9	3	1	44

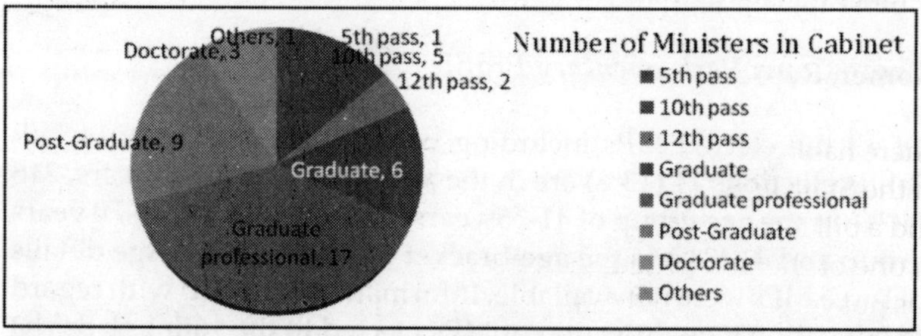

Fig. 3.3: Number of Ministers in Cabinet

Nine (20%) have declared their age to be between 51-70 years and two Ministers are above the age of 70 years (ADR report). The age group and the number of Ministers falling therein is indicated below.

Table 3.19: The Age group of Ministers

Age group	*31-40*	*41-50*	*51-60*	*61-70*	*71-80*	*Total*
No. of Ministers	1	8	16	17	2	44

Profession-wise, the number of elected Lok Sabha members is estimated at Agriculture 144 (26%), Political and social services 132 (24%), Businessmen 111 (20%), Lawyers 38 (7%), Teachers and Educationists 24 (4%), Medical practitioners 24 (4%), Artists 18 (3%), Journalists 4 (1%), Civil police. This Lok Sabha seems to be represented by a cross-section of people adding vibrance and

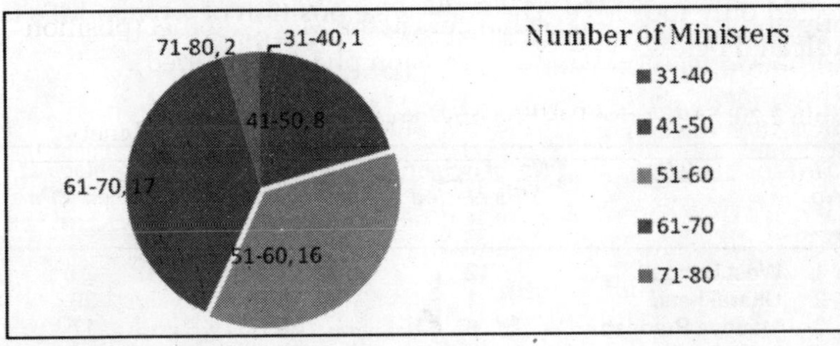

Fig. 3.4: Number of Ministers

sectoral representation which augurs well for strengthening India's democratic credentials.

Women Representation

There has been constant clamour for reservation of seats for women in the State legislatures and the Parliament. In spite of best efforts and a bill introduced by the outgoing UPA government and passed in one of the houses of Parliament, the final bill enacted to an Act has not yet seen the light. The often alleged clamour for reservation of seats through legislative mandate has failed. Prolonged lobbying with and enticement to political parties for distribution of more tickets to women candidates evoked little positive response. However, during the last three elections to the Lok Sabha (2004, 2009 and 2014) the number of women candidates fielded by various political parties has increased leading to an increase in the number of women candidates elected. In 2004 election, 45 women MPs were elected whereas in 2009 elections, the number rose to 59. The current Lok Sabha (2014) will have 61 females constituting 11 per cent and 482 males constituting 89 per cent of the 543 total seats in the Lok Sabha.

From a mere five per cent of women representation in 1952 elections, the percentage has gone up to 11 per cent in the 2014 elections. The notable feature of 2014 elections is the increased percentage of women representation in the 16th Lok Sabha. One-third of West Bengal MPs are women while States like Karnataka, Rajasthan, Kerala and Punjab have just one M.P. each. Although Tamil Nadu is headed by a woman Chief Minister, the state has elected only four MPs. The State-wise position of women MPs is indicated below.

Table 3.20: State-wise Position of Women MPs

Sl. No.	*States*	*No. of women MPs elected*	*Total No. of MP seats in the State*	*Percentage of women MPs*
1.	West Bengal	12	42	29
2.	Uttarakhand	1	5	20
3.	Madhya Pradesh	5	29	17
4.	Uttar Pradesh	13	80	16
5.	Gujarat	4	26	15
6.	Delhi	1	7	14
7.	Assam	2	14	14
8.	Maharashtra	5	48	10
9.	Tamil Nadu	4	39	10
10.	Bihar	3	40	8
11.	Punjab	1	13	8
12.	Andhra Pradesh	3	42	7
13.	Kerala	1	20	5
14.	Odisha	2	21	10
15.	Rajasthan	1	25	4
16.	Karnataka	1	28	4
17.	Chandigarh	1	1	100
	Total	**61**	**543**	**11**

Although women make up 49 per cent of the population, only 7.8 per cent women of the total candidates (8163) contested in 2014 election. One-third of 631 women candidates are independents. Congress had the largest number (57) with BJP only 37. Women now often out-number men in polling queues but clearly political parties have not woken up to the new scenario. The following table will indicate that the number of women candidates has risen significantly since 1952 elections but they still form a tiny percentage of the contestants. The number of women MPs has been rising but it is still way below the global average. Our record, therefore, is a dismal and distinctly much below the position compared even to South Africa's 44.8 per cent. Women electors have always constituted less than half the electorate and continue to do so. But the encouraging trend noticed in our country is that more and more women are voting in the elections.

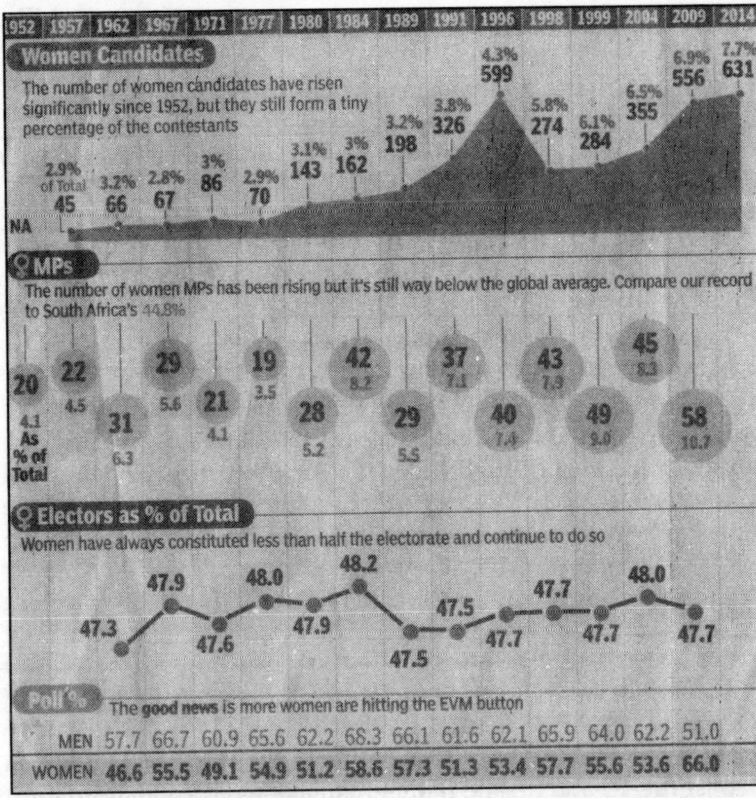

Fig. 3.5: Women Candidates

Thus, during the last three elections 2004, 2009 and 2014, the percentage of women who stood for election was respectively 6.53 per cent, 6.89 per cent and 7.83 per cent. The percentage of women who were elected to Parliament (Lok Sabha) were 8.28 per cent, 10.86 per cent and 11 per cent respectively. The party-wise position of women who contested and won during the last three elections 2004, 2009 and 2014 is reflected in Table 3.20.

The overall increase in the number and percentage of women representation in the Lok Sabha, therefore, is very minimal and not that encouraging.

Importance of High Turnout

The 2014 elections saw many previous records shattered,

Table 3.21: Party-wise position of women : contested and won in 2004, 2009 and 2014

Sl. No.	Name of the Party	Seats contested during			Seats Own		
		2004	2009	2014	2004	2009	2014
1.	BJP	30	44	36	10	13	29
2.	Congress	45	43	57	12	23	4
3.	Independents	117	207	191	—	—	3
4.	Others	163	262	347	23	23	25
	Total	**355**	**556**	**631**	**45**	**59**	**61**

participation of voters being prominent among them. At 66.4 per cent, the overall turnout was the highest that has ever seen in a national election. Compared to the turnout in 2009, the 2014 turnout was eight percentage points higher. This rise is also the highest ever between two successive parliamentary elections. An analysis of the constituency-level turnout data released by EC does indicate a link between the success rate of NDA and the increase in the turnout. Comparing the percentage point increase in turnout at the constituency level with the winning party at that constituency, the BJP and its allies had a greater likelihood of winning seats where the turnout increase was higher. A state-wise disagreegated look at the turnout figures show an interesting mix of constituency and drastic change. Nagaland recorded the highest turnout at 87.8 per cent followed by Tripura (84.7%) and Sikkim (83.4%). These were the top three turnout states in 2009 also. Assam and West Bengal too recorded very impressive turnouts. Overall, 17 States recorded turnouts higher than the national average. At the bottom of the list was J&K again but here too the turnout jumped by ten percentage points. But the increase was largely due to the effect of a huge rise in voter participation in Udhampur and Jammu. While both UP and Bihar recorded below 60 per cent polling, the turnout rise in both states was good with 11 percentage points. Interestingly, of all States, Goa recorded the biggest percentage point jump (+21) in turnout. In fact, barring Nagaland which saw its turnout fall marginally, every state saw its turnout rise.

One of the major reasons for the poll percentage going up has been the increased participation of women. Nationally, 65.6 per cent of all registered female voters turned out to vote, a rise of 10 per cent points. Men were only marginally ahead at 67.1 per cent. In as many as ten states, women's participation was greater than that of men. Another interesting feature of this 2014 elections is that in seats with high SC & ST population proportions, the overall polling was higher compared to turnout in seats with less SC & ST proportions. This pattern seems to indicate high voting by non-ST & non-SC communities in seats where SCs and STs dominate. The overall locality-wise pattern also remains the same with semi-urban seats recording the highest turnout (68.7%) followed by rural area seats (66. 7%). Highly urban seats recorded the lowest turnout (61.1%) yet again, although it must be added that the percentage point increase in turnout was much higher in urban seats compared to semi-urban and rural areas. This perhaps indicates greater participation by middle and upper class voters in cities.

2014 Sweep Index

One of the outstanding features of India's 16th general elections is the degree of coordination among voters both at the national as well as the state level. At the national level, the so-called "Modi Wave" and its Prime Ministerial Candidate Narendra Modi led to the BJP getting an unprecedented a non-Congress majority in Parliament. What is also interesting is that various states have delivered resounding verdicts in favour of a particular party or formation. This has been attributed to a "State-Wide" sweep. The sweep index for the 2014 elections was the second highest ever, second only to the 1984 election when Congress got over 400 seats in Parliament. It was not just the BJP and its allies that swept the 2014 election, the All India Anna Dravida Munnetra Kazhagam (AIADMK) got 37 out of 39 in Tamil Nadu, the Biju Janata Dal got 20 out of 21 in Odisha and the Trinamool Congress got 34 out of 42 seats in West Bengal. Incidentally, these are the States where the BJP does not have much of a presence though it has won at least one seat from each of these states. The extent of sweeps shows that the BJP and its allies have virtually maxed out on their performance in the states they are strong in. That the sweep index was the highest in 1984 and the second to follow in the recently held elections in 2014 can be seen from a comprehensive sweep index in India placed in Figure 3.6.

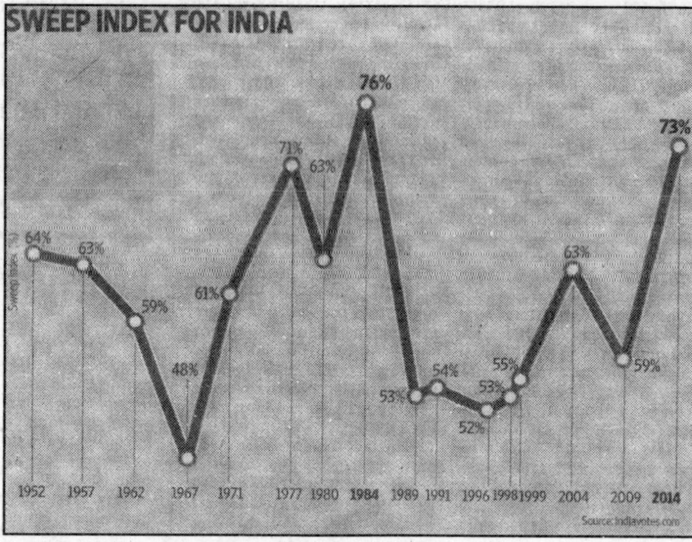

Source: The Mint, 23rd May, 2014 (indiavotes.com)
Fig 3.6: Sweep Index for India

Beyond Modi wave, a greater wave swept India. In 502 constituencies out of 543 studied and audited it was found that the turnout of voters had been an unprecedented record show of more than 66 per cent voting. The 2014 elections has turned out to be the greatest ballot in India's electoral history, nay world history, irrespective of its outcome. It is already two per cent higher than the previous record of almost 64 per cent clocked in 1984 on an extraordinary sympathy wave after Indira Gandhi was assassinated and her son Rajiv Gandhi elected as the Prime Minister. The 2014 turnout is 8 per cent higher than 2009, another record. The highest increase in turn out so far has never exceeded 7 per cent. Of the 814 million voters, 443 million voters voted. The turn out in the election 2014 is more against the population of US which is only 319 million. By global standards even, election 2014 is according to some, a "Tsunami Turnout", an unprecedented and formidable electoral exercise.

Youth Votes

High voter turnouts are frequently believed to be indicative of anti-incumbency. Following the record-breaking 66.7 per cent voter turnout this time, political parties and some in the media declared that the country had voted for change. But analysis made by *"The Hindu"* shows that there is no such relationship in this election. Using constituency level voter turnout data, *"The Hindu"* compared turnouts with the likelihood of an incumbent getting re-elected or losing his or her seat. This means that constituencies which witnessed high turnouts were actually slightly more likely to return an incumbent. The likelihood of losing one's seat was also very weakly correlated and statistically insignificant with an increase in turnout. Constituencies that suddenly witnessed a higher turnout than in 2009, were not decisively voting for a change in leadership. Sanjay Kumar, Director of the "Centre for the Study of Developing Societies" (CSDS) leads its national election studies and observes. "I do not know how this idea that high turnout is associated with anti-incumbency has persisted from generation to generation. This relationship has never existed...." Looking at the 30 Assembly elections that have taken place over the last 5 years, he found that 24 elections saw a high voter turnout but 12 returned the incumbent and 12 brought in a new party. Going back 20 more years and looking at 110 more Assembly elections, he found the data equally inconclusive.

The second most commonly repeated story of this 2014 election was that youth were going to swing this election. *"The Hindu"* found that in all but one of the 20 Assembly segments across the country with highest proportion of 18-19 year old first-time voters (all from MP & Jharkhand) belong to parliamentary constituencies that voted for the BJP. Given the scale of party's win, the number, on its own, does not tell the complete story. Historically, the vote share of parties has always been the same among youth voters and the general population, i.e. the youth of a constituency vote largely in the same proportion as older voters for each party. Young voters also do not appear to want different things from candidates than the other voters. In the 2014 election, young voters were expected to vote for decisive leadership. But the post-poll survey by CSDS found that vote share for the BJP among the youth was five per cent (5%) higher than the general population showing that the youth did indeed particularly prefer the party and the Prime Ministerial candidate Narendra Modi. With just over 10 per cent points separating the vote shares of the BJP, the incumbent Congress, the youth vote could have made a big part of the difference in this election. With the exception of West Bengal, ten big states with highest proportion of youth voters, the others being Chhattisgarh, Jharakhand, MP, Delhi, UP, Assam, Rajasthan, AP and Bihar, all saw big swings towards the BJP while aging Tamil Nadu and Kerala largely resisted the Modi-wave. The following Table 3.22 indicates the state-wise position of higher percentage of votes given by youth to parties.

Table 3.22: State-wise Youth higher percentage of voting to parties

Name of the State	*Name of the Party*	*Percentage of Youth Voters*
Chhattisgarh	BJP	29.11
Jharkhand	BJP	20.88
Madhya Pradesh	BJP	20.74
Delhi	BJP	19.60
West Bengal	TMC	18.51
Uttar Pradesh	BJP	17.27
Assam	BJP	16.60
Andhra Pradesh	TDP	16.59
Rajasthan	BJP	16.32
Bihar	BJP	15.86

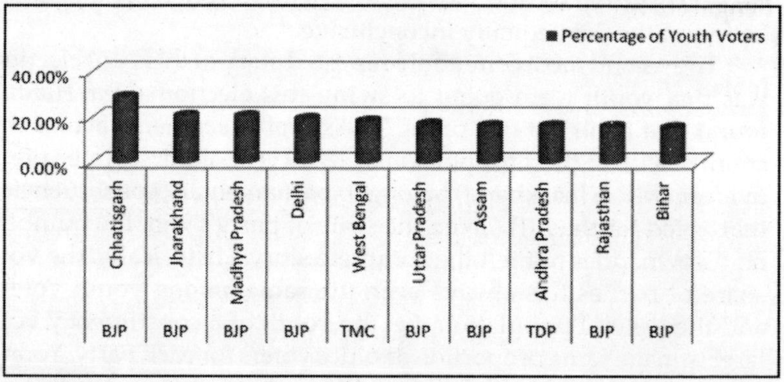

Fig. 3.7: Percentage of Youth Voters

Note: Complete figures were not available in respect of Maharashtra, Uttarakhand, Jammu & Kashmir.

First-Timer and Re-elected MPs

The newly elected 16th Lok Sabha has the highest number of first-time MPs in the last three decades. The AIADMK tops the list with

34 of its 37 MPs elected to Parliament for the first time. In the 543 member Lok Sabha, 315 MPs (58%) have been elected for the first time in 2014 general elections. These members include those MPs who might have been members of the Rajya Sabha before but have been elected to the Lok Sabha for the first-time. About 226 MPs (42%) have been elected to the 16th Lok Sabha (PRS Legislative Research) with prior Lok Sabha experience. Ram Vilas Paswan from Bihar, Kamal Nath from MP, P.A. Sangama from Meghalaya have been elected to the Lok Sabha for the ninth time. Kariya Munda and Sibu Soren from Jharkhand, Sumitra Mahajan (now elected as speaker of 16th Lok Sabha) from Madhya Pradesh, Arjun Charan Sethi from Odisha have been elected to Lok Sabha for the eighth time. Of the 281 BJP MPs elected to the 16th Lok Sabha, 116 (41%) were MPs before and 165 MPs (59%) have been elected for the first-time. Of the 44 Congress MPs, 35 (80%) have been MPs before. The AIADMK has 34 first-timer MPs (90%). The Trinamul Congress has 19 first-timers (56%) while the BJD has 12 (60%). *In toto*, 171 MPs who were part of the 15th Lok Sabha, are now part of the 16th Lok Sabha. The largest number of MPs who continue from the 15th Lok Sabha to the 16th Lok Sabha are from West Bengal (18 MPs), followed by Karnataka (17 MPs) and Maharshtra

Table 3.23: Percentage of First-Time MPs

Name of the Party	*NC*	*ANC*	*BJP*	*BJD*	*SHIVSENA*	*AAP*	*AIADMK*
Percentage	20 (%)	56 (%)	59 (%)	60 (%)	67 (%)	75 (%)	92 (%)

Source: PRS Legislative Research.

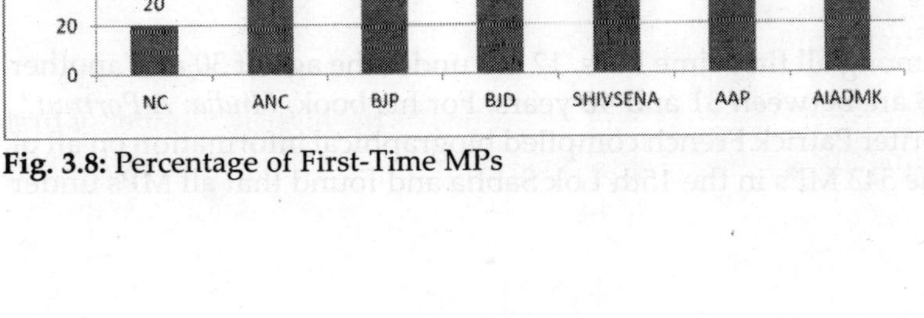

Fig. 3.8: Percentage of First-Time MPs

(16 MPs). The percentage of first-timer MPs party-wise is placed in the Table 3.21 and Fig. 3.9.

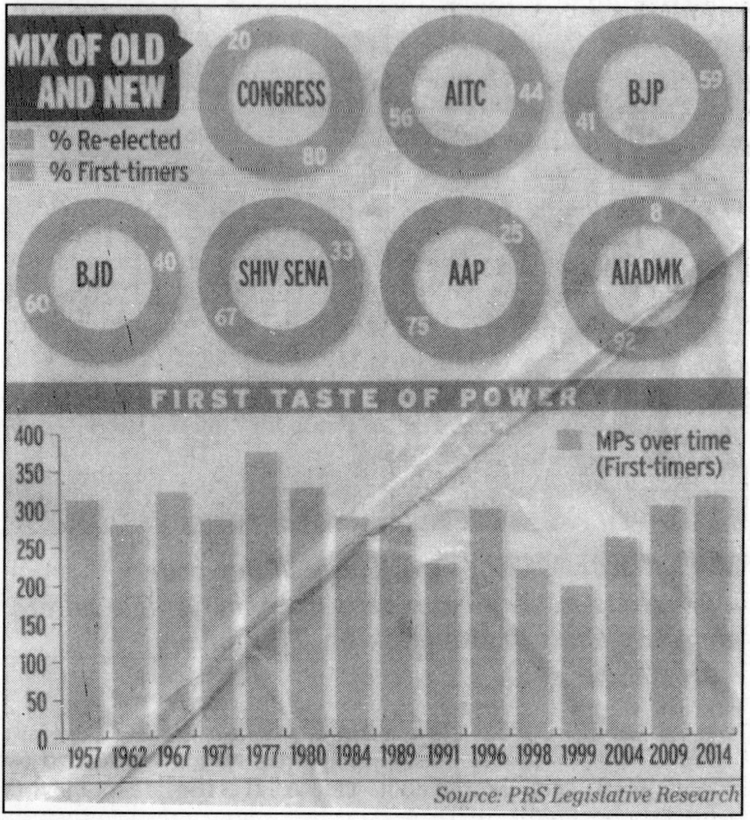

Fig. 3.9: Mix of Old and New

Although the 16th Lok Sabha sees the highest number of first-timer MPs over 30 years, family connections remain an important entry point in politics this time around too.

Age Factor

Among all first-time MPs, 12 are under the age of 30 and another 48 are between 31 and 40 years. For his book, *"India: A Portrait"*, writer Patrick French compiled biographical information on all of the 543 MPs in the 15th Lok Sabha and found that all MPs under the age of 30 and more than two-thirds under the age of 40 had, in effect, inherited their seats. For the new Lok Sabha, the *"Hindu"* found that the number of MPs under the age of 30 grew substantially from six to 12. However, nine of these 12 first-timers are relatives of politicians. The list of MPs under the age of 30 with family connections includes those from the BJP, the Shiv Sena, the AIADMK, the TDP, the INLD and the YSR Congress Party. Of the MPs aged between 31 and 40, at least 20 are sons and daughters of politicians, the *"Hindu"* found.

The BJP has the highest number of re-elected MPs 79 (28%) of the total MPs of BJP elected in the 2014 elections. The Congress has 31 (71%) of total 44, the TMC 13 (38%) of 34, the BJD 8 (40%) of 20, Shiv Sena 7 (39%) of 18, CPM 5 (56%) of 9, Samajvadi Party 4 (80%) of 5, TDP 4 (25%) of 16, AUDF 2 (67%) of 3, IUML 2 (100%) of 2, JD(S) 2 (100%) of 2 NCP 2 (33%) of 6, Akali Dal 2 (50%) of 4, YSR (Congress) 2 (22%) of 9 and others 8 (9%) of 89.

India's young and first time voters seemed to be quite handful as an aggregate but very unpredictable as individual voters. The situation before the 2014 elections seemed to be even more complicated as the bulk of these voters was concentrated in the election battle ground states and had a greater proportion residing in rural areas. Interestingly, the male to female ratio of this group of young and first-time voters was a little less than the equal. The total voters estimated by the Election Commission was 725 million initially (*Source:* Census of India). The population of these young and first-timers with their dispensation in rural and urban areas in top ten states as percentage to the total voters in these states is reflected in Table 3.22 and 3.23.

Table 3.24: Lokasabha-wise Ist Timer and Pre-electred MPs

Sl. No.	*Lok Sabha*	*Number of First timers*	*No. of re-elected MPs*	*Sl. No.*	*Lok Sabha*	*Number of First timers*	*No. of re-elected MPs*
1.	2nd	316	222	**9.**	10th	225	258
2.	3rd	280	228	**10.**	11th	299	196
3.	4th	321	202	**11.**	12th	217	250
4.	5th	311	228	**12.**	13th	185	262
5.	6th	377	144	**13.**	14th	271	220
6.	7th	329	157	**14.**	15th	302	181
7.	8th	290	243	**15.**	16th	NA	NA
8.	9th	274	165				

The history of Parliament elections indicates that it is rare for a majority of outgoing MPs to be chosen again even through some get re-elected repeatedly even up to 8-9 consecutive terms of five years each. The following Table 3.24 indicates the Lok Sabha-wise position of first timers and those re-elected as MPs.

Table 3.25: Top 10 States for First-Time Voters

Name of the Country/State	Total			Rural			Urban		
	Male	Female	Total	Male	Female	Total	Male	Female	Total
India	10.87	9.73	20.60	7.56	6.76	14.32	3.31	2.97	6.28
1. UP	2.09	1.81	3.90	1.61	1.39	3.00	0.48	0.42	0.90
2. Maharashtra	0.97	0.85	1.82	0.54	0.48	1.02	0.43	0.37	0.80
3. Bihar	0.90	0.73	1.63	0.79	0.63	1.42	0.11	0.10	0.21
4. WB	0.79	0.75	1.54	0.56	0.53	1.09	0.23	0.22	0.45
5. AP	0.73	0.69	1.42	0.49	0.45	0.94	0.24	0.24	0.48
6. MP	0.68	0.60	1.28	0.49	0.43	0.92	0.19	0.17	0.36
7. Rajasthan	0.67	0.59	1.26	0.50	0.44	0.94	0.17	0.15	0.32
8. TN	0.55	0.52	1.07	0.30	0.28	0.58	0.25	0.24	0.49
9. Karnataka	0.52	0.49	1.01	0.33	0.30	0.63	0.19	0.19	0.38
10. Gujarat	0.53	0.47	1.00	0.30	0.28	0.58	0.23	0.19	0.42

Note: Total voters estimated by the Election Commission was 725 million.

The Census of India had calculated the region-wise/state-wise total number of voters and voters in the age-group of 18-35 and percentage of voters in the age-group of 18-35. The Census figures estimated the total number of voters at 833124487 and 395088197 in the age-group of 18-35. The following Table 3.26 indicates the region-wise/state-wise percentage of these voters.

Rise and Decline of Independent Candidates

Independent candidates make up the largest block of contestants in the Lok Sabha election. Starting from 1952 election till 2009 elections, the number of independent candidates fluctuated and varied differently. Table 3.27 indicates the year-wise number of independent candidates contesting in percentage to total contestants.

Table 3.27 indicates that 1996 election recorded the highest number of independent candidates comprising 76 per cent of contestants that fought elections. But 1950s was the golden age of independent candidates when non-Congress parties were mostly in their infancy and many prominent politicians contested as

Table 3.26: Region-wise 18-35 age group-voters and percentage

Sl. No.	*Name of the Region/State*	*Total Voters*	*Voters in 18-35 age group*	*Percentage of voters in 18-35 age group*
1.	Andaman & Nicobar Islands	287436	135216	47
2.	Andhra Pradesh	61990569	28695665	46
3.	Arunachal Pradesh	888364	483021	54
4.	Assam	20926631	10466193	50
5.	Bihar	61936119	30515267	49
6.	Chandigarh	788339	396924	50
7.	Chhattisgarh	17331242	8276056	48
8.	Dadra & Nagar Haveli	235455	138159	59
9.	Daman & Diu	187849	114926	61
10.	Goa	1137897	458434	40
11.	Gujarat	42728134	20112317	47
12.	Haryana	17779444	8768778	49
13.	Himachal Pradesh	5075535	2222965	44
14.	Jammu & Kashmir	8275991	4131719	50
15.	Jharkhand	20971418	10368166	49
16.	Karnataka	45001815	20969626	47
17.	Kerala	25535170	9411790	37
18.	Lakshadweep	47887	20899	44
19.	Madhya Pradesh	48209533	23571631	49
20.	Maharashtra	81991472	37885864	46
21.	Manipur	1794519	876710	49
22.	Meghalaya	1782540	991351	56
23.	Mizoram	740453	380880	51
24.	Nagaland	1297651	713205	55
25.	Delhi	12201982	6085904	50
26.	Odisha	29762336	13432350	45
27.	Pudducherry	948288	399604	42
28.	Punjab	20597825	9488693	46
29.	Rajasthan	44532790	22428036	50
30.	Sikkim	443369	233599	53
31.	Tamil Nadu	55060068	23201879	42
32.	Tripura	2652442	1271426	48
33.	Uttar Pradesh	126682415	64491692	51
34.	Uttarakhand	6934506	3383881	49
35.	West Bengal	66367003	30565371	46
	India	**833124487**	**395088197**	**47**

Source: Census of India.

independents. They were the largest block of non-congress MPs in the fifties. In the elections of recent years, most of the independent candidates lose their deposits. The number of independent candidates who lost their deposits as percentage of independent candidates during the last four elections is reflected in Table 3.28.

Table 3.27: Year-wise number independent candidates contesting

Sl. No.	Year	No. of Candidates	Percentage of total candidates	No. of independent candidates elected	Sl. No.	Year	No. of Candidates	Percentage of total candidates	No. of independent candidates elected
1.	1952	533	28.4	37	9.	1989	3713	60.3	12
2.	1957	542	34.0	42	10.	1991	5514	63.6	1
3.	1962	479	24.1	20	11.	1996	10636	76.2	9
4.	1967	854	36.3	35	12.	1998	1915	40.3	6
5.	1971	1134	40.7	14	13.	1999	1945	41.8	6
6.	1977	1224	50.2	9	14.	2004	2385	43.9	5
7.	1980	2826	61.0	9	15.	2009	3830	47.5	9
8.	1984	3894	71.0	13	16.	2014	N.A	N.A	N.A

Table 3.28 : The number independent candidates who lost their deposits in last four elections

Year	1998	1999	2004	2009
No. of candidates who lost deposits	1898	1928	2370	3805
Percentage	99.11	99.13	99.37	99.35

From the figures of 1952-2009, it transpires that collective share of independent candidates in percentage level was much more which looks impossible now. From a percentage of 15.9 per cent it has come down to 5.2 per cent in 2009 elections (*Source*: eci.nic.in).

Broad Highlights of 2014 Elections

The 2014 elections to the 16th Lok Sabha witnessed use of abysmal personal attacks although Indian elections have demonstrated exemplary domestically and internationally. By resorting to negative through personal attacks by candidates and parties, India has rather lost a glorious opportunity to present to the world the immanent positives of a democratic franchising exercise that encompassed an electorate of more than 800 million voters. It appeared that political parties are incapable of addressing the challenges of finding out solutions to the model code of conduct. The 2014 election campaign has perhaps witnessed more violations of the model code by the political parties and their candidates than ever before. The largest numbers of criminal cases for violation of the provisions of RP Act have been registered by the executive at the behest of EC during the campaign. Those accused of violating the code of conduct include the principal opposition party's Prime Ministerial candidate himself, Chief Ministers of several states and quite a few union and State Ministers. The matter did not end there. Most of the political parties and their leaders openly resorted to accusing the EC itself. Apart from Narendra Modi, several others including TMC Chief Mamata Banerjee and Samajwadi Party Supremo Mulayam Singh Yadav had run-ins with the EC during the poll campaign. The reason why political parties are irksome is because the EC has expanded its regulatory authority under Article 324 of the Constitution ever since the model code of conduct was introduced since 1960 in Kerala Assembly elections which became a potent regulatory tool from 1990's. Earlier, the EC was primarily concerned with ensuring free and fair elections. But unlike the RP Act which has provisions to penalize individual electoral offences and corrupt practices, the code is a set of moral principles meant to guide the conduct of parties during the campaign period. Though the code had no legal force, it was during T.N. Seshan's tenure, as historian David Gilmartin put it, that it was brought "into public consciousness as a symbol of the underlying notion that elections required a different kind of morality from everyday politics." The EC has been ambivalent about turning the code in to law since this could lead to protracted legal battles in court as it happens with RPA related cases and thereby undermine its authority during elections. Some have argued that by taking on sweeping powers during the election period, there is a danger of EC restoring to populism. So long as the code does not have legal sanctions, EC can take immediate remedial action. But at the same, lack of legal sanction has led to gaps in the enforcement of the code. Some of the provisions in the code are also hard to enforce. For example it says that criticism of other political parties "shall be confined to their policies and programmes, past record and work" and that it must "refrain from criticism of all aspects of private life". This is simply being ignored as experience of pre-poll campaign of 2014 elections demonstrates. Therefore, the EC must specify what an "electorally legitimate and procedurally correct" a candidate's speech could be. The EC should, therefore, be given adequate powers to enforce the model code of conduct.

References

Angan Kaw (1996). *Bhagat Election and Electoral Reforms in India,* Vikash Publishing House.

Benziger, T. Joseph, *Criminalisations of Politics in India,* Dynamic Youth.

Committee on Electoral Reforms, (Dinesh Goswami) (1990), *Report on Electoral Reforms.*

Core Committee on electoral reforms (2010). *Back ground paper on electoral reforms* GoI.

Committee on State Funding of Elections (1998). Indrajit Gupta Committee.

Election Commission of India 1992. *Proposals of the Election Commission of India for Electoral Reforms.*

Election Commission of India, *Proposed Electoral Reforms* (2004).

EPW, Katju, Manjari, *Election Commission and changing contours of politics.*

EPW, *Vote power and lobby power,* 1994.

EPW, *Electoral reforms and citizens initiative: Some breakthroughs.*

Financial Express, Dhaka 2008, *Election without money and muscle power.*

Gopal Swamy, N. *Elections, a democratic festival, The Hindu.*

G.N. Ray, *Role of Money Power in Elections.*

Goswami Committee Report, 1990.

Hussian, Maybe, *Election without Money and Muscle Power.*

Jay Prakash Narayan, *Electoral and political party reforms in India.*

Journal of Constitutional and Parliamentary Studies (2000), Electoral Reforms, Plea for a fresh look.

Jayatilak Guha Ray, *Electoral Reforms in the Context of recent Supreme Court Judgements,* IIPA.

Law Commission of India (1999)—*Report on Reforms of Electoral Laws.*

L.K. Advani (2003). *Electoral System in India, Need for reforms: Panchayat.*

Lijiphart, A., *Electoral System and Party Systems,* 1994.

Madhav, Godbole, *India's Parliamentary Democracy on Trial,* Rupa & Co.

Main Stream, 2008, Proactive Role of Election Commission.

National Commission to Review working of the Constitution, 2002.

Report on electoral process and political parties, 2002.

Suman Deep Kaur (2008). *Electoral Reforms in India, Pro-active Role of Election Commission* (Main stream).

S.M. Krishnan, *Role of money power in elections,* Seminar Paper.

S.R. Sen, Vote power and lobby power, *EWS.*

The Hindu (February 1999), Proportional representation is the answer to quota problem.

T.M. Joseph, *Proportional representation, a case for electoral reforms in India.*

Tarkunde Committee Report, 1975.

Vorrha Committee Report, 1993.

4
Judicial Reform

The Constitution of India contain several noble features of which the highest place was accorded to "justice" by the "Founding Fathers" of the Constitution. A reading of the Preamble to the Constitution significantly envisages that higher priority is given to justice than the other principles of liberty, equality and fraternity. Social and economic justice enjoin precedence over political justice. The Constitution prescribes the broad structure and defines, delimits and demarcates the role and function of every organ of the state including the judiciary and establishes norms for their inter-relationship, checks and balances. After all, independence of judiciary is essential to the rule of law and Constitutional norms.

A lot of concern has been expressed in the present past about excessive judicial activism. These concerns have been expressed even by the Supreme Court itself in the past when it urged caution on lower courts over excessive judicial activism. The former Lok Sabha Speaker Somanath Chatterjee, while addressing a function of the High Court Bar Association in Nagpur, warned that attempts by the judiciary to usurp the onerous responsibility of the country's governance would have serious implications if some organs of democracy encroach on the jurisdiction of other organs, particularly the legislature. Meaning the judiciary, he even went to the extent of saying that about twenty per cent of judicial officers are corrupt. He called upon courts to dispense affordable and speedy justice to the poor. The discomfort of activism is not confined to a few now. It has been causing discomfort among analysts, politicians and even the Supreme Court itself. This type of Judicial romanticism as some have put in now springs from civil society, political cowardice of political leaders and parties and of course, judicial over-reach on the part of some judges and courts. Judicial romanticism is the habit of mind that always looks to courts as a solution to any problem. This has, in fact of late, become a habit.

The functions of rule-making, rule-enforcing and rule-interpreting are the functions of legislature, the executive and the judiciary respectively each supposed to operate in its demarcated jurisdictions. Unfortunately, in recent decades, any problem political or otherwise, which should have been solved by any of the organs of government, is tempted to be solved by any of the organs of government through a fresh piece of legislation even though the country has plethora of existing laws. Many a time, problems and conflicts that require resolution in the political arena are transferred to judicial arena. One such telling example would be the reference to the Supreme Court of India for rendering advisory opinion in any question of fact or law by the President of India. This definitely differs from ordinary adjudication since it involves no litigation between parties. Moreover, the advisory opinion of the Court is neither binding on the government nor executable as a judgement of the court. The U.S. Supreme Court has decided that in such a role of the court giving advisory opinion on the argument would tantamount to encroaching upon the legislative function and thereby negate the separation of powers that underpins the US Constitution. In India, the judiciary exists to interpret laws, expound the Constitution and ensure that the rule of law prevails. The responsibility of maintaining law and order vests with executive arm of the government. It is the Cabinet which should weigh popular opinion before deciding upon any issue/issues of public policy. It cannot shift the burden of responsibility to the courts for matters of policy. The judiciary cannot decide upon questions of belief, opinion, political wisdom nor pronounce upon questions relating to history, archaeology and mythology etc. It cannot compensate for the inadequacies of governments or the failure of the political process. In the Babri Masjid dispute case when the government made a reference to the Apex Court, although there was no legal point, the court, on the point of reference as to whether a temple existed at the disputed site in Ayodhya, clearly held that the reference was "superfluous", unnecessary and does not require to be answered.

Judicial Over-reach

In recent years, the courts seem to be shedding such inhibitions. Judicial over-reach may be rooted partly in the flattery of public faith in the judiciary in certain specific situations like the notorious emergency in 1975-1977 and partly by the failure of governments to address and redress serious ills afflicting society. But these would not be merely compelling situations for judiciary to play the role of activists. If the judiciary wishes to be activist, it has enough of agenda within their own sphere of activities without encroaching upon the legislative and executive jurisdictions. The most serious shortcoming of the judiciary is its excruciating slowness. In fact, these are almost 1000 times more annually accepted by Indian courts as compared to their U.S. counterparts. Part of the explanation for the multiplying backlog of cases is attributed to the politicisation of the judiciary at all levels and part in its corruption at lower levels. The more the delay, greater is the benefit that goes to pockets of others. Indian litigants have not only fondness for filing cases but to linger them. Considering the frequency and number of cases filed in courts by the people, it testifies that the people have great faith in the judicial system compared to other institutions of government. Even then frivolous, motivated and mischievous cases at times are launched at little or no cost to plaintiffs that exact a heavy toll on the defendants. The cases relating to Sania Mirza, India's tennis icon and the prolific writer Taslima Nasreen in recent periods amply testify the way cases are filed in courts on flimsy and frivolous grounds. In such circumstances, the courts have a great role to play.

Judicial Activism

In the present day disposition of our socio-political dispensation, there is much of a talk about judicial activism. But nothing spectacular is clearly witnessed in this direction. Ofcourse, there are traditional judges who stick to the precedents. Many socially important matters come before the Appex Court. Obviously, the judge takes into consideration all the relevant factors, the environment, our eco-system, our lack of facilities for public etc. The judge appreciates these things and takes a positive view. Such judges are, therefore, called activist judges. Another perception that prevails is that the judiciary tends even to legislate. But in many of these matters of serious complaint the court gives directions and sometimes refers to Parliament to do something and have a legislation. Even then, sometimes, these legislations either take a long time or are not done at all. For example, smoking in public places is injurious to health. Parliament is not coming out with any legislation on this. In situations like this, courts give some directions so that the public will have some protection. It is not that the courts are functioning as a parallel to Parliament. Of course, in some of the recent directions, the Apex Court seems to be worried of the machinations of politicians and the executive in protecting the interest of citizens and their Fundamental Rights. In spite of all that is said good of the judiciary, there are allegations of corruption which should be carefully handled with because the whole judicial system depends on faith and confidence of people in the system. Once that is lost, the system losses it justification for existence. Therefore, the allegations against judiciary are to be addressed very seriously.

In the recent past, a two-judge bench of the Apex Court consisting of Justice A.K. Mathur and Justice Markandey Katju in their judgement held that judges should not over-reach or encroach on the areas of the legislature and the executive. Subsequent to this judgement, another two-judge bench of the Apex Court referred a PIL to a three-judge bench. A couple of days thereafter, the Chief Justice of the Apex Court clarified that the judgement of the two bench court was not binding on a three-judge bench of the Apex Court and indicated that suitable guidelines will be framed with regard to entering PILs. Many legal luminaries hold the view that judges should not stray into the exclusive domain of other branches A few instances of judicial activism gives an impression that the judiciary is probably transgressing its jurisdiction to the domain of other branches. In the case of the PIL filed by Congress MLA Sanyam Lodha challenging the discretionary power enjoyed by the Chief Minister of Rajasthan to award higher compensation to adult rape victims than to minors, a division bench of the High Court struck down the relevant rule in the Chief Minister's Relief Fund Rules, 1999 which empowers the Chief Minister to award monetary relief to an unlimited extent to rape, flood and drought victims. The bench judicially substituted the phrase "unlimited extent" with "equality and without discrimination" effectively curtailing the powers of the Chief Minister to award relief arbitrarily. Now the moot question is whether the High Court was right in a pure legislative issue like this. The judiciary has the power to review any legislation but whether the judiciary should entertain and act on a PIL case like the above to tell the executive and the legislature is the point for greater debate. In another case, the Municipal Corporation of Delhi curtly told the Delhi High Court to dispose of the case relating to demolition of authorized buildings and scrap the court-appointed monitoring committee and Court Commissioners. Quoting a judgement of the Apex Court the MCD virtually asked the High Court to "lay off" the demolition case as it falls within the domain of executive and legislature. It is a fact that most of the constructions in the nation's capital are illegal and unauthorisedly sanctioned by corrupt officials under the patronage of *netas*, causing suffering to the common man. Here both the executive and the legislature have failed to perform their duties. In such cases, the Court should intervene to set things right in issuing guidelines.

Lively criticism of judicial activism encroaching upon the powers of the legislature and the executive, has been voiced by many including the former Lok Sabha Speaker Somanath Chatterjee. Such controversies are the life blood of democracy and should be welcomed. On March 12, 2007, Marshals were summoned in the Lok Sabha as Communist Party of India (Marxist) members stormed the well menacingly advancing towards Shipping Minister T.R. Baalu. DMK members formed a human wall to protect him. On March 19, 2007, another scuffle took place in Rajya Sabha when BJP member S.S. Ahluwalia and other opposition members rushed threateningly towards Finance Minister P. Chidambaram who was protected by a cordon of Congressmen. The Indian citizen's perception of the political class is overwhelmingly coloured by the above images. It is, in this context, that judicial activism has flourished in India and has acquired enormous legitimacy with the Indian public. Some instances of the past may be of worth recounting.

Instances of judicial activism in India are greatly influenced by incidents of other democracries. Stuart King James I of England who claimed absolute power in 1608 wanted to remove any case from the royal courts and decide himself as a royal person. This was objected to by the Chief Justice Coke on the ground that the

King cannot do as the case ought to be determined and adjudged in a court of justice according to the law and custom of England. Being greatly offended, the King replied: This means that "I shall be under law which is treason to affirm" but the Chief Justice replied that "Bracton says that the King should not be under man but should be under God and Law". During that period of British legal system, judges were removable by the King and had no security of tenure. Chief Justice Coke's reply to the King was an affirmation of the judicial power while upholding the rule of law against arbitrary decisions of the sovereign. This was judicial activism at its finest. Not only in England but in the United States, such reaffirmation of judicial power was demonstrated in 1801 when Chief Justice John Marshall highlighted and reaffirmed the power of American Supreme Court in invalidating congressional statutes in the celebrated case of *Marbury vs. Madison.* Chief Justice Earl Warren of the U.S. was one of the activist Judges who has profoundly influenced the Indian Supreme Court. By his decision, he legitimised affirmative action by the courts and removed racial discrimination in schools by segregation, reapportioned obsolete electoral districts and enhanced the rights of poor accused and defendants. Justice Warren and the judges supporting him cameout in conflict with their colleagues who championed judicial restraint. In *Stewart vs. United States,* a bare majority reversed a murder conviction because of improper questioning by the prosecution. After the majority opinion was read, Frankfurter in open court characterized it as an indefensible example of "Judicial nit-picking and excessively flinchy appellate review".

In India the most prominent case of high water mark of judicial activism was the judgement of the majority in the *Keshavananda Bharati case* relating to Fundamental Rights. For the first time, a court held that a constitutional amendment duly passed by the legislature was invalid as it was damaging or destroying its basic structure. This was a gigantic innovative judicial leap unknown to any legal system. The master-stroke was that judgement could not be annulled by any amendment to be made by Parliament because the basic structure doctrine was vague and amorphous. The judgement was severely and passionately criticized by the executive and many eminent lawyers. The immediate response of the executive was the supersession of three senior-most judges (Justices Shelat, Hegde and Grover) while the fourth judge Justice

A.N. Ray who had decided major cases in favour of Government, was appointed Chief Justice. However, the critics were soon silenced. The excesses of internal emergency of 1975 completely legitimized this judgement and one of its severest critics, the great Jurist H.M. Seervai changed his views. Judicial activism earned a human face in India by liberalizing access to justice and giving relief to disadvantaged groups and the have-nots under the leadership of V.R. Krishna Ayer and P.N. Bhagwati. The Supreme Court gained in structure and legitimacy. Later, when the independence of judiciary was threatened by punitive transfers, the Court entered the arena of judicial appointments and transfers. With the increasing criminalisation and mis-governance and the complete apathy of the executive, the Court under the leadership of Chief Justice Verma and Justices Bharucha and Sen, took up the case of terrorist funding linked to political corruption through the "*hawala* route" in the *Vinet Narayan case*, (*Jain hawala case*). A cover up by the CBI to protect its political masters was exposed and the Court monitored the investigation upholding the principle "Be you ever show high the law is above you". In this case, during hearing, there were reports that Prime Minister P.V. Narasimha Rao was interfering with the investigation and the Court passed an interim order on March 1st, 1996. It was directed that "the CBI would not take any instruction from, report to or furnish any particular thereof to any authority personally interested in or likely to be affected by the outcome of the investigation into any accusation. This direction applied even in relation to any authority which exercises administrative control over the CBI by virtue of the office he holds, without any exception." In substance, Prime Minister Rao was forbidden from exercising control over the CBI in relation to that case. It was a bold and courageous order and carried judicial activism to hitherto un-scaled height. The fall-out of the case was resignations following initiation of prosecutions against high profile political personalities including three Cabinet Ministers, two Governors and the leader of the opposition. In consequence, probably the ruling Congress lost power in the next general election.

The Court, on several occasions, have issued direction in Public Interest Litigation (PIL) cases covering a wide spectrum such as road safety, pollution, illegal structures in VIP Zones, money menace, dog menace, unpaid dues by former and serving legislators, nursery admissions and admissions in institutes of higher learning. There is no doubt that some times these orders are triggered by righteous indignation and emotional responses. The common citizens have discovered that the administration has become so apathetic and non-performing and corruption and criminality so widespread that they have no recourse expect to move the courts through PIL enlarging the field for judicial intervention. The great contribution of judicial activism in India has been to provide safety valve in a democracy and sustain a hope that justice is not beyond reach. Judicial activism has come to stay in India and will continue to stay as long as the judiciary is respected and not undermined by negative perceptions, which have overtaken the executive and the legislature. There is, however, a concern among the public about lack of transparency in judicial appointments and a sense of increasing unease because of a lack of a credible mechanism to deal with serious complaints against the higher judiciary.

Indian democracy has several reasons for congratulating itself for the vitality of its public discourse in several cases of recent times. The more important issue has been the judicial activism. The high profile politician Sibu Soren was convicted for a murder committed in 1994. Bollywood celebrity Sanjay Dutt was convicted of offences under the Arms Act, Navjot Singh Sidhu, an ex-cricketer was convicted for a road rage killing committed some 20 years ago. The most interesting case relates to *Jessica Lall murder case* where the Delhi High Court reversed a perverse decision of a lower court. The acquittal of the accused Manu Sharma by the lower court was a patent miscarriage of justice which the High Court identified correctly and reassuringly. More important than the decisions in individual cases is a path-breaking recent ruling of the Supreme Court which has creatively interpreted section 197 of the Criminal Procedure Code and section 19 of the Prevention of Corruption Act in favour of citizens. These sections provide that no court can take cognizance of charges against public servants without prior sanction of the Government. The obvious intention behind this provision was to prevent frivolous litigation by interested individuals or groups against honest civil servants and legislators. Similarly, in two other cases, namely *Lalu Prasad vs. State of Bihar* and *Prakash Singh Badal vs. The State of Punjab* justice was sought to be thwarted by the plea that statutory permission had not been obtained before the launch of prosecutions. This protective wall has now been breached by the judgement of the Supreme Court in the aforesaid two cases. The Court has held that the protection provided by these two sections are not meant to provide "absolute and unqualified immunity" against criminal prosecution. A public servant is entitled to immunity only in the context of his official duties. In *Sibu Soren's case*, the special court of CBI rejected Soren's plea of immunity under Article 105 (2) of the Constitution which says that "no member of Parliament shall be liable to proceedings in any court in respect of anything said or any vote given by him in Parliament." The Delhi High Court confirmed this ruling but surprisingly the Supreme Court in April 1998, in a majority decision of 3 to 2 held that Soren and others were immune from prosecution by virtue of their membership in Parliament. This anomaly in law has now been corrected in the latest judgement in the *Lalu Prasad Yadav's case*. The minority judgement in this case made an important point that immunity given to members of Parliament is only in respect of their speeches or votes on public matters and not for a corrupt practice that precedes the speech or vote.

Judicial Review

Many Chief Justices of India agree with the recent Supreme Court ruling subjecting the power of pardon of a Governor and President to judicial review but they differ on the application of the judicial review yardstick. Justice J.S. Verma was candid in holding the position that "every action of the executive is subject to judicial review but such review should be exercised with great circumspection." In his own judgement in *S.R. Bommai case* he had held that "even if there is an element of subjectivity (in an executive decision and action) judicial hands should be off". Justice Verma's views came in case of the Apex Court judgement gushing the pardon granted to a convicted Congressman in Andhra Pradesh on the ground that it was subject to judicial review. Justice Verma was categorical that judicial review of executive action was not new. In the *Indira Gandhi assassination case*, this point was debated and it was settled that the pardon power of Governor or that of the President is justiciable. In the *case of Mohammed Afzal* whose hanging has been ordered in *Parliament attack case* and was long pending has resulted at last awaiting in rejection by the President but surprisingly there has been a sudden twist in the case. The Madras High Court surprisingly stayed operation of execution order and therefore, was under further judicial review. Justice K.N. Singh held this case of attack on Parliament as one of the rarest of rare cases as an attack on the country's sovereignty and therefore, could not be pardoned. Justice Singh observed that pardoning a convict after all the courts have adjudicated him to be hanged should be on consideration, reasonable and not whims or likes or dislikes. In general, courts do not interfere with pardoning but if it is found there was no ground at all, courts need to interfere.

India, unlike the United States, does not have separate hierarchies of federal and states. Although Indian polity is dual, the judiciary is integrated. There is only one unified judicial system. One hierarchy of courts with the Supreme Court at the apex to arbiter in matter-relations between the Union and the States and the States *inter se*. The Supreme Court and the High Courts, as custodians and watch-dog of Fundamental Rights and freedom of the people and their constitutional rights, have tremendous and awesome responsibility. The superior judiciary, of course, has preserved and protected the Fundamental Rights of citizens drawing substantially upon the "Directive Principles". In recent years, there have been voices of detraction. Judicial activism has not gone well with groups of democratic theorists who object to the kind of judicial activism which has tended to turn social and political process to legal process and obliterating the thin-line of demarcation between interpretation and adjudication and exhibiting an ever eager tendency to intervene in the governing process. Constitutional adjudications do have an inevitable legislative element. Judges need great wisdom and restraint in wielding this great judicial powerless they erect their own predilections into principles. The importance and need of judicial review has been very well explained by one judge who said "the irreplaceable value of the power of judicial review lies in the protection which it has accorded to constitutional rights that has maintained public esteem for the judiciary and has permitted peaceful existence of counter majoritarian implications of judicial review and the democratic principles on which our federal government rests."

The judiciary should face challenges in this era of liberalization, privatization and globalization and should not be left behind, said the former Chief Justice of India Mr. R.C. Lahoti in the recent past. The judiciary should strive for excellence and be prepared to learn to face new challenges. He said that judiciary was very conservative and lived in ivory towers earlier. To face the new challenges, when new issues were emerging in the fields of development, science and technology, governance and economics that had global consequences, the judiciary should be ready to set an example. Setting up of the National Judicial Academy (NJA) for imparting training to judges is a right step in the right direction. The Chief Justice of India declared 2005 as "the year of excellence in judiciary" and expected the highest judiciary to be fully functional in providing quality in justice by stimulating knowledge. In this connection he stressed the need to introduce information and communication technology in the judicial system for which funds should be available. For complete computerization of the judiciary in the country, Rs. 667 crore were estimated as the need for modernization. Considering the enormous size of the judiciary and the huge volume of litigation, there is need for building alternate dispute resolution system. Cases being normally tried in courts could also be settled through mediation, conciliation and settlement.

The Courts are saddled with bundles of cases leading to abnormal and inordinate delays in their disposal. An approximate number of about 3 lakh under-trial prisoners are confined to the sordid environment of prison cells, most of them possibly innocent, because of the delay in disposal of cases. It is estimated that about 80 per cent of the prisoners might have been released had their trials been completed on time. Most of them are languishing in jail for periods more than the one they would have faced had they been sentenced even for the highest period prescribed under the law. Because of the ineffectiveness in the functioning of the judicial courts, most of the criminals accused of severe crimes somehow secure bail and get easy access to political and bureaucratic power circles and freely roam about and continue to perpetrate similar or even more grievous crimes even while they are freed on bail. The colossal amount running to hundred of crores spent on under-trial prisoners could be saved if they are released on personal security and the money saved on account of this could be used to establish additional courts for speedy dispensation. To make the judiciary functional and remedy injustice through delayed justice, it is not enough to set up special tribunals to try politicians and bureaucrats expeditiously. It is necessary to increase the number of courts many times more to ensure that they function as efficiently as in other developed countries. In America, the number of courts is about 10 times more than in India. We may not increase the number of courts to that extent, but to overhaul the system, resources should be found-out at least to increase the number of courts and the judges many times more than what is existing now.

Recruitment Mechanism

Judges in democratic countries are presumed to be independent and impartial. In countries like Great Britain they enjoy vast powers by convention. In the United States, they wield wide-ranging powers by constitutional provision. So, is the case in India. There are powers and autonomy in the executive and the legislature that are inviolable by the judiciary. The final pronouncements by the highest court on disputes are binding on the civil authorities; violation or non-compliance is subjected to contempt power of courts. Thus, there is paramountcy for the jurisprudence of judicial action which provides practical guarantee to the civil rights of citizens. In this context, the appointment, performance and removal of judges at all levels assumes a great deal of importance because sometimes the judges play such roles which are dangerous and antagonistic to the social and secular values as enshrined in the Preamble to the Constitution. Even Parliament can be belittled and victimized by judicial excesses and class biases. The highest court in our system suffers public scrutiny and criticism from a constructive angle although courts should not shy at exposure if true and responsibly presented. Some feel that it is dangerous and unwise to expose the truth of judiciary. But, it is always better to have all citizens informed as to how the judicial system works and functions in our country.

The totality of administration of our country is vested in the trinity of executive, legislature and the judiciary. The actions of the executive are subject to judicial review when there is injustice social, economic and political or aberration from the provisions of Law and the Constitution. When the legislature makes laws beyond constitutional bounds or acts arbitrarily, contrary to its basic structure, the highest court examines and corrects. But when the judiciary is guilty of excesses, either a larger bench or a Constitutional amendment can intervene. The supremacy of the judiciary, its finality and presumed infallibility make it obligatory to control its operation by an instrumentality accessible to the people. Therefore, it becomes necessary to control and preserve the judiciary from going beyond what the Constitution provides. In fact Parts III, IV and IVA contain the soul of the Constitution and the court has a solemn duty to accept its social philosophy, culture and imperatives. In this context, comes the question of appointment of those who occupy the high office of administration of law and justice. While public servants are chosen by Public Service Commissions, recruitment of judges is of greatest constitutional importance. Therefore, the selecting body of judges must, in its composition, be beyond question. The present process of selection through the collegium of judges of Supreme Court is not infallible. Its performance in the last few years has been hardly creditable. The choice of selection is not based on any rational principle or comprehensive investigation or opportunity for the opinion of the Bar or the public. No objective study is done on the social background or commitment of the candidates. No opportunity is also given to the Bar or public organizations concerned with justice—social, economic and political. The appointment of judges must be a public purpose, not a matter of secrecy as it is now. There must be guidelines based on which the selection may be made and the principle must be implementation of the values of the Constitution. The independence of judiciary must be reflected in the independence of selecting the instrumentality and its processes. When the appointment is to the Supreme Court, whether by direct selection from the Bar or by elevation from among judges, there should be an investigation in to the professional capacity, character, performance and social background of the candidates. A two thirds majority of the commission must support the selection. In view of the increasing communal lunacy and insidious corruption in public life, court must be impeccable in integrity, intelligence and constitutional wisdom. In our republic, the justice system is the principal instrumentality in satisfying the objectives and undertakings in the Constitution. The people generally would expect to be assured of integrity, efficiency and moral responsibility of easy access to the court as well as early finality of dispute resolution. All these would constitute the successful performance of the judicature for which the judges should be chosen rightly keeping in view the values and ideals of the Constitution and the rights of the people. To realize these, there must be a machinery to guarantee the good performance of the judiciary. This could be achieved by means of what Justice V.R. Krishna Aiyer suggests, through a "Performance Commission". Citing about such a system existing in United States, Justice Aiyer presumes and suggests why this system should not be replicated in our country. The transfer and promotion of judges of the High Courts could be based on its recommendations. We should have nationally sensitive and supremely impartial judges. There is, however, a concern among the public about lack of transparency in judicial appointments and a sense of increasing unease because of a lack of credible mechanism to deal with serious complaints against higher judiciary.

The Supreme Court appointed the CBI to investigate the *Ghaziabad "Provident Fund Scam" case* apparently on the plea that both the UP police and State government themselves desired a CBI investigation. The response of the executive was direct and strident. The then Union Law Minister H.R. Bharadwaj reported to have said (*Hindustan Times*, 25th September, 2008) that "the quality of some of the judges selected over the years was questionable and the system of selection by a Committee of judges (Collegium) has failed." He further observed that "in a bid to maintain its supremacy, the judiciary tried to rewrite the law through a Supreme Court judgement in 1993 which gave them the powers for appointment and transfers. Merit has been ignored while give and take has thrived in the collegiums system." He continued to observe that "it is the right time to have a relook at the collegiums system which has failed. There was a time when the judiciary was above suspicion and people had great respect for it. The same cannot be said today. Serious allegations of corruption against judges are in the public domain. It needs to be corrected." But the most alarming and disturbing factor in this issue was the solution offered by him. He suggested that "a committee of judges could recommend names which should be finalized after discussion between the CJI and President. The decision of the President should be final on the advice of the Union Cabinet".

The views of the then Law Minister seem to be naïve and disingenuous. The Central Government is always consulted before appointment of judges to the High Courts and the Supreme Court. In fact the Central Government has the infrastructure and capacity to gather and verify information through the intelligence bureaus, the police and other sources about the anticidents and otherwise of persons proposed to be appointed as judges. In fact, on many occasions, the executive equally failed when undesirable appointments were made by it in the past. Therefore, the attack by the Law Minister was slanted in favour of the executive. In fact, it is an attempt to restore a failed and discredited executive without any definite mechanism. The Supreme Court of India has earned the enviable reputation by enlarging human rights jurisprudence for disadvantaged groups. It has been a bulwark against excesses of the executive and the legislature and a pillar supporting the rule of law and our democratic freedoms. Its contributions in protecting journalistic freedom against legislative privileges, electoral reforms and its rulings against arbitrary dismissal of State Governments, censorship, gender discrimination are outstanding. It stands tall among constitutional courts in new democracies.

Looking at the historical background it is seen that there have been tensions between the executive and the judiciary. When judicial review invalidated progressive land reform legislation in the early 1950s, Constitutional amendments were fashioned to nullify the decisions. The judiciary was under criticism by the legislature and the executive as being too conservative in its approach. There was no attack on the honesty, integrity and probity of the Court. After the judgement in *Kesavanand Bharati case* delivered on April 24,1973, a powerful executive struck back when on the retirement of Chief Justice Sikri on April 25, 1973, Justice A.N. Ray was made Chief Justice superseding three senior most judges, namely Justice Shelat, Justice Hegde and Justice Grover who promptly resigned. The executive said it wanted "forward-looking" judges. This was resented all over India. As a sarcasm Chief Justice Hidayatullah said one will have Judges "looking forward" rather than "forward looking". The executive resorted to mass transfer of independent High Court judges who stood up during the emergency. Constitutional amendments were rushed through while all major opposition leaders were preventively detained without trial. The powers of the Supreme Court and High Courts were drastically reduced and judicial review was sought to be outsted almost completely. With the Janata Government coming to power in the 1977 elections, the 44th Constitutional Amendment restored back the powers of higher judiciary including judicial review. With fall of the Janata Government in 1980 and Indira Gandhi being voted to power again, attempts were made to exercise powers of transfer against High Court Judges. This was widely perceived as a threat to Independence of the judiciary and it was in this background that the Supreme Court over-ruled the earlier decisions and held negative the primacy of the Union executive in appointments to the High Courts and the Supreme Court as well as transfer of High Court Judges. The final word rested with the Chief Justice of India subject, of course, to the plurality of consultations constituting the Collegiums of Judges. Although these decisions were subject to criticism then, with the radically changed situations now particularly in the era of coalitions, the decisions seem to be timely and relevant.

In the present situation of scams, the judiciary was likely to come under a cloud. Even the former Attorney General of India G.E. Vahanvati some time back told the Supreme Court unambiguously that "impeccable integrity" was not a feasible proposition in the matter of appointment while arguing in the case relating to the selection of P.J. Thomas as the Central Vigilance Commissioner whose past conduct had been questioned. To confirm the preponderance of dubious individuals in virtually all walks of life, the Apex Court lashed out in an unprecedented manner against the Allahabad High Court by accusing it in an echo from Hamlet of harbouring "something rotten" in its precincts. This criticism emanated from a case of High Court's allotment of a plot of land to a circus company although the Lucknow Bench of the same court had earlier dismissed the petition. The Supreme Court requested the Chief Justice of High Court to do some "cleaning" by taking strong measures including the transfer of incorrigibles. These 'incorrigibles' obviously referred to the "uncle judges" under whom their kith and kins are practicing in the same court. To arrest this trend in the judiciary, the Law Commission had observed that just as government officers were kept away from their home districts, Judges should not be posted in courts where their relatives were lawyers. Keeping this in view, even the Law Ministry had drafted a bill to remedy the situation and proposed to secure a commitment from the judges that they will not function in courts where their relatives practiced. But this seemed to be not feasible. In spite of the view of the former Chief Justice of India C.P. Bharucha that one-fifth of the judiciary was corrupt, the uncle-nephew factor is not the only concern but greater transparency on appointments and close scrutiny of assets of judges could act as a check.

The Constitution (120 Amendment) Bill, 2013 and the Judicial Appointment Commission Bill, 2013 seek to reform the appointment of High Courts and Supreme Court Judges by establishing a Judicial Appointment Commission (JAC). This is a significant shift towards strengthening "Independence of Judiciary" and the "rule of law". Despite different opinions expressed by many including legal luminaries, about the bill, the fact remains that the present proposal seriously misunderstands the minimum level of constitutional entrenchment of judicial appointment as well as optimal level of institutionalization of protocol and process of appointment. From some of the recent arguments that the rule of law and the independence of judiciary necessarily means that judiciary must have primacy among the constitutional institutions in the judicial appointment process is not historically sound and valid considering the discussions held in the Constituent Assembly. While discussing the issue of appointment of High Court Judges, under Article 217, Dr. Ambedkar said: "with regard to the concurrence of Chief Justice, it seems to me that those who advocate that proposition seem to rely implicitly both the impartiality of the Chief Justice and the soundness of his judgement. I personally feel no doubt that the Chief Justice is a very eminent person. But after all, the Chief Justice is a man with all the failings, all the sentiments and all the prejudices which we as common people have; and I think, to allow the Chief Justice practically a veto upon the appointment of judges is really to transfer the authority of the Chief Justice which we are not prepared to vest in the President of the Government of the day. I, therefore, think that that is also a dangerous proposition." In 1982, Justice P.N. Bhagawati speaking for the majority in *S.P. Gupta case* (1982) held that Articles 124 and 217 provided the exclusive power of appointment of judges fettered by the need to consult with the Chief Justice. While reviewing the arguments for judicial supremacy in this process, he cautioned that "in cases of this kind.... a considerable amount of passion has been injected into arguments on both sides and sometimes passion may appear to lend strength to an argument; but sitting as judges, we have to be careful to see that passion does not blind us to logic and predilections pervert proper interpretation of the constitutional provisions. We can always find some reason for bending the language of the Constitution to our will, if we want, but that would be rewriting the Constitution".

Although the observations of both Dr. Ambedkar and much thereafter, Justice Bhagawati had cautioned against the executive role and the judicial pre-eminence, the Supreme Court in the Advocates Record Association (ARC 1993) changed the track to conclude that the principle of separation of powers and doctrine of basic structure requires that the court, acting through the Chief Justice, must concur with every judicial appointment. The Presidential Reference (1999) displaced the Chief Justice acting solo by allowing a review to emerge from the collective decision-making among senior members of the judiciary through the collegiums process. The court method of appointment is only two decades old. There is little evidence that the change in the appointment process in the last two decades has enabled the higher judiciary to become a forum for principle rather than partisan decision-making or a meritocratic institution representative of India's diversity. Therefore, the proposed bill is a timely interventation to reform critical aspect of our Constitution by paying attention to the first principle of constitutional design. Many countries have adopted the principle of separation of powers to design an inter-institutional process to constitute the judiciary. These institutions operate as a check and balance to ensure that no single institution has an overweening influence on judicial composition. In fact, in the contemporary constitutional design, two inter-institutional designs dominate, i.e. the judiciary and executive acting in concert and the executive and the legislature. While the bill envisages collaboration of the executive and judiciary in the appointment process, a few more important issues need to be kept in view.

Pendency of Cases

The judicial system depends more on the faith of the common man, said K.G. Balakrishnan, the 37th Chief Justice of India. A large number of cases are pending in different courts of India particularly the High Courts. If the High Courts take initiative, these can be impressively reduced. In one year in Kerala, about 61000 cases were reduced. Setting up of additional courts and as part of that, appointment of adequate number of judges and judicial officers in the subordinate judiciary can reduce the large number of pendency of cases. The Centre should provide adequate funds to the States for the purpose of constituting special courts. Even in evening courts some petty cases can be disposed of. It is not easy to have courts for "Alternation Dispute Resolution" in India unlike foreign countries. The cases have to be identified and arbitrators and conciliators or mediators have to be selected and a mind set for this developed. Pendency of cases can be reduced if High Courts and other courts pay urgent attention. In fact, a system should be developed where instead of judges giving priority to dispose of cases, the system should create an environment and infrastructure built up which should facilitate expeditious disposal of cases. The criticism that under the "Judges Enquiry Bill" the National Judicial Council is completely managed by the judiciary is not really fallacious. After all, somebody else scrutinizing the activities of judges may have the problem of affecting the Independence of the Judiciary. That is why senior judges themselves make a sort of enquiry. This is only a prelude to any impeachment that may sometimes become absolutely necessary. It is not anti-impeachment. It is only a correction process. If any serious impropriety is noticed, the judge can be asked to go on leave or the judge may voluntarily quit. To the general criticism as to why the Chief Justice of India was not covered by the bill had a point but considering the fact that Indian Courts are viewed by the outside world with high respect, the CJI, in fact, should not be an exception for he also can face the impeachment procedure. Another point is often compared to the transparency obtaining in the appointment procedure of a judge in the United States. Why that system cannot be adopted in India? The answer could be simple on a strong and positive note in case of India. In America it is a political appointment, which comes through a particular channel but in our case, the CJI of the Apex Court and CJIs of High Courts are appointed and everybody knows his performance.

Contempt of Court

It is being observed now that at times political leaders criticise the judges if the court verdicts go against their interests although the Constitution has expressly prohibited such denigration of the judiciary for political reasons. Article 129 of the Constitution reads "The Supreme Court shall be a court of record and shall have all the powers of such a court, including the power to punish for a contempt of itself." Similarly, every High Court is, under Article 215, a "Court of Record" and as such, it too can penalize a person for a Contempt of Court. No other institution acting under the Constitution has been accorded such a status. But the Lok Sabha and the State Assemblies have occasionally summoned people for an alleged breach of privilege. This punitive authority has been derived from the British source for a temporary period as the Constitution makers did not intend to vest in them such authority as an original right or perpetual gift. It is necessary to determine what constitutes contempt of Court. The Constitution has not defined it in any way. But section 2 of the Contempt of Court Act, 1971 makes the matter sufficiently clear. Wilful disobedience or a scandalous remark about a judge constitutes a contempt of Court and in such a case, a penal measure can be adopted against the offender. But the Constitution or Law has not in anyway prohibited any genuine and well-intentioned criticism of the judicial process or verdict nor has it denied the right of others to point out the technical flaw of a judge in his interpretation of the Constitution or Law. In other words, fair and reasonable criticism of the judiciary in the interest of public good does not, in anyway, constitute a Contempt of Court. What is prohibited is tendentious and malicious criticism of the judge or imputation of motive behind the judgement. In case of such wilful aspersions on a judge, the law will take its course. Therefore, an academic criticism must be differentiated from planned malice or calculated tirade which creates a summary contempt of the judiciary. In this way, the superior courts enjoy a penal power, which intends to uphold the dignity and independence of the judiciary.

For practical reasons, the above mentioned powers should be used properly, carefully and with circumspection. In case of *Hiralal vs. UP* (1953), the Supreme Court observed that such punitive power should, of course, be exercised honestly, sparingly and remain limited to cases involving prejudice. In case of *Hasan vs. UP* (1959), the Supreme Court held that when such offence had been proved beyond doubt, the affected court can impose punishment where mere facts seems to be inadequate. It is stark reality that our judiciary has rarely dealt with such affairs and leniently inflicted punishment upon the offenders. Some years back, CPI-M leader, the late EMS Namboodiripad remarked that as judges come from affluent families, they have a particular class interest, and as such, the working people cannot find justice and fair play from them. This comment originating from the Marxian doctrine of class struggle, amounted to Contempt of court. But the Supreme Court imposed a nominal token fine on him. The late Jatin Chakraborty, RSP leader and former West Bengal Minister, made some adverse comments on the attitude of Mr. Justice Barooah of Calcutta High Court in connection with the verdict on a petition filed by a singer. This comment also seemed to be a Contempt of Court. But instead of taking stern action, the Judge observed that in the interest of maintaining happy relationship between the executive and judicial branches of the Government, he would pass by the matter and would only expect such dignitaries refrain from making irresponsible and malicious remarks against Judges. It is only in case of CPI-M leader Biman Bose that Calcutta High Court sentenced him to three days' simple imprisonment and a fine of Rs. 10,000. To reduce the huge backlog of pending cases, emergent measures are required. It should be made mandatory that every case be disposed of within six months. In this background exercise of power of contempt by courts seems reasonable.

Attack on Judiciary

The attack on the judiciary is not a new thing in Indian politics. When in 1969, the Supreme Court invalidated the Bank Nationalization Bill and Privy Purse issue by a majority, some judges were condemned as the apostles of conservatism and agents of capitalism. Even signatures of MPs were collected to sack them under Article 124(4) of the Constitution. Thereafter, Judges were generally looked upon and classified into two categories "forward looking" and "Conservatives". Instead of dismissing any Judge, a scheme of favouritism was promptly adopted. In 1975, A.N. Ray was made the Chief Justice of India superseding three senior Judges A.N. Grover, J.M. Shelat and K.S. Hegde. Mr. Justice H.M. Beg was similarly promoted by rejecting the rightful claim of Mr. Justice H.R. Khanna. This is certainly not a Contempt of Court but before doing such mischief, certain people at the helm of affairs dubbed some judges as the root of all evils. Above all, what seems to be a judicial mistake or an act of conservatism may subsequently prove to be an important matter of public welfare. This can be supported by an American example. To fight the evils of the Great Depression of 1929, President Franklin D. Roosevelt adopted the "New Deal". Though people regarded this as a necessary step towards economic recovery, the Supreme Court, by a majority, invalidated most of the provisions of the "New Deal" as *"Ultra-Vires"* of the Constitution. Naturally, public reaction was vehement and judges were regarded as "agents of vested interests" and champions of conservatism". Encouraged by such public support, President Roosevelt raised the Supreme Court Reorganization Bill in Congress, which sought to empower the President to appoint a new judge against each of the sitting judges who were above 70 years of age. At this time, only three judges, i.e. Owen Roberts, Benjamin Cardo-go and Fisk Stone were below 70 or so and the President was likely to find an opportunity of inducting six new judges. It was hoped that now the "New Deal" would be regarded by the Supreme Court's majority verdict as *"Intra-Vires"* of the Constitution and that the President would find an opportunity to go on with his recovery scheme. But suddenly, public opinion swung to the opposition direction. It was realized that the "New Deal" was not all conducive. If the Supreme Court was packed in this way, it would become an adjunct to the executive and, thus, democracy and rule of law would dangerously be at stake. In the face of such country-wide resentment, the U.S. Congress withdrew the bill and retained the court's original structure. It indicates that the Americans regard the judiciary's independence as the bastion of democracy and personal liberty.

But the fact remains that the judges necessarily don't represent all wisdom. To err is human and judges too are human beings. So, a verdict may be constitutionally wrong but an appeal against the verdict of High Court can be filed in the Supreme Court. Even the Supreme Court may err but its error can, under Article 137, be rectified by itself on a future occasion. In this way, it has pronounced different verdicts on the right to property in the case of *Sankari Prasad vs. Union* (1950), *Golaknath vs. Punjab* (1967), and *Keshavananda Bharati vs. Kerala* (1973) to modify its earlier stand. Therefore, instead of attacking the judiciary, it would be proper to appeal for a revision of the judgement or to wait for a change of judicial opinion. Denigration of the judiciary by political leaders is highly objectionable because it goes against the letter and spirit of the Constitution. A climate should rather be built for sustaining the dignity and independence of the judiciary. It occupies a significant and dignified position in our constitutional system. It is the cornerstone of democracy and the symbol of liberty. Therefore, its honour and dignity should be maintained and not damaged in anyway.

Some time back in April 2007, senior political elite came face to face with the higher judicial hierarchy at the annual joint convention of Chief Ministers and Chief Justices. Much notice had been taken on the exceptionally sagacious observation of the Prime Minister that all the three organs of the Indian State, i.e. the legislative, the executive and the judiciary ought to respect institutional boundaries. The then Chief Justice of India K.G. Balakrishnan demonstrated an agreeable stubbornness speaking for the judiciary, its independence and its constitutional obligation to interpret authoritatively the Constitution. Even he went a step further and suggested that if the judiciary's discharge of its functions created tension with the legislature or the executive, such tension is but natural and to some extent, it could be desirable. The statement of the Chief Justice should not be construed as a confrontation but as one with sobering effect on the judiciary-legislature-executive matrix. Unfortunately, in recent years, the public discourse has tended to see only differences between Parliament and the Supreme Court as a "confrontation". In view of the above remarks of the Chief Justice, it should now be presumed that any occasional differences will, and should, in good time get sorted out in a dignified manner. There could be no disagreement with the observation of Mr. Justice Balakrishnan's delineation of the court's power of judicial review for in any democratic political system, the citizen must feel that he or she has the ultimate protection by an independent judiciary against the state whose activities are prone to trample upon the individual's political and civil rights. But in our judicial system one important thing is missing, i.e. the jurisprudential discipline, which is being increasingly felt beyond the occasional individualistic behaviour of a judge.

It is true that "the Constitution is what the judges (higher Judiciary) say it is". But in our democratic republic, the taste of defining the Constitution is being performed by as many as 400 odd empowered men and women spread across the Apex Court and 21 High Courts each technically on a par and unanswerable to any brother judge. They are under no obligation to accept the intellectual or jurisprudential leadership of any superior judge. The result is periodic out-break of judicial way-forwardness in one or the other High Court. For example, a single judge declared that Muslims have ceased to be a minority in Uttar Pradesh. This raised explosive political issues. Of course, the order was stayed. Regrettably many failed attempts have been made by many Chief Justices of High Courts to impose some kind of behavioural discipline on brother judges. All these flaws could be attributed to process of selection of judges in the higher judiciary. It is now widely debated that the existing selection and promotion process does not necessarily favour the best and the brightest. The individual inadequacies and institutional habits cumulatively detract from ideal image of a wide and independent judiciary. But simultaneously too much criticism of the judiciary and its functioning should also be avoided otherwise, as Mr. Justice K.G. Balakrishnan pointed out and probably rightly, this could do incalculable damage to the institution of judiciary. Therefore, much of the onus lies on the judiciary itself to reclaim its glory. Delineating the contours of this responsibility, the late Chief Justice Ismail Mohomed of South Africa had said "the independence of judiciary and the legitimacy of its claim to credibility and esteem must in the last instance rest in the integrity and the judicial temper of the judges, the intellectual and emotional equipment they bring to bear upon the process of adjudication, the personal qualities of character they project and the parameters they seek to identify on the exercise of judicial power. Judicial power is prudentially no more immune from vulnerability to abuse than legislature or executive power but the difference in this is that the abuse of legislative or executive power can be policed by an independent judiciary but there is no effective constitutional mechanism to police the abuse of judiciary power. It is, therefore, crucial for all judges to remain vigilantly alive to the truth that the potentially awesome breadth of judicial power is matched by the real depth of judicial responsibility. Judicial responsibility becomes all the more onerous upon judges constitutionally protected in a state of jurisprudential solitude where there is no constructional referee to review their own wrongs."

In view of the position outlined above, the judges have to resist the temptation of getting swayed by the political partnership of the day. Some Judges do tend to render themselves vulnerable to such temptation given the selection process as also the creeping institutional arrogance. This occasional propensity to partnership, however, is easily traceable to the wider absence of jurisprudential discipline. It is good that a section of the judicial leadership has now initiated to re-think on the all-too-apparent abuse of the Public Interest Litigation (PIL) device. Rather than getting bogged down in the debate over the extent of judicial over-reach, or rather than remaining satisfied with the checking of the executive's way-wardness, it is time that those in the helm of the judiciary also gave thought to bringing about some kind of jurisprudential coherence in the pronouncements of the 400 odd higher judges in the country. But this coherence will remain excusive as long as the judiciary does not re-discover the fundamental promise made in the Constitution to the people of India, the promise of an egalitarian social and economic order. In fact, the judiciary takes its brief from a constitution framed in 1950. But the political class, especially since 1991, has redefined the purpose of the Indian state to the disadvantage of the vast majority of Indians. The judiciary has gone along with this short-changing. What is probably worse that large segments of the judicial hierarchy have come to subscribe to the new middle class instigated ideas and prejudices. Social and economic biases have come to difine the working philosophy of many of a judges. India is changing at a rapid pace and parts of this change appear to be calibrated by global forces, beyond the reach of the Indian state. Public policy-making in such a situation entails different choices, invariably pitting one section of society against the other. The judiciary finds itself embroiled in the making or unmaking of these different choices, and the nature of judicial intervention is often defined less by any pronounced jurisprudential doctrine and more by the judge's personal predilections. The reservation for Other Backward Classes (OBC) controversy and the court-driven painful sealing drive in Delhi are two prime examples of an individualistic approach. The problem is part structural as at no time is a judge (either at the time of appointment to a High Court or on elevation to the Apex Court) judged in terms of his or her philosophy or ideas. A calculation of seniority becomes the prime, if not the only, yardstick of eligibility. And since the process of selection and promotion is a closed affair, the public at large never gets to know, leave alone question, the judicial nominee's philosophy. Ability or willingness to make the executive bend at the knee seems to have become the only working or preferred philosophy.

In the current situation of our democracy, citizens will rejoice in many more institutional victories of the judiciary as long as it is willing to function as an enlightened friend of democratic India. The judiciary cannot function nor can it retain its independence or credibility in total isolation from the demands and hopes generated by democratic churning. While the judicial leadership is certainly entitled to assert its rights and autonomy, it is also obliged to work towards producing an enlightened jurisprudential philosophy. The remarks of the then Prime Minister (Man Mohan Singh) that the judiciary enjoyed enormous power and its primary obligation was to enforce the rule of law and to uphold the constitution, were clear. But his remarks that the judiciary cannot substitute its power of mandamus to take over the functions of another organ meaning the legislature and the executive, created a lot of uproar. Cautioning the judiciary against over-stepping the functions of the other organs, he said that such takeover of the functions of another organ may, at times, become a case of overreach. But the remarks of the then Chief Justice K.G. Balakrishnan were a marvelous balancing of the situation when he expressed that the perceived tension between courts, legislature and executive was natural and inevitable corollary of a healthy democracy.

Alternative Action

The exchange of views between the then Prime Minister and the Chief Justice of India represents divergent views of the executive and the judiciary on the affirmative action taken by the courts in recent times. In fact, the debate is not new. It had started ever since the Constitution came into being. There has been open confrontation on land reform laws, abolition of princely privileges, bank nationalization and other sectors. Therefore, the perceived tension is a natural and inevitable corollary of a healthy democracy as the Chief Justice of India remarked. But the more important aspect which did not get adequate attention of the critics in the Cinderella treatment meted out to the judiciary is the provision for judiciary in Central and State budgets. The country is already suffering from the neglect of health, education and land reforms over the past decades. The disaster awaiting the judicial system due to budgetary starvation is already in sight. The arrears of cases are in crores and the judge-case-ratio is abominably low. Jails are over-crowded with under-trials. According to a 2000 estimate, the expenditure on judiciary was only 0.2 per cent of the GNP as compared to 4.3 per cent in the UK. More than half of it is generated by litigation itself like court fees and fines. This revenue is not spent on the government's populist schemes. Almost every Chief Justice has lamented this state of affairs. Retired Chief Justice Y.K. Sabharwal had observed: "Most of the courts function from dingy, dilapidated and outdated structures with poor hygienic conditions even for judicial officers". Former Chief justice A.S. Anand said "Till such financial and administrative powers are vested in the judiciary, the state should not hesitate to lay more expenditure for the efficient management of the judiciary. As the position stands at present, every High Court and the judicial system itself is starved of funds. The retired incumbent K.G. Balakrishnan had also spoken of this predicament of the judiciary sometime back."

Financial Autonomy

In a consultation paper on the financial autonomy of the judiciary released by the "Commission to Review the Constitution" suggested that the judiciary must be included separately in the plan by the Planning Commission and separate allotment be made by the Planning Commission and the Finance Commission. The National Judicial Council and the State Judicial Councils and their respective administrative offices are to be established. The National Judicial Council will deal generally with the over-all needs of the judiciary. The State Judicial Councils will deal with the policy making, budget and implementation of the same. So far as the subordinate judiciary is concerned, budgets are to be prepared by the National Judicial Council or the State Judicial Council initially and should be presented to the executive and finalized at that stage by mutual and effective consultation keeping in mind that expenditure on the demands of the judiciary are no less important than other development expenditure and thereafter, the budget as finally settled, is to be presented in Parliament or the State Legislature, as the case may be. A convention is to be made that the budget estimates so finalized shall be published through the Parliament or State Legislature without the downward revision. Financial advisers from the CAG office should monitor expenditure and keep a check and take suitable action according to normal procedure in their annual reports. A convention is to be accepted that officers nominated by the Judicial Council can appear before the Public Accounts Committee. If necessary, the relevant rules made by the Speaker/Chairman of the legislatures, may be amended. Within the budget, the Judicial Council must have full freedom for re-appropriation. This should be made clear in the statute. The Registrar of the High Court need not run to the Secretariat for obtaining sanction whenever the expenditure crosses a particular amount, as is the procedure currently. The Central Government should not throw the entire burden of establishing the subordinate courts and maintaining the subordinate judiciary on the State Governments. There is a concurrent obligation on the Centre to meet the expenditure for subordinate courts. Therefore, the Planning Commission and the Finance Commission must allocate sufficient funds from national resources to meet the demands of the subordinate judiciary in each state. Regrettably, very few suggestions have been accepted or implemented in spirit. In consequence, innocents suffer and poor service conditions breed corruption. This aspect is hardly realized either by the consumers of justice or the critics of the judiciary. Now, that the Planning Commission is dissolved, the substituted mechanism should be in place.

The third issue of course, relates to expenditure. The amount which the country is spending on judiciary is one of the lowest compared to the income from court fees earned on administration of justice as observed by the Apex Court in Judge's Case. The Law Commission, in its 127th report, observed that "the state today spends precious little, or to say the least, practically nothing on the administration of justice. The First National Judicial Pay Commission, chaired by K.J. Sethy, states in its report of November 11, 1999 that the expenditure on the judiciary in India is just 0.2 per cent of the Gross National Product (GNP). The National Commission to Review the Working of the Constitution laments: "there is no exclusive grant by the Centre for court expenditure. All that we have is an insignificant centrally sponsored scheme for the courts prepared by the Planning Commission while allotting some monies for the state on population basis." While some steps have been taken in the past few years to increase spending on the judiciary and the then Prime Minister had agreed to grant Rs. 10000.00 crore to improve infrastructure, it is yet to be seen if any significant improvement takes place.

Supremacy Controversy

While bidding good-bye to the members after the Constitution was finally passed in the last sitting of India's Constituent Assembly, Chairman Rajendra Prasad said that it was the best of Constitution which the "best of minds" in the country would interpret and the "best of minds" would adjudge what was what. But it was a pity that those who would frame the law need not have to possess any educational qualification, he said. The Constitution has enfranchised the illiterate. In reply, Prime Minister Jawaharlal Nehru said that he reciprocated Rajendra Prasad's sentiments but his predicament was that when they were fighting for independence, the best of minds were on the side of the British. But the illiterate, the "teeming millions" as he put it, were on our-side and had staked everything on freedom. Therefore, how could they be denied vote in a free India when their sacrifice was due most? In the backdrop of ever-running debate between parliament and the judiciary to determine who is supreme, one is reminded of the parliament and the "the teeming millions". To think that parliament is not supreme is to betray the trust of people who return MPs. It will be a sad day when there is confrontation between the two because both are independent in their own way. The Supreme Court is supreme, viewed former Chief Justice of India Y.K. Sabharwal. But the fact remains that its supremacy ends where the supremacy of Parliament begins. Of late, the judiciary primarily the Supreme

Court, is alleged to be violating the "*Laxman Rekha*" and expanding its boundary and going beyond it. For this, the executive is partly to blame because it has become lethargic and ineffective. Therefore, in the name of judicial review, the Supreme Court is adjudging such government's measures, which are purely administrative, it is alleged. There is no doubt that the judiciary has, by and large, interpreted the Constitution to benefit the vulnerable sections of the society. At times, the executive has been rightly taken to task and the aggrieved party given relief. In cases like the *Babri Masjid*, the Supreme Court directive was just and categorical but the executive failed to comply with it. As a result, the unfortunate demolition took place. It has been noticed that in the process of reaching its judgement in certain cases, the judiciary has tended to arrogate itself the doctrine of "separation of powers" enunciated in the Constitution. It is time that the judiciary did some introspection. However superior, the "best of minds", i.e. the judges are not accountable whereas the executive is answerable to parliament, i.e. "the teeming millions". This is what Indian democratic system is all about.

There was a great deal of controversy sometime back with regard to the expansion of Ninth Schedule of the Constitution. This Schedule is a lock room available in the Constitution to stash any law that Parliament wants to insulate from judicial review. The provision mandates that none of the laws specified in the Ninth Schedule shall be deemed to be void on the ground that it was inconsistent with any of the Fundamental Rights, notwithstanding any judgement, decree or order of any court or tribunal of the country. The Constitution has a grey area, which a determined Supreme Court can use to register its primacy. In the absence of the Schedule, the confrontation between the judiciary and Parliament is inevitable. Therefore, there is lot of justification for Schedule Nine (Ninth Schedule) to stay, however faulty the Ninth Schedule is. Even though this Schedule was not in the Constitution when it was passed, it was added subsequently in the background of several cases filed in courts challenging the land reforms. It was then almost a battle between the conservative judiciary and the progressive executive. In fact, Nehru did not want the Courts to get in the way of welfare schemes like land reforms. The judiciary of course, is required to ensure that the laws framed do not violate the Constitution, but the courts cannot function as a kind of super legislature or supreme super. At times, the "*obiter dicta*" by judges give the impression that they are running down the elected representatives in the State Assembly or Parliament. This is bad in law and bad in ethics. Mr. Somanath Chatterjee, former Speaker of the Lok Sabha once rightly observed. "In the interest of harmonious functioning I believe that no one organ of the State should usurp the functions which essentially belong to another, nor should it abdicate its essential functions and thereby upset the well-cherished principles of separation of power and checks and balances provided by our Constitution."

Not long ago, the Supreme Court caused a flutter in demanding the report by a Parliamentary Standing Committee on a bail consideration. The division bench which made the demand wanted Parliament not to proceed with the bill till the Court had considered the matter. The situation was saved when the Government's own lawyer pointing out to the bench that it could not pass such an order. Even then, the additional Solicitor General had to give an assurance that "a copy of the Standing Committee's report shall be placed in a sealed cover before this Court." The judges did not realize that even if they were to make a case of Judicial review, the examination was to be after the bill had been passed, not at the stage of consideration. The independence of judiciary is essential in a democratic country. It strengthens the pillars on which the structure of democracy stands. But the judiciary should work within its limitations. It cannot give any direction to Parliament to demand any law. Nor can it intervene in any matter pending before the Speaker or the House. India's first Speaker G.V. Mavalankar always stressed that the Parliament was the supreme law-making body. For him, no one was above Parliament although he wanted an effective judiciary for a meaningful functioning of democracy. It is true that people have vested interests in maintaining and sustaining a strong and independent judiciary, but they have equal interest in keeping the role of Parliament and State Assemblies preeminent. People are sovereign and their representatives act with same confidence to articulate their problems and try to find solutions. It is another matter that politicians have degraded the role assigned to MPs and MLAs. Still the judiciary could be well advised to leave them alone.

The confrontation between the Judiciary and the Parliament in the recent past and in the remote past is not a new phenomenon. It is only the tilting of balance to varying degrees at different times.

In fact, apart from being exhibited as an apolitical institution of wisdom, the judiciary eminently remains as apolitical institution also. The social times, economic policies, clouts of various sections of society, the nature of the polity, the stability of the Central Government and a long list of unforeseen factors, in fact, impinge on judicial making. The unanimous judgement throwing open Ninth Schedule legislations to judicial scrutiny cannot be looked upon purely in terms of principles. In fact, the basic structure of the Constitution which is the basis of the said judgement, was propounded in the *Kesavananda Bharati* case as far back as 1973. The device of "creators" of the Constitution in the shape of laws passed by Parliament requiring protection from the very Constitution was put in place by the first amendment. The placing of the laws in the Ninth Schedule and keeping them out of the purview of judicial scrutiny on the ground of violation of Fundamental Rights, was introduced in 1951. For more than half a century the provision has been staring us in face. It might, therefore, be more instructive to look at the issue historically.

After Independence, the abolition of *Zamindari* system and the implementation of land reforms was the agenda of the Government. Land reform laws were passed in most of the States. Landlords challenged the validity of these Acts in courts. A number of such laws were struck down by the courts. This led to the creation of Ninth Schedule by first amendment, immunizing laws from attack on the ground of violation of Fundamental Rights. Therefore, the courts struck down as discriminatory the nationalization of banks which had been done with laudatory object of public control of national wealth. Similarly, the abolition of Privy Purses to erstwhile rulers of Princely States was held to be violative of Fundamental Rights. In fact, P. Shiv Shankar, then Law Minister, at a meeting of Bar Council of Hyderabad in 1987 stated that "*Mahadhipatis* like *Kesavananda* and *Zamindars* like *Golaknath* evoked a sympathetic cord nowhere in the whole country except in the Supreme Court of India, and the bank magnets and a whole lot of reactionaries found their haven in the Supreme Court". The Supreme Court, in an admirable display of wisdom held that this statement did not amount to contempt of court in 1988. It is noticed that there has been a disquieting shift in judicial pronouncements from the 1990s. There was a time when courts would provide relief from the harsh actions of executive. Today, demolitions of slums are being carried out on the orders of the courts with little concern for the Fundamental Right to shelter. The change in orientation is stark in the area of PILs which began as a fructification of Fundamental Rights for the poor and the exploited. In the decision to shift industry out of Delhi, the Court heard the Public Interest Litigants, the Industrialists and the government but not the workers, when right to life was directly affected. The track record of the courts in the area of civil liberties from upholding the preventive detention law in 1950 to upholding the suspension of the right to life during the emergency in 1976 speaks for itself.

At a conceptual level, there can be no quarrel with the principle that Parliament should not be allowed to enact laws violating Fundamental Rights and then protect them by putting in the Ninth Schedule. The fact remains that 90 per cent of the 284 laws in the Schedule still pertain to land reforms. Laws grossly violative of the Fundamental Rights like TADA, POTA and the AFSP Act were not put in the Schedule. They were upheld by the Supreme Court as Constitutional. It is Parliament which allowed two of these laws to lapse. This must be borne in mind while evaluating judicial scrutiny as a safeguard against laws violative of Fundamental Rights. The fact of declining authority and credibility of the legislature and executive with an increasingly activist judiciary should temper the enthusiastic welcome accorded to the judgement.

In a sufficient judgement, a nine-judge bench of the Supreme Court has held that there could not be any blanket immunity from judicial review of laws inserted in the Ninth Schedule the Constitution. Once a law is enacted and included in the Ninth Schedule, it gets protection under Article 31-B (Validation of some Acts and Regulations) and is not subject to judicial scrutiny. The nine-judge bench consisting of Chief Justice Y.K. Sabharwal, Justices Ashok Bhan, Arajit Pasayat, B.P. Singh, S.H. Kapadia, C. K. Thakker, P.K. Balasubramanya, Altamas Kabir and D.K. Jain examined the validity of inclusion of several Central and State laws including the Tamil Nadu Reservation Act providing for 69 per cent quota in jobs and in educational institution. After examining the scope and power of Parliament to enact laws and include them in the Ninth Schedule, it was held that the power of judicial review could not be taken away by putting a law under Ninth Schedule.

In its unanimous verdict the Bench, while recognising the supremacy of the court to examine the validity of inclusion of law in the Ninth Schedule, did not accept the argument that introduction of Article 31-B was just a one-time measure to protect agrarian laws after the abolition of *Zamindari* system and that it out-lived its purpose. The Bench held that the power to grant immunity at will, is not compatible with the basic structure doctrine and therefore, after April 24, 1973, the laws included in the Ninth Schedule would not have absolute immunity. The validity of such laws can be challenged on the touch-stone of basic structure such as reflected in Article 21 read with Article 14, Article 19 and Article 15 and the principles underlying these Articles. The bench also held that insertion in the Ninth Schedule is not controlled by any defined criteria or standards by which the exercise of power may be evaluated. The congruence of the insertion is that it nullifies entire Part-III (relating to Fundamental Rights) of the Constitution. The supremacy of the Constitution mandates that all Constitutional bodies are required to comply with the provision of the Constitution. It also mandates a mechanism for testing the validity of legislative acts through an independent organ, i.e. the judiciary.

Mr. M.C. Setalvad, the longest serving Attorney General of India and one of the distinguished legal luminaries of India had offered his views to say "We have in truth not the supremacy of the courts but the supremacy of the Constitution". But curiously the Apex Court observed on September 29, 2006 that "Rule of law is part of the basic structure of the Constitution. So, long as laws are there, government and the authorities have to see to it that they are implemented. If not implemented, it is for us to implement them otherwise; we will be violating the Oath." From a mandate to interpret law, the courts have redefined their role as wanting to correct aberrations and shortcomings in every walk of life. Not even animals are beyond the courts eye inasmuch as that sometime back the Apex Court passed directions on breeding of animals in the zoos. A day later, the same court felt obliged to give directions on translocating monkeys from the capital (New Delhi) region to Madhya Pradesh forests. Could M.C. Setalvad have thought this to be an over-involvement of judiciary? A concerned and sensitive judiciary is no doubt the most valuable asset of any democratic system. The Indian judiciary has indisputably deepened the rule of law arrangement. This contribution becomes more critical when we remember that respect for law, its restraint and obligation does not come easily either to the ruler or the ruled in a traditional society like ours. The rich and the powerful believe they have the licence to get away with defying the letter and the spirit of rule of law. The poor and the vulnerable seem to believe that injustice is their lot. The Supreme Court and the High Courts in India can justifiably take credit for having hammered the ideas of restraints to poor and authority into the minds of those who claim to represent "the people". In the post-1991 era of economic reforms, the newly empowered middle classes have applauded the judiciary as it questioned the political leadership's legitimacy as the sole representative of the popular will. As the polity has become more and more fractious, judges have been inclined to practice Setalvad's disapprovingly "supremacy of judiciary".

In the dispute over reservation for the Other Backward Classes, the Cupreme Court almost came closer to passing an order that Parliament would not take any decision until the bench examined the matter as explained earlier. Unless our polity and all its branches and official including all judiciary find the wisdom to reverse the trend, the rule of law or rather the Constitution will be in danger of being supplanted by the rule of judges. The recent years have become eventful years for the Supreme Court in having passed orders almost on every facet of day-to-day life. Some of the judicial interventions in very important cases like the Bihar Assembly dissolution, sealing operations in the National Capital, notice to the office of the Speaker on expulsion of ten Lok Sabha members evoked strong reaction from the executive and politicians. A flash point was reached in the forest matter when the Central Government said "the Supreme Court should not think it is the only institution that is protecting the environment as the Centre too has a responsibility. Mr. Justice Sabharwal refuted the criticism saying judicial activism was not new to India. The judiciary intervened only when the executive or the legislature failed the confidence reposed in it." Similarly, the Andhra Pradesh Government suffered a setback after the Apex Court refused to stay the operation of a full bench judgement of the High Court striking down legislation providing five per cent quota for Muslims in public appointment and admission to educational institutions. In the matter of reservation, the Court held that the "creamy layer" among the Scheduled Castes and the Scheduled Tribes must be excluded from the purview of reservation in the public employment and promotions and that the total reservation in public employment and promotions and the total reservation for the SCs and STs and Other Backward Classes, must not exceed 50 per cent. In the dissolution of Bihar Assembly case, the Court pulled up Bihar Governor Buta Singh for recommending dissolution of the Assembly. In the matter of student's issue, the Court constituted a high-powered committee headed by R.K. Raghavan, former Director of CBI to look into ragging and suggest remedial measures. The Court also gave its nod for implementing the suggestions given by J.M. Lyngdoh Committee on the conduct of Union election in universities and affiliated colleges. In the controversy case in the Mullaperiyar dam, the Court asked Kerala to raise the water level of the dam from 136 to 142ft. In *the Taj Corridor case,* the Court set aside a CBI status report for closing the case against the former UP Chief Minister Mayawati in the Rs. 175 crore scam. In a case of far-reaching consequences, the Court held that no prior sanction from the competent authority was required to prosecute a public servant including present and former Ministers in corruption cases. In a series of directions, the Court ordered the Centre and the States to implement sweeping reforms to ensure complete autonomy of the police administration.

Transparency and Accountability

Justice V.R. Krishna Ayer, in one of his articles published in *"The Hindu"* clearly and confidently asserted that judges are public servants and not bosses. Contrary to what the Chief Justice of the Supreme Court said about the Chief Justice as not a public servant but a Constitutional authority, Justice Krishna Ayer said that public justice is public service and therefore, judges are public servants. It may be true that Chief Justice is not a public servant but a Constitutional authority but every judge is oath-bound to dispense public justice, without fear or favour, affection or ill-will. Therefore, the Right to Information Act does cover Constitutional authorities. It may be that judges are categorised as a higher category of public functionaries or a nobler group of public servants democratically more accountable and qualitatively more liable than others to furnish information to the people about themselves and their functions if it is relevant to the public interest. Similarly, all important Constitutional authorities like the Judges, Ministers, the CAG, the EC and the Speaker of the Legislature are *fortiori* public servants with superior and more profound obligations but these are not two antithetical categories. In fact, one of the great judges Jerome Frank in his book *"Courts on Trial"* had said that he had little patience with or respect for, the view that it is dangerous to tell the public unpalatable truths about the judiciary. He wrote "I am unable to conceive that in a democracy, it can never be unwise to acquaint the public with the truth about the working of any branch of government. It is wholly undemocratic to treat the public as children who are unable to accept the inescapable shortcomings of man-made institutions. The best way to bring about the elimination of those shortcomings of our judicial systems which are capable of being eliminated is to have all our citizens informed as to how that system now functions. It is a mistake, therefore, to try establish and maintain through ignorance, public esteem for our courts."

The judiciary should function as a democratic instrumentality but not as an occult class of divinity. To quote David Pannick "we need judges who are trained for the job, whose conduct can be freely criticized and could be subject to investigation by a Judicial Performance Commissions, judges who abandon wigs, gowns and unnecessary linguistic legalisms, judges who welcome rather than shun publicity for their activities. Information about Judge wealth, other activities and even private doings if they affect judicial duties, cannot be kept secret." To cite David Pannick again "The judiciary is not the least dangerous bench of government. They send people to prison and decide the scope and application of all manner of rights and duties with important consequences for individual and for society. Because the judiciary has such a Central role in the government of society, we should, (in the words of Justice Oliver Wendell Holmes) wash with clinical acid this aspect of public life. Unless and until we treat judges as fallible human beings whose official conduct is subject to same critical analysis as that of other organs of government, judges will remain members of a priesthood who have great powers over the rest of community, but who are otherwise isolated from them and misunderstood by them to their actual advantage." In fact Judges like Ministers, Governors, Presidents, Speakers and host of other functionaries are Constitutional Authorities. Most emphatically they are public servants and not absolute bosses with vast political power but above democratic accountability. Therefore, they should have functional transparency and be fundamentally incorruptible. Judges must be free from graft, nepotism, abuse of power and arrogance. They should be paradigm of clean personal life, open and accessible custodians of public justice and paragon of moral excellence and humanist simplicity. They are supposed to be of a higher cadre with a more sublime calibre.

The Supreme Court, in a ruling of the constitution bench in K. *Veeraswami vs. Union of India* (1991 SCC P-655) held that the expression "Public Servant" used in the Prevention of Corruption Act, is undoubtedly wide enough to denote that every judge including judges of the High Court and the Supreme Court are under the law, not above it. Judge's public and even private life to the extent it influences and their judicial role should be accountable and transparent to the public. Democracy becomes a disaster if the President, the Speaker, the Prime Minister and the Chief Justice hide their wealth and dealings from the scrutiny of the people who are sovereign. Indian judiciary should, therefore, accept the observation of US Justice Frankfurter that "judges as persons are courts, as institutions are entitled to no greater immunity from criticism than other persons or institutions. Just because the holders of Judicial Office are identified with the interests of justice, they forget their common human frailties and fallibilities. There have sometimes been martinets upon the bench as there have also been pompous wielders of authority who have used the paraphernalia of power in support of what they called their dignity. Therefore, judges must be kept mindful of their limitations and of their ultimate public responsibility by a vigorous stream of criticism expressed with candor however blunt." In this background, our judges should realize that our republic is essentially socialist, secular and democratic. Therefore, what is needed is a Judicial Appointments and Performance Commission of supreme stature, its members selected from amongst the highest judicial, political and public-spirited wonders of popular confidence.

Judicial Accountability Bill

Some time back eminent citizens from various walks of life appealed to the then Chief Justice of India G.K. Balakrishnan and judges of Supreme Court and High Courts to voluntarily disclose their assets to advance the cause of transparency and probity in public life. The appeal invited reference to 1997 Code of Conduct (Re-statement of Judicial Values) in which the Supreme Court decided that each judge would declare his/her assets in confidence to the CJI. This was also reiterated in 1999. These resolutions were adopted in the light of growing public perception that there was lack of accountability of the higher judiciary. This was in line with the requirement of declaration of assets by all civil servants to the government. The rationale given by the Supreme Court for the need for disclosure of assets of candidates contesting election would equally apply to all public servants occupying crucial positions of authority. Although information on the voluntary disclosure of assets by judges could now be available through RTI, it would greatly advance the cause of transparency and probity in public life if the judges publicly declare their assets. Such a view was also expressed by eminent former judges and Chief Justices of the Supreme Court including Justice Krishna Iyer and Justice J.S. Verma.

Plea Bargaining

Plea bargaining is another attempt intended to bring reform in the judicial systems. Even as the legal system in the country is in a desperate need for reforms, the response to such initiative among the stakeholders has not been encouraging and forthcoming. The response of bars' has been particularly lukewarm. The justice delivery system in the country still had to bank on the 200 year old statutes like the IPC and CrPC formulated by the British rulers. These have become obsolete and need to be changed to suit contemporary requirements. Therefore, the bench and the bar have to come together to ensure a smooth make over. Plea-bargaining was a small step towards improving the justice system and help ease the pendency. To make it a success, members of the legal fraternity would have to shoulder the responsibility. In fact, a plea bargain is an agreement in which a prosecutor and defendant arrange to settle the case against the former. Under this system, an accused in a criminal case will be able to plead guilty in exchange for a reduced sentence. As more than 2.80 Crore backlog cases are pending in the country which would take years together to arrive at conclusion, plea bargaining could be effective in speeding up cases. But there is a lack of awareness on this method. In fact, if properly adopted and implemented, maximum number of UTP cases in petty offences can be resolved by this system. Now, that jails are being overcrowded by under-trial prisoners arrested for petty offences, plea bargaining can be put to fruitful use in deciding such cases and thereby lessening pendency as well as improving jail administration.

Corruption

The allegation of high irregularities branded as corrupt practices committed by Justice Ramaswamy some years ago leading to an impeachment motion moved in Parliament against him and the Ghaziabad "Provident Fund Scam" where Rs. 15 lakh was being sent by a law officer to a sitting judge of the Punjab and Haryana High Court allegedly meant for another women judge and some other cases of fraud and corruption in higher judiciary have come to notice in recent years. Justice Soumitra Sen, a serving judge of the Calcutta High Court was identified by the Chief Justice of India as a fit case for impeachment. A few years ago, Justice Shamit Mukherjee of the Delhi High Court was accidentally discovered to be indulging in dubious transactions when phones of other officials were under surveillance by the police. Thus, the reputation of the higher judiciary was at the low ebb at a particular point of time. Unless vigorous in-house action is taken by the judiciary to repair the damage, public opinion may call for legislative intervention by Parliament. Therefore, a legislative mechanism has to be properly framed. The present system of appointment requires radical restructuring. The final ward in appointments can never be safely entrusted to fractious Coalition Governments which are weak on governance, soft on terrorism and high on corruption. Each Coalition partner will demand its quota in the highest judiciary as well as the High Courts, on occasions threatening withdrawal of support. Therefore, in the effort to criticise the present system of selection through collegiums, let not the silver be stolen. The way forward should be for a transparent, accountable, open and merit-based system of judiciary in the country. The recent cases of corruption levelled against two judges of Andhra Pradesh in the mine scam some time back allegedly accepting bribe from mining barrons have brought direct and glaring discredit to the Judiciary.

The Supreme Court passed devastating strictures against some of the judges of Allahabad High Court some time back which speaks of the dangerous decline of image and credibility of the judiciary. Even Supreme Court Judges are allegedly tainted. Eight former Chief Justices of India were facing corruption charges in court cases as alleged by a very senior advocate of Supreme Court. Not only judges have been discovered to be corrupt, court judgements too often are reportedly bizarre and sometimes irrational. All these make the most damaging dent on India's judicial system. The human quality of judges appears to be wanting. Therefore, reformatory measures are essential. As a measure of reform it has been pleaded that the judiciary must be insulated from the political class. To achieve this, it was suggested that a judicial commission comprising retired judges and legal luminaries should be constituted to decide the appointment, promotion, demotion and transfer of judges. Judges must be freed from the power of Cabinet. The Judicial Commission must be made accountable to the President of India as was the Election Commission during the tenure of Mr. T.N. Seshan as the Chief Election Commissioner. The judges must be given special moral support as being enjoyed by Priests. Judges should be role models in the democratic set-up for which they need to be given specialized training imparted by recognized training institutions and should be put to a test before qualifying for life-long judicial service. They should not be allowed from entering any other service, business or employment after retirement. It has been suggested to raise the age of retirement to 70 years and the decision to retire them before this age should be left to the discretion of the Judicial Commission.

Structural Deficiencies

There are three main structural deficiencies in our judicial administration : (i) Lack of co-operation between the multi-power centres in appointments to the higher judiciary; (ii) A pathetically low population-to-judge ratio; and (iii) Abysmally low spending on the judiciary. The first issue could be examined in the context of former President K.R. Narayanan's reference in 1998 to the

Supreme Court after the Union Government returned recommendations sent by the former Chief Justice of India M.M. Punchhi with respect to certain appointments of judges to the Supreme Court for reconsideration. At this time, the government resorted to the Presidential reference to the Supreme Court. The Union Government agreed to accept and treat as binding the Court's answers to the questions set out in the reference. In this case, while answering the reference, the Apex Court held that "consultation with the Chief Justice of India" in Articles 217(1) and 222(1) of the Constitution required consultation with the collegium of judges in the Supreme Court. The collegium should consist of the CJI and the four senior most puisne judges. With reference to appointment of judges to High Courts the Apex Court held that the Chief Justice of High Court in consultation with two senior most puisne judges of the High Court should recommend persons to be appointed to the High Court. On receipt of such recommendation, the Chief Justice of Supreme Court would, in turn, consult two senior most puisne judges of the Supreme Court while confirming the recommendation. Further the CJI would consult and elicit the views of the senior most judge in the Supreme Court who has come from the court to which a prospective candidate belonged. The Apex Court sought to ensure transparency in the consultation process by insisting that the opinion of all members of the collegium in respect of each recommendation should be given in writing. The CJI must convey these opinions along with his recommendation to the government. The answer to the nine questions posed in the Presidential reference has set the broad framework within which appointment of judges to the Supreme Court and the High Courts and also the transfer of judges should be effected. While the above scheme appears comprehensive to cover issues relating to appointment of judges, particularly High Court judges, one aspect that has contributed to delay in finalizing appointments is the issue of lack of prompt response by the government on the recommendations. Although, it is expected that government will act with speed and dispatch in such matters, such expectation does not materialize expeditiously normally. To eliminate such unnecessary delays, it was suggested to consider introducing deeming provision that if the government does not respond within a fixed period, it will be deemed that it has no objection to the names suggested by the

Supreme Court. If the government is in the process of investigating any aspect of the proposed candidate's merit or credibility, it may seek extension of time but all these should be done in a stipulated time-frame. In the current system, it is possible for the government to take unlimited time to verify the credentials of the candidates but retention of such files/proposals will seriously undermine judicial independence.

The second issue relates to the inadequate population-to-judge ratio. Professor Wolfgang Koehling of the University of Bonn, in one of his interesting studies of the Indian Legal System published under the title *"The Economic Consequences of a Weak Judiciary: Insights from India"* has tried to establish an empirical relationship between the quality of Indian judiciary and the economic development of Indian States. In his study, he points out that a judiciary that is weakly staffed and inadequately funded, as in India, will inevitably lead to, (a) a lower per capita income, (b) higher poverty rates, (c) lower private economic activity, (d) poorer public infrastructure, and (e) higher crime rates and more riots. The 120th Law Commission report recommends a five-fold increase in judicial strength at all levels. Comparing India's population to judge ratio with other countries, it points out that it is one of the lowest in India. While the United States and the United Kingdom have about 100 to 150 judges per million population, India has a mere 10.5 judges per million population. While legislative representation and adequacy of staff in other civil services, in the police etc. are planned on the basis of population, the same norm is not applied while sanctioning judicial strength, the report points-out. When it comes to appointment of judges, the government wants to apply the number-of-cases-filed to the number-of-judges ratio. This is unfortunately not an equitable norm to apply. It is unfair to say that sanctioning of judicial posts will depend on the number of cases filed. It is, therefore, imperative that Law Commission's recommendation to increase the strength of judges in the country at least 50 per million population sounds reasonable to start with.

Political Nexus

In India, our system is peculiar as compared to American system of judicial arrangement. We hardly know of our judges, their background details whereas in America, the citizen has the satisfaction of knowing the men and women on the bench before they retreat to becoming anonymity after confirmation. No one has ever argued that American democracy stands diminished or the American citizen's faith in the judicial system gets shaken by knowledge about a judge's thought process. By contrast, we know so little about our judicial benefactors that anyone who can purchase a copy of the judges list can find-out who will be the Chief Justice of India on a probable specific date. In American system, whereas a person is appointed and continues as a judge for life or till he chooses to announce his retirement, in Indian system the position is different. Judge John Roberts appointed sometime back as Chief Justice of America will continue for life or till he resigns. The Chief Justice William Rehnquist presided over the American Supreme Court for 18 years till his death. As a sad contrast, in India, we have had Chief Justices with tenures ending in just over three weeks, sometimes in a few months rather than long judicial innings of years and years. In the second judge's case, adoption of the principle of seniority gives us a Chief Justice almost every other year, if not more often. It is not that pronouncements of our judges are no less consequential nor our judiciary any less autonomous, independent or powerful than the American courts but unlike the American courts, the Indian judiciary has been arrogating to itself the right to monitor the morals and manners of political class. Unfortunately, this monitoring now tends to produce consequences that belong to the politician's domain. We maintain that judges are above politics. But this façade began cracking up in the post-Nehru era. The first crack appeared when a sitting Chief Justice of India (K. Subba Rao) allowed himself to become the opposition's presidential candidate against Dr. Zakir Hussain in May 1967. To quote Mr. M.C. Setalvad, no sitting judge had ever committed such a "grave impropriety" nonetheless, the evidence suggests existence of private ties of political congruence. Otherwise, we would have not had retired judges getting elected Members of Parliament from party quotas, or accepting gubernatorial assignment. Even a retired Chief Justice of Supreme Court (Justice Ranganath Mishra) was elected to Rajya Sabha on party ticket. In consequence, the present situation is that there are any number of post-retirement appointments the government of the day can dangle before the judiciary fraternity. Those who preside over the higher courts are deemed *ipso facto* to have the temperament, expertise and rectitude developed over decades that somehow insulate judges from the temptation of political partnership. However, if soon after leaving the bench so many judges are willing to break bread with the political crowd, can it be presumed that all of them are totally devoid of political predilections and prejudices? Curiously enough in our political discourse, the politician is invariably blamed for wanting to suborn judicial integrity, as if the judge concerned is not making a choice. In 1967, Justice Subbha Rao clearly made an ideological-*cum*-political choice. He was approached by the Swatantra Party's Minoo Masani and others only because few months earlier, on February 27, 1967, he had given a judgement (in *I.C. Golak Nath vs. State of Punjab*) that was hailed by the forces of the right in India. Political circles were agog with speculation whether or not, the electoral process in Bihar will be rolled back, even after the Election Commission, under Article 324, had notified an election schedule before the elections (2005). Beyond Bihar, there is the larger question whether or not, the judiciary is allowing itself to be dragged into the political arena by this or that section of the political crowd. The last known straw that struck Camel's neck was the gubernatorial assignment gladly accepted by former CJI Sathasivam as Governor of Kerala State.

Public Interest Litigation (PIL)

Politicians have cunningly spotted this judicial inclination wanting to clean our system. Public interest litigation was a creative innovation. It was meant to provide relief to the hapless citizen against an insensitive state. It has now become a tactical tool available to any politician or party that has lost a battle in the political arena. Many High Courts have even got embroiled in matters that belong to the executive domain which can be well-understood. But now this judicial foray into the political arena has induced another institutional weakness, i.e. the temptation to play to the gallery which would not, in fact, be bad if the 'gallery' were a level playing mechanism. Media attention or applause in an unequal society like ours ought to be inherently suspect. The media in India are at-best an unreliable guide to public opinion and at times an unworthy custodian of public interest. The media are prone to lap up "oral observations" as abiding and binding judicial pronouncements, especially those directed against politicians and governments. These "oral observations" have no legal sanctity nor are they reflected in any court record. Yet, these invariably cause embarrassment or consequences for this or that section of the political class. At one time, a judge has shown an awareness of the scope for misunderstanding of his "oral observation" when justice S.N. Variava issued a clarification about an observation of his (March 15, 2005) that suggested that someone had sought (unfairly) to transfer a trial judge in the fodder scam case. Otherwise, the observations produce screaming headlines for their hit-and-run spicy flavour and become part of political propaganda for or against this or that leader or party. There is another danger. The media discourse tends to be dominated by middle class professionals who are in the thrall of middle class values and interests. Nothing would be more tragic than any constitutional institution to be swayed by media coverage as a true reflector of the public interest. When it comes to political reporting, the media have very suspect credentials in terms of objectivity or fairness.

The essence of the democratic spirit enjoins the political leadership to act responsibly and reasonably. Democracy insists that power be exercised without becoming restraint. By increasingly making itself available and ready to correct the alleged wrong doing of political leaders, judicial intervention has the effect of absolving the political class of the obligation of responsible behaviour and wise conduct. The judiciary should, therefore, arbitrate on Constitutional and legal issues and not settle political disputes. Judicial rebukes for politicians and governments cumulatively lower public esteem for the elected executive and unkind observations about Constitutional functionaries do not strengthen the democratic institutional edifices that include a genuinely independent judiciary.

The Chief Justice of India has stated that there are about 27 million cases pending in courts. This is an alarming situation. After all what the society expects from lawyers and judges? What happens to the long-neglected plight of litigants in such situations? Some years ago, the Chief Justice of America Warren Burger, in one of his hard-hitting speeches to the American Bar Association told the audience that the entire legal profession-lawyers, judges and law teachers—had become so mesmerized with the stimulation of the court room contest that they tended to forget that they ought to be "healers of conflicts". The doctors, in spite of astronomical costs, still retain a high degree of public confidence because they are perceived as healers. Should lawyers not be healers? He asked rhetorically. In this backdrop, in a developing society, to cater to the needs of the unprivileged as well as the privileged few, all judges, lawyers in our country need to cultivate the healing touch. For this, those in legal profession possessing such attributes need to convince the public by action that they are not only disposers of disputation inside courts only but resolvers of conflicts outside the courts as well. After all, "litigation is an activity that has not markedly contributed to the happiness of mankind" as has been said by an old judge. Therefore, courts must strive to be litigant-friendly which, in practice, they are not.

Most of the courts in our country are like public hospitals where people come and go with much trepidation because they have to do that. The court-rooms are generally dirty, unkempt and there are any facilities such as adequate waiting rooms for parties, witnesses and those who need to have recourse to court services. Speedy disposal of cases, which we all glibly talk about, is more easily said than done, simply because adjudication is a very complex and time-consuming task. The least, then, the litigants are entitled to expect is that their cases get decided ultimately in God's good time with as little personal inconvenience as possible. Today, regrettably, court houses are badly built, hopelessly located, and have very few amenities for those who frequent them. Courts appear to operate in a world of their own, without apparent regard to the needs of the litigating public. Each court issues from day to-day its own long-very long-case-list. The judge is only able to go through a few cases in the list but litigants and witnesses must attend and wait on every single date. The case which cannot be taken up are then adjourned to a date several months in the future when litigants and witnesses must again assemble. At this time too, more often than not, the case does not reach and has to be again put off. The vicious circle of adjournments gets even more oppressive when senior lawyers are involved. As was recalled by President Zail Singh at a law conference held in Mumbai some years ago "*Bade bade vakil ki lambi tarikh padti hai*". The admonition was meant first for judges who accommodated senior lawyers by granting them longer dates and secondly, for senior lawyers who neglected the cases of their too numerous clients. There is no syndicated programme of caseload management in courts, even after the introduction of sophisticated IT technique. Therefore, there must be a better system of court management for handling 27 million pending cases. The presiding judge of every court must spend some thought and time as was done by a former Chief Justice of Bombay, High Court in devising ways and means to ensure a more litigant-friendly atmosphere in court premises. We already have a very efficient legal services authority functioning under a statute designed to promote legal literacy; but the convenience of unfortunate litigants is not on its list of priorities. The principal participant in the legal process is simply not treated.

Interest in Cases—Recuse Plea

The question as to when a judge who has either a pecuniary interest in the litigation or non-pecuniary interest in the litigation or non-pecuniary connection with a party to the litigation should recuse himself from a case has been raised and debated. Many of the judges before entering into the judicial service have had several interests in share investments, in companies, corporates and other organizations. In all such cases, what moral principle could be laid-down? The decision to recuse from the case is left to the wisdom and sagacity of the concerned Judge/Judges. In one case, Justice S.H. Kapadia sitting on a bench of three judges having disclosed his interest as a shareholder in Sterlite Industries, a party before the proceeding, heard the case and delivered judgement. In case of Justice Raveendran hearing the *Reliance Company case* at the very outset disclosed that he holds share, in both the companies, and upon both parties, expressing no objection, proceeded to hear the case with other judge. After six days of hearing, Justice Raveendran recused himself from the case as had discovered that his daughter was a lawyer in a firm which was doing legal work not connected with litigation before him but for one of the Reliance companies. In another part-heard case, Justice M. Katju recused himself as his wife held share in a company which was a litigation case before the bench. Justice Kapadia recused himself from a case in which Sterilite industries, a sister concern of Vedant industries was an applicant in the Court.

The basic principle of judicial conduct is that a judge should not have an interest in the litigation before him which could give rise to an apprehension of his deciding a matter in favour of one of the parties. It has been almost a hoary rule of judicial propriety that even the smallest pecuniary interest will disqualify a judge automatically. This rule is mostly applicable in cases where judges own shares in companies who are parties before him. Such a rule was reportedly laid down in a celebrated case in 1952 in the House of Lords where the court held that Lord Chancellor Lord Cottonenham ought not a have decided a case in which he held the shares of a company which was a litigant before him. If this rule is applied in the present day situation, a large number of judges are likely to be disqualified causing considerable disruption of judicial work. Therefore, the question arises should a judge recuse himself from a case even if his or his spouse's share holding is minimal or his judgement would have a remote or no effect on the company? The answer could be that in all fairenes, "justice should not only be done but seen to be done." Where the judges interest is not pecuniary, there should be no automatic disqualification. In this connection, the instance of statement of Recusal Policy of US could be cited. In 1993, the statement of Judges of US were recorded as follows, "we do not think it would serve the public interest to recuse ourselves, out of an excess of caution, whenever a relative is a partner in the firm before us or acted as a lawyer at an earlier stage." In another instance, Justice Anotin Scalia of the US Supreme Court in 2003 firmly declined to recuse himself even when one of the parties objected to his taking a case in which Vice-President Dick Cheny with whom he had gone on a duck-hunting holiday. Justice Scalia dismissed the objection stating "since I do not believe my impartiality can reasonably be questioned, I do not think it would be proper for me to recues....". As compared to this, Justice Raveendran's case is of exceptionally high standard of moral justice which prompted him to recue himself from high profiled *Reliance case*.

References

D.D. Basu—*Indian Constitution*.
Harold Laski—*British Constitution*.
Judicial Appointment Commission Bill, 2013.
Law Commission, *Reports on Judicial Reform*.
N. Vankatachallah Commission to Review Working of the Constitution.

5
Police Reforms

Introduction

The Police is the foundation of any country's socio-economic polity. Its functions are based on the willing acceptance of people. Unfortunately, over the periods of history, it has been loosing its faith in discharging its duties and functions in accordance with the laws framed. Therefore, people doubt the *bona fides* of police in fulfilling the aspirations of common aggregated interests of the community. The problems of criminal justice administration in India are compounded by the country's vastness, lack of homogeneity of people and accumulated dissatisfaction with the policies and programmes and their implementation. Maintenance of public order and the rule of law is the key function of any sovereign state that would defend the nation from external aggression or maintain unity and integrity of the state. Dicey defined rule of law as the absolute supremacy and pre-dominance of regular law as opposed to the influence of arbitrary powers. There can be no peace and tranquility without enforcement of law. It is said that "wherever law ends, tyranny begins" (John Locke). Therefore, police have always been recognized as the vital arm of the state. In ancient kingdoms, maintenance of public tranquility even through the use of armed police force was the duty of the state.

India inherited a transitional police structure created and established by the British Raj in the mid nineteenth century with the main aim of keeping the Indian natives under control. This structure never preferred to provide services to the community. The present police system is broadly based on the antiquated law of

1861. The first Police Commission (Fraser Commission) was constituted in 1902-03. This Commission made several recommendations based on which certain new wings of Police administration like the CID came into being, but there was no change in the basic structure and framework of law. The Police Act of 1861 was legislated by the British after the Indian Mutiny of 1857 imposing a police force upon their subjects (Indians) which could be used solely to consolidate and perpetuate their rule. Even the 1902-03 Police Commission found the "Police Force" throughout the country in a most unsatisfactory condition inasmuch as that the abuses were common everywhere causing great injury to the people and bringing discredit to the government. These factors, therefore, called for radical reforms in police. Several committees and commissions although strongly recommended for major changes, the political executive and even to some extent, the bureaucracy continued to retain their stronghold on the police. The Police Act of 1861 and some other State Acts framed later modelled on the 1861 Act, vested powers on the Superintendent of Police (SP) directly but subject to control of the political executive ultimately. The colonial Police Act required the police to detect, apprehend and prosecute offenders, collect intelligence, maintain traffic, control disorders and finally obey lawful orders of various authorities. It was known very clearly that the police organization was not meant to serve the people of India but principally to maintain the authority of the Crown and to protect the British interests. But virtually the police remained to be a valid agency of governance. As such, the role of police did not take into account or envisioned the community's expectations like helping persons in distress, resolving conflicts and creating a sense of security. The emphasis on carrying out orders of authorities virtually resulted the Police to be seen as an appendage to those in power who, in turn, expected their orders to be carried out. Even though the police was seen to be using the "Bullet" and the "*Lathi*" throughout the freedom struggle. Sardar Patel held the view that if the police could serve the British efficiently and effectively, why should they not be expected to serve more efficiently and effectively, with greater sense of dedication to their own country? The expectation of Sardar Patel is yet to be achieved even after more than half a century of our independence.

The National Police Commission (second) (1977-81) set-up to suggest measures on police reforms made several recommendations including a Model Police Act to replace the outdated Police Act, 1861. It was mandated to suggest measures to improve the professional efficiency of Police and ensure its accountability to the people and the law. The Commission observed that "increasing violence is seen as the most disturbing feature of the contemporary law and order situation in the country. News papers frequently report details of violent incidents involving large groups of agitators who clash with the police while articulating some issues of discontent and frustration. Police actions to restore order in such a situation frequently involve use of force including fire-arms and some occasions, which, in turn, draw adverse public reaction and escalates tensions and hostility between the public and the law enforcement agency." Lack of effective accountability mechanism and periodic performance review has been causing loss of public confidence in the police. Widespread indiscipline, contempt for law and procedures and naked corruption have weakened faith in the police institution. It has been alleged that police brutality is unchecked. Incidentally, India has not ratified the UN Convention against torture and other cruel, inhuman or degrading treatment or punishment after signing it on October 14, 1997. Nothing has been done to replace the law framed over a century ago (1861) by a structure which should be compatible with our democratic framework, our plural society, multi-religious, multi-casteist, multi-lingual, multi-cultural communities and societies. The National Police Commission deliberated over this and other important issues which included responsibility of states, mode of selection of police chiefs, establishment of State Security Commission and replacement of the archaic Police Act, 1861. Sections 3 and 4 of the Police Act, in fact, define police accountability. These sections lay down that the Superintendent of Police rests with the State Governments and its administration with the DGP. At the district level, it vests with the Superintendent of Police subject to the overall control and direction of the District Magistrate. Although the Act itself does not define the degree of Superintendence or directional control which the State Government or the District Magistrate shall exercise, but these functions have been utilized by the executive over a period of years to establish some kind of a complete control over the police. The Fraser Commission (1902-03) had also recorded that successive governments have wrongly interpreted these sections to carry out "a degree of interference which the law did not contemplate and which has been prejudicial to the interests of the police establishment." But nothing happened on this and the trend continued till the dawn of Independence. Even after Independence, successive governments found the continuing system convenient to them in serving their political interests and partisan objectives.

The National Police Commission made several recommendations in almost eight volumes but nothing of the sort was done to reform the police administration. Both the National Commission and the Shah Commission above everything, sounded a note of warning for the unfettered use of police by successive governments to their convenience and to serve political interests and partisan objectives. In actual practice, the Police is accountable to the political authority at the first place. It is also accountable to the civil service in the second place and to the laws of the land and the judiciary thereafter and then to their own organization and lastly to the people although it should have been the reverse. The National Police Commission deliberated over these and many other issues. Peculiarly, while almost all states uniformly responded that "Police and Public Order" are state subjects and it was not the business of Central Home Ministry to interfere in this domain, it remained a fact that the evolution of a systematic change in police administration and involvement of society in it, could not be guaranteed. As to how to generate political will or compulsion still remains a problem. That the police is crucial, vital and most important element of our entire criminal justice system should be undisputed. But the question of autonomy and accountability requires to be viewed not only in terms of the singular role of the police but all other elements which, along with the police, comprise the entire criminal justice system. Due to inherent failures of various elements which are required to support the functioning of the police including all civil services, the entire political executive, the investing system and the judiciary framework, the police system has not been adorned by various groups in the society. As such, people seem to have lost the trust in the police so also the intelligentsia. Several ills have plagued the functioning of police cadre starting from initial recruitments, punishments, trainings, appointments, promotions and lack of accountability which has emerged because of continuous politicization. Therefore, much of the maladies in the system could be removed through an effective and efficient political and administrative management.

The National Police Commission had clearly and categorically said that the police should be accountable at the first place to the people, then to the law of the land and thirdly to the organization. Although the Commission did not figure the political authority and the civil service anywhere in its report, it was very clear from some of the instances like the Muzaffar Nagar, the Ayodhya incident (1992), the Hindu Sikh Riots in Delhi, 1984. The Commission among other things, had recommended for setting up of a "State Security Commission" consisting of a panel of three names with the Chief Minister given the option of selecting one of the three and insulating the investigative machinery from the law and order functions and to have a new Police Act which would reflect the values, democratic aspirations of the people which will make the police accountable to the laws of the land. While there have been suggestions that police should earn the confidence of people, the public also have peculiar perceptions about police functions. The functions of modern police is not confined to mere maintenance of law and order in society but is expected to perform even duties of election and expected to render multifarious services to the people even though people still carry the usual distrust and non-confidence against the police. This is a peculiar development in police administration *vis-à-vis* the public. The public expect that the police station should not be a mere law and order or crime detection or prevention agency, it should be a public grievance redressal machinery for all aliments of the society.

The National Police Commission (1977-81) also recommended that police role should be re-defined in order to include participation in legal proceedings, identifying in advance, brewing problems and situations and making attempts to resolve them, take preventive measures and aid other government agencies, helping and counselling individuals in distress, facilitate orderly movement of people and vehicles, resolve conflicts and promote amity and play other social roles expected by the community. As such, there was need to remodel and redefine the role of police and make colateral provisions to achieve these ideals. Although outwardly the police appear to be a monolithic organization, it is beset with controls exercised by numerous authorities at various levels. Added to these, is the problem of extraneous pressure often described as "an overdose of petty interference". Both the 1902-03 as well the 1977-81 Police Commissions felt that executive have expanded their powers over police far in excess of what had been contemplated in the 1861 Act. After separation of judiciary from the executive, the problems of police have been compounded inasmuch as that authorities expect their wishes to be carried out even though every action of police is ultimately subjected to judicial scrutiny. The Commission also examined the role of elected State Governments with regard to superintendence over the police on the one hand and above realities on the other and came out with the concept of "State Security Commission" to be chaired by the Chief Minister and composed of others like one MLA from each of the ruling parties and opposition, a retired bureaucrat and judge, one academician with the DGP as its secretary. The "Security Commission" was to exercise control over the police in regard to "preventative and service-oriented functions". The Commission was expected to follow a rigorous process of selection of the "Police Chief" who would have a statutory tenure and to take care of the responsibility of the elected government and free the organization from extraneous influences with a view to restore the command structure of the police which had been described as "totally disputed if not destroyed" in the words of the then Home Minister late Indrajit Gupta.

The National Police Commission observed that "increasing violence is seen as the most disturbing feature of the contemporary law and order situation in the country. Newspapers frequently report details of violent incidents involving large groups of agitators who clash with the police while articulating some issues of discontent and frustration. Police action to restore order in such sites frequently involves the use of force including firearms on some occasions which, in turn, draws adverse public reaction and escalates tension and hostility between the public and the law enforcement agency." These observations seem to be matters of reality in a more accelerated pace in the present day situation when law and order assumes greater priority and attention in governance.

The Padmanabhaiah Committee also observed in the same renewed pace that "internal security is an important element of national security. Therefore, it would be prudent for the policy-makers to realize that the present day challenges to internal security especially those posed by covet designs of Pakistan ISI, or Maoist Marxist extremist groups and of the religious fundamentalists are of such a nature that to meet them squarely, meaningfully and effectively, the society and the country need a highly motivated, professionally skilled, infrastructurally self-sufficient and sophistically trained police force." But under the present background of atrocious and precarious law and order situation, mere efficient policing alone cannot enforce effective rule of law and public order unless there exists an equally effective and impartial criminal justice system to maintain order and harmony in society.

On a writ petition filed in 1996 by Prakash Singh, a former DG of BSF, the Supreme Court issued comprehensive directions in September 2006 which included that (i) the DGP should be selected by the states from amongst the three senior most officers on the basis of their length of service, very good record and range of experience. Police officers on operational duties like the I.G. of Police in charge of a range, Superintendent of Police-in-charge of a District and "Station House Officer" in-charge of a police station should have minimum tenure of two years. The Centre and the States were to set-up security commissions for selection and appointment of personnel and ensure complete autonomy in police administration. The investigating police should be separated from the law and order police/ensure speedier investigation, better expertise and improved rapport with the people. There should be a "Police Establishment Board" in each state to decide all transfers, postings, promotions and other service-related matters of officers. A district level "Police Complaints Authority" headed by a retired District Judge will look into complaints against officers of and up to the rank of Deputy Superintendent of Police. The State Security Commission is to ensure that the State government does not exercise unwarranted influence or pressure on police, lays down broad policy-guidelines and evaluate performance. The appointment of DGP should be done through merit-based transparent process with a minimum tenure of two years for the DGP and other Police Officers on operational duties. The National Security Commission at Union level was to prepare a panel of officers for selection and placement as Chiefs of Central Police Organizations with minimum two-year tenure. From a report by the "Commonwealth Human Rights Initiative" (CHRI) it has transpired that though most of the States set-up "State Security Commissions", they did not reflect the court's criteria. At least States like Andhra Pradesh, Jammu & Kashmir, Odisha and Tamil Nadu had not complied with the directives. Of late, the Odisha Government. have gone for amendments and the Odisha Police Act, 2013 in providing for the State Security Commission, Police Establishment Board and the Police Complaints Authority. Arunachal Pradesh, Goa and Meghalaya had, of course, complied with the directives of the Court. At least, till about March 2013, no State Government had established "Police Complaints Authorities" at district and state levels that fully complied with court directives. In fact, a significant minority of States like Uttar Pradesh, Tamil Nadu, Mizoram, Madhya Pradesh, Jammu & Kashmir and Andhra Pradesh completely ignored the directions initially.

The Justice J.S. Verma Committee which was appointed in the wake of the Delhi Gang Rape incident had recommended a comprehensive set of measures one of those related to full compliance of Supreme Court's directions on police reforms as of utmost priority to national welfare including the welfare of women and children. It is a pity that State Governments like Maharashtra in their affidavits to the Supreme Court had taken the stand that the court's directions are "inconsistent with and contrary to the procedure laid-down by the Constitution". Fifteen states passed legislation following the Supreme Court's judgement of September 22, 2006. Instead of these laws (state laws) coming in the nature of compliance of the Supreme Court's directions, states passed these laws essentially to circumvent the implementation of court's direction. The 2006 judgement contained mandatory provisions that Union, State and UTs were required to comply with by framing appropriate legislations. They enacted hurriedly laws which they did not in the last six decades to perpetuate the *status quo* and frustrate court's intention to reform the police. How the court tackles the recalcitrant states which passed executive orders only in partial compliance of the court's directions was the question in debate. The other dilema related to the issue whether the Apex Court would allow the states to hoodwink the judiciary by-passing laws to legitimatize the *status quo*. Fortunately, a leading advocate of the country had challenged the constitutional validity of these Acts and urged the Supreme Court to declare the legislations enacted by the 15 states as null and void.

The model police bill prepared in 2006 by the Police Act Drafting Committee (PADC) of the Home Ministry complements the courts judgement. Only 12 states were reported to have enacted their own versions of the New Police Act. CHRI's coordinator (Police Reforms Programme) Navaz Kotwal was of the view that most of these new pieces of legislation are as regressive as the archaic laws replaced. Interesting is that new laws are being drafted in complete secrecy by a small lobby of Police Officers and bureaucrats without involving the public or intelligentsia as a result of which the Acts tend to reduce or dilute accountability. The whole system from recruitment to training, promotions, transfer, appointments and accountability has eroded and got rotten that a complete makeover is needed. This view was almost corroborated when former Union Home Secretary G.K. Pillai said that "today less than 30 per cent of those recruited in police have got in through merit...." Therefore, the first and foremost challenge is how to ensure that those recruited come through a transparent and merit-based system. Politicians and political parties should not feel that the police are instruments in their hands to further their interests. This has to change. In fact the police is meant for all citizens. People do not trust the police as they are rude, badly behaved, corrupt and tend to abuse their power. Therefore, they need to make conscious efforts to bridge the gap with the public.

Three important and relevant issues surround the entire police administration and its governance. These can be broadly classified as : (i) police accountability, (ii) police professionalism, and (iii) police, human rights and community policing. The National Police Commission had given categorical recommendations to insulate police from extraneous influence so that it can function within the framework of law. Setting up of a State Security Commission was one of the major recommendations. As regards improvement of police professionalism, the Commission had highlighted the need for orientation of training of police personnel, strengthening of the investigating machinery and modernizing the police force to reduce its response time. In recent years, violation of human rights has assumed significant proportion. In fact, thousands of complaints are received by the NHRC and the SHRCs every year of which about 60 per cent complaints relate to police only. Human rights violation takes place not only in respect of an accused or criminal but also in respect of women, children, minorities and backward classes. To redress many of these issues, community policing becomes significant.

The National Police Commission had recommended several measures needed to strengthen police administration. There was hardly any political will to implement them. Therefore, such will has to be found elsewhere principally in two ways, namely within the institution itself and the involvement of the society. As far as autonomy of police force is concerned, the judgement of Lord Denning in the Metropolitan Police Commissioner's Case (1968) is considered very relevant inasmuch as that this judgement has been followed by the Supreme Court in *Abhi Nandan Jha (Bihar) case* with regard to independence of police in the field of investigation. As such, there is need to reverse the current trend and institutionalize the mechanism which will purge the police force of the existing infirmities and convert it into an institution commanding the highest respect alongside the judiciary because both are equally important for implementation of the rule of law which is the bedrock of democracy. There is an urgent need, therefore, for state governments to set up a credible mechanism for selection of the police chief in the states and mechanism for their selection, appointment, tenure, transfer and posting. This includes not only the chief of the State Police but also all police officers in the rank of Superintendent of Police and above. There is no gainsaying that police officers are transferred very often which greatly demoralizes them. Instances are not rare where the average tenure of a Superintendent of Police is not even six months or even two months in some states. Transfers are made on whimsical reasons. Apart from demoralizing the police force, there is also the adverse effect of politicking the police force. The National Police Commission had alarmed the Central Government to take strong measures within the ambit of its Constitutional powers in informing the State Governments that such practices are alien to the envisaged Constitutional machinery. Things seem to have gone further down.

In order that a systematic mechanism is not available, top level senior officers could help in the evolution of an internal mechanism towards achieving transparency and accountability basing on their internal guidelines and guidelines based on the judgements of courts and the NHRC. That the police should exercise its paramount discretion following certain principles has been elaborated in the Supreme Court judgement in *Joginder Kumar and D.K. Basu cases*, need not be over emphasized. The determination of the framework and the extent of autonomy is dependent on the environment in which it will operate since it is not merely a structural or legal matter but a question as to how the improved structure in the frame work of legal hierarchical and authoritative position will be allowed to function on a day-to-day basis. Regrettably the police functions in the police force throughout the country need reform. As things continue to happen in police administration, things will not be remedied merely by a few judgements like *Hawala judgement* or the judgement in *Prakash Singh's case*. There should also be radical change in the behaviour and attitude of the people towards police including the political masters who were, in many cases, rather very unfair if nor rude, towards police personnel at the apex level for which instances of police brass committed even suicide. In the *Hawala judgement*, Justice J.S. Verma observed as follows : "in view of the problems in the states being more acute, I was being troubled by the incidents which I had heard during arguments. As elaborately discussed in the report of the National Police Commission there is an urgent need for the State governments also to set up a credible mechanism for selection of the police Chief in the States."

Crime and Investigation

In any country, criminal justice system is the *sinequanon* of the prosecution (prosecution wing) and the courts (trial) and the prison (punishment and reform). The essence of criminal justice system is that the trial of an accused should be swift and punishment for the criminal should be certain and deterrent. But regrettably in our country, track record has been rather dismal with abnormal delay in disposal, increasing and mounting pendency and falling in conviction rates. With huge pendency of criminal cases in different courts and disproportionate rate of judges to pendency, it is unfathomable to measure the quantity and quality of criminal justice in the country. Right from the stage of filing of FIR, its registration and framing of charge sheet, it takes several years for the conclusion of trial. The frequent visits of victims and witnesses to courts creates unpleasant and disquieting experiences. Trials continue to linger because witnesses resile from original statements. Prosecution becomes ineffective due to lack of coordination between prosecution and investigation leading to acquittal of culprits in many cases. These, however, create of sense of cynicism among the law abiding citizens losing faith in the criminal justice system. Keeping these in view, it has been suggested to go for large scale reforms in the criminal justice system covering important areas of access to justice, proper investigation, effective prosecution, better and swift trial and improvement in the prison system.

In the recent past, some efforts were taken for effecting reform in criminal justice system. By the 2005 Criminal Law Amendment Act, "Plea-bargaining" has been recognized. On the recommendations of the Eleventh Finance Commission, several "First Track" courts have been set up to expedite trial of pending cases by appointing *ad hoc* judges. As early as 1988, the Law Commission in its 125th report had recommended for extension of functioning time of courts and setting up of additional courts beyond normal hours of present courts. Some States like Gujarat started the system of evening courts for hearing and disposal of petty cases. The *Lok Adalats* constituted under the Legal Services Authority Act, 1987 and the "First Track" Courts have done excellent work in settling large number of cases, particularly claim settlements under Motor Vehicles Act. The former Chief Justice of India Justice Y.K. Sabharwal had suggested several reformatory measures for reforming the criminal justice administration in the country which, *interalia* included "Judicial Impact Assessment" (JIA) of each new legislation, summary disposal of weak cases involving trivial issues, allocation of cases to specific track courts, alternate dispute resolution methods, video-conferencing, use of modern means of communication for service of summons, conduct of pre-trial hearing etc. The Law Commission in its 120th Report (1987) had recommended for increase in the number of judges. The Supreme Court in the *All India Judges Association Case* (2003) directed the Government to increase the strength of judges from the ratio of 10.5 or 13 per 10 lakh people to 50 judges for 10 lakh people.

In the area of investigation, when a case is registered, it must lead to the process of investigation which may result in eventual prosecution. While going through these processes the police is alleged to be committing several omissions and commissions.

These omissions and commissions could be even deliberate. It is also alleged that police is invariably reluctant to register cases as "First Information Report" (FIR). This is the practice all-over India which is otherwise called "Burking of Crime". But in the normal work relating to heinous and sensational cases having public knowledge, such burking can hardly be resorted to particularly in serious cases like-murder. Reluctance to register cases is attributed mainly to, (i) free registration of all cases which may lead to a sharp jump in crime figures, and (ii) if registered, the case has to be investigated and detected. This would attract hard work to select the crime roots and may reflect the competence of the officer concerned including supervising officer if not properly investigated. Therefore, an *inertia* is likely to prevail in the minds of police officers to avoid registration of cases relatively in ordinary cases. Little is realized then that burking can lead to long-term effects on police administration because crime thereby, is artificially controlled and resources of the department do not increase but public dissatisfaction and anger precipitates leading to almost criminalization of society, increase in corruption and police officers particularly in-charge, get away with their responsibility, as a result "small criminals graduate to big criminals."

It is often held that non-regisration is a negative human rights. In fact, non-registration of crime is the highest in the category of property crimes and crimes against women and girls. One of the best examples of fudging of crime records can be seen when number of burglary cases came down up to only 6 cases per lakh in 1997. At one point of time it was even suggested to entrust the work of registration of crime to an officer other than the investigating officer. This, of course, could not work. One of the alternatives was to remove excessive weightage given to crime data while assessing officer's work and treat "burking" as a serious dereliction of duty. To avoid registration of cases, police is alleged to be avoiding by asking the complainant or even victim to bring stationary for writing the report. The fact remains that many State governments fail to supply even adequate stationary to police for which the police seeks supply from complainants/victims. Even though investigation work does not entail expenses largely, but undertaking journey with witnesses and suspects to various sites, cost of accommodation, food, materials for covering dead bodies etc. require funds which most of the police stations do not have adequately. Very often, lack of sufficient funds for use of vehicles for the purpose of investigation work adversely affects the credibility for which police officers stoop low for collecting illegal money. This leads to police minimizing the nature and gravity of the seriousness of the crime. For this, instances are not rare where a dacoity is shown robbery and a robbery as burglary and even a burglary to a theft. In fact, the priorities of the police has remained almost the same in the last several decades. Cases of murder, dacoity, rubbery, rape, kidnapping, burglary and theft in their number bring in greater ignomity than their increase in number. With the increased public opinion through media, human right groups and opposition parties, the police is placed now-a-days in greater dilemma to address various crimes issues.

One of the main constraints of a transparent criminal justice system is the prevailing distrust of police built into the system itself. For example, under the provisions of CrPC, a statement made before the police shall not be signed by the person making the statement and that it could be used in the court only to contradict the witness and not to corroborate. The main objective of this provision was to ensure that the police does not obtain statements through coercion. While the CrPC (Chapter XIV) and the Indian Evidence Act, 1872 (Section 145) elaborate the procedure of examination of witnesses by police and statements to police are not to be signed and such statements could be used in evidence, the Law Commissions and the "Committee On Reforms" in the criminal justice system recommended that section 161 should be amended to make it obligatory to record statements made by the witnesses during investigation in the narrative or in question and in another form, a copy of the statement be given to witness immediately. Similarly, section 162 of CrPC be amended so that the statement can be used both for corroboration and contradiction.

Human rights have surfaced in different forms now and their violence by law-enforcing agencies primarily relate to physical torture and third degree action. Human rights activists and even some sections of media try to display that police does this type of torture although this is not always true. The police depends such action on the ground of "professional objectives" for extracting information or confession in order to either solve a case or recover stolen property or weapon or unearth other crimes or ascertain the whereabouts of other criminals. Another professional objective of police is to terminate the criminality of a professional criminal. As courts often grant bail or anticipatory bail very early; cases linger on and punishment normally results in short-term jail. Therefore, different coercive methods are used by police although crime is contained temporarily as a result of this but not stopped altogether. The fact that the suspect is to be produced in the court within 24 hours of arrest can hardly guarantee the police to complete interrogation thoroughly. Since, courts do not easily grant remand to police custody of the suspect, there has been a perceptible tendency to apprehend the suspect and keep him in illegal custody on the plea of detailed interrogation. In major and serious crimes like robbery or burglary, the police has a normal tendency to sweep over all suspects in the vicinity, round them up with the intention to escape immediate and effective detection. Although the police is normally not comfortable in keeping a man in police custody because of fear of the judiciary, magistracy, the media or the human rights courts, human rights groups and activists, it tends to resort to the shortcut method of third-degree to secure easy confessions except a few cases of hardened criminals. Therefore, the system of investigation by police needs change in the existing system.

While reforms in judiciary is indispensable to ensure better, fast and speedier criminal justice administration, reforms in investigation is also vital. With commencement of a crime begins the process of investigation and even though State Government have their prescribed procedures for crimes investigation, rarely do the investigating officers follow the provisions of law and rule. The initial importance of criminal investigation is recording of "First Information Report" (FIR). The normal procedure of recording the first information given in writing or oral is to reduce it to writing and read over to the informant complainant and handover copy of the same is an important stage of criminal investigation. This is mandatory duty of the officer-in-charge of police station which is said to be very often not followed. The National Police Commission in its report (Fourth Report, 1980) observed as to how 50 per cent of the complainants reported about non-registration of complaints by police stations. The Commission had suggested setting up of reporting centres in urban areas where authorized citizens could register FIRs. The procedure of recording FIR is clearly spelt out in section 154 of

CrPC 1973. In spite of this, police stations continue to err the procedure. With rapid development of communication facilities, many states have attempted to use technology to bring in transparency in registration of cases. Rajasthan introduced "*Aarakshi*" to improve police efficiency in police procedure. Andhra Pradesh introduced "e-cops" programme for computerization of police services. Kerala has tried to develop a system of 'web-based electronic complaint registration'. The National Police Commission (1980) recommended to bring in amendments to section 154 CrPC, namely (i) police should be allowed to obtain additional Information from the informant; (ii) should make FIR registration mandatory irrespective of whether the alleged offer was committed within the P.S. jurisdiction or not; and (iii) allow constituents of police stations like police outposts to also record F.I.R. But in reality, these recommendations have not been sincerely acted upon. On the other hand, emphasis has been given on crime statistics rather than successful number of cases defected and prosecuted. Keeping these in view, the second Administrative Reforms Commission (Moily Commission) recommended for registration of citizen-friendly FIRs with use of technology to improve accessibility of police stations to the public establishment of "call centres" and "public kiosks". It also recommended to equip police stations with CCTV cameras to prevent malpractices and ensure transparency.

The issue of large pendency of criminal cases has been discussed at various fora in the past. In the conference of Chief Justices held on 9th and Tenth March, 2006, it was also suggested that petty offences including traffic and municipal cases can be transferred to "Special Metropolitan Magistrates". In recent periods of criminal justice history, it has been often suggested to introduce and apply computerization programme in the Supreme Court, High Courts and Subordinate Courts to regulate and monitor pending cases, case list status, report, daily case list and judgement information. A committee under the Chairmanship of Dr. Justice G.C. Bharuka in 2004 was constituted to assist the Supreme Court is formulating a national plan for computerization, communication and management reforms in judiciary. On the basis of recommendations of the Committee, a five year programme was prepared and launched in 2005 for implementation in phases.

The Second Administrative Reforms Commission also reiterated that the recommendations of the aforementioned committee be implemented in phases.

There were times when due to delay in judicial verdict in many cases, a parallel system of "justice" mostly dominated and fine-tuned by gangsters and *mafias* had sprung up mostly in some of the metro cities. Many legal celebrities had said that the criminal justice system in the country was on the verge of collapse. The idea that crime rate appreciably diminishes more in a society which is more literate has been vividly falsified from crime statistics collected from some of so-called more literate States. That there is scant respect of political forces to judicial process is best exemplified in the sensational cases of Jayalalitha (Tamil Nadu Chief Minister) in disproportionate wealth cases, the famous Hawala case, the Best Bakery riot in 2002 etc. which demonstrated the blatant failure of law and order authority and the carelessness shown by the State Governments to the investigation and prosecution agencies that the police and the prosecution reportedly conspired to sabotage the justice system which raised active debate for separating prosecution from investigation by police. The recommendations of the National Police Commission 1977 to set up a separate State Security Commission and to replace the archaic Police Act of 1861 by a new Act has now come to fruition but not in full measure. The National Human Rights Commission observed that it was aware of the melancholy history of failure and lack of political and administrative will that signifies to revive the quality of policing in this country and save it from the catastrophic extraneous influences that are ruining the investigative work of the police. The Malimath (Justice V.S. Malimath) Committee's recommendations primarily intended to enable easier conviction, reduce threshold of evidence, effective removal of right to silence, reverse burden of proof and increase momentum of summary trials. A dispassionate analysis of the recommendations tended to establish that the Committee tried to repose unflinching faith in the police administration but seemed to have sidelined the vast data of police abuses that stand recorded in the criminal justice administration of the country. The suggestion of the Committee to amend section 167 CrPC appeared to be unconvincing as release of a person on bail on grounds of non-submission of charge sheet within the prescribed statutory period was not in anyway, either to affect the investigation or trial. After all, why should a citizen suffer for delay in investigation? Similarly, the recommendation to amend sections 161 and 162 of CrPC in regard to statements recorded by police admissible as evidence invited serious criticism and debate. Similarly, suggestions for amendments to section 25 of Evidence Act and section 313 of CrPC and some of the sweeping changes with regard to burden of proof and presumption of innocence also attracted criticism. A few even argued that implementation of some of the recommendations may revive archaic laws which have been buried in the graveyard of history. Our legal profession and legal educational system need a lot of improvement. The Committee's attempt to incorporate some of the inquestorial system to the existing adversial system aiming to pin-down the defence of the accused to take a stand during the early stages of the trial itself has also found positive reactions from some quarters. Many human rights activists and legal luminaries came out openly against some of the recommendations of the Malimath Committee on the ground that these recommendations would strengthen more the high-handedness of the police.

Crime Investigation: CBI and Police

The Code of Criminal Procedure (CrPC) categorically mentions the circumstances under which freedom of an individual may be restricted by lawful arrest and judicially ordered detention. Any restriction, arrest or detention which is contrary to the basic principle of law, is strictly prohibited. Article 21 of the Constitution states that "no person shall be deprived of his life or personal liberty except according to procedure established by law". This applies to every agency including police having legal power to detain or restrict any person's movement. The CrPC lays down as to how an arrest is made, before whom an arrested person must be produced within 24 hours and how the crime will be investigated and completed etc. In the division of powers between the Union and the States, the VIIth Schedule is framed under Article 246. List I under it is the Union list in which Parliament has the legislative competence. List 2 is the State list for which State legislatures have the legislative competence and List 3 is the Concurrent list in which both Parliament and State Legislatures have legislative competence. Entry 8 of list I empowers Parliament to enact legislation on the CBI and IB. Hither to, Parliament has not enacted a law for either of the agencies although the I.B. has been in existence since the British era. The CBI was set up in 1963. Public order and police find place at entries 1 and 2 of the State list and therefore, legislative jurisdiction exclusively vests in the State legislatures. Parliament may legislate under entry 2 of List I for both the military armed forces and the civil armed forces of the Union. The Border Security Force (BSF) Act legally creates BSF as a legally entitya civil armed force of the Union. But the Police can only be created by the State Legislature. The Constitution recognizes only the police as an agency competent to both prevent crime and investigate it.

To circumvent this problem, the Union Government enacted the Delhi Special Police Establishment (DSPE). It is a legal entity, a police force and an agency competent to investigate. It acts as a duly empowered force and enjoys full police powers as prescribed under CrPC while probing offences entrusted to it. But the CBI was created by a resolution dated. 01.04.1963 of Government of India with the stated objective of handling cases then under investigation by DSPE. Therefore, the recent judgement of the Gauhati High Court that CBI has no legal status and no legal powers seems to be correct. Instead of providing legal cover to CBI, it was constituted with six divisions such as, technical, crime records, research, law and administration meaning that it is only an executive agency. Therefore, it has been held that the Central Government needs to enact legislation creating a CBI subsuming DSPE into it and giving a specific jurisdiction within a framework of legality.

That the CBI has poor record of investigation particularly in the *Coalgate scam case*, was reinforced by the Supreme Court when it held the entity of CBI as "a caged parrot" with no autonomy whatsoever. This remark was provoked by the poor record of investigation into the *Coalgate scam*. The autonomy of CBI involves internal administration, investigations unhindered by political factors and financial autonomy. Internal administration of this organisation involves the selection of the Director and the staff, annual assessment of staff by superiors, transfer and disciplinary action. The normal practice followed in selection of Director, Special Director and Joint Director involves the "Appointment Committee" of Cabinet and the CVC. Officers below the level of the Joint Director are chosen by the CVC on the recommendation of the Director CBI whose views are generally accepted. Non-IPS officers such as Deputy Superintendent of Police and Inspectors are chosen by the Director CBI. This system worked well till about 1990s. But the deterioration started after 1990 when political interference surfaced to grapple the organization.

In the Indian Penal Code, sections 161 to 165 deal with acts of corruption. In terms of procedure, they are non-cognizable offences in which case the CBI needs to obtain permission of Magistrate First Class. Such permission was used to be granted automatically. Both the Acts of 1947 and 1988 (The Prevention of Corruption) Act made act of corruption cognizable. But the government issued orders to CBI not to take cognizance in respect of creamy layers in politics and bureaucracy without its permission. The judiciary also passed orders that to take cognizance of an act of corruption of a judge, the permission of a High Court or Supreme Court would be required. Five important areas of functional autonomy of CBI are essentially related to, (i) taking cognizance of an act of corruption; (ii) fair investigation and prosecution; (iii) disposal of investigation resulting in closure due to want of substantiation of allegation; and (iv) discretion in referring investigated case for departmental act or rigorous option of prosecution in court and option of appeal etc. Taking cognizance of offence involves two aspects. One is to take cognizance of an act of corruption by a Minister and Senior Governmental Officers of the rank of Joint Secretary and above. Here, the functional autonomy is already restricted in that prior permission is required before taking cognizance. Of course, cognizance can be taken by court orders. The CBI cannot *suomotu* take cognizance of an offence. The executive instructions of the government exempting senior officials and judicial officials exempting senior officials and entire class of judges and Magistrates from taking cognizance of offence amounts to legalizing corruption. That political interference has started playing in the area of CBI autonomy can be better demonstrated in the case of Vincent George which was pending over a decade in the disproportionate case. The fallacy is that while cases are pending involving senior officers and politicians, the subordinate courts have parallel power of taking cognizance of offences under sections 190, 192, 200 of Cr PC 1973. Any final report of investigation by the police or CBI under sections 156, 157 CrPC such as closure of case, needs to be sent to the Judicial Magistrate First-Class under section 159 of CrPC and the Magistrate has the power to order reinvestigation.

The other deficiency in the structure of CBI is that unlike the CVC, the CBI is not an organization created through an Act of Parliament. It has been suggested that the organization needs to be placed on a legal anchor like the Election Commission. It may be composed of three members headed by a Chief Justice of a High Court or a judge of the Supreme Court, one IPS Officer and another from the civil society. The members of CBI Directorate may be chosen by a committee consisting of the Prime Minister, leader of the Principal Opposition, leader of third political force and a representative of civil society. The Directorate should have full independent power of taking cognizance of offences against all ranks of officers. The work of CBI may be reviewed by a Parliamentary Committee instead of leaving it to an unelected institution like the CVC.

The CBI's crises of credibility has been exposed recently when the Supreme Court was seized with the allegations against the former Director of CBI Ranjit Sinha for meeting persons linked with the 2G scam and coal scam at his residence. The Court on September 8, 2014 described the allegations filed by the senior lawyer Prashant Bhusan, as serious. It is a matter of grave concern that the agency is facing such crises of credibility although it is equally grave that a section of people continue to bring disrepute and discredit to the professional wisdom and expertise of CBI. This is in clear contrast to the earlier observations of the court that the CBI is a "Caged Parrot" which speaks in its "master's voice". During hearing, the Court had asked the Centre whether it was contemplating a law to make the working of CBI independent and insulate it from extraneous intrusions and interferences. The Group of Ministers (GOM) was set up by the Central Government in May 2013 to submit a proposal on law to safeguard the CBI's autonomy. Nothing specific has come out on this issue. With regard to meaning of autonomy, views expressed in some quarters seem to be misleading since autonomy does not mean complete freedom or unbridled independence. As far as autonomy of CBI is concerned, it should, in fact, have complete freedom to investigate crime even though it continues to be under the administrative control of government of the day. In fact, section 4(2) of DSPE Act vests superintendence of CBI in the Central Government. This Act also provides legal power to the CBI whereas under the Act, the Special Police Establishment (SPE) conducts Investigative work. Therefore, the agency does not function in isolation. It needs cooperation of other government agencies like Income Tax Department, Enforcement Directorate, also of foreign governments through Ministry of External Affairs. Therefore, the line between superintendence and interference in its investigation work is rather thin but by no means vague. In our existing legal system, every branch of governance should remain and function, within its limits, more so the political executive. In view of the fact that the police and the CBI undertake investigation under the CrPC, they ought to be accountable to law and law alone. This interpretation is amply exemplified in the judgement/observation of English Judge Lord Denning in the case *Regina vs. Metropolitan Police Commissioner* in 1988 demarcating the duties of the Commissioner of Police and Secretary of the State (Home Minister). The above judgement has been quoted by the Indian Supreme Court in several cases including the *Vineet Narain Case* in 1997. The Central Vigilance Commission Act of 2003 was the outcome of the order of the Supreme Court. But regrettably, the Apex Court brought back the "Single Directive" requiring the CBI to obtain prior permission of the government before initiating enquiries into allegations of corruption against government officers in the rank of Joint Secretaries and above which had been quashed by the Supreme Court earlier. But surprisingly the Apex Court has again in its order on May 6, 2014 has quashed section 6(A) of DSPE Act (DSPEA) of 1946 in reiteration of its earlier order dated 18.12.1997.

The recently enacted Lok Pal Act provides appointment of the Director of CBI by a collegium comprising the Prime Minister, Leader of Opposition and Chief Justice of India. While this provision seeks to meet the requirements of proper selection, the problem lies with the manner in which the CBI is liberated from extraneous consideration and interference. Under the Act, the services of the CBI would be placed at the disposal of the Lok Pal for investigation over which the Lok Pal will have the power to oversee and supervise. But the new CBI Act has to substitute the archaic DSEP Act. In November 2014, the Lok Sabha passed a bill to amend the DSEP Act, 1946 to include the leader of the largest opposition party in the lower house of Parliament as a member of the selection committee to appointment of the CBI Chief as the Lok Sabha did not have a recognised leader of opposition. The Committee will now have the Prime Minister, Chief Justice of India and the leader of the single largest party as its members. The amendment has removed the mandatory requirement of quorum in the selection committee. It has also provided that no appointment of a director (CBI) shall be invalid merely by reason of any vacancy in the selection committee.

Lok Pal and the CBI

With the passing of the new Lok Pal Bill becoming an Act of Parliament, finally the dream for an empowered and high-profile Ombudsman seems to be a reality now. This exercise started nearly four and half decades. Because of lack of political will and the fear of an unknown factor, it did not take any stride. The prospect of facing an angry electorate in the next few months had probably persuaded the main political parties to sink their differences and go for smooth passage of the Lok Pal Bill in both houses of Parliament on the eve of the 15th Lok Sabha Elections. The continuing pressure and stellar role played by Anna Hazare in keeping up the pressure on the executive had to be acknowledged gracefully. Even though he sounded sometimes unreasonable and stubborn, this had to be acknowledged with conviction that a corruption-ridden nation needed an Ombudsman with single focus on restoring the credibility of a much-abused public service. In the new Ombudsman system, the Chairman and eight members of the essentially anti-graft body are to be selected by a collegiums comprising : (i) the Prime Minister, (ii) the Speaker of the Lok Sabha, (iii) the Leader of the Opposition in the Lok Sabha, and (iv) the Chief Justice of India or a sitting Supreme Court Judge nominated by the CJI and an eminent jurist. The Lok Pal will have jurisdiction over all public servants under the Union Government including the Prime Minister. A probe against the Prime Minister could be initiated only with the approval of two-thirds of the Lok Pal's members with a view to prevent likely attempt to cause instability in the Government on frivolous complaints. While the Lok Pal will have its own investigative wing empowered to conduct a preliminary inquiry into a complaint received by it, the Lok Pal can entrust such an enquiry to the CBI or to any other agency.

The most novel and distinguishing feature of the Lok Pal is its empowerment to provisionally attach any property suspected to have been acquired by an accused through illegal means without waiting for establishment of the charge in the court of law. But some suspect that under this new dispensation not much is likely to change. Instead, the CBI will have one more master. Although the Director CBI will be appointed by a larger collegium as against the present arrangement of being chosen by the appointments Committee of the Cabinet comprising the Prime Minister and the Home Minister after the CVC forwards a panel of usually three names under the CVC Act and the Delhi Special Police establishment Act, the CVC has the authority of superintendence over the CBI in respect of anti-corruption matters, while induction to the CBI of and above the rank of Joint Director will still need the CVC's approval. In the past, questionable inductions and rejections of names suggested by the Director CBI has taken place. Now under the Lok Pal dispensation, another restraint on the Director CBI will take place when proposals of induction and rejection will be subject to Lok Pal's approval. This is likely to create another hurdle leading even to situations of divided loyalties. The other point of likely embarrassment may arise out of the infamous "single directive" issue under which no officer of the Union Government can be subjected even to a preliminary enquiry by the CBI without the nod of the Ministry concerned except in trap cases where an officer is caught red-handed while accepting a bribe. Officers below the rank of Joint Secretary unfortunately are discriminated who do not enjoy the benefits of "single directive". The single directive has the potential to compromise the confidentiality of information collected by the CBI against an officer. When an officer has engaged in dubious transactions in collusion with or to favour a Minister, how can the later could give green signal to the CBI to go ahead with the inquiry? This is, in fact, the most persuasive argument against the "single directive' which has been incorporated into the Delhi Special Police Establishment (DSPE) Act and is, therefore, inviolable. Therefore, the Lok Pal may not materially alter the situation in respect of corruption in high places unless appropriate changes are effected in the existing process and procedure.

The silver lining is the placement of the Director of Prosecution of CBI under the control of DCBI who is at present, an officer drawn from the Ministry of Law owning his loyalties to the Law Minister rather than the DCBI. After the new law coming into force, the DCBI may ignore overtures of meddling Law Minister wanting to bailout his government from a different situation as in case of coal block allocation. There are certain grey areas in the new Lok Pal Law. The Law is not clear as to what should be the relationship between the CVC and the Lok Pal. There could be situation of conflict between the two authorities when the CVC and the Lok Pal refer the same matter to CBI for enquiry. Both are statutory authorities and each one would like to maintain its ego. In such situation, the DCBI is likely to be hard-pressed to please two authorities besides the department of personnel. It was earlier suggested by some that the Lok Pal should only look after personnel matters of the CBI (inductions and transfers) and the Department of Personnel to look after only budgetary allocations to the CBI. In such a situation, the CVC seems to be a needless appendage particularly after the creation of Lok Pal. On the whole, the Lok Pal cannot be viewed as anything but a cosmetic imposition on the CBI which pleads for greater autonomy. The support of Supreme Court to CBI is still in the realm of theory.

Security and Infrastructure Development

It seems to be the right time to transform Police and security system in the country in order to bring it in tune with the requirements of a modern democratic nation. Political leadership needs to be more attentive in this regard. Police officers must ensure that grievances of the common man are addressed and readdressed. The rule of law which is the cardinal principle on which a modern state rests, must be strictly enforced in a prompt, fair and equitable manner. Leaders of security forces must provide good and able leadership through their actions and values. The police force must strengthen external and internal communications to deal with increasing communal tensions. Communication with the people and within the police organization right down to the beat level must be improved. District and local police administration must take notice of communal tensions in their initial stages. Steps to prevent corruption and ensure accountability and probity in public life be taken at appropriate level and time. With growing urbanization, dimensions of crime have increased. The worst sufferers of this malady are the women and children. Violence against these vulnerable sections of population has to be dealt with firmly. There is also need to ensure that affirmative police action is taken in respect of marginalized sections of society. Although police in our country face varied security challenges and have manpower and logistics deficiencies, it has stood the test of the time on many a challenging situations. Besides playing the role of proactive service provider, a law enforcing body and a partner in growth and development and peace, it must take care of the welfare of the constabulary and their families lauding its men and women for their commitment, dedication and service to the nation and pay homage to those who have made the supreme sacrifice in the cause of the nation. Although the Supreme Court in *the Prakash Singh vs. Union of India* made landmark judgement asking the Union and State Governments to furnish before it details of action taken to establish Security Commission as ordered in court's verdict in 2006, many states go by default even today.

It remains a fact that the police, as often as not, abdicate their responsibility and act at the behest of the ruling dispensation. Therefore, there is need for structural reform. The Supreme Court in the above mentioned case issued a seven-point directive to the centre and states to counter the political stronghold over the police and make the law-enforcement authorities efficient and accountable. The striking features of the Supreme Court directives are : (i) to set up a State Security Commission to ensure that the police functions in a neutral manner and in accordance with law and government does not exert unwarranted pressure on the police; (ii) there will be a "Police Establishment Board" headed by the State's Director General of Police and Senior Officers to decide on transfers, postings and other service related matters pertaining to officers of and below the rank of Dy. Superintendent of Police; (iii) setting up of a "Police Complaints Authority" to probe allegations of misconduct against the police; and (iv) states to separate the investigation and law and order functions of the police force. A committee was appointed under Justice K.T. Thomas to examine the affidavits filed by State Governments regarding the measures taken to implement the directives of the court. The ground realities of four States, namely Uttar Pradesh, Karnataka, West Bengal and Maharashtra were analysed. The position was found to be dismal. In absence of police reforms, insulation of the police from political pressures and smashing of the nexus between the police and politicians may be extremely difficult. Therefore, it is necessary for the media, police and civil society to raise the pitch for police reforms. In the United Kingdom, Lord Denning in the famous case of *R vs. Metropolitan Police Commissioner* emphasized the independence of the police constables who ought to be "answerable to the law and law alone". The insulation of the executive functions of the police from extraneous interference was also stressed by the Supreme Court in the case of *Abhinandan Jha vs. Dinesh Mehta* (AIR 1968, Supreme Court 117).

The Government constituted a committee in the *post-Nirbhaya gang rape case* headed by late Justice J.S. Verma to suggest amendments in laws for quicker trial and enhanced punishment to criminals committing sexual assault against women resulted in the amendment to Criminal Law (Amendment) Act, 2013. Although not much seems to have changed thereafter except for a large number of victims in such cases are now coming forward to lodge complaints. The arrests of Asaram Bapu and Tarun Tejpal and even allegations of sexual assault against a former Judge of Supreme Court are positive indications, but the overall environment has not changed because government has not paid serious attention to the subject of police reforms. One full chapter running into 28 pages was devoted by the Verma Committee on Police reforms. The Committee observed that "full compliance with this judgement across all-over India is of utmost priority to national welfare, including the welfare of women and children and towards the weaker sections of the community." The Committee urged upon all States "to fully comply with all six Supreme Court directions in order to tackle systematic problems in policing which exist today .... If the Supreme Court's directions are implemented, there will be a crucial modernization of the police to be service-oriented for the citizenry in a manner which is efficient, scientific, and consistent with human dignity."

Regretably, the recommendations were conveniently ignored both by the political class and the bureaucracy putting up fierce resistance to the proposed reforms probably with the expectation that these would dilute their hold over the police and to that extent, reduce their powers. Although the Supreme Court has been monitoring the implementation of its directives given on September 22, 2006, the States have been coming with one excuse or the other. About fifteen States have passed Acts which violate the letter and spirit of the court's orders. The impasse continues. In consequence, the country even after 66 years of Independence continues with an archaic, feudal, colonial police essentially designed to subverse the interests of the rulers. But the fact remains that the police is capable of dealing with law and order problems, terrorism, Maoist insurgency, militancy and even separatist movements but is really not geared to deal with these issues. It has very poor infrastructure in terms of transport, communication and forensic support. With huge short-falls of man power the leadership is mostly of indifferent quality. What is worse is the day-to-day interference by politicians in its functioning. Therefore, the police is simply unable to deliver, let alone meet the expectations of the people. Therefore, police needs to be recognized, restructured and reformed in order that it becomes sensitive, responsive, humane and accountable. What the country needs now is a democratic police for our democracy.

From the data collected and complied by the Bureau of Police Research and Development (BPR&D), it was seen that over 5 lakh posts were lying vacant in the police departments in the country at a point of time with UP topping the list followed by Maharashtra, Gujarat, and Andhra Pradesh, approximately 1.95 lakh vacancies in UP, 47000 in Maharashtra, 45000 in Gujarat and over 43000 in the Andhra Pradesh. In the wake of December 16, 2013 gang rape incident, the Supreme Court had slammed the State governments over dwindling Police-Public ratio. The Centre had earlier informed in February that only 137 police personnel are available for every one lakh of the population and over 25 per cent police posts were lying vacant in the country. The total sanctioned strength of police personnel in all 35 States and Union Territories was over 21 lakhs but the actual strength was approximately 16 lakhs.

The national average of number of vehicles per 100 police men was 6.78 vehicles. In other words, only six vehicles are available for movement of 100 personnel at any given time. In UP only, three vehicles are available for 100 police men, four in Tripura, five for Himachal Pradesh. A total of 1.43 lakh vehicles were available with the States and Union Territories in 2012 which included 10000 heavy duty, 13000 medium duty, 58000 light vehicles and 59000 three and two-wheelers. With regard to coverage area for police personnel as per report of BPR&D 2012, only one constable was available to secure 1.49 sq K.m. but in less population states like Arunachal Pradesh, the ratio was highest at one constable for 7.27 sq. Km. As regards officers on board, Himachal Pradesh had only 12 (IGPs) against sanctioned strength of 22, West Bengal had only 28 serving DIGs in 2012 against sanctioned strength of 55. Interestingly the study results of BPR & D 2012 indicate that 296 police stations across the country did not have any telephone facility and 39 police stations were functioning without wireless sets. Although police and "law and order" are state subjects, the Centre has been focusing on training infrastructure for police personnel in the State. According to the aforesaid study of BPR&D 2012, an amount of Rs. 912 crore was spent on police training at all-India level (2011-12) which was only 1.64 per cent of total police expenditure of Rs. 55,747 crore. The Union Home Ministry is also looking in to modernisation of police force (MPF) and had already earmarked Rs. 1400 crore under the scheme for Twelfth Five Year Plan.

The landmark judgement on Police reform in 2006 doubled the willingness of political parties to implement the sweeping reforms. Despite the Court's order on police reform, no State appears to have implemented it in letter and spirit. People want a good police force and a clean and efficient bureaucracy which the court ordered for but our political masters seem to be not ready for this big change. The fact remains that the image of an honest civil servant subjected to arbitrary transfer or suspension by the political executive at the behest of vested interests, is etched in the public consciousness as a key archetype of Indian bureaucracy. The rising public awareness of the importance of the bureaucracy in the delivery of basic services to citizens received a welcome boost from the Supreme Court's reformative verdict on insulating officers from political interface but questions might be raised as to whether the Supreme Court was not over stepping its ambit by directing the constitution of a mechanism to regulate transfers and postings especially when draft bills were in circulation on such reforms? But it is evident that the court has taken judicial note of various official reports and studies like the reports of the K. Santhanam Committee on Prevention of Corruption, the Hota Committee and the second Administrative Reforms Commission that addressed these issues which were not taken forward. The failure of the executive to frame a legislative framework to address the key concerns forced the court to step in. The reality is that the phenomenon of the political-bureaucrat-industrialist's nexus is so entrenched that it requires a sustained systematic effort to cleanse the administrative system. The real gain for citizen out of this historic verdict of the Supreme Court has raised the bar for good governance in this country by providing a framework to insulate bureaucrats from the pressures of a clutch of vested interests which act through the political system. But right or wrong, as a result of this verdict, public confidence is bound to rise. The judgement is significant because reforms are necessary as most of the public servants silently endure the sufferings at the hands of politicians. After all, public servants are not private servants. The decision of the court has reaffirmed faith in the strength of democracy. With political morality in the country touching its lowest ebb, the ruling establishments have been using bureaucrats increasingly to bestow favours on themselves and their kin and to share the spots with the corrupt elements within the bureaucracy. The governments have also been using the bureaucracy to hound political and other rivals to settle scores. That perhaps explains why the CBI demands to confer on its director the status of secretary to the government that would enable the incumbent to report directly to the Minister in-charge of the department.

That personnel and training evoked such a strong "no" from the Centre that going by the manner in which police reforms have been subverted over the years despite Supreme Court directives, the fear is not unreal that unless civil society and courts are watchful, the governments at the Centre and the States would do everything to frustrate the well-meaning intent of the Apex Court to reform the bureaucracy. The fact remains that transfers are a political industry in many states depending upon the degree and extent of political culture and the bureaucratic participation in it. But can a secured tenure guarantee performance? We can know now that subtle tenure does not necessarily translate into delivery. The real issue is that there are laws and rules on what bureaucrats should not do but what about those who dwell in the safety of no-action zone? What about those who choose to do nothing and have come to institutionalise the phrase "pending" in government? Can politicians be held accountable while the permanent government is not? In theory, it is well to say that honest bureaucrats should resist illegal orders but in reality, the tribe of honest bureaucrats is an endangered species especially when there is no protection offered to the bureaucrat against his transfer or suspension because of the termity displayed in asking for written instructions and not for acting on oral directions. An independent bureaucracy is the backbone of probity in administration and can be an effective antidote to corruption. Therefore, if implemented in true letter and spirit, the judgement of the Supreme Court is likely to promote professionalism and help to ensure accountability. The governments of both the Centre and states should not have any reservation about implementation of the judgement in letter and spirit.

Autonomy and Accountability

In totalitarian states, police exercises absolute powers, enjoys unlimited and unbridled authority and therefore, these states are normally branded as police states; even police remains totally vulnerable to extra-legal pressures and influence. The Police Act of 1861 which is the foundation bible for police administration in India when reviewed by the Frazer Commission in 1902-03, founded many of the rules and regulations framed by the provincial governments which were contrary to the spirit of the Police Act of 1861. Contrary to the expectations that the degree of interference in the police would be minimal after Independence, the opposite has really happened which has eroded its autonomy. Therefore, there is need for autonomy as well as accountability in police. The National Police Commission made a number of recommendations important of them being, (i) insulating investigation wing of the police from external pressures and providing freedom in operational areas of investigation; (ii) removing the Damocles sword of transfer constantly hovering on the head of Chief Police and assuring a statutory tenure and proper and careful selection; and (iii) construction of State Security Commission to help the state government for effective discharge of its supervising responsibility under the framework of law. The National Human Rights Commission, while endorsing the aforesaid recommendations, strongly upheld that police autonomy should be balanced by police accountability. The Police has to be ultimately accountable to the people and has the responsibility to the law of the land which is the expression of popular will. The relationship of the people to law is instrumental as well as professional.

Late Justice J.S. Verma, as Chairman of National Human Rights Commission, in a workshop organized by Institute of Social Sciences (ISS), New Delhi in 2001 emphasized the view that the independence or autonomy of the police is as important as independence of judiciary. But with autonomy goes accountability. In a republican democracy like ours, there can be no absolute power vested in anyone and there has to be accountability of everyone who is invested with any public power. The police should be seen as a protector of the society and not a persecutor. But the present situation is different. In the justice delivery system, the police is an important as the judiciary. If the judiciary is taken for granted as independent, why not the police which comes to the fore before the judiciary steps in the justice administration system? Unless the police force detects the crime, properly investigates it and conducts the prosecution, how canthere be a fair trial by the judiciary? This is the bedrock of our criminal justice administration.

The independence and autonomy of the police is as important as the independence of judiciary. Along with independence and autonomy goes accountability as there can be no absolute power vested in anyone and as such, there has to be accountability of everyone who is invested with any public power. Therefore, independence and autonomy go hand-in-hand like two sides of the same coin as one without the other cannot be democratic. Hence, there should be an effective mechanism for enforcing accountability so that public power invested in any public servant is misused or used arbitrarily. A time may come when it is not the police force which complains of provisions like sections 25 to 27 of the Evidence Act but a public clamour for doing away with such provisions may be raised. This can happen when police officer at every level including a constable at the lowest level is seen as not a protector of the society but as a persecutor which is unfortunately the current image. Police being the principal law enforcing agency and one of the essential constituents of the criminal justice administration has to be understood as distinctly different from general administration otherwise understood as good governance transcending human governance. As a constituent of the justice delivery system of criminal justice administration, police force is as important as the judiciary.

Judiciary comes to the picture of criminal justice administration much after the police force steps in. Since, police is the principal law-enforcement agency, its role in the implementation of the rule of law is vital. In this background, it is clear that the police force must be an autonomous force which is uninfluenced by any extraneous factor. To achieve this, is needed several measures to ensure its proper structuring. The source of recruitment for example at the lowest level of police force, i.e. the constable, needs change. Change at the recruitment stage followed by consistent training updating from time to time is required which should come from within the institution itself and the society itself since political will is not be forthcoming.

The judgement of Lord Denning in *the Metropolitan Police Commissioner's case* (1968) was not only famous and path-finding but was followed by many judicial systems although the Supreme Court of India in a case from Bihar (*Abhinandan Jha*) pronounced the same thing in matters relating to autonomy. Therefore, there is urgent need to reverse the current trend and to institutionalize the mechanism which will purge the police force of the existing infirmities and convert it to an institution commanding highest respect alongside the judiciary because both are equally important for implementation of the rule of law which is the bedrock of democracy. The fact remains that the public opinion about police has not changed although people have expressed enough confidence in judiciary. Probably people have not realized the significance of the role of the police. They do not perceive the police as the protector as they perceive the judiciary to be. Therefore, it is a need to bring about a qualitative change in the functioning of the police force.

Training

The primary objective of training is to improve and increase knowledge, skill and aptitude of individuals. It is intended to develop personal skill as well as to improve capacity for shouldering higher responsibilities and challenges. Although police was the first civil service in India, for a long period of time it had no systematic training framework and infrastructure. Due to historical reasons, Indian police like other diverse systems in other countries, had its moorings in the military heritage. During the administration of kings and emperors and even during the middle ages, the police functions had some form of military overtone or the other. Even during troubled times of history, the challenges of internal security were mixed up with the perils of external integrity which reasoned out virtually the need for police role in maintaining internal security and rendering justice. But the emergence of a truly professional approach to policing is of recent origin. The advent of East India Company followed by proclamation of the Queen Victoria in 1857 created some sort of an organized system in the wake of the Police Act of 1861. Compared to the armed forces, the police took a back seat resulting the police being treated with a step-motherly attitude. Due to this low priority to "policing" the growth and development of police system got a setback as it could not create any impact in society, its credibility and public image remaining at a lower level. In spite of the fundamental inadequacies of the police system in India, it definitely continued to contribute substantially to the internal security needs of the community. Gradually, a slow and perceptible change took place in designing workable methods of police training predominantly in the use of arms, crowd control and regulatory work. Crime prevention and crime detection work started to get increasing attention. As early as 1859, a training school for the constables was established in Vellor and similar institutions were set up in Phillaur (Punjab) and Moradabad (UP) in early 1890s. In fact from 1900, a steady and systematic effort was made to stabilise police working through the concept of police training. The urge for change in police system was not given the needed thrust after Independence although the national focus was on development and planning. The courts of law, the media and public opinion were clearly unhappy with the policing in general.

The Government of India constituted a committee on police training in 1971 headed by Professor M.S. Gore which, besides several other recommendations, asserted that "training" in the police system was utterly ignored and neglected due to lack of any conviction in the utility value of training. The committee *inter alia* pointed out precisely that "Police Training" was consigned as a non-development oriented and non-plan activity and therefore, no systematic funding was available both at the national and state level. The fact remains that prior to 1970, the inadequacies in police system were predominantly visible and the shortcomings were mostly due to lack of internalization of the needed faith in the efficacy of systematic training of police force due to inadequate response of the government, the civil service and the police hierarchy. The recommendations of the Gore Committee (1971) coupled with the recommendations of the 3rd National Police Commission (1982) evoked positive response towards needed reforms in criminal justice system in general and the police organization in particular. The police work has been undergoing unprecedented transformation with newly emerging issues such as emergence of new varieties of crimes, technological revolution, liberalization and globalization of economy with intense impact on life including problems of crime and maintenance of law and order and rising public expectations from public institutions including police organization. Data on crimes in India definitely indicate an increasing trend in cognizable cases under the Indian penal code, in offences relating to rape, kidnapping and cases registered under special and local laws. The police is unable to investigate in all cases and about 70 per cent of cases of the cases investigated, are charge sheeted. Therefore, over the years, the backlog of cases mounts at the level of police station itself. Although other investigating agencies/departments like the CBI, ED, customs and income tax departments and the CBDT etc. do take up investigation in certain cases, these have no direct bearing on the work of the regular civil service in various States and Union Territories.

Statistics relating to various years since 1995 till 2010 disclose that the volume of violent crimes have practically not changed much but such crimes affecting life such as murder, homicide etc. have shown increase. The instance of Bombay underworld dons which ganged up at the instance and prodding of our hostile neighbour causing enormous loss of life and incalculable damage to property in the early part of 90s, the 'Securities Scam', the Urea Scam, the Hawala episode, the Bofors scandal, several instances of *supari* killings, kidnappings, extortion, black-mailing etc. are virtually common place. Betting and horse-racing or forms of gambling, fixed matches (cricket) etc. are engulfing. The Vohra Committee (1993) report highlighted about the nexus between criminals and politicians and bureaucrats including the police. Besides reflecting on the nexus, the report also highlighted problem arising out of organized crime. The report, however, did not dwell much on the emerging technology and its impact on crime control. Besides the issue of organized crime, the unpredictable and unseen poison of money-laundering and other forms of organized and unorganized crime in recent years across countries including India, has been the alarming issue which has posed a great threat to police administration. The impact of money-laundering can have far reaching adverse effects on the society from both social and economical points of view. Money laundering impacts a substantial position of the Gross Domestic Product (GDP) of any country. A study revealed that spread of money laundering alone accounted for about 4 to 12 per cent of GDP in Australia, 11 to 33 per cent in Italy, 1 to 15 per cent in UK and 4 to 33 per cent in USA. The impact of the aforesaid problems leads to inflationary pressures on the economy, creates uneven distribution of resource, imaginations on the tax base, generates black money, entrenches parallel economy, undermines development programmes, breeds corruption and disturbs the economic balance and orders public value and standards.

Emergence of scientific and technological advancements have imposed great consequences on the human life itself. True, a large number of technological and improvements have played a major role in making human lives better and meaningful but these have also used the potential to subjugate other countries subverting that knowledge to perpetrate crimes or acts conveying harm, injury, damage or loss to others. Innovation and introduction of computers have not only enhanced human ingenuity but has also posed serious security risks. Computer crimes are bracketed under hacking, interruption, time theft and frauds. Software piracy, computer sabotage and crimes add to the above list and ending with the cyber crimes. Therefore, all police activities in any form call for police competency to face all these challenges and devise ways and means to meet these challenges. The available police training infrastructure and institutional mechanism is rid with an unmindful long-nurtured and consciously imposed colonial ignorance. Apart from various in-service police training courses, the police colleges offering training courses to police personnel from the lowest ranks of Constables, direct cadet Sub-Inspectors, Sub-Inspectors, Deputy Superintendents etc. These training groups are responsible for forming the essential psychological, anatomical and morphological entities of the state police force members.

Members of Indian Police Service receive their state-level induction training after passing out from the National Police Academy, Hyderabad. Right from the rank of DIG of Police, senior officers are kept in-charge of training at the state level. But police training has not been accorded that much importance as is being given to police in other national and international organizations like the United Nations Peace-Keeping Operations. Police training, police trainers and police training managers are accorded utmost importance by Multi-national UN police contingents and the police force of the country of deployment. In fact, best of the experienced police officers are invariably chosen for police training management and instructional purposes. With increasing recognition of the need for well-educated liberally and technologically sound police force to meet the emerging challenges, police training must be given due importance in view of the fast-changing social, economic, political, cultural and jurisprudencial scenario at the national and international levels. Mere talk of police reform or modernization without holding police training in highest esteem becomes meaningless.

It is, therefore, absolutely necessary to set up an ideal police training mechanism to promote a healthy administrative apparatus. A lot depends on the personal qualities and abilities of the heads of these institutions, their administrative and faculty members. Unfortunately, it has been customary to construe a posting in a training institute as a penal assignment. Where police officers either being incapable of or unwilling to take on field assignments, take refuge in training centres. Most police trainers regrettably lack aptitude, adequate education and enlightenment. Therefore, it is time to set common standards for selecting a police trainer/manager from experienced officers with proven track record. This would require strict research-oriented standards of proven qualifications and aptitude for appointment of police trainers at all levels of police organizations. It may also be necessary to align the status of police trainers with educators at the academic institutions. Periodical mandatory performance appraisal and rating by trainers should be ensured. Compulsory training of trainers in collaboration with Central police training institutions, foreign police academic and institutions, scholarships for police trainers for undertaking advanced studies, specializations or topical research should be encouraged. Since, the procure of recruitment and training of police suffers from intrinsic infirmities and police work require skills with high degree of basic and advanced mental, physical, moral and intellectual fitness even spiritual soundness, it is necessary that modern day policing keeps abreast of contemporary criminal tendencies. It must rise successfully to the challenges of modern day delinquency.

A Modern Mechanism of Advanced Skill

Predictive Policing

"Predictive Policing" is a futuristic crime control method which would allow the police to foretell not just the nature of crime but also indicate the place where such a felony is to take place. In common understanding, post-adoption of the method, the police would be able to reach the crime scene before the crime is committed. This system is based on a sophisticated algorithms and behavioural science which complies crime related data of past years. The software then analyses the crime data and produces results predicting future crime in terms of location, and nature of crime. Several police departments of developed world are gradually taking help of software for predictive policing with impressive success. Use of the software "Pred Pol" has resulted in a 25 per cent drop in burglaries, in areas under the Los Angeles police department of USA. A similar software is developed by the IBM for the South Carolina police which has led to decreasing crime rate. The Scotland Yard in Britain has popularized "Face watch"—a smart phone application that provides the viewer the picture of suspects who may be in their areas. Coming across such a suspect, people can alert the police department by simply tapping on the suspect's image.

Many States in India have, in the meantime, prepared blue prints to adopt the predictive policing system. Jharkhand government is implementing such a system. But staunch believers in and investment on practitioners of conventional policing still hold that investment prediction of crime through computer will be a wasteful exercise. They believe that computers would be ineffective instruments for peeping into the unpredictable 'human' nature of the criminals. It has been made out that there is no alternative to the strengthening of the police station, the basic structure of policing and empowering the beat constable. While some of these arguments are valid, to write off the role of technology in future crime prevention may not be a good idea at all. The critiques of future policing also argue that analytical capacities of the software infuses no additional expertise. Police officials use past data and their own analysis to identify crime patterns. But the ability to identify crime patterns is intrinsically linked to capacity of individual officers which is not standardized. In fact, benefits from the software could be immense especially for states which have dearth of officials and ground-level personnel vacancies at times running as high as 25 per cent. The software system would provide instantaneous analysis free from the vagaries of delays and follies associated with human planning. Besides, police department would be able to optimize force deployment by the new mechanism.

But the proposed system would receive the greatest challenge from the believers of conventional policing and the prevailing legal system. Would the courts prosecute suspected arrested persons on the basis of a software prediction? Would the new system prevent crimes in new areas? Whatever be the apprehensions, after all, the predictive policing software dose not replace the conventional policing but acts merely as an enabler. It facilitates the seamless integration of the merits of technology with the skills of the police personnel. It aims at not solving crimes but preventing them. More number of crimes being prevented, would produce less criminals in the courts and aid over-burdened judiciary. The experiment in Jharkhand could be watched not as a common model applicable to many states but tried on experimental basis by different State Government police establishments.

Women in Police—The Gender Question

Induction of more women in the police force as an essential component has been well acknowledged in the ongoing police reform efforts in India. Encouraging more women to access its services without inhibition tends to secure positive outcomes in policing process. Entry of women to police force was witnessed even before Independence. The princely State of Travancore appointed women as special police constables in 1933 for the first time in modern India. But the progress and percentage of entry of women to police establ· hment has been negligible and tardy. In spite of repeated recommendations in the past to raise the number of women police at least up to a third of civil police force up to the level of Sub-Inspector, only 93887 women of the total 16.6 lakh personnel had been inducted till 2011 in the country. This accounts for a mere 5.65 per cent marking an increase of 4.6 per cent points over the two decades since 1991. Among the states, Maharashtra has made a transible surge by doubling its number between 2009 to 2011 from 12813 to 24219 which account for an increase of 13.2 per cent of the total 1.82 lakh strong force. Tamil Nadu with 15864 has doubled the number in the two-year period. On the other hand, in Mizoram and Union Territory of Daman and Diu, not a single women is traceable in the police force. In the Central Reserve Police Forces, regrettably the representation of women is dismal. Women personnel and officers constituted a mere two per cent of the total two lakh troopers recruited by paramilitary forces in the last three years and in the initial few months of 2013. Although 207348 personnel were recruited in various ranks in the CRPF, BSF, ITBP, SSB, CISF, Assam Rifles etc. between 2010 and 2013, the number of women was a mere 4733. The interesting fact is that of all the states, and Union Territories, in 13 States and Union Territories only there is no women police stations at all. As per data of the Bureau of Police Research and Development (BPRD), there were only 442 such police stations across India as in June 2011 Tamil Nadu had the maximum number of stations (196) followed by UP (71). There are several issues including training, sound working conditions and facilities that surround the women police force in order to bring them to the mainstream and empower them for effective policing.

The *Nirbhaya Gang Rape case* led to the setting up of a committee headed by Justice J.S. Verma which suggested to amend laws to ensure quicker trial and enhanced punishment to criminals committing sexual assault against women. The recommendations of this committee resulted in the passage of the Criminal Law (Amendment) Act, 2013. First traçt courts were set up to deal exclusively with cases relating to offences, against women. In spite of this, not much seems to have changed and there are daily reports on sexual assaults. The only significant change has been that such type of victims are now aggressively coming forward to lodge complaint. The arrests of Asaram Bapu and his son Narayan and

Tarun Tejpal are positive indications of widespread indignation. The main reason for recurrence of such incidents can be attributed to government's inaction on police reforms. The Verma Committee devoted almost 28 pages to police reforms alone. It was clearly stated therein that full compliance with the aforesaid judgement across all of India is of utmost priority to national welfare of women and children and towards the weaker sections of the community. The Committee urged upon all the state, "to fully comply with all six Supreme Court directives in order to tackle systematic problems in policing which exist today. But these recommendations seem to have been conveniently ignored. It is alleged that the political clan and the bureaucracy have been putting fierce resistance to the implementation of police reform because it would dilute their hold over the police and to that extent, reduce their powers. The police would need certain measures of functional autonomy to perform its function effectively but it is grossly wanting. Although the Apex Court has been monitoring the implementation of its directions given on September 22, 2006, states have come up with one excuse or the other. Till December 2013, only fifteen states had passed legislation which actually violated the letter and spirit of Court's orders. Regrettably, even after 66 years of Independence, the country in saddled with an archaic, feudal, colonial police originally designed to subserve the interest of the rulers.

In spite of continuous and continuing criticism against police, the bare fact remains that police is the key to dealing with problems relating to women's safety, law and order, terrorism, Maoist insurgency, militancy in J&K, separatist movements in North-East etc. Therefore, the professional competency of police need to be strengthened in terms of infrastructure development relating to transport, communication, forensic support, manpower, leadership quality etc. The worst is that police functioning is handicapped due to interference from politicians and bureaucracy. Therefore, it should be reorganized, restructured and reformed in order that it becomes sensitive, responsive human, accountable and people-friendly. The country needs people's police instead of ruler's police.

A modern democratic country like ours needs a transformed police and security system. The changing requirements of our institutions need more attention of political leadership for formulating conducive policy legislation. The police must address the grievances of common man. The rule of law must be strictly enforced in a prompt, fair and equitable manner. Leaders of security forces should also provide good and able leadership through their action values. The police force need to be strengthened both external and internal communication to deal with the worrying increase in communal tensions. Efforts need to be in place for preventing corruption and ensuring accountability and probity in public life. With growing urbanization, dimensions of crime have increased. The worst sufferers of the malady are mostly the women and children. Violence against these vulnerable groups needs to be dealt with firmly and curbed. Affirmative police action is required in respect of marginalized sections of society. Despite challenges and constrains of manpower and logistics, the police has acquitted itself well and attained significant success in addressing them. What is needed of it is that there must be a proactive service provider, a law enforcing body and a partner in growth, development and peace.

The Prime Minister Narendra Modi while addressing the Director Generals of Police in Guwahati on November 30, 2014 enunciated a new concept of "SMART Police" which should be strict and sensitive, modern and mobile, alert and accountable, reliable and responsible, techno-savy and trained (SMART). Instead of normal advocacy for a smart police hither to used, Modi has given a new dimension with very comprehensive implication which, if implemented sincerely, would bring a sea-change in the functioning of police and may usher in a revolutionary change in the police force and its administration. But, is it possible to achieve this in the existing colonial structure of the police and political influence which the police is obliged to carryout *diktats* of the political executive? That the police should be mobile or modern goes without saying. But whom shall the police be accountable? The National Police Commission had recommended the police to be accountable to the people and law of the country. The Supreme Court had tried to enforce this concept by directing states to establish Security Commission comprising men from different walks of life to ensure that there is no undue interference in the day-to-day functioning of the police and that the police must function within the limits of law. While some States have set up such commissions even diluting its character, composition and functions, many other States have shown least interest in insulating the police from extraneous pressures. The response of the Centre is also lukewarm in that the Model Police Act drafted by Soli Sorabjee in 2006 still remains in the cold-storage.

Restructuring Metropolitan and Rural Policing

In the present law and order situation, the potential victims are the women and the children. The Indian state needs to factor the speed and efficacy of response as a structural imperative within a recast law and order landscape of the land. Unfortunately, instead of ensuring a more responsive metropolitan policing in India's major cities, the state agencies involved in law enforcement are over-burdened with VVIP security. Without downgrading VVIP security, India must comprehensively upgrade the quality of policing response for preserving and protecting the safety and security of people living in cities, towns and even rural areas.

One of the key features of metropolitan policing in emergent India must be sensitization of police men towards security of women at work place and in public place. Raising issues relating to women's safety, Prime Minister Man Mohan Singh some time back in the annual conference of police chiefs asked the police chiefs of all states to put in place institutional mechanisms to ensure the safety and security of women and children. The concern of the Prime Minister come at a time when owner-editor "Tehelka" Tarun Tejpal was facing arrest in a sordid affair of alleged sexual assault on a junior colleague. Unless the contours of metropolitan and rural policing are restructured, the annual conference of state police chiefs will remain self-defeating. The Centre and States must evolve a common strategy in terms of police logistics, modernization strategies and acquisitions. Urban, rural and national security issues can be more effectively dealt with through systematic involvement of Chief Ministers with Union Government on a structured and regular basis. With the support of the Central Paramilitary Forces, the state police are protecting a whole range of national assets such as airports, seaports, defence installations and highways. The police are also facing terrorists threats from air and sea which the centre is more competent to handle. Maintenance of law and order comes within the jurisdiction of States under the Constitutional provisions. But given the current inefficiencies and inadequacies of state police forces and the financial burden involved, the Centre cannot wash its hands off the responsibility. Therefore, periodical interactions with the rank and file may pave way towards modernization of police forces in order to bring about a qualitative change in their working culture.

Village and Community Policing

Historically speaking, protection of lives and properties of community normally rested with the village heads and officials. Village "*Durbar*" or "*Sabha*" was all powerful. The Police Commission of 1902 (Fraser Commission) recommended rural policing by "Headman" through *Choukidars*, but no uniform system was suggested because of varieties of ethnic and customary cultures. The Mughal era pre-eminence of *Zamindars* as Collector, head of revenue, head of *Thanedar* system consisted of military force, regular force under *Thanedars*, *Naib Thanedar*, *Choukidar Chowki* (Outposts) assisted by peons or *Paiks*. *Paiks* collected rent and acted as village watchman. *Thanedars* and *Choukidars* were provided *Chakran* land for services provided.

After the Mughals, *Zamindars* became powerful as land collectors and head of *Thanedari* system. The British East India Company obtained *Dewani* right (right of land revenue) in 1765. With the *Zamindars* being greedy and rapacious, came the famine of 1770 which deteriorated the economic situation. In 1772, Warren Hastings took over marginalised *Zamindars* and entrusted revenue collection to collectors but *Zamindars* continued administrative control over *Thanedars* and village watch system. *Fouzdars* used to help *Zamindars*, but this system disappeared with Mughal exit. *Thanedari* system was delinked from *zamindari* system. *Zamindars* became mere revenue collection agents without any role in Company's administration. The decennial settlement (1784-1790) established state right to collect rent as primary domain of state with land holding *Malguzari* (Land paying rent) and *Lakhraj* (rent-free land). Even *Chakran* land was not rent-free and therefore *Malguzari*. The *Thanedars* were treated as private servants of *Zamindars* and were substituted by public servant system later on. Lord Cornwalis introduced the police system. The civil police force of Collector against *Zamindars* was established and extended to village level by regulation No. XIII of 1793. With the collapsed *Zamindars* through *Chakran* (service) lands, difficulty arose for *Darogas* of *Thanas* to control situation. Nomenclature of watchmen varied from place to place like Birbhum *Kotwals*, Bihar *Paswans*, *Paiks* in Burdwan Midnapur and *Choukidars* of Odisha. By 1793 regulation, *Choukidars* were treated as public servants maintained by *Zamindars* through service land, but the company refused to acknowledge *Choukidars* as public servants but did not object to *Chakran* land. They remained under the control of Darogas. So, also the *Pharidars, Samandaras, Ghatowals* etc. In 1837, the Bird Committee suggested reform for regulating the role of *Zamindars* and appointment of *Zamindars* by Magistrate.

The Police Commission of 1860 recommended enactment to professionalise police and devolve distinct responsibility in rural areas. The village watchman system was brought under the control of police and administration. The *Choukidars* were people of the villages but not official functionaries with responsibility to collect ground-level information. Nexus with local police station was recommended but ultimately *Choukidari system* failed due to, (i) inadequate and perfunctory supervision, (ii) meagre remuneration, and (iii) most of *Chakran* landholding being under the control of *Zamindars*. Some analysed the view that *Choukidari* system should be integral part of police administration where as some other have held that it should not be part of police administration.

Village Choukidari Act of 1870

Under this Act, the appointment, dismissal and control structure was provided with pay, equipment, powers and privileges linked with police station. The *Choukidar* was basically an informer and helper to the police in matters of enforcement of law, collection of taxes. The Panchayats and local bodies exercised general control and arranged payment of their salaries. In 1892, District Magistrates were made responsible for fixing number of *Choukidars*, their salary and disciplinary power but the system failed.

The Police Commission of 1902-03 rejected the idea of placing the village police under Station House Officer as it would be out of touch of custom, usage and interest of villagers. None of the recommendations of the committees, commissions was successful. With the passing of Bengal Village Local-Self Government Act, 1919, the Union Boards were created which were authorised to nominate persons for the job of *Daffadar* and *Choukidar* and were pay masters with disciplinary control although the District Magistrates were to determine their number, salary and equipment. This system of dual control over the *Choukidars* was the bone of contention between the administration and the Union Boards particularly after Government of India Act, 1935.

The Choukidari Inquiry Committee of 1938, although identified some of the key problems like, (i) *Choukidar* to be regarded as a village servant appointed, paid and controlled by villagers; (ii) policing of the village should be the direct responsibility of the government; (iii) *Choukidari* system should be abolished; and (iv) existing dual control system as best working arrangement, it did not recommend direct control of police over *Choukidars*. On the other hand, it recommended that *Choukidar* and *Daffadar* would continue to be paid by the Union Boards but the District Magistrate and the Officer-in-Charge of Police Station would continue to have control over them as before.

The British legacy including the archaic Police Act of 1861 continued to remain in force after Independence. The *Choukidars* and *Daffadars* were required to report information at the Police Stations about crimes, criminals and matters of general administration. The Police Commissions set-up by various states in 1960s and 1970s commended this system and the National Police Commission (1971-1981) was in favour of continuance of the system. Adoption of Panchayati Raj system by State Governments and Constitutional Amendments (73rd and 74th) witnessed gradual withering away of the *Choukidari* System and other village officers discharging police functions at the village level. With gradual democratisation of village level institutions, the *Choukidari* system witnessed a gradual decay in spite of recommendation of National Police Commission and other Committees.

The Police Act, 1861 was the result of emergence of conceptual suspicion by the British of possible future threats, agitations or revolts from its subjects on the backdrop of 1857 uprising (Sepoy Mutiny). Therefore, it was but natural that the Police Act 1861 was designed and drafted to make it an effective instrument to curb the voices of protest against the British oppressive rule. As India's struggle for Independence gathered momentum, the British wanted to crush and suppress the freedom movement through use of police force. Many of the problems of the present-day Indian police like the poor relationship with public and indifference to their interests, had in fact, their roots in the colonial past. Consequently, the image of police in the society was perceived to be one of corrupt, misbehaved and discourteous outfits of government structure. With passage of time, the situation has not improved either; rather the trust deficit between the police and the public has gone up. With guarantee of Fundamental Rights of citizens in the Constitution, the excesses committed by the police has been construed as a glaring breach of trust between the people and the government affecting the dignity of citizens. These probably led to a paradigm shift in policing, i.e. the need for conceptualising the concept of "community policing."

Community policing has been a buzzword in recent periods, Community policing has been defined as "an area specific proactive process of working with the community for prevention and detection of crime, maintenance of public order and solving local conflicts and with the objective of providing a better quality of life and sense of security". David Bayley identified four basic elements of community policing, namely; (i) community-based crime prevention; (ii) Patrol deployment for non-emergency interaction with the public; (iii) active solicitation of requests for service not involving criminal matters; and (iv) creation of mechanism for grassroots feedback from the community. It has been held that community policing is a philosophy in which the police and citizens act as partners in providing security to the community and controlling crime. This involves close working relationship between the police and the people. In fact, community policing provides decentralized and personalized police service to the community. This envisages that police cannot always impose order on the community. Instead, people must be encouraged to think police as a resource to help solving community problems and concerns. This would require creation and development of new breed of officers who can act as direct links between the police and the people in the community. The essence of community policing is to minimise the distance/gap between the policemen and the citizens.

Many States in India have tried to introduce community policing in some form or the other. In Andhra Pradesh it is branded as "*Maithri*", in Tamil Nadu it is named as "Friends of Police". In Maharashtra community policing through Mahala Committees in places like Bhiwandi is reported to have done excellent progress.

The Odisha police has launched the "Ama Police" project since April 2013 with a three-tier structure, i.e., (i) "Ama Police Beat" at the bottom, (ii) "Ama Police Samiti" at the middle, and (iii) "the District Advisory Committee" at the apex. It would take more time to these experiments to stabilise for which governments of the day should have commitment to adopt community policing as an organisational philosophy for which resources should be earmarked with additional manpower, frequent and repeated interaction with the community through "Community Liaison Group" or "Citizenship Committee". Community policing needs to be people-driven rather than Police-driven in convergence with other departments of government. But mere budgeting or additional manpower may not be exclusively conducive to the working of this new system. This would require involvement and designing of the system in a way in which the community will be oriented towards a degree of self-policing through the process of empowerment. Can our existing police system address this? In fact two major factors stand in the way, i.e. (i) the present hierarchical bureaucratic structure and management through command and control in police system which should be compatible with the spirit and substance of community policing; and (ii) the community must respond positively to the needs of such policing. Opportunities must be created for releasing community's intrinsic efforts to articulate its own security perceptions. Police officers and policemen should be going closure to the community for meeting security needs and helping the community in solving problems relating to crimes and prevention of crime.

Role of Armed Police—Central and State Reserves

The need for Armed Reserve in present day police system need not be over-emphasized. The Indian Police Commission in 1902-03 observed that 11 armed reserves are necessitated by the principle that it is the function of an efficient police not only to prevent and detect crime but also to secure the peace and tranquility of the country. The Commission also observed that the number, organization and equipment of the force must, therefore, be such as would enable it to deal with promptly and effectively with tumults and local disturbances without the aid of the military aim. This led to the creation of "District Armed Reserve Police" in all districts and in some provinces like Bihar, Bengal, Assam, Madras more or less on the infantry pattern. The British also gave greater attention to maintenance of law and order. The Simon Commission also emphasized the importance of the Army, the police and the Indian Civil Service. The Indian Police during the British Raj was very efficient in restoring order so much so that Lloyd had observed "No force in the empire stands higher than the Indian Police. They maintain, in royal support of the government they serve, peace and order without which no political structure can subsist. To the self-governing India of the future, the Indian Police is not the least of the gifts which Britain has to offer. Truly, the Indian Police has been one of the great organizations achieved under British leadership and developed by the Indian ranks. It has always stood by the side of the government in most difficult times."

In the pre-Independence period, the armed police consisted of the district armed police whose task was to guard government treasury, escorting cash from treasuries and bank, escorting prisoners and function as a small striking force. At the provincial level, armed police units were maintained and kept at the disposal of the Inspector General of Police. The importance of District Armed Reserve and Armed Police Battalions was acknowledged even after independence as frequent use of military force for law and order situation was not considered always desirable. Hence, it was the realization for the police to have their own armed units. The process of strengthening armed police at district and state levels picked up momentum. While the army was maintained for the defence of the country, the States were urged to raise adequate number of armed police battalions. Till the present times, the structure of civil and police has remained almost static. Maintenance of law and order remains district-centric but in actual practice, centralized advice and instruction on operational matters affects the independence and autonomy of police. The principle of supervision by civil administrative authority has been sedulously preserved except in a few metropolitan cities where the system of commissionrates of police have been implemented. The laws, rules, regulations being followed by the police in the country have virtually remained static. The observations of David Baley in one of his books *"Police and Political Development in India"* were probably very appropriate to the functioning of police in India. It reads "In India today, a dual system of criminal justice has grown up; the one law and the other of politics. With respect at least to police, decisions made by the police officials about the application of law are frequently subject to partisan review or direction from elected representatives. Thus autonomy of police officials in specific and routine applications of law has been severely curtailed.... Police officers throughout India have grown accustomed to calculating the likely political effect of any enforcement action they contemplate. Altogether, then, the rule of law in modern India, the frame upon which justice hangs, has been undermined by the rule of politics. Supervision in the name of democracy has eroded the foundation upon which impartiality depends in the criminal justice system." Some time in the recent past, the Group of Ministers of the Central Government recommended that the laws which are archaic have to be identified and rewritten or deleted from the statute book.

In view of increased number of registered and unregistered crimes almost in all states, the local police can hardly handle them although state security apparatus is mandated to adequately deal with law and order situations. Due to more widespread militancy, insurgency or terrorism aided and abetted by countries hostile to India, the task of the state security apparatus becomes very difficult and pervasive. The structure and scheme of internal security management has not been able to keep pace with time, and therefore, reform measures for improvement of national security system is considered indispensable. There is need to restore the fitment, capacity and morale of state police through a transparent recruitment and promotion process and improvement in the living and working conditions of police forces. Although the district armed reserves have remained almost relatively static over the last several decades there has been a gradual growth in the number of armed police battalions in many states in the meantime. The number of State Armed Battalions, the India Reserve Battalions, BSF, the CRPF as reflected in the VIIth report of the National Police Commission in respect of years 1963, 1981 and 1998 and on the recommendations of the Fifth Pay Commission seemed to be a hopeful beginning. Although the National Police Commission had indicated the numerical strength of officers in the armed battalions and their disposition under different police command officers, the overall supervision remaining with the State Police Chief, the quality of leadership of the force is of paramount importance. The

Commission also recommended for creation of two Central IPS Cadres for liberal exchange between states and those two cadres. It also emphasized the need for reflecting a proper mix of the society in the composition of the police force in general and the armed police in particular. The Commission highlighted the imperative need for periodical refreshers training course. It was observed that armed police were not used only for law and order need, but also in 'ones and twos' for jobs which fall primarily in the domain of civil service. The character of armed police battalions as striking force seems to have been diluted on many occasions. Unjustified demands for additional State Armed Police on several events by even the District Magistrates and Divisional Commissions seemed to be inflated and unjustified. Normally, the Army is trained to fight and destroy the enemy from outside inside the country but instances are not rare when Army personnel have been engaged in maintaining "Internal Security."

Many State Governments have established armed constabulary since before Independence. In 1947, the Police Reorganization Committee chaired by Sir Sitaram recommended merger of the Royal Military Police and the State Armed Constabulary into Provincial Armed Constabulary. In 1948 (December 13), the United Provincial Armed Constabulary Act was passed. In 1956, the nomenclature was altered to "Pradeshik Armed Constabulary" (PAC). The duties and functions of the PAC were basically enumerated as, (i) deal with law and order "*Bandobast*" situations arising out of riots, agitations and strikes; (ii) carryout duties at religious congregations, elections, traditional fairs and VVIP visits; (iii) conduct anti-dacoity operations; (iv) maintain communal peace during festivals; and (v) defence related duties. Although PAC was mandated to deal with cases of emergency, with changing situations of crimes and security, some other specialized jobs like checking infiltration, smuggling, bomb detection etc. have been entrusted to this force. Consequently, the PAC as a mobile striking reserve has been severely mauled and its role diluted to a great extent. As if, this force suffers from adequate infrastructural facilities, regular training, process of recruitment, lack of adequate communication facilities, challenges of multiple nature of its intervention not only in the internal security situations, but also its being utilized in rescue and rehabilitation work during floods, cyclone and other natural calamity situations, senior officer's reluctance to avoid postings in the battalions and deputation of officers with indifferent record of service to this force and abdication of responsibility of senior officers of the force in operational situations.

The States of Madhya Pradesh and Andhra Pradesh had been maintaining Special Armed Forces for quite some time. The then Central Provinces (CP) had provision for Special Armed Reserve for six cities of Nagpur, Jabalpur, Sagar, Nimar, Raipur and Sambalpur since 1889 with additional number of forces attached. The Indian Police Commission (1902-03) had recommended for training of staff. But the Special Armed Force came into being in 1939 with specified number of forces and the number was augmented subsequently from time to time. Following the recommendations of a Committee in 1951, the Special Armed Constabulary was merged with the Special Armed Force and when in 1956 M.P. was born as a separate State of India, it inherited the forces from all the four constituent states. It may be mentioned that during the first ten years of Independence, the role of armed police forces of all states in the country changed from that of state police to that of armed force for performing semi-military duties. In Andhra Pradesh, a special armed police force was created to assist the local police in maintenance of law and order. Long periods of deployment in hostile and emotionally disturbing environment take a large toll of lives of this force. Continuous absence from their families and long hours of duty with depleted operational strength leads to causalities or stress related diseases. The use of special force on routine pickets, VIP and some police station security duties has affected the morale of the force to some extent. These shortcomings need remedy.

Border Security Force (BSF)

This force was created to guard the country's borders following the 1965 war with Pakistan. This force played a very crucial role in 1971 war with Pakistan and extended valuable support to Army. Following the recommendations of a Working Group on Border Management in 1992, the strength of this force was fixed and changed from time to time. The distinguishing lacunae of this force is that it has been employed continuously in different situations not directly connected with the duties and functions envisaged.

Its morals and efficiency is, therefore, greatly jeopardazied. The battalion composition is broken mostly which restricts the supervisory and structure of the force.

Central Reserve Police Force (CRPF)

The Central Reserve Police Force (CRPF) started with a mere single battalion in 1939 christened as "His Excellency The Crown Representative's Police" which had grown over the years to about 140 battalions with 10 Rapid Action Force, 2 Mahial, 5 signal battalions and a Special Duty Group. The strength has been augmented subsequently. The CRPF has a saga of sacrifice, and sustained dedication to the cause of national integration. Composed of personnel belonging to almost every state in the country, this force has universal presence across the country which manages diverse range of sensitive internal security concerns as an unarmed civil police as well an armed combat force. The functions of this force are characterised by hard working conditions with multiple problems without adequate logistic support from the State Governments. This force is often asked to perform duties of routine law and order which, in the normal course, should be handled by the state police. On the other extreme end, this force is called upon to deal with extreme forms of terrorism and insurgency requiring them to adopt changes in their roles and locations resulting in unnecessary loss of life. That problems relating to anti-terrorist and counter-insurgency operation and handling of internal security duties should be left to the security apparatus of states had been recommended by the Group of Ministers on reforming the National Security System. The GOM reiterated that this force should function as a "striking reserve" for providing assistance to states on terms and conditions notified by MHA already. A growing tendency on the part of State Governments to circumvent the prescriptions given in the "Standard Operation Procedures" needs to be checked. The policy decisions of the State Governments are required to involve district administration as responsible for implementation of police decisions.

The other important challenge relates to executive deployment of the force. State governments continue to make *ad hoc* demands for deployment of this force without proper scrutiny. This trend needs to be arrested. At least some specific services like court processes, examination and cinema hall duties and escorting of prisoners should not be entrusted to this force. Frequent deployment of the force, therefore, seems irrational. Because of these, forces are frequently given as a political largesse and professional advice is not always available or sought for and the forces do not stand scrutiny for which the morale and efficiency of this force gets diluted. Due to dispersed deployment in large areas under immediate supervision of State authorities, the close touch and active supervision and guidance is not always visible. In view of these adverse situations, it has been suggested that a minimum indivisible unit of deployment should be worked out. Because of the present tendency of States and the Centre functioning in watertight compartments, the optimal results of the efforts and achievements of the CRPF are not being properly chronicled. Although IPS officers from different states are deputed to Central Police Organizations, regrettably these officers from state cadres are not offering their services readily. Therefore, some element of compulsion should be tagged to the conditions of their deputation in order to achieve best results in the management of internal security as recommended by the National Police Commission.

To strengthen and consolidate the command structure of the Central Police Force, the role of officers at the level of commandants and other superior officers need redefining in the context of operational autonomy. The control and guidance of State authorities, over the Central Police Force when deployed in States need to be clearly spelt out. Since, Central Police Force work with unanimity and in a body, they need close supervision of experienced officers of armed police forces which is normally not available. Added to this, the spectrum of duties of armed battalions need to be clearly reviewed and defined so that they are not mis-utilized or under-utilized while engaged in different nature of duties whether as 'Rapid Action Force' or in any other action. Keeping in view the existing structure and state of expertise of the central force, it has been suggested that the moral of the personnel should be kept high and upgradation of surveillance and intelligence need re-review and refining.

The CRPF, India's largest Armed Police Force with about 230 battalions now has been doing commendable work in fighting insurgents in Kashmir, Maoists in Chhattisgarh, Jharkhand,

Odisha, Andhra Pradesh and other terrorists in the strife-stricken areas including protection of borders of Punjab. But despite their valiant services to the nation, unfortunately they get a raw deal. The CRPF Act, 1949 which provides for the constitution and regulation of CRPF is a colonial inheritance of the Crown's Representative Police Force Law, 1939. Even after Independence of the country, some of the provisions in the CRPF Act, 1949 seem to be violative of fundamental freedoms like the right to equality, equal protection in public employment and the right to protection of life and personal liberty which should have been provided to the CRPF personnel. That has not happened. On the contrary, CRPF personnel have been subjected to the judgement of the commandant of a battalion endowed with Judicial powers of a Judicial Magistrate to try heinous offences in accordance with the procedure laid down in the CrPC, 1898 even though the CrPC, 1898 was amended in 1973 but not effected in CRPF Act. This continuing practice violates the provisions of Article 50 of Constitution of India Mandating separation of judiciary from the executive. The peculiar dilemma in the CRPF Act is that it empowers the commandant both the judicial powers of trial and executive powers of departmental action against CRPF personnel even though as per provision both in the amended CrPC, 1973 and the Constitution, it is necessary to go for appropriate revision in the CRPF Act and rules thereunder. It has been suggested that legal practices adopted by BSF, the Indian Army, Navy and Air Force can be emulated without compromising on the need for an independent disciplinary procedure. Even creation of a separate judicial forum can be legislatively made in the CRPF to provide just and proper justice to the cause of CRPF personnel who sacrifice their lives for the nation.

Prison Reforms

India's prisons are normally over-crowded. Of the various categories of jails, i.e. central jails, district jails, sub-jails, juvenile and women jails, some jails have also low population in terms of prisoners and under-trial prisoners. Compared to United States and China, India's jail population is quite low both as a proportion of the population and in absolute terms. Despite this, India's jails suffer from over-crowding of prisoners who are involved both in serious and major offences as well as minor and technical violations of law. The situation in many prisons has become such that these could be tantamounting to violation of human dignity and basic human rights—The "All India Committee on Jail Reforms" (1980-83) headed by Justice A.N. Mulla had observed that "over-crowded prisons, prolonged detention of under-trial prisoners, unsatisfactory living conditions, lack of treatment programmes and allegations of an indifferent and even in-human approach of prison staff, have repeatedly attracted the attention of critics over the years." In fact, modern prison reforms in the country started right from the Indian Jails Committee in 1919-20 which identified reform and rehabilitation as the true objective of prison administration. It made several important recommendations which included : (i) establishment of separate jails for different categories of prisoners; (ii) minimum area of 75 square yards per inmate within the jail walls; (iii) creation of special courts for hearing of juvenile delinquents and their housing in remand homes; (iv) holding of separate conference of Inspector Generals of Prison every alternate year; and (v) segregation of child juveniles from adult prisoners within the jail walls. Regrettably, no conspicuous efforts could be taken for integrated and comprehensive reforms in jails. It is incidentally the courts that have intervened to lay down specific rules and guidelines for prison reforms from time-to-time.

The Supreme Court in *Joginder Kumar vs. State of UP and others* (1994) cited the findings of National Police Commission that 60 per cent of all arrests were either unnecessary or unjustified and laid down four requirements to be strictly followed. These were, (i) the right of the arrested person to request that a friend, relative or other persons of the delinquent be informed of his arrest and the place of such arrest; (ii) the duty of the police officer to inform the arrested persons of this right; (iii) the need for an entry to be made in the police station diary as to who was informed of the arrest; and (iv) the duty of the Magistrate before whom the arrested person is produced to satisfy himself that these requirements have been complied with. On the whole, the police officer making an arrest should record in the case diary the reasons for making the arrest. This means that every arrest by the police has to be justified in law.

Despite judicial interventions, suggestions and recommendations made on prison reforms, the conditions of prisoners in most of the jails continue to be old, antiquated, inhuman and even overstretched.

Even though prison population is low in India by international standards, the low rate of conviction may be the result of passive and regressive steps taken for reform in jails. Better and effective reforms, of course, call for providing better facilities to inmates and promoting professional competency in prison administration. This, in turn, would require adequate funds for modernization of jail infrastructure as well as procedural reforms including changes in existing statutes and rules. Reforms in jail administration would be more effective if reforms in corresponding areas in entire criminal justice administration takes place particularly in certain possible areas like reducing the number of arrests for petty offences, increase the possibility and availability of bail, speeding of trials, providing alternative modes of dispute resolution in few areas like heinous offences and creation of an impartial and professional system to consider remission of sentences, parole etc. The Mulla Commission made some wide ranging recommendations on organizational structure of prison services, adoption of a jail manual and involvement of experts and NGOs in the field of treatment, care and rehabilitation of offenders, establishment of more open prison etc. The NHRC also prepared a model Prison Bill. In 1998, the Ministry of Home Affairs circulated a model bill to the states which some States like Rajasthan adopted. A new model Jail Manual was also circulated to all states by the Union Government in 2003. Keeping the above in view, the Moily Commission (Second ARC) recommended that, (i) Union and State Governments should workout to arrange funds for modernization of prison system; (ii) necessary legislations should be enacted and adopted; and (iii) existing rules on parole and remission of sentences be reviewed by an Advisory Board headed by a retired judge of the High Court, the DGP and the Inspector General of Prisons of the State. The recommendations of the Board should be normally accepted. For remission of sentences, a separate board of the same Advisory Board may be empowered to deal with.

That the status of prisons in our country can be well imagined from the latest report of National Crime Records Bureau (NCRB). Overcrowding, under-staffed and rising number of undetrials is the sorry state of affairs that continues in Indian jails as per latest government statistics showing 4.18 lakh people in jail with 117 sharing the space meant for 100, (Prison Statistics India, 2014). The National Crime Records Bureau showed that nothing much has changed in Jails. Our Jails could accommodate only about 3.56 lakh people. The States could increase the capacity only by 8702 in 2014 as against increase in the number of prisoners by 6544. Although the occupancy rate has come down from 118.4 per cent to 117.4 per cent compared to 2013 figures, overcrowding continues to be the main problem faced by most of the jails in the country. While 12 States including Andhra Pradesh, Bihar, Gujarat, J&K, Odisha, Tamil Nadu, Telengana and West Bengal have an occupancy rate less than 100 per cent, States like Chhattisgarh, Uttar Pradesh, Madhya Pradesh, Assam, Jharkhand and Delhi, have more than 100 per cent of national average. Dadra and Nagar Haveli is reported for having the highest overcrowding at 33.7 per cent (199 prisoners occupying space of 60) followed by Chhattisgarh 258.9 per cent and Delhi 221.6 per cent. In Chhattisgarh jails, 16525 prisoners are cramped in space for just 6382 while Delhi has 13850 in the space of 6250 showing an increase of 4.8 percentage points from 216.8 of 2013. Karnataka jails had a capacity of 13381 housing 14221 prisoners by the end of 2014 compared to an increased capacity of 281 and 103 prisoners during 2013. The report, however, indicates that Uttar Pradesh had the highest number of 18221 inmates followed by MP (36433), Bihar (31295), Maharashtra (27868) and Punjab (26007). The number of convicted prisoners has increased by 15 per cent in 2014 (1.31 lakh) over 2013. Number of persons convicted for rape charge has increased by 8.4 per cent in 2014 (8879) over 2013 (8188).

The report also reveals that over 3500 under-trial prisoners at the end of 2014 are in jails across the country for more than five years without closure of their cases. This is 16 per cent increase from the previous year 2013. Of them, 176 are women. During 2013, there were only 3047 such prisoners and 2028 in 2012. The figures of last few years indicate that the pace of growth of prisoners has been increasing. Uttar Pradesh contributed 1022 persons (28%) in 2014 against 914 in 2013, Bihar 477 in 2014 as against 464 in 2013. Punjab is the only major state which has shown decrease in number at 294 during 2013 and 180 during 2014. The overall profile of jails, number of inmate convicts, under-trials and occupancy status is reflected in Table 5.1.

Table 5.1: Occupancy Status of all jails in India including inmates convicts and under-trials

No.of Jails	Capacity	Inmates			Convicts			Education Status	
		Total	Male	Female	Total	Male	Female		
1387	356561	418536	400855	17681 (4.2%)	131517	126114	5403	Illiterate	3522
								Below X class	56469
								Above class X	28853
								Graduates	96993
								Post graduates	2219
								Tech Degree/ Diploma	1781

Under trials	282879	Occupancy	
Male	270783	2012	112.2%
Female	12096	2013	118.4%
Illiterates	82735	2014	117.4%
Up to X class	119370	As on 31st December, 2014	
Above class X			
Graduation	55605		
Graduates	17000		
Post-graduates	5202		
Tech Degree/Diploma	2967		

Government figures indicate that there has been a steady decline in death penalties when voices against death penalty are getting louder these days. The number of death-row convicts in Indian jails and awarding of capital punishment have decreased in the past couple of years. The figures of last three years, i.e. 2012, 2013 and 2014 are shown in Table 5.2 below :

Table 5.2 : Death-row convicts in Indian Jails

Year	No. of prisoners housed in jails on death row	Percentage of death row convicts compared to total no of convicts	Percentage of convicts given capital punishment
2012	414 (women-13)	UP- 82% (0.1%)	UP —25.8
2013	382 (women-10)	(Karnataka in top five)	Maharashtra —36
2014	318 (women-8)		MP —33
			Bihar —28
			Karnataka —24

The figures show that the number/percentage of awarding of capital punishment is also decreasing. While 125 people were awarded death sentence in 2013, it came down to 95 in 2014 as against 97 in 2012. During 2014, Bihar awarded the highest number of capital punishment at 17 followed by UP 16, MP 12, Maharashtra 9, Chhattisgarh 8, Gujarat, Jharkhand, MP (5 each) and Karnataka with one only.

The overall position explains that there has not been any spectacular change in the decrease in number of capital punishments although the Law Commission had recommended for abolition of death penalty. The Union Home Ministry is learnt to be not in favour of abolition death penalty on the ground that the time is not ripe for such a move. The report also shows that the number of commuting death sentence to life also increased during 2012 (64) and 2013 (115) but during 2014 only 112 cases were reported.

Reforms in Crimes Against Vulnerable Sections and Children

It has been often reported that certain sections of society like the Scheduled Castes, Scheduled Tribes, women and children are more vulnerable to different types of exploitation and become victims of crimes. Protection and enforcement of rights of these sections of society is the primary duty of the administration and the police. Besides being victims of other crimes, they are also victims of atrocities, discrimination, exploitation, prejudices etc. Although Article 17 of the Constitution abolished untouchability and protection of civil rights was enacted in the year 1955 providing punishment for untouchability offences followed by the Scheduled Castes and Scheduled Tribes (Prevention of Atrocities) Act in 1989 to curb atrocities on these sections of people, nothing tangible has happened. The Commission for Scheduled Castes and Scheduled Tribes was established in 1978 with Constitutional status given in 1992 (65th Amendment of Constitution). But a separate Commission was constituted for Scheduled Tribes exclusively in 2004 (Eighty Ninth Amendment) to assist both Central and State Governments for better and effective implementation of the aforesaid Acts. But implementation of the provisions of these Acts have not been spectacular either in terms of speedy disposal of cases or in terms of investigation, conviction rate and pendency of such cases. Similar is the position with regard to crime against children. Working children in different areas of occupation including street children are more vulnerable. Different data reveal that there has been a general increase in all categories of crimes particularly those relating to trafficking of girls for prostitution as well as child marriage and rape. In spite of comprehensive amendments to the Juvenile Justice Act, 2000 and the recently enacted legislation enhancing the juvenile age from 18 years to 16 years, tackling of such crimes requires a combination of professionalism and sensitivity to ensure that the victims are not subjected to secondary or repeated victimization due to their suffering from post-traumatic stress. Therefore, government should take concrete and salutary steps to increase awareness in the administration and among the police in particular regarding crimes against children to tackle such crimes.

References

A.K. Samanta, *Village Watch System in India, Perspective and Prospect*.

Bibhu Prasad Routray, *NIE* 09.09.2012.

Biswajit Chakraborty (2012). Training day, *The Statesman*, 8th July.

Editorial – Political powerness, *NIE*.

J.C. Chaturvedi, *Police Administration and Investigation of Crime* (Edited).

J. Venkatesan, *The Hindu*, March 29, 2013, States drug their feet.

Mohan Das Menon, *NIE* Dt. 01.12.2013, Restructuring Metropolitan and Rural Policing.

Mohanty, Satyajit, Rural Policing and Community Policing, *Political & Business Daily*, April 2013.

N.K. Singh, *The Hindu*, September 12, 2014; The CBI's Crisis of Credibility.

Prakash Singh, *NIE*, India needs people's police instead of present ruler's police.

Prakash Singh, *NIE*, Dt. 14.12.2014, Translate Words in to action to make SMART reality.

R.K. Raghuvan, *The Hindu*, 06.02.2015, The Price of indiscretion.

R.K. Raghuvan, *The Hindu*, December 21, 2013, Lok Pal and the CBI, A cure worse than malady.

Sankar Sen, Unresponsive Police, *Statesman*, 10.05.2013.

S.V.M. Tripathy, *Status of Armed Police Battalion in India*.

The Hindu (P. Jacob), March 24, 2013, *Women in Police, The Gender question*.

6
Corruption—Transparency and Accountability

Bureaucratic Corruption

Corruption is one of the most vital issues that surround the bureaucratic system today. Transparency International's Corruption Perception Index (2002) places India in the 71st position in a list of 102 countries with a score of 2.7 in a 10-point scale which shows hardly any improvement over its past scores of 2.78 (1995), 2.63 (1996), 2.78 (1997), 2.9 (1998), 2.9 (1999), and 2.8 (2000). In spite of all noble impulses and recommendations of Surinder Nath Committee on Civil Services Reforms there was every anticipation that the reports will be allowed to gather dust in the corridors of power and that almost came to be true. The real danger anticipated was that only cosmetic changes would receive with a so low a voice that the recommendations would be irrelevant in practical sphere. The much hyped "objective personal appraisal", even if resorted to, the normal expectation was that the system may degenerate into one of dysfunction only and the system may not be self-sufficient to correct itself from degeneration. Therefore, it has been often suggested that periodic test of civil servants is necessary to prove their professional competence. There seems to be feeling that corruption breeds where incompetence and nepotism prevail. Another suggestion which normally is placed was to ensure wholesale ban on re-employment after retirement. It is a fact that some bureaucrats spend their last few years of service networking and obliging people who matter to ensure post-retirement rehabilitation for themselves often at the cost of public interest. In this area no amount of criticism would actually work to thwart these efforts unless public opinion through the media is alert and knowledgeable NGOs are moulded effectively together to demand transparency through "Right to Information". This exercise would result in effective reform in administration. A lot of discussion about corruption, nepotism and criminalisation concerning the bureaucrats goes on. Thick-skinned as they are in the system, many reportedly get away scot-free under the cliché of red-tap. Therefore, in spite of several attempts of occasional reform impulses, the end result has not been encouraging indeed.

As part of the administrative reform initiatives, the UPA Government was reportedly contemplating to amend All India Service Rules to prevent corrupt IAS/IPS officers from taking refuge under the State Government they work for. As per the proposed amendment to Rule 6, officers shall be deemed to be on Central deputation a month after a request in this regard has been sent to the State Government concerned. The idea behind this reformatory step was to bring corrupt officers to the centre so that action can be initiated against them. As of now, Rule 6 states that in case of differences between the Centre and the State over deputation of an officer, the views of centre will prevail. But very often it is noticed that States do not allow the officer concerned to proceed to the Centre. Instances are many. The amendment was likely to expand the scope of Central Vigilance Commission (CVC), empowering it to monitor activities of all IAS/IPS officers and just not those serving at the Centre. If the amendment was to take effect, the CVC and internal security agencies can prepare monthly reports on IAS/IPS officers who are under their scanner. Once those officers are placed under Central deputation, taking action against them would be rather easier. On the basis of reports by the CVC, it will consult respective State Vigilance Commissions and Internal Security Agencies without any interference from the State. Currently State Governments can refuse to go along with Centre's move to order, for instance, a CBI inquiry against a particular IAS/IPS officer. The case of UP's former Chief Secretary Akhand Pratap Singh is the glaring example. Mr. Singh was voted as the most corrupt officer by the UP IAS Officers' Association and the Centre initiated a probe against him and a CBI inquiry was ordered in 1999 by Atal Behari Vajpayee's office. For three years, the State

Government sat on the request and Singh went on to become UP Chief Secretary and was even cleared for extension till the courts intervened on the basis on a PIL filed. It is only after his retirement that Mr. Singh was raided by the CBI. The CBI reportedly unearthed more than Rs. 100 crore, said to be the ill-gotten wealth of Mr. Singh. He reportedly owned more than 42 properties spread across three states in the names of his family members. Apart from voting him as the most corrupt officer of the state, when a delegation of IAS officers met the then Chief Minister Kalyan Singh and mentioned to him for probing the acquisition of assets of A.P. Singh, Kalyan Singh straight away refused to hold such a probe. On the other hand, A.P. Singh continued to hold important posts under successive Chief Ministers and his career progressed uninterrupted until Mulayam Singh Yadav made him the Chief Secretary of the State and even went on to grant him an extension. A.P. Singh's case is a typical of political and bureaucratic corruption in India making it more sinister and damaging than corruption in other parts of the world. It is alleged that corruption in India occurs more upstream and probably less downstream. This type of corruption at the top distorts fundamental decisions about policies, projects and developments. Very often corrupt gains are smuggled to safe havens abroad and not ploughed back to domestic production and investments and this is done both by venile bureaucrats and corrupt politicians. The case of A.P. Singh is a typically illustrated case which established that corruption often leads to promotion and not prison.

In advanced industrial countries of South East Asia notably Japan and South Korea, even top leaders are not spared for corruption charges. The former Italian Prime Minister Bettino Craxi had to leave the country in exile in Tunisia to escape his extradition due to corruption charges against him at home. But unfortunately, in India, corrupt persons are too powerful and beyond accountability. Government departments have built up institutional mechanisms that perpetuate and not eliminate corruption. Upright officers are frequently transferred to unimportant posts or marginalized so that the corruption chain is not disturbed. One of the main reasons why corruption has become so endemic and pervasive, especially among public servants, is that it has become a high reward and low-risk activity. Very few public servants are ultimately punished. Some kind of a "law of the jungle" as a sociologist puts it, prevails. A large number of cases (more than 4000) under the Prevention of Corruption Act were reportedly pending at one point of time in different courts in the country. Peculiarly, sometimes junior officers or clerks are only punished but senior officers are seldom brought to book. It is difficult to find IAS or IPS officers except a very few in recent years being charge-sheeted, tried and convicted and serving a jail sentence under various provisions of the Prevention of Corruption Act. In recent years, a few cases like the former Police Commissioner of Mumbai and the former Collector of Patna that some action was reportedly taken, thanks to the media for highlighting the gravity of incidents that the errant public servants were involved in. It is reported that at one point of time since 1990, the Central Vigilance Commission (CVC) granted sanction for prosecution against about 100 civil servants and only one was reportedly convicted by a court of law. Besides criminal cases, departmental proceedings have become a long-drawn and time-consuming matter. While disciplinary proceedings applicable to civil servants, observes Santhanam Committee in its report, "are not dissimilar to those in several other countries, the proceedings for implementing dismissal, removal or reduction in ranks are far more elaborate and formal." There is a considerable weight in the recommendation of the Santhanam Committee that "it should not be unreasonable clarification to treat in a separate category of charges of bribery, corruption and lack of integrity and provide for simplified procedure." Unfortunately, bureaucratic corruption prevails because of political corruption. The unholy nexus between corrupt politicians and venal civil servants is well known.

The growing nexus between politicians and civil servants becomes apparent from the Central Vigilance Commission Bill, 2003, passed by Parliament. The Central Vigilance Commission (CVC) Bill, 2003 provides for a three-member Vigilance Commission, but makes the employees of the Central Government at the level of Joint Secretary and above immune from any enquiry for any offence allegedly committed by them except with the prior approval of Central Government. The only rationale given by the government for this differentiation is that it is essential to protect officers at the decision-making levels and relieve them of anxiety and the likelihood of harassment. Thus, in the newly enacted law there are two groups of government servants, one comprising those below the level of Joint Secretary, and others above who are to be treated by different yardsticks and on this basis, the officers at the decision-making levels, must be protected. The Central Vigilance Bill is indeed an unconcealed attempt to detail the judgement of the Supreme Court in the *Vineet Narain case*, which had earlier declared null and void the direction of the Central Government known as the "Single Directive". Similarly, more or less akin to the above exceptional provisions, steps are also being followed by some State Governments in respect of State Government employees.

The problem of political corruption which gives rise to bureaucratic corruption, has been further compounded by the entry of criminals in politics. Many powerful criminals, instead of playing the role of king-makers behind the scene, are jumping into the areas of politics and trying to become political leaders themselves. They have both muscle powers and money power. At one point of time, there were about 40 tainted Ministers of Parliament in the Thirteenth Lok Sabha itself and in the Fourteenth Lok Sabha, there were about 100 such tainted members. The "National Commission to Review the Working of the Constitution" recommended that any person charged with any offence punishable with imprisonment which may extend to five years or more, should be disqualified from contesting the election. If a political party puts up such a candidate with knowledge of his antecedents, it should be de-recognised and de-registered. The Commission also recommended that the criminal cases against politicians pending for trial or in appeal must be disposed of by appointing special courts. But the political masters are in no mood to pay any heed to these recommendations. Considering the prevailing situation one gets the impression that the instruments for fighting corruption are getting blurred. The character for the premier investigating agency of the country, namely the Central Bureau of Investigation (CBI), has been widened to deal with various other forms of crimes not connected with corruption. It is now saddled with all kinds of cases by the government and also the courts. With a strength of 600 to 700 officers spread all over the country, the CBI is not in a position to investigate and prosecute more than 1000 cases in a year. Anti-corruption wings in different states have also become politicised and fail to play any useful role in preventing corruption. The heads of anti-corruption wings of different states are used to further partisan ends of the ruling party.

The Vigilance Chief is not permitted to submit charge-sheets against senior government servants without the clearance of the government, and if the assigned government servant is close to the powers that be, the permission is invariably withheld. Some years back the Central Vigilance Commission had made public a "black list" of officers against whom sanction for prosecution had been needlessly delayed. In the majority of cases, the CBI has sent repeated reminders to Ministry and the departments concerned to give the sanction but without any success. At one point of time the Customs Department alone, as reported in the press, was holding up sanction in as many as 12 cases involving 55 officers who had been booked by the CBI in the year 2003. In the case of *Vineet Narayan*, known popularly as the "*Hawala Case*", the Supreme Court laid-down some procedure to insulate the CBI and Enforcement Directorate from extraneous pressures. There is a similar need to identify other sensitive posts in the government which can be filled up from a panel of names recommended by an objective and independent committee. The composition of the committee can be different for different posts. Once selected, the incumbent should have a minimum tenure of 2-3 years. This may bring about a change in the present system in which corrupt elements literally bribe their way to important posts. In a forthright interview, one of the ex-directors of CBI clearly admitted that the autonomy of the agency (CBI) is a myth and there are constant pulls and pressures to go soft in sensitive areas. Nevertheless, the fixed term will give some elbow room to the upright officers to withstand pressures. Further, the Prevention of Corruption Act (PCA), 1986, should be revised to make it more effective. The provision to attach properties of government servants who are facing trials for acts of serious corruption and in possession of disproportionate assets should be more emphatic. The hard-fact, however, remains that the foremost requirement in the battle against corruption is a strong political will and no anti-corruption effort will be successful if this is missing. There lies the rub where the political will is missing. The bill to set up the institution of Lok Pal gathered dust because of lack of political consensus. Of late, due to sustained effort of an activist group led by the social worker Anna Hazare that a new Jan Lok Pal Bill had been attempted and in turn, a new Lok Pal Bill has been passed by Paliament under the UPA-II Government. A powerful, independent and effective institutional mechanism can play a significant role in curbing corruption. In this connection, a few instances of other countries could provide sufficient evidence to our politicians and bureaucrats to go for change of mind in bringing real reforms in administration. The Independent Commission Against Corruption (ICAC) set-up in 1974 in Hong Kong did a remarkable job in reducing corruption and enabling Hong Kong to break out of the corruption trap. The then Governor, Sir Murray Machehose, made the commission independent of any department and responsible only to him. From its inception, the ICAC has adopted a policy that anti-corruption work requires more than just investigation and prosecution. It has also a branch concerned with prevention which seems to reduce opportunity for corruption and to involve the public in it. The government indicated its commitment by appointing a person of impeaccable integrity to head the ICAC. Singapore has also devised similar institutions to bring down high corruption to a low corruption economy.

Another disquieting factor is that corruption has become legitimised in India and particularly among public servants. It no longer provokes a sense of outrage or moral indignation. A corrupt public servant, particularly if he is rich and powerful, is no longer held in disrespect or ostracized. This deadening of social conscience and lack of disapproval has provided further stimulant for corruption by public servants. The biggest factor behind the cancerous growth of corruption in civil service has been the unholy nexus that has grown up between the corrupt politicians and corrupt civil servants, the so-called "*Babu-Neta* Syndrome". This explains the rare unanimity among the politicians to nullify the Supreme Court's direction in the '*Hawala Case*' declaring the single directive null and void. It was a set of executive instructions issued by the Central Government, prohibiting the CBI from undertaking an enquiry or investigation against an officer of Joint Secretary and above in the Central Government, including those in public sector undertaking and nationalized banks, without prior sanction of the head of the department. However, all political parties agreed to bring the single directive back on the ground that officers at the decision-making level of the government require protection. The Vigilance Commission Bill, which has been passed by Parliament contains this vicious clause and seeks to detail the judgement of the Supreme Court. Politicians perhaps have their own compulsions. Today elections have become prohibitively expensive and also entry points for criminals in politics. Election expenditure is 20 to 30 times more than the legal ceiling prescribed. All over India, it is estimated that Rs. 7000 crore or even more are spent on elections to Parliament and State Assemblies in five years. This figure has swelled up in the meantime. This expenditure can be sustained only when the return can be high and the return can be high only when high levels of corruption are sustained over a long period of time leading to institutionalisation of corruption. In consequence, political masters rely on civil servants considered pliable and dependable. Honest officers are marginalized and dishonest officers get plum postings. Corruption in India, as the UNDP report says, leads to promotion and not to prison. Because of organizational and infrastructural deficiencies, the CBI is hardly capable to make any dent when such cases are decided long years after trial. Besides and unfortunately the Anti-Corruption Agencies or Vigilance Commissions of different states seem to be politicised and often utilized for political witch-hunts rather than preventing corruption. In some states it has become a practice to launch criminal cases against political opponents when a new party comes to power. Very few cases are thoroughly investigated and resolutely pursued in the courts of law. As a result, political leaders charged with corruption are seldom brought to book. Even without a crystal ball, one can foresee the fate of cases launched by the Punjab Government against Prakash Singh Badal. The head of the anti-corruption units in the states also acts as a hatchet man of the government. Of course in some states like Maharashtra and Odisha the vigilance and anti-corruption chiefs have done comparatively good work. Even in some states, the vigilance chief is not permitted to submit a charge sheet against any senior government officer without clearance by the government, and if the government servant is involved (as is very often the case) is close to the powers-that-be, the permission is withheld. While overall control of the government over anti-corruption wings is understandable, control over the registration of cases and submission of final forms is contrary to the provisions of Criminal Procedure Code.

Today corruption has become so widespread and all pervasive that many people cynically believe that it is not possible to get out of the corruption trap. In spite of this general feeling of distrust and disappointment, there are a few success stories in some of the

Asian countries like Hong Kong and Singapore as mentioned earlier which have been able to complete the transition from high-corruption societies to low corruption ones. A small country like Bhutan has succeeded in keeping corruption at a low level. The foremost requirement in the battle against corruption is to have a strong political will. No anti-corruption agenda will be successful if this is missing. So far, the political masters have not displayed any resolute-will to combat corruption. However, it is hoped that growing pressure of public opinion and international concern will force the hands of politicians to act. The World Bank and the IMF have openly condemned corruption and decided to accord greater priority to combat it in their programmes. In December 1996, the UN General Assembly adopted a resolution calling upon its member-states to take effective concrete action "to combat all forms of corruption, bribery and related illegal practices in international commercial transactions". Therefore, successful anti-corruption strategies to stem the rot in the civil services must include : (i) A mechanism to identify the corrupt public servants without disclosing their names publicly. A provision to this effect in the Prevention of Corruption Act should help drawal of list of corrupt public servants without legal acrimony; (ii) Confiscation of ill-gotten property. The Benami Prohibition Act, 1988 has remained a dead letter because the rules laying down the manner and procedures of acquiring benami property under the Act have not been inexplicably framed; (iii) Public officials must submit every year a detailed break up of their assets position and tax returns. If the returns are carefully scrutinized and followed by swift inquiries against some of the known public servants living beyond their means, it will have a deterrent impact. The existing provision in the Government Servants Conduct Rules regarding submission of annual property returns is honoured more in the breach than action. Therefore, any attempt to trace and trap corrupt ones ends in a failure; (iv) Establishment of exclusive anti-corruption courts for completion of trials within a time-frame; and (v) Provide immunity to the informers. There was a need to have Whistle Blowers Act to ensure that whistle blowers are protected against retributive action. Many Western countries have the Whistle Blowers Act to prevent employers from taking retributive action against the Whistle Blowers. In our country the tragic *case of Satyander Dubey* is still fresh in public memory. The Government of India's resolution of April 2004 now empowers the Chief Vigilance Commissioner (CVC) to act on the complaints of the whistle blowers and to protect them. Of late, the Whistle Blowers Act is in place but implementation not materialised. However, it is futile to hope that corruption can be eradicated by the government's efforts alone. Public Vigilance, therefore, is the cornerstone of any anti-corruption strategy. In the United Kingdom, bodies known as anti-corruption leagues have done useful work in educating the people and consolidating their will to resist corrupt practices. Citizens are fertile sources of information about where corruption is occurring. It is also necessary to evolve sound group norms and service ethics based upon twin concepts of honesty and efficiency. The Service Associations, instead of concerning themselves solely with the improvement of pay and career prospects mainly must take initiatives in establishing such group norms.

The arrest of a senior IAS Officer of the Haryana cadre sometime back by the CBI for acquisition of properties disproportionate to the known sources of income was shocking but no longer surprising. In this case the CBI made a record of sorts in terms of cash recovery from public servants. It could recover Rs. 2 crore cash from the residence and bank lockers of the officer. Of late, a number of officers of All India Services, both IAS and IPS, have been detected for involvement in brazen acts of corruption. Intervening in a debate in the Rajya Sabha (7 May, 2004) on corruption in bureaucracy, the then Deputy Prime Minister L.K. Advani said "out of 186 cases pending against IAS and IPS officers the overwhelming majority related to corruption charges. The decline in the standards of probity of the senior civil services has become more pronounced during the last three decades. In August 1947, when India became Independent, the country's bureaucracy was, by and large, regarded as efficient, disciplined and devoted to its responsibilities. It was subjected to rigorous Government Servants Conduct Rules. Even in the early sixties, the number of officers of dubious reputation in All India Services could be counted on the fingers on one hand, but by 1998, the Indian Bureaucracy was adjudged as one of the worst in Asia, let alone, in the world. This was the verdict of a Hong Kong based think-tank called Political and Economic Risk Consultancy (PERC) and was based on its annual survey of businessmen who have been interacting with the bureaucracies of Asian countries. On a 10-point scale, Singapore was rated the best at 2.53 and Vietnam the worst at nine. India with 8 points was occupying the ninth position among the 12 Asian countries. This is indeed a very depressing state of affairs for a country, once proud of the quality of administration and dedication of its senior bureaucrats.

The *Telgi Stamp Scam* appeared as gargantuan dimension as this shamed the once-famed police force of Mumbai which came to be dubbed as "gangsters in uniform". An officer of the rank of Inspector-General of Police was arrested and put in a police lock-up for complicity in the very crime he was paid to prevent and investigate. The long interrogation of the Police Commissioner of Mumbai by the special investigating team that forced him to go on leave days before his retirement surely could not provide any comfort to the morale of a uniformed force. It was tentatively estimated initially that above Rs. 30,000 crore was involved in the crime and may go up as investigation proceeds. The complicity of police with the criminal appeared to be unmistakable. The Mumbai police doubtlessly allowed the criminal to spend his days not in a grimy police lock-up in Dharavi but in posh Mumbai hotels or in his equally swanky flat in Cuffe Parade amid his favourite herbal baths. The trade was payment of huge sums of money to the custodian and upholder of law. The case, at the preliminary investigation stage revealed that an Assistant Police Inspector with a monthly salary of barely Rs. 10,000 was found with assets upward of Rs. 100 crore; an IG of Police with a monthly Salary of Rs. 30,000 held an asset of Rs. 25 crore. The SIT reported that the culprit Abdul Karim Telgi had been comfortably allowed to spend time in his own flat instead of in the police lock-up. Therefore, the so-called "Steel Frame" has become "Steal Frame" today. The answers to all these demeaning values in bureaucracy probably accounts for lack of accountability and transparency, which have spawned a culture that has made corruption a "risk-free high-return industry" in India. The litany of culpable public servants in recent memory is rather endless: starting from Chairman of Punjab Public Service Commission to a Chairman of Central Board of Excise and Customs to a former Vice-Chairman of Delhi Development Authority and sweeping in its embrace a whole string of system-busters. Regrettably in the system people are alarmed but not shocked. In fact, public memory is lamentably short and people in general are apt to forget these incidents in due course of time.

Some time back in a report it was said that about 20000 central services officers control the collection and disbursement of over Rs. 325000 crore every year. They take decisions that can encourage competitiveness or destroy it in favour of a particular corporate. A small reduction in customs duty can lead to a windfall for one company and catastrophe for another. If these officials allow about 10 per cent leakage in revenue, it means a loss of Rs. 30000 crore to the government. If the officials get a cut of even 10 per cent, the Indian bureaucracy gets over Rs. 3000 crore. This, practice is well-known to the power corridors and the Prime Minister's office was so alarmed with the volumes of complaints that it set up a special anti-corruption unit in 1996 and 2000. The CBI pitched in with 2256 cases under the PCA between 1998 and 2001, the conviction number though is a different story. It is, in fact, pathetic. But more than this, what is truly alarming is the fact that these very public officials facing prosecution circumvent the system by admirable management of their networking skill. While the rule of law and natural justice should and must have a place in the system, they have little place where the basic tenets of such a society are violated. While the law can be exploited to delay prosecution and gain valuable time, bureaucratic networking can be trusted to forge new equations to enable the so-called questionable characters to surge ahead. While some of the most corrupt officials are rewarded with prize, postings, and transfers continue to become a flourishing industry, this continues to promote openly and encourage criminalisation of the system. In the backdrop of this situation, many questions are apt to be raised. Given the anatomy of corrupt personnel, why is that they manage to find berths in those very sensitive assignments that should be singularly denied to them? Do honesty and efficiency not go hand in hand? Are not people bright and honest in the same breath? The reality is that while most of the dishonest are bright, the arrested Inspector-General of Police of Mumbai was reported to have graduated from IIT and IIM. These people are self-doers keen to over-achieve for themselves. Not that the honest are any less bright and brilliant than their dishonest counterparts; they are inhibited to act in the same cavalier way because the system and its manners do not help them perform. Unlike the dishonest who are excellently networked to achieve their objectives, the honest are self in their own little pockets without a clue on the happenings in the other part of the world.

N. Vittal, former Central Vigilance Commissioner highlighted five factors as the root of corruption in India. These are : (i) Scarcity of goods and services; (ii) Red tape and delays which give rise to the phenomenon of speed money; (iii) Lack of transparency in decision making; (iv) Cushions of safety built into our legal and administrative systems/procedures and a very healthy principle that every man is innocent till proved guilty prompting the corrupt to use their ill-gotten wealth to engage the best legal brains and escape the clutches of laws; and (v) Tribalism or a sense of "*biradari*". The UNDP lists India way down at rank 135 out of 175 countries when it comes to human development. The World Economic Forum, Geneva has rated India 50 out of 53 when it comes to global competitiveness. The significant fact is that India's performance is worse than that of China (59th position), Ghana (50th position), Mauritius (40th position) and South Africa (36th position). The most surprising fact is that China ranked as the second most corrupt country with a score of 2.15 in 1995 has over the last 7-8 years improved its score to 3.5. Some other countries like Brazil and the four Nordic countries (Denmark, Finland, Norway and Sweden) have always led the index. The UNDP report on Human Development 1999 on South Asia avers that if corruption level in India goes down to that of Scandinavian countries, the GDP will grow by 1.5 per cent and foreign direct investment will go up by 12 per cent.

All the above indices mean that corruption is the cancer that is sapping India's governance. This has led people to dub India a 'Kleptocracy' whose political, social and economic philosophy has thievery, robbery and thuggery written all over it—a word that has now found a place in the 2002 edition of the New Oxford English Dictionary. We should be aware and conscious of the South Asian countries that once registered an economic growth belied its growth potential to eventually crash in 1997. It is high time we showed up transparency, accountability and better governance. Generally, there are two aspects of corruption : (i) money paid for favours done; and (ii) money paid for doing what should have been done on its own. The first is clearly political corruption. For example, an industrial licence granted out of turn, a preferred location, favoured access to a scarce resource, a privileged appointment, inside information divulged, showing the booth in mammoth government contracts, i.e. defence, oil, railways etc. The stakes involved are gigantic. Ostensibly, the funds are amassed for the party, although one would never know the truth. The magnitude of political corruption is mind-blowing. Bofors, the submarine purchase, 2G spectrum, Coal, CWG and Adarsh Housing scams are good examples. Every major government purchase lends itself to abuse. At the state level, Electricity Boards, State Transport Corporations and various State co-operatives are in the same league. The nation loses several thousand crores each year from smuggling and of course the Hawala. The Telgi scam is a clear, unadulterated loss of precious government revenue. The greatest benefit of liberalization process is the elimination of quasi-rent in a number of areas that were the hot-beds of corruption. The motivations of all these types of abuse could be twofold; power and a variance political power costs a lot of money. It is sad but true. Late Rohington, Chairman of Thenmax had suggested, may be justifiably, to legitimize donations to political funds. Any individual or company can donate funds to a recognized political party and claim tax deduction. The political party will be required to maintain a strict audit of the party's funds by impartial auditors and a defalcation of funds would merit criminal strictures in the same way as one would do in a business organization. There could be no limit to the amount the party can spend for an election so long as it is vouched and audited.

The other facet of corruption is administrative corruption. It has been very succinctly, said that "the act of bribing is, in many ways, reminiscent of the act of love, a subtle overture, a gentle response, a mild flutter, a turn of phrase, a little body language and a partnership begins to develop." A good bit of administrative corruption stems from lack of proper homework. There are several areas in and reasons for which administrative corruption takes place even because of defective system in-built. It could, if the scope of supply of a project is unclear, if terms of contract are subject to interpretation, if strict record of alternation is not maintained, if the project is not regularly followed up and reviewed etc. At the turn of twentieth century, in Europe and United States, sanctified corruption due to acquisitive capitalism born of possessive individualism was almost a way of life. Even though over the decades, there has been appreciable changes in procedures, practices, the reformatory measures are sadly breached with impunity. In such situation, remedy in criminal procedure and first-track legal system is warranted. Edward De Bono had the idea of lateral thinking to find-out a solution to the problems by considering various options. N. Vittal, the former CVC India recommended several measures to overcome delays in our legal system. He observed, "There are 30 million cases pending in various courts. The average time span for a dispute to be resolved through the court system is about 20 years. Litigation has become a convenient method for avoiding prompt retribution by many people on the wrong side of law. The Bible says that the path to hell is paved with good intentions. The legal system is meant to punish the criminal and protecting the law abiding citizen." He said, "many a time, the criminal exploits the legal process itself to escape punishment. Take for example the widespread crime of corruption. One reason why we cannot check corruption is because the corrupt, with the financial clout of their ill-gotten wealth, are able to engage the best legal brains and quibble their way through the legal system and laugh all the way to the bank. I would recommend strongly a result oriented managerial approach. If the entire legal system can be approached from the point of view of a well run company whose focus is on productivity and the bottom line in terms of achieving objectives, such a managerial approach to legal reform, instead of a purely legalistic approach, may yield new and better results." He adds: "the corrupt and the criminal escape punishment by taking advantage of the delays in the process." The CVC for instance finds that many a time, before the departmental action is taken and the guilty is to be punished, the charged officials have already retired. At times, it may not be even possible to effect a deduction in pension. Then, of course, the ultimate end is death. At least four files are put up to the CVC every month where the charged officers have expired." Therefore, the only deterrent that can be of any consequence is to arm the civil society with the Right to Information Act which has been passed by Parliament in 2005. In addition, a mass upsurge with "Quit Corruption Movement" is also wanted in our country today. The people must rise against the marauders of public money and morality. The "Anna" (Anna Hazare) movement is a direct pointer to all these malaise in recent years.

In our country, nobody seems to be accountable to the country itself. Why is it happening in our country whereas in developed countries like Singapore there seems to be better discipline? N. Vittal, in one of his articles, has identified seven factors responsible for poor governance. The first of course is the cast-iron protection given to all public servants, thanks to the Article 311 of the Constitution. It was provided with the best intention that nobody must be penalized without due enquiry and a chance to defend himself/herself. The net result is while it may be easy to engage a person, it is very difficult to throw him out. This led to what Vittal calls the first law. The law says that in any organization, those who work get more work, and those who do not work, get pay and promotions. The second factor is that state of Indian judiciary and the judicial system. Our judiciary is the most protected one in the world. It is even protected from the truth, thanks to the Contempt of Court Act, 1971. As a result, any intelligent, effective and objective discussion about improving the judiciary is out of question. Punishment of the guilty ultimately depends on the process of law and the judicial system. Already the public servants are protected by the shield of Article 311. So, why should anybody be responsible at all? The third aspect of our governance which promotes irresponsibility is the culture of secrecy, thanks to the Official Secret Act. Our laws provide tremendous scope for discretion which is the fourth factor leading to not only growth of corruption, but also a sense of irresponsibility. One need not be fair as a public servant because one is already protected, thanks to the culture of secrecy causing from the Official Secret Act or alternatively, the slow moving process of punishment. In fact, irresponsibility has become a part of our democratic system because we have a process of democracy based on corruption. In the fifth sector, all political parties collect funds in the form of cash. Black money is generated by evasion of taxes and illegal activities and black money is the oxygen for corruption and corruption is the oxygen for black money. Money is the engine which makes the political parties function.

The dilution of the strength of national parties has led to the present era of coalition politics. Every political party seems to be keen on "making hay while the sun-shines". Because of the peculiar development of our fractured politics and "coalition *dharma*" parties have started insisting on not only their representatives in the Cabinet but asking for "lucrative Ministries". In the UPA-II coalition government, many small state-level constituent parties had done that whether it is for the Telecommunication Ministry or the Railway Ministry. The entire system is being shaped for exploitation and looting of public money openly by design. This has been possible because of coming together of the corrupt elements in politics and the corrupt elements in bureaucracy. When the Central Vigilance Commission (CVC) published the names of the corrupt officials in the website in the year 2000, one dramatic fact that came out was that many corrupt officials were occupying sensitive posts. This is the sixth factor. Apart from the natural attractions between corrupt politicians and corrupt bureaucrats, the politicians have also perfected the art of breaking the backbone of the honest and straight-forward civil servants by two weapons. These are the weapons of transfer and suspension. This is the seventh factor. Thus, we have a system of bad governance in the country where nobody is responsible. Due to the above seven factors, the system is designed to lack accountability. Noises were being made about setting up of Second Administrative Reforms Commission and the same was established which has, in the meantime, submitted its report with recommendations. A separate Commission for judiciary and also enacting the perpetually evading Holy Grail of the Lok Pal was also being vociferously pleaded for. It is almost certain that none of these measures is going to ever succeed unless the above mentioned seven factors which are at the root of irresponsibility and lack of accountability in our system are tackled.

Political Corruption

Corruption has admittedly grown to monstrous proportions and taken its deep roots in our body-politic. Corruption is not merely process of monetary transactions of give and take. It has greater ethical and moral dimensions too. That this has declined or disappeared from our mind could be substantiated if an example of the action of Khan Abdul Gaffar Khan, the "Frontier Gandhi" as he was commonly called, could be cited. Mr. L.C. Jain gives an account in one of his writings as to how Gaffar Khan had to travel from Peshwar to Delhi Railway Station covering almost about 50 journey hours and even did not stretch his legs although all the seats in his compartment were vacant because he had paid for one seat only. Such an instance of rare quality of honesty can never be found these days. That was the Gandhian legacy for which no prescription was required unlike the present-day Lokayuktas which have been setup in some states to watch people's conduct. True, India has more than a billion people and we cannot expect all these individually to be as clean as the Frontier Gandhi. Not all, not even a microspic of it could be like Satya Sai Baba, Sri Sri Ravi Shankar or Swami Ranganathan Nandaji. But, do we have a guaranteed state mechanism to contain and curb corruption or should we have more of legislation in shape of anti-corruption laws, corruption-detection squards, prosecutors or Lokpals, Lokayuktas, the CBI, the CVC, the states' agencies of vigilance and Intelligence Bureaus? In the entire country one finds a few Lokayuktas and less Lok Pals obviously to spare political masters (Ministers, MPs, MLAs etc.) to catch the small fish, i.e. the clerks instead of big guns (senior bureaucrats). That in spite of several agencies available for anti-corruption drive, there is no compelling sword against the Ministers is evident from a past statement of Mr. Pranab Mukherji that no action could be taken against a charge-sheeted Minister for the fear that the then Central Government might fall.

The often quoted definition of corruption, i.e. use of public office for private gain sounds so ancient and casual because of all-pervasive nature of corruption that people in general find it to be simply funny. That corruption is not a new phenomenon and it is seen in increased proportions in higher echelons of bureaucracy and elected political functionaries is evidently clear. This happens often in collusion of or in nexus with criminal elements. The best eye opener evidence is traceable in the report of Vora Committee. Reports of various agencies clearly indicate that corruption is mostly rampant in Administration of Revenue, Public Works, Public Distribution System, Welfare Schemes, Irrigation and Police departments of state governments and in the major tender and contract deals of Central and State Governments. Corruption reportedly takes the form of speed money for expediting approval/ sanction of providing legitimate services or bribes for doing illegal acts including twisting of rules/instructions mostly at lower levels and this happens more often because of the vertical integration between officials and politicians. The top functionaries are unable to check the prevalence and growth of corruption in public life because of the malaise of black money and erosion of moral value of people in society. A startling report of Transparency International (India) has revealed after survey that Rs. 26,728 crore is wasted every year due to corruption in our country for which the poor suffers the most. The Indian public pay this as bribe to avail of public service. The areas in which maximum amount is given as bribe include Health (Rs. 7,578 crore), Power (Rs. 5,764 crore), Education (Rs. 3,552 crore). The "India Corruption Study 2005" released by Transparency International reports that ordinary citizen pay bribes to the tune of Rs. 21,068 crore annually for availing of public services. Sixty-two per cent of the people surveyed said that corruption was real. One-third of them said that corruption was on the rise compared to the previous year 2004-05. Among the 159 countries surveyed by the aforesaid agency, India is placed at 88th position in the Corruption Perception Index (CPI). In the ten-point scale, its position is 2.9 which is compared to countries like Mali, Benin, Gabon and Tanzania.

India's recent past corruption and scam-spangled history beginning with the security scam of 1992 involving an amount of about Rs. 5000 crore is a pointer to the series of scams that unfolded their severity in the nineties. The sugar scams of 1994 (Rs. 650 crore), the fodder scam (Rs. 920 crore) of Bihar, housing scam (Rs. 17.4 crore), Hawala scam (Rs. 65 crore), JM bribery case (Rs. 3 crore) were detected in 1995. The urea scam (Rs. 133 crore), medical equipment scam, telecom scam (Rs. 1200 crore) all happening during 1996. The Bofors and the Submarine deals, the great bank scam and the multi-crore Telgi stamp paper scam of 2003 have shown how vulnerable the nation has become merely because the men in key positions could not resist the lure of money. The latest two major scams of Commonwealth Games (CWG), 2G Spectrum and the Adarsh Housing scam (Mumbai) have exceeded all past records.

Diaries seized from Hawala dealer S.K. Jain and his brother revealed the recorded payment of Rs. 65 crore to 115 persons. The Jains had acted as nodal points, allegedly passing laundered money to a wide-range of politicians including L.K. Advani, V.C. Shukla, Devi Lal, Shard Yadav, Rajesh Pilot, Madhav Rao Scindia, N.D. Tewari, M.L. Khurana, Yashwant Sinha, Ajit Kumar Panja, R.K.

Dhawan and Arjun Singh. All the accused politicians were later on let off as the Supreme Court ruled that diary entries of the Jains were insufficient for conviction without corroborative evidence. Pt. Sukhram created a sensation when currency notes worth Rs. 4 crore were discovered during a CBI raid at his residence in 1996. Besides, Sukharam was booked in cases related to telecom deals for disproportionate assets. In 2002, a Delhi Court convicted and sentenced him to three years RI for causing a loss of Rs. 1.68 crore to government in a telecom equipment deal. But the Delhi High Court, later on, suspended his sentence and granted him bail. Several MPS of Jharkhand Mukti Morcha and break-away faction of Janata Dal were paid bribes in 1993 to help defeat a no-trust-motion against P.V. Narasimha Rao Government. In October 2000, Rao and Buta Singh were sentenced to three years RI. On their appeal, the Delhi High Court first stayed the order and later acquitted them. The Supreme Court had ruled that the bribe-takers who voted for Rao enjoyed immunity. The Rs. 950 crore fodder scam was unearthed in Bihar in 1996 involving Lalu Prasad Yadav, Jagannath Mishra and a slew of officials. Lalu Prasad resigned as CM and was jailed several times as an undertrial. Lalu and his wife were also booked for possessing unaccounted assets worth Rs. 42 lakh. Charges were framed against Lalu Prasad Yadav and Jagannath Mishra in two fodder scam cases. The sting conducted by Tehelka.com on defence deals in March 2001 led to the resignation of former BJP Chief Bangaru Laxman and former Defence Minister George Fernadandes. Bangaru Laxman was sentenced to a 4 years term in prision by special court of CBI. The NDA Government ordered departmental action against defence officials and a judicial probe into various issues including the *bona fides* of the news portal. The UPA Government abruptly terminated the judicial probe and initiated action against politicians during the Tehelka tapes. In the 1970s, Jayaprakash Narayan's anti-corruption agitation called "Nav Nirman", brought down Chiman Bhai Patel's Government in Gujarat. Rajiv Gandhi lost the 1989 polls over Bofors. The Congress party was identified with corruption and non-performance while the BJP later projected itself as a party with a difference. After six years of NDA rule and a host of scams that failed to dislodge any Minister, anti-corruption campaigns no longer fire the public imagination. The UPA-II Government has been charged of corruption in 2G Spectrum, Coal and Commonwealth Games (CWG). Criminal cases are pending against the then Minister A. Raja and some MPs and Ministers.

It is a tragedy that our political leaders and Ministers were the enemies of our own people who elect them as their representatives. The combination of political corruption and bureaucratic collusion has been the undoing of the Indian polity. The Supreme Court had criticised the Union Government for inaction of the Rs. 1000 crore Indian bank scam. Corruption in high places involving "big fish" (as the former Chief Justice of India J.S. Verma observed in Hawala cases) is not possible without the active assistance and complicity of the bureaucratic brass. When Sukharam was booked in the telecom deal, nobody asked at that time as to why any action was not taken by the functionaries of the concerned department who were charged with the responsibility of preventing large-scale loss of public funds from the Consolidated Fund of India. Did anybody question as to whether the tenders were evaluated according to the prescribed norms and whether the Secretary and other officers of the department advised the Minister of the consequences of finalising the tenders against their advice recorded in the file? Therefore, greater transparency strikes at the root of corrupt and criminal politics. That politics is criminally corrupt is established from one example at least. On May 2, 2002, the Supreme Court of India passed a landmark judgement mandating candidates contesting Parliamentary or Assembly elections to disclose in the public their criminal records (convictions, acquittals, charges etc.) if any; their assets and liabilities, their educational qualifications etc. This was indeed, a rare opportunity for the silent majority to make itself heard. People have a right to know, if they still elect corrupt politicians. Peculiarly, all major political parties resisted the Chief Election Commissioner's efforts to get the Supreme Court directive implemented by demonstrating rare unanimity to set at naught the Supreme Court directive. In an all-party meeting on state funding of elections convened by the Chief Election Commissioner in February 15, 2006, there could be no consensus among political parties although there was agreement that money and muscle power should be eliminated. The Indrajit Gupta Committee had clearly underlined that arrangements should be made in such a way that there should be full state funding, with no loopholes left to be exploited by the parties and a level playing filed ensured for all candidates. In this, the Centre and the State must share. Funding should be through political parties and not directly to candidate. There should be strict enforcement of the limit of expenditure.

Corruption is one of the damaging consequences of poor governance characterised by lack of transparency and accountability. It lowers investment and hinders economic growth and human development by limiting access to basic social services as well as increasing the cost of their delivery. It also increases poverty, subverts financial system and undermines the legitimacy of the State. Therefore, corruption is anti-poor, anti-development, anti-growth, anti-investment and inequitable. The cost of corruption to a nation is, therefore, very high. Transparency International's definition of corruption as "use of public offices for private gains" displays an inadequate appreciation of the nature and dimension of corruption in India and other developing countries. This definition is limited in scope as it refers to individuals only. In our system, political partronage and middlemen exploit for personal gain. They may not hold public office but are greately responsible for corruption in siphoning public money. Therefore, a broader definition of corruption has to be devised. Normally, the strategy for bringing out transparency is neither focused nor effective. It is true that as transparency increases, corruption is reduced. But a direct approach for tackling corruption is required so that quick results are obtained for bringing about a demonstrative effect to ensure a credibility in the system. The efforts of government to curb corruption through the Prevention of Corruption Act (PCA), 1988 and through its vigilance machinery have become almost ineffective. The defect apparently lies in the approach of government's vigilance machinery which is basically a *postmortem* activity for which it hardly has any contribution to combat corruption and increase transparency. The main activity of vigilance machinery is to nab culprits and bring them to justice departmentally and criminally. This implies as if the vigilance machinery waits with patience and indulges while giving opportunity to take bribe and commit the crime. After the crime is committed, a much of funfare and publicity is made and effort to punish the guilty rarely succeeds. There is hardly any preventive action and proper vigilance to reduce incidents of corruption. Moreover, vigilance personnel do not have the ability for fool-proof and expertise to deal with white-collar crimes. The investigation becomes tardy and prosecution is half-hearted. The century-old police machinery designed for law and order have neither the expertise nor temperament to tackle corruption cases with expediency. Disciplinary proceedings and court cases continue years and success rate of conviction is extremely low. The big fish thrive with impunity, whereas the police covers up its ineffectiveness by catching small fry giving high voltage publicity to inconsequential cases relating to lower employees and operatives. The hardened corrupt officials go scot-free. On the contrary, lack of knowledge and expertise as well as lack of integrity on the part of investigating machinery results in harassment of honest officers and act as a dampener for taking bold-decisions.

The other intriguing issue which relates to corruption is the role of politicians. In poor and developing countries citizens normally look up to the government for everything. In the course of time, government consisting of political leadership and bureaucratic apparatus has become all powerful. In India, politicians have arrogated limitless powers to themselves. They seem to be omnipresent and omnipotent dominating all aspects of economy, administration and activities concerning and affecting the people. Today, the politician is the most dominant element of a corrupt system. Many political leaders are fountain-heads of corruption. Electoral politics is the most corrupting aspect of Indian political system. Politics has become a lucrative profession. A politician has the final say directly or indirectly for every major decision, whether it is policy-making, law implementation or administration. He is entitled to take decisions without professional expertise and moral basis and many a time without holding public office. The decisions are dictated by short-term considerations. Unless their role is restricted only to the specific responsibility of representing the voice and interest of the people, there is no hope to achieve a transparent and honest government system. The civil society institutions must be proactive in combating such widespread corruption in the country. Otherwise, no measure of administrative reform in India would be effective and fruitful for a successful and vibrant democracy of ours as we claim to be. The Anna movement and Kejariwal's tirade against corruption and passionate zeal for bringing out "Jan Lok Pal" Bill are positive efforts towards cleansing the existing corruption climate in the country.

The Central Vigilance Commission had raised the issue of some Union Ministers' corrupt practices—putting pressure on chief of various public sector undertakings to grant them undue favours. Nothing happened on this score although some of the Ministers had directly/indirectly accepted such allegations as partly correct or completely incorrect. Absence of clear evidence helped equivocation and obfuscation and the hatchet was quietly sought to be buried. In another incident, a prominent Minister in the past demanded everything for himself at the cost of public exchequer, toilet, fancy floors, a fountain at his official residence, re-doing of the residential lawn, residential lighting and paintings, air-conditions, geysers, mobiles, photographs, interior decorations, payment of bill for a banquet and so on. The Goa, holiday in a five-star hotel seemed to have stoked the Minister's feel-good instincts. Slightest acquaintance with government functioning may enable to know that such things go on with impunity literally everyday. They know that it is easier to ramdown such things the throats of PSU's than the Ministries/Departments. And that is why most of the political masters are keen that the structure of PSUs is not changed through disinvestments. The India shining advertisements given-out in the past by Ministries fall in this category. The demand for grants sanctioning appropriation from the voted expenditure is nothing but trust reposed on the executive by the highest body of people's representatives to spend money collected through taxes and revenues that the public has paid. Long ago Kalidas quite perceptively wrote: "The state took taxes and revenues from the people only to ensure their own prosperity in return, like the sun takes moisture from the earth only to give it back in thousand fold measure." This means that civil servants including political masters who draw their powers from the people must necessarily use them for the welfare of the people and not for their own enrichment. In today's India, sadly the "fence merrily eats the crop it is meant to protect."

To say that India is changing is to hide the truth. But it is also obvious that it is not changing for all its citizens. Even a casual observer cannot miss the squalour in which a large number of the poor and the deprived live. Economic reforms have, no doubt, given new buoyancy to the Indian economy, but it is also a fact that they have not touched a large section of the Indian people. To do that, government needs to undertake basic political and administrative reforms. The economic reforms undertaken so far have neatly skirted this issue. This option is not available if the goal now is to reach the marginal sections of the society. The privatisation route on its own will not be able to accelerate the developmental process for them. Even the NGO route has very limited scope in large parts of the country. Many NGOs are doing wonderful work in some areas, but where they are needed most, a large number of them have become as inefficient and corrupt as the governmental structures. In the North-East for example, it is alleged that many Ministers have floated NGOs under the control of their wives and children to siphon public funds. For some times to come, government agencies will continue to be the main channel for reaching people in these areas. Since, there is little possibility of initiating any meaningful political reforms in the near future, former Prime Minister Man Mohan Singh had done well to concentrate on administrative reforms. Successive governments have been talking about administrative reforms ever since independence, but the exercise has remained mostly on paper. Politics and politicians are the main hurdles as the *status quo* suits them. The administrative system has become progressively worse. It is today neither professional nor neutral. Clearly, no substantive administrative reforms are possible without some consensus, informal if not formal, in the political class. But our polity is more divided today than before. And there are no signs that this trend is likely to be reversed in the near future. Some leaders like Lalu Prasad Yadav have become role models for ambitious new comers in this highly lucrative profession of politics, cutting across party lines. His brand of politics is being practiced in more than one state. Self-seekers who dominate today's political scene call the shots. They are busy destroying every democratic institution that comes in the way of their single-minded pursuit for power and money. But the solace is that Indian judicial system, in spite of several deformities, could put Lalu Prasad Yadav in Ranchi jail in the fodder scam and defranchising him from the political career. To say this is not to paint all political leaders black. Many of the senior leaders in every political party are persons of high integrity. Unfortunately, they find themselves helpless in controlling their rank and file.

The Supreme Court on 6th May, 2014 held as invalid the legal provision that makes prior sanction mandatory for the CBI to conduct a probe against senior bureaucrats in corruption cases under the Prevention of Corruption Act. On the petition filed by BJP leader Subramaniam Swamy and the Centre for Public Interest Litigation (CPIL) the Court held that section 6A of the Delhi Special Police Establishment (DSPE) Act which granted protection to Joint Secretary and above officers from facing even a preliminary inquiry by the CBI in the corruption cases, was violative of Article 14 of the Constitution. This was a landmark judgement in that it would now empower the CBI in the investigation into several cases pending due to the provision that has now been struck down by the Constitution Bench. It is noteworthy to cite what the Appex Court observed in this case. To quote "Corruption is an enemy of the nation and tracking down a corrupt public servant, however high he may be, and punishing such person is necessary mandate under the PC Act, 1988. The status or position of a public servant does not qualify the person exemption from equal treatment. The decision-making power does not segregate corrupt officers in to two classes as they are common crime doers and have to be tracked down by the same process of inquiry and investigation." The bench observed that section 6A of DSPE Act granting protection to one set of officers is directly destructive and run counter to the object and reason of the PC Act, 1988. It also undermines the object of detecting and punishing high-level corruption. How can two public servants against whom there are allegations of corruption, graft or bribe-taking or criminal misconduct under the PC Act, 1988 be made to be treated differently because one happens to be a junior officer and the other a senior decision-maker? Therefore, section 6A of DSPE Act has propensity of shielding the corrupt. There could not be any protection to corrupt public servants because the aim and objective of investigation is ultimately to search for the truth and any law that impedes that objective may not stand the test of Article 14 of the Constitution. Therefore, breach of rule of law amounts to negation of equality under Article 14 of the Constitution. Section 6A, therefore, fails in the context of these facts of Article 14.

Overview

In the above context, the former Prime Minister's (Man Mohan Singh) new initiative for administrative reforms could be considered timely. Undaunted by the failures of the past attempts, he had taken two major decisions: setting up of a second Administrative Reforms Commission (ARC) and a complete revamp of the appraisal system for the IAS, as a starting point to reform the senior bureaucracy. There is little doubt that he was really serious as he had not to wait even for the constitution of the second ARC before announcing the second step. He rightly separated the process for the higher bureaucracy from the mid-level and lower bureaucracy. One could only hope that he proved the skeptics wrong; as he did in case of economic reforms. A step-by-step approach, which does not ruffle too many feathers, is more likely to succeed. All past attempts failed miserably, because they attempted too much and stepped on too many toes. The problem may be phrased in terms of control, accountability and responsibility. They are all inter-linked. Accountability to the people will be an illusory goal if the political executive keeps on strengthening its hold on the administrative machinery at all levels. Posting, transfers, and promotions are mostly left in the hands of the political leaders. The system, as it has developed since Independence, is today neither neutral nor effective. The obsession to make it neutral at all levels, higher and lower, has not worked and is unlikely to work in the foreseeable future. Maybe, the time has come to think of an alternative model of administration where central and local bureaucracies are organized differently. The process of reform can be very different for the lower and the higher bureaucracy. The merit criteria cannot be uniformly applied for all civil services at the higher level and it may be a basic requirement in a country with such diversity; it need not be so in case of the local bureaucracy where partisan behaviour could be less of a handicap and prove more effective, if the goal is empowerment of the deprived sections and to speed up development in the rural areas. Local government is expected to be mission-driven and not rule-bound. Even a partisan bureaucracy at the village level can be more accountable and committed if monitored properly at the political level. The acceptance of hierarchy and rational-legal authority in the villages is formalistic at best. Such a pattern of authority conflicts with the traditional basis of authority in most other relationships. Personal authority constitutes a crucial component of administrative structure in the rural areas. This is not going to change very soon. Strong loyalties to caste, religion, language and ethnic groups dismiss commitment to the national political system and have the potential for political unrest and instability. A system which includes the expertise of the career civil servant and the commitment of the political appointee, and is able to exercise a delicate balance between rules and discretion, is more likely to succeed at the local level. The district administration is the cutting-edge of the delivery system of government services and programmes, and that is where reform process should start. More than one innovative alternative model, excluding the judiciary and police could be tried on an experimental basis in different parts of the country to get proper feedback.

Of late, there has been considerable focus on the issue of civil service reforms following the report of the "committee on civil service reforms" headed by P.C. Hota as Chairman and the undercurrent of growing dissatisfaction on the effectiveness of public delivery systems. However, by no means, the disenchantment with the system is new as amply demonstrated by the number of committees and commissions set up from 1947 onwards. The Hota Committee re-identified many a reason for the 'poor' performance of the civil services. A number of recommendations such as reducing the recruitment age to 18 (from the present 21), periodical reviews for weeding out the inefficient and the corrupt, etc, are proposed for improving the system. However, this report, like many of the earlier ones, glossed over the structure of the civil services itself. Surprisingly, even the very definition of the civil service itself is restricted to those who are recruited through the combined civil services examination, which constitutes 1.5 per cent of the Central Civil Service. Furthermorc, there is an overwhelming emphasis on the Indian Administrative Service, which constitutes less than 10 per cent of the group "A" services; an explicit recognition that we are not ready to move forward from the much-maligned 'colonial legacy'.

The internal structure of the civil services is such an anachronism that any discussion of reforms without totally destroying the same and recreating a modern structure is bound to fail. The Hota Committce itself quotes Jawaharlal Nehru's statement of 1954 vintage: "Administration is meant to achieve something and not to exist in some kind of an ivory tower following certain rules of procedure and narcissus-like looking on itself with complete satisfaction. The test after all is the human being and their welfare." Unfortunately, the civil services are not even able to look at themselves with self-satisfaction as the internal structure has been so blatantly destroyed in the years that followed Nehru's statement. These internal contradictions originated with the basic rules and regulations governing the civil services themselves, pet named the Fundamental Rules (FRs) framed in 1921 and adopted, as it were, on the eve of the country becoming a republic. These rules are 95 years old and still going strong. Any attempt to decipher them by reading the volumes written in the colonial legal language must be very challenging task. With the 1921 foundation, which was tailor made for colonial monolithic civil service structure, we went in for specialization post-republic. Then it became the duty of the "administrators" to perpetuate their hegemony over the new found specialized cadres with the old distinction between "line and staff" which was used by the colonial system to demarcate field organizations from the rule/policy makers. Successive minor attempts have been made to maintain the edge of one service over the rest, in pay and perks, posts and promotions. The inter-service and intra-service rivalries have cast long shadows over administrative efficiency. Thus, even within the top echelons of the civil services (1.5%) which were so earnestly trying to 'reform' the caste and *dharma* wars being fought are even so destructive to the very foundation of the system.

Coming to the rest 98.5 per cent, it is the story of "a million mutinies a day". As in a feudal hierarchy they constitute the bottom pyramid meant to serve the top. With further divisions into many groups and sub-groups with varying service conditions in terms of promotion, pay and perks, a regular fratricidal war is ensured. Without proper training and right ethos they are expected to perform inaccordance with the changing times and expectations. If civil services are to be reformed and the delivery system is to be enhanced, the existing structures need to be destroyed and the 1921 vintage rules governing the civil services wiped-out. The objectives and goals need to be recast and modern structure created on the principle of equity and non-discrimination. A well-trained structure without intra-service, line staff differences and a clear statement of rewards and punishment for performance and non-performance is the remedy. Performance evaluation has to be based on pre-set, transparent, objective criteria. In short, what we need is a Schumpeterian creative destruction rather than building extensions or pillars for extra support to a dilapidated old structure. Such a revamping will be possible only from above, not by committees housing vested interests—retired or otherwise.

Reforms in administration are over-due in India. The half-century-old bureaucracy after independence needs overhauling inorder to shoulder the emerging commitments. Therefore, the tasks are more comprehensive and demanding due to conditions created by changing situations between private and public sector economy. Therefore, the present system of governance needs to provide for a change from power-shift to a people-centric governance. Rightly or wrongly India's planning model was greately influenced as much by the Western prescriptions as by the Russian pattern of planning the whole economy. The private sector had merely an indicative target of investment with no specific mechanism of monitoring. The whole of agriculture, much of industry, commerce, bulk of civil, electrical and other construction works remained with private companies and the public sector had to be contented with a variety of institutions, boards, consultative committees, co-ordination committees. Consequently, the system of governance remained in utter jeopardy devoid of a clear channel of accountability.

The "Founding Fathers" of our republic chartered out sustainability to democracy and development, economic welfare and social change. The whole infrastructure of planning was an administrative undertaking without wholesale displacement of the private sector from agriculture or commercial sectors. Both public and the private sectors had the opportunity to grow and develop capacity together even with some risk of inefficiency. With passing of time the approach appeared to introduce imbalances. Unfortunately, politics intervened and public offices became the means for running parties and amassing personal wealth. There was decline in the framework of public policy for change and clarity about the accelerators of development. Controls imposed selectively and periodically became a regular feature. In the process, the public sector over-reached its capacity while capability developed in the private sector remained under-utilized. Consequently, the needed balance of the public sector working essentially as a countervailing force to moderate the capitalist greed eluded us. Similarly, the private sector inducing efficiency in public sector for a more competitive economy did not materialize. Even in a limited space, the private sector failed to remove the exploitative image with the common people. Although correction was needed, nothing tangible happened in that direction and ultimately the administration had to be blamed for the tardy progress although greater responsibility lied elsewhere. Indian administration has failed to develop lobby for change. Its diversity prevents a coherent class approach. It is a house divided within. It has failed to resist political intrusion in its cadre management and the decision-making apparatus. It has also allowed the dependency syndrome to overwhelm it. Piecemeal development has distorted its capacity for improving its identity and relevance.

Administrative reform that overcomes the aforesaid hurdles is clearly in the executive domain. Judicial intervention in the executive domain has been rationalized on lack of executive manageability which cannot do without effective and efficient administration. Delayed overdue reform has brought the administration to a standstill. We are atbest having a maintenance administration. Although discretion built into the system has a purpose but its use for good has to be applied very cautiously as large part of the use is tainted. Speed in decision-making and in implementation is thwarted by complex procedures but given the existing environment, use of discretion adds to risks. Therefore, any reform must weigh the risk-propensity environment if efficiency and effectiveness are to be ensured. Therefore, attitudinal change in the political and judicial spheres and removal of adversarial postures is complementary to administrative reform.

In private sector, despite so much of hype about human resource, reduction of manpower is the first and easiest way to improve profits. It is not so easy in the public sphere. The reform strategy to downsize establishment in many countries under the World Bank recommendation was found to have increased costs. The staff salaries and modernization of working increased costs of more than reductions from downsizing. In India the improved remuneration on Pay Commission recommendations is often quoted as having played mischief in managing the fiscal situation. However, the reactive rationale in first having removed all restraints on managerial remuneration in the private sector and value change for life style under the liberalized economic management are presented as productive. A performing public service will seek some sense of parity with segments that thrive on tax concessions, subsidies and other sops in the name of competitiveness. Economy in revenue expenditure and cost effectiveness has to be precisely defined. Administrative reform has to be projected within a clear context that suits the governance needs and the challenge of growing global integration.

It is misconceived to plead that economic and commercial globalization is leading the way. Globalization in terms of security, culture, regional identity proceeds a pace. Domestic developments have focused on the spread of the cult of violence, ideological assets on cultural diversity, economic and social disparities and declining levels of social discipline. All these are not purely administrative tasks but involved interests that have grown into the habit of engaging the administration to settle scores. Under these situations can the administration be expected to take on the task that belong to the political and social leadership? Will it ever be effective as a conciliator as in the past, if the current trends are not arrested? If not then, how will administrative reform be influenced by these cross currents? Finally, does not the country's political class has the stomach for realistic reforms that address these critical issues? The progress of the "Right To Information" legislation and its operationalisation, the progress on controlling the spread of corruption in high places, the progress on electoral reforms, the progress on even the highly selective measures to tighten the administrative leadership debated during 1997 do not provide any hope. The government has been good in setting up commissions and committees but it is quick to develop a cool feet when the reports are furnished. The Mallimath Committee report on various aspects of criminal justice reform and the Hota Committee report on civil service reform are more recent examples of negative political commitment. It is well recognized that major reforms require broad political consensus and strong government commitment. The Prime Minister had, therefore, realistically stated that reforms beyond a point need legislation, that is to say a political agreement.

Now, the question arises as to who shall bell the cat? The issue therefore, boils down to debate the matter threadbare at the political level. A coalition system provides the best opportunity. If the Central Government picks up courage, the States will have to respond. Now, that different political parties are participating in governments either at the Centre or in the States, there is enough scope for initiating political dialogue. Reform has ideological, constitutional as well as technical dimensions. Major political parties appear on record to support reforms. The agenda of both the NDA and the UPA in the past shows this. Other political parties would agree except for what they have grievances about the way the administration functions. Therefore, the issue boils down to defining what reforms are politically digestible and to prepare common minimum objectives and directions for public debate. The Constitutional aspect may need for a proposal to amend provisions in existing legislation and procedure in the light of the experience in the last half a century. Subordinate legislation appears to have expanded the discretionary authority a lot. There has been an undercurrent of demand to curtail it. This is the job of the government and the technical aspect of the issue needs to be gone through by an expert committee/commission. The constitution of the Administrative Reforms Commission headed by Mr. Moilly is a step in the right direction. The National Common Minimum Programme (NCMP) provides for short-term action and long-term deliberation only. However, a consultancy has been commissioned in respect of the Food Corporation of India (FCI) to control inefficiencies that increase the subsidy burden. This seems to be an economy rather than an administrative reforms undertaking. The Central Government has succeeded in persuading State Governments for a decentralized PDS, improving coverage and containing costs.

The long-term measure is covered by setting up of an Administrative Reform Commission which has been done. Going by the experience of the previous Commission (1966), it would take a long time and unless a character has gone through a process of debate and consensus, it would remain a bureaucratic exercise only in the technical domain. To provide an administration that is responsible and responsive at all times can only draw cynicism without action on real reforms that have been made repeatedly by knowledgeable teams and persons and lie buried in the record rooms. The former Prime Minister, as reported in the media, is reported to have suggested restoration of the relationship of trust between the Minister and public servants. He mentioned the commitment to provide transparent, citizen-friendly and accountable government. In his address to the Secretaries some time back he emphasized on their working according to their mission and feeling and said they were free to meet him if there were hurdles in doing so. He also suggested that opportunities within department reforms of the administration should be identified and advantage taken to accomplish. But about restructuring, he has hardly articulated. The still-born idea of early recruitment and training according to the French system and the panel system with personal interview, in the footsteps of private companies for filling up top management posts are counted in that category. He has not referred to the liberalization era proposals such as contracting, larger lateral entry, exchange of executive positions between business and public administration and the like.

Budget power is another source of reform of procedures, delegation of financial authority for expeditious implementation, flexibility in hiring manpower and its deployment and shift in allocations for cost-cutting. Budgetary entry into the administrative reform focuses on the card objectives of financial prudence, allocative efficiency, budgetary integrity, revenue-consciousness. But pretty little is being done for this. Even though exhaustive inputs are provided by the Comptroller and Auditor General as well as financial committees of Parliament and State legislatures, the budget fails to reflect in the enhancement of quality of financial management. Another area of reform is the process of plan-making and implementation. More than a decade of liberalization has not been able to establish a changed role for the Planning Commission. The Planning Commission is almost placed in a subservient position in micro-managing of national finances and economic reforms which is in-charge of the Finance Ministry. A methodology may have to be developed to bring about co-ordination of the private sector in the monitoring mechanism of economic policies, structure of public-private partnership etc. The present NDA Government has replaced the Planning Commission by a "NITI AYOGA" the structure, function and policy initiatives of which are to be watched now. The administrative departments must make their duties clearly known. Each department must have a task force to examine how to ensure efficiency, economy and integrity. The Department of Administrative Reform at the higher level should define tasks, enter into dialogue with the departments and other groups to solicit views as to how departments should move. The New Employment Guarantee Act, the Rural Health Mission, the Right to Education Bill, the Food Security Bill and a few other schemes of the Central Government bear pious intentions but their administrative implications have to be understood for successful implementation. After all, administrative reform is not merely for efficiency and economy but also capacity building, structural modernization, procedure simplification, financial delegation and some other critical problems of management. Therefore, thought should be given to making administration redesign systems, redefine responsibility and relocate accountability and display limits of delivery.

For all the ills attributed to it, the bureaucrats cannot be wished away. For lack of any alternative, it will remain the interface between policy and its implementation, between promise and its deliverance. Imbuing the appraisal process with expertise and impartiality is thus a good start. But much else needs to be done speedily to restore the 'Steel Frame' to even a semblance of its envisioned self. The latest proposal for bureaucratic reform originated from the former Prime Minister himself which would acquire more substance if it dovetails with a cascade of appraisal process. There is, for instance, the recommendation by the P.C. Hota Committee on civil services reform that mid-career appraisals be made more meaningful. Ways and means of shifting the worthy from the incompetent and the corrupt must be evolved. Bureaucrats are endemically susceptible to hierarchies. To be viable and efficient, checks against the unwieldiness and inaction, need to be constantly upgraded.

The P.C. Hota Committee suggested catching IAS potentials young. Prabir Sen, an ex-Secretary to the Government of India puts the emphasis on a set of core values and purposeful training. Certainly desirable, but in 50 years ethos neither has had any recognition. Can these be isolated from the total environment in which corruption is ubiquitous, brazen and rampant; where there are no proper performance criteria, no objective performance decisions. About 85 per cent of the people are dissatisfied with all the public services. We are attempting to fool young All-India Service aspirants and the public, but only fooling ourselves, disregarding the hard facts of the wider environment. The IAS and IPS are contrasted unfavourably with the ICS of Phillip Woodruff's "The Guardians". The unfavourable comparisons are flawed. The ICS of the British pre-1947 period was both civil service and government. Not so after 1947. Even the ICS after 1947 was far from "The Guardians". They refused to have a joint ICS/IAS Association after 1947. They failed to convey to their new masters the true civil service relationship with the political executive on the Westminster model, a crucial failure. They knew they would die-out in the next 25 years. They failed to give the IAS the training and traditions they received from the British ICS. In the early 1950s, long before Indira Gandhi's compelling "commitment"—the first senior official to "mind-read" political minds was an ICS officer in Bihar cadre. When an excellent ICS officer like L.P. Singh, Chief Secretary, Bihar was abruptly shunted to Delhi by the Chief Minister, that short shrift should have at least rung a bell in the ICS cadre. But it did not. The era of political "commitment" had begun. When the commitment era came with the emergency, ICS officers were seen criticising the then Cabinet Secretary who was also an ICS officer. Similarly, when one of the last Cabinet Secretaries failed to stand up for an honest IAS Secretary of Petroleum and Chemicals, he was demeaned by an unprecedented arrest by a Police inspector in his office, in the ephemeral regime of Charan Singh, it was the financial confirmation that the ICS was not even "The Guardian" of the civil service, not to speak of the people of India. In spite of this, there was a few of the best of the Indian ramp of the ICS namely H.M. Patel, L.P. Singh and Bhagwan Sahai, but they were a too few.

Neither nationalist politicians crying for the *Swaraj* since 1920s nor the ICS examined the historical nature of 25 centuries of Indian governance since the Mauryas to realise that, (i) there were Central Governments for only five of 25 centuries, and that too by foreigners, the Mughals and the British for three of five centuries; (ii) those 25 centuries showed India was strong in all forms of art and culture and trade, but weak in good, institutional government; and (iii) there was a mere "transfer of power" from the British to Indian hands with virtually the entire laws, traditional and systems of the pre-1947 colonial governments, together with Second World War economic control. Neither the politicians nor the ICS thought of better indigenous forms of *Swaraj* especially the centuries-old customary management of local resources of land, water, forests by local communities destroyed by centralising governments in last two centuries. If the present IAS and other post-1947 services are to function in an Indian environment, what are the characteristics of that Indianness, as admitted and recognised by

Indian themselves? The progressive increase in Indianness cutting across old political parties and all sections of Indian society may be summarised in: (a) low public and organisational work ethic from legislature to public office; (b) low civic mindedness; (c) self-hood, caste and community superseding any public or national interest; (d) the continuance of the "*jagmahi*" government; and (e) opportunist and criminalized politics to the near total exclusion of public, national and long-term interests. These conditions are sustained because of the lack of active sustained interest of business leadership in good governance, beyond their sectional interests.

In the above backdrop of wide, weak and historical background, much more, than "catch them young" is to infuse value systems. "Better Training" is India's need. Where are those larger, effective, purposeful answers? Is there any honest analysis of past government failures leading to the dissatisfaction of 85 per cent of the people? Is it a case of ungovernable governments with ungovernable people, the problems magnified by size and plurality? In her famous study of violence, Hannah Arendt has pointed out to the disintegration of public's services—"schools, police, garbage, public transport, traffic problems, pollution etc in mass societies." Large political and administrative bureaucracies cannot cope. They become self-interest, not public service groups. Therefore, representative democracy is no substitute for participative democracy. Prolonged failures of good governance leads to loss of legitimacy, credibility and then power itself. When power without legitimacy and credibility is exercised, it fails. Such repeated failures lead to mass violence in the form of riots and insurgencies, now terrorism. So, there is no alternative to the widening and deepening of meaningful participatory governance at all levels from village to town, to State and Centre. Citizens must govern local governments. Their representatives must ensure that. Representative government through more functional legislatures is a part of this participatory process of real democracy. Or else, there would be tyranny of invisible tyrants, masquerading as democratic government behind the political and administrative bureaucracies. All these require a belief in constructive democratic opposition, in freedom and right to information, e-governance, respect for human rights organizations and NGOs, the CAG and the Central and State vigilance bodies like Lok Pal and Lokayuktas etc. and by the political and administrative executive.

References

Central Vigilance Commission Bill 2003.
Civil Service Fundamental Rules.
Constitution of India.
Lok Pal and Lokayukta Bill.
National Commission to Review the Working of the Constitution.
Official Secrets Act, 1923.
Prevention of Corruption Act, 1988.
RTI Act, 2005.
Transparency International Corruption Perception Index Reports.

Bibliography

Administrative Reforms Commission Reports, 1966.

Administrative Reforms Commission Reports, 2005.

Advani, L.K. (2003). *Electoral System in India, Need for Reforms: Panchayat*.

Appleby, Paul (1953). *Public Administration in India*; Report of a Survey.

Appleby, Paul (1956). *Recognition of India's Administrative system* with special reference to administration of government's industrial and commercial enterprises.

Armstrong, Robert, *Management in Civil Service*.

B.N. Yugandhar Committee on Administrative Reforms (2003).

Basu, D.D., *Indian Constitution*.

Benziger, T. Joseph, *Criminalisations of Politics in India*, Dynamic Youth.

Central Vigilance Commission Bill 2003.

Chaturvedi, B.K., *Core Group Report on Administrative Reforms*.

Chaturvedi and Maheswari, (1984). *Administrative Reforms*.

Civil Service Fundamental Rules.

Goswami, Dinesh (1990) Committee on Electoral Reforms, *Report on Electoral Reforms*.

Indrajit Gupta Committee, (1998). *Committee on State Funding of Elections*.

Constitution of India.

Core Committee on Electoral Reforms (2010). *Back ground paper on Electoral Reforms*, GoI.

Core Group on Administrative Reforms under Chairmanship of Cabinet Secretary.

Coupland, R. (1941). *Britain and India*.

Dixon, J. and Kouzmin, A., *Management Innovations for Improving Governance*.

Election Commission of India (1992). *Proposals of the Election Commission of India for Electoral Reforms*.

Election Commission of India (2004). *Proposed Electoral Reforms*.

EPW, *Electoral Reforms and Citizens Initiative: Some breakthroughs*.

EPW (1994), *Vote Power and Lobby Power*.

Fifth Pay Commission Report.

Financial Express, 2008, *Election without Money and Muscle Power*, Dhaka.

Fulton Report, 1968.

Godbole, Madhav, *India's Parliamentary Democracy on Trial*, Rupa & Co.

Gopal Swamy, N. Elections, a democratic festival, *The Hindu*.

Gorwala, A.D., *Report on Administrative Reform.*

Goswami Committee Report, 1990.

Hota, P.C. (2004). *Committee Report on Civil Service Reforms.*

Hussian, Maybe, *Election without Money and Muscle Power.*

Jennings, Sir Ivor (1961). *Cabinet Government.*

Jennings, Sir Ivor (1961). *Parliament.*

Joseph, T.M., *Proportional Representation, A Case for Electoral Reforms in India.*

Journal of Constitutional and Parliamentary Studies (2000), Electoral Reforms, Plea for a fresh look.

Judicial Appointment Commission Bill, 2013.

Katju, Manjari, Election Commission and changing contours of Politics. *EPW*,

Kaul, M.N. and Shakdar, S.L., *Practice and Procedure of Parliament* with particular reference to Lok Sabha.

Kaur, Suman Deep (2008). *Electoral Reforms in India, Pro-active Role of Election Commission* (Main stream).

Kaw, Angan (1996). *Bhagat Election and Electoral Reforms in India*, Vikas Publishing House.

Krishnan, K.P. Geetha, 2000-01 *Expenditure Reforms Commission.*

Krishnan, S.M., *Role of Money power in Elections*, Seminar Paper.

L.K. Jha Commission, *Report on Performance Appraisal and Management.*

Laski, Harold, *British Constitution.*

Law Commission of India (1999)—*Report on Reforms of Electoral Laws.*

Law Commission, *Reports on Judicial Reform.*

Lijiphart, A. (1994). *Electoral System and Party Systems.*

Lok Pal and Lokayukta Bill.

Main Stream, 2008, Proactive Role of Election Commission.

Mathur, H.C. (2004). *British Civil Service.*

N. Vankatachallah Commission to Review Working of the Constitution.

Narayan, Jay Prakash, *Electoral and Political party reforms in India.*

National Commission to Review the Working of the Constitution.

National Commission to Review working of the Constitution, 2002.

Official Secrecy Act, 1923.

P.C. Hota Committee (2004) on *Civil Service Reform.*

P.C. Jain Committee Report on *"Review of Administrative Laws"* — 1998.

Pay Commission Reports—1946 and 1958.

Prevention of Corruption Act, 1988.

R.B. Denhart and Denhart—*Public Administration and the Critique of Domination.*

Ray, G.N., *Role of Money Power in Elections.*

Ray, Jayatilak Guha, *Electoral Reforms in the Context of recent Supreme Court Judgements*, IIPA.

Report on Electoral Process and Political Parties, 2002.

Review of Working of the Constitution (2002). *Vankatachaliah Commission Report*.

Rodney, Brazier, *Constitutional Reforms* (1998).

RTI Act, 2005.

Santhanam, K. (1964). *Report on Prevention of Corruption.*

Saxena, Pradeep, *Administrative Reforms*—A study of major countries.

Second Administrative Reforms Commission, 2005—*Moily Commission Report*.

Sen, S.R., *Vote Power and Lobby Power, EWS.*

Surindernath Committee (2002) *Report on Administrative Reforms.*

Tarkunde Committee Report, 1975.

The Hindu (February 1999), Proportional representation is the answer to quota problem.

Transparency International Corruption Perception Index Reports.

Vajpayee, G.S. (1947) *Committee on Secretarial Reorganization.*

Vohra Committee Report, 1993.

Index